In the Interest of Others

In the Interest of Others

ORGANIZATIONS AND SOCIAL ACTIVISM

John S. Ahlquist and
Margaret Levi

PRINCETON UNIVERSITY PRESS

Princeton & Oxford

LIBRARY OF CONGRESS CATALOGING-IN-PUBLICATION DATA

Ahlquist, John S.
In the interest of others : organizations and social activism / John S. Ahlquist
and Margaret Levi.
pages cm
Includes bibliographical references and index.
ISBN 978-0-691-15856-3 (hardback : alk. paper) — ISBN 978-0-691-15857-0
(pbk. : alk. paper) 1. Labor unions—Political activity. I. Levi, Margaret. II. Title.
HD8031.A45 2013
322'.2—dc23   2013009155

British Library Cataloging-in-Publication Data is available

This book has been composed in Sabon LT

Printed on acid-free paper ∞

Printed in the United States of America

1 3 5 7 9 10 8 6 4 2

For David J. Olson

Comrade, Colleague, and Friend

Contents

Figures

Tables

Acknowledgments

Dedication of this book to David Olson hardly captures our debt to him. As the first Harry Bridges Chair in Labor Studies, he began an enduring relationship with the International Longshore and Warehouse Union (ILWU) that piqued our interest in this remarkable union and led to extraordinary access to people, archives, and information. David co-directed "Union Democracy Reexamined" with Margaret and approved John's appointment to help manage the project in the summer before John officially became a graduate student at the University of Washington. He was a collaborator and co-author with Margaret for nearly forty years and a mentor and friend to both of us. He read and commented constructively on everything either of us wrote that dealt with labor or unions or workers. He advised us, prodded us, and praised us. He marched with us and drank with us. He was there for our celebratory moments and for those times when we needed a lift. He opened doors others could not. One of his last acts of friendship was his reading of the final manuscript, which bears his thoughts and influence—and corrections.

The ILWU is an organization where work is done in teams. We took their lesson to heart and benefited from the contributions of a very large team of graduate and undergraduate students who searched archives, undertook interviews, engaged in surveys, and wrote memos and papers that we draw upon extensively. Jon Agnone was the primary research assistant for more than four years. It was he who negotiated the contribution of the invaluable interview tapes from Howard Kimeldorf and William Finlay, two distinguished authors of earlier books on longshore work, and it was Jon who ensured the tapes were transcribed and coded for use not only by us but for future generations of scholars as well. He helped frame the survey and supervised it until, upon receiving his PhD in Sociology, he passed the torch on to Amanda Clayton. It was Amanda's initiative and persistence that finally earned us the cooperation of all the locals we wished to include in the survey. Equally important, she decided to write her master's thesis on the changing residential patterns of three unions and the consequences for occupational community. Her maps and thinking gave us new insights into the various forms of social networks that develop (or fail to develop) as a consequence of membership. Other graduate students also played key roles in supervising undergraduates and providing research of their own: Barry Eidlin, on loan from Berkeley, researched the Minneapolis Teamsters; Devin Kelley wrote up the responses of different longshore unions to containerization; Rebecca Szper helped with the electoral data collection and analysis; Juliana Rigg and Alison Waggener Boyd ran focus groups; Antonina Gentile shared her knowledge of European waterfront unions; and John Hermanson supervised group interviews with pensioners. Anne Greenleaf and Jennifer Noveck provided additional assistance with the polishing of the final manuscript.

The undergraduates (many now long graduated) constitute an even longer list. Nowell Bamberger, Chris Croker, Byron Haworth, Morgen Myrdahl, George Robertson, Carrie Sachse, and Elizabeth Zamora wrote papers from which we draw heavily. Others engaged in essential coding, transcribing, survey analysis, and bibliographic work: Alex Aldea, Hester Angus, Angeli Bhatt, Kristin Ebeling, Randy Eng, Elizabeth Fawthrop, Max Frieda, Adam Goodwin, Jun Hwang, Tyler Jones, Ashleigh King, Brendan McDavid, Natalie Quist, Cheryl Ream, Michael Rodriguez, Armontae Smith, Igor Voloshin, and Lila Zucker.

We could not have built such a team without the funding of the National Science Foundation through SES-0717454, SES-0517735, and an REU (Research Experience for Undergraduates) grant. Additional funding came from the United States Studies Centre at the University of Sydney and from the Harry Bridges Center for Labor Studies for working groups on Union Democracy Revisited (with David Olson) and Waterfront Workers' History (with James Gregory) and, through the Center, a Washington State Labor Research Grant. Levi received a seed grant for a preliminary and related project from the Russell Sage Foundation. *Politics & Society* provided funding for an early conference and Florida State University for a later one. The Jere L. Bacharach Professorship supported some travel and other expenses, as did both Florida State University and the University of Wisconsin. The Helen Riaboff Whiteley Center at Friday Harbor provided additional research time and space and a lovely atmosphere in which to cogitate, collaborate, and write. We also relied heavily on the staff and resources of the Noel Butlin Archives Centre of Australian National University, the International Longshore and Warehouse Union archives, the Cal State Northridge special collections, the archives of the Harry Bridges Institute, and the special collections of the University of Washington.

Numerous colleagues shared their time and expertise. We benefited immensely from their feedback, questions, and tough love. Michael McGinnis and the late Elinor Ostrom sponsored a "book party" at the Workshop for Political Theory and Policy Analysis, Indiana University, to discuss our penultimate draft. Their comments proved invaluable, as did those of the discussants, especially Torben Iversen and Elisabeth Wood, who read the entire manuscript and continued to engage with us after the workshop ended. Christopher Adolph, Ron Magden, David Olson, Shane White, Eugene Vrana, Joe Wenzel, and, of course, the reviewers, Mark Lichbach, Gary Miller, Ignacio (Pacho) Sanchez-Cuenca, and Kathleen Thelen, commented on the final draft. Indeed, we owe a special thanks to Pacho, who advised us at the outset and was there to give us feedback at the end. Others who provided useful comments on particular chapters and arguments were Matt Baggetta, Matt Baretto, Tim Bartley, Dan Cole, Cliff Carrubra, Kathy Cramer-Walsh, Torun Dewan, Eric Dickson, Scott Gehlbach, Avner Greif, Jeff Hart, Macartan Humphreys, Edgar Kiser, Edmund Malesky, Greg Mallory, Steve Pfaff, David Soskice, and Erik Olin Wright. Lew Bateman and Chuck Myers, two of the best editors in the business, also offered good advice and support.

Equally important to the development of our argument were the responses of audiences where one or both of us presented papers drawn from the book. University and institute venues included Bergen, Berkeley, CEACS (Center for Advanced Study in the Social Sciences) of the Juan March in Madrid, Columbia, Colorado, Dartmouth, Florida State, Gothenburg, Harvard, Kobe, Mahanirban Calcutta Research Group, Max Planck Institute in Cologne, MIT, Oxford, Penn State, Stanford, Sydney, Texas, Virginia, Washington, Wisconsin (Havens Center, La Follette School), Yale, UCLA, and the World Bank Institute. Meetings included those of the American Political Science Association (2010 and 2011), Brisbane Labour History Association, International Political Economy Society (2011), International Society of the New Institutional Economics (2012), International Studies Association (2012), Midwest Political Science Association (2012), and Southern Political Science Association (2011).

Without the help of members, officers, and others connected to the Maritime Union of Australia and of the International Longshore and Warehouse Union, this book could not be. They inspired us, but they also provided us with access and practical support. At the MUA, we benefited from the assistance of Paddy Crumlin, Paul McAleer, Warren Smith, and Zoe Reynolds. At the ILWU, we owe special thanks to those who helped convince the International and local leadership of the value of the survey. We would not have had access without the active commitments of Holly Hulscher, Bobby Olvera Jr., Conrad Spell, Herald Ugles, and Joe Wenzl. We also recognize the invaluable assistance of David Arian, Sarah Faker, Jodi Itman, Scott Mason, Danajo Montez, Chris Romischer, Paul Pemberton, Peter Peyton, Joan Rettinger, Tony Salcido, Randy Vekich, Matt Ventoza, Robin Walker, and Cameron Williams. Also deserving of our gratitude are Bob Hasegawa, Teamsters, Andrew Hedden, Harry Bridges

Center for Labor Studies, Conor M. Casey, Labor Archives of Washington, University of Washington Libraries, and Goetz Wolf, Harry Bridges Institute. We owe a special debt of gratitude to Geoffrey Garrett and Sean Gallagher and the staff of the U.S. Studies Centre, who created a home base in Australia for us. Ron Magden literally opened his basement, full of decades of interviews, films, documents, and notes, most of which are now housed at the University of Washington, and he gave freely of his vast knowledge and experience. Gene Vrana, formerly director of Education and archivist/librarian of the ILWU, made materials available throughout and corrected our errors, both in terms of history and protocol. Any faults rest on us, despite Gene's and Ron's best efforts to eliminate them.

This project has been more than a decade in the making, spanning John's entire graduate school career and then some. He would like to extend personal thanks and recognition to his parents, Deborah and Stephen, his siblings, Andrew, Elisabeth, and Joel, as well as Andrew Lewis. He could not have completed this project without the love and support of a large and widely dispersed group of friends who are thankfully too numerous to mention by name. Special thanks, however, are directed to those whose hospitality he has abused over the years: James Henrickson and Jennifer Zee-Henrickson; Jason Tsai and Charlotte Rhode; Maia Piccagali and Scott Steiger; and Peter Dilello.

Margaret thanks her great friends, Bea Kelleigh, Katrina Pflaumer, Jennifer Isaacs, and Marah Brah, who continually demonstrated interest in a project so different from the important contributions they make daily. Both of us are in debt to Pat Troy and Sandy MacKenzie and to Lindie Clark and Kerry Schott for intellectual and caloric sustenance plus, when needed, shelter in Australia. Margaret's family, Beatrice Levi, Alice Duncan, Jane Kaplan and Don Bonato, Nick Duncan, and Caroline Duncan, remain a continuous and never-ending source of support.

Finally, we both thank Bob Kaplan who survived—gracefully—another book project of Margaret's and a first one of John's, adopted as part of the family. Bob ensured, as best he could, that writing and collaboration were made even more pleasurable by providing us with good food and great wine at the end of long days at the academic mill.

In the Interest of Others

CHAPTER 1

Beyond Economism

Workers flood the streets to protest government policy. They shut down businesses and public offices. This describes moments in nineteenth-century America; it certainly captures recent events in parts of Europe, Asia, and the American Midwest. While all unions are involved in politics to some degree, large-scale political strikes are rare in the contemporary Anglo-Saxon democracies, and rarer still is the use of industrial action for political ends. Variation in the size, form, and goals of political mobilization is the subject of countless studies. The most interesting tend to focus on the collective actions of those who are marginalized—be they African Americans in the United States or peasant farmers in China—or those engaged in out-and-out rebellion or revolution against the state. This book raises a somewhat different puzzle.

We ask why some organizations move beyond the particular and particularized grievances that are the raison d'être of the organization and engage in political actions, especially those that have little or nothing to do with members' reasons for belonging. For example, in the late 1930s, dockworker unions in Australia and on the West Coast of the United States refused to load scrap iron bound for Japan, in protest against the Japanese invasion of Manchuria. These unions continue to periodically engage in work stoppages or boycotts in opposition to national foreign policy or to assist in freedom struggles overseas.

We explore the variation in organizational norms, governance arrangements, and social networks that produce systematic differences in aggregate behavior. We also explain why members go along. Left-wing longshore union members give up time and money to fight on behalf of social justice causes from which they can expect no material return. Parishioners of churches throughout the United States risk jail to shelter asylum seekers. Altruism is common enough, and so are volunteering, political commitment, and unselfish service to others. Yet, we know that there are environments that evoke such behavior and those that depress it. Why and how do some organizations produce membership willingness to self-sacrifice on behalf of a wide range of political and social justice issues? In some instances, the answer may be simple: self-selection. Those who want to act on behalf of others join the church or the interest group or the activist organization that encourages, indeed advertises, such behavior. The more interesting cases are those in which individuals join for one reason but come to pursue goals they may not have considered previously. Membership changes them. It shapes their identity and choices.

Part of the answer lies in how an organization defines its community of fate (Levi and Olson 2000), those with whom individuals come to perceive their own interests as bound and with whom they are willing to act in solidarity.[1] This term is more than a rhetorical flourish. It embodies two distinct but interrelated concepts. The community identifies those whose situations organizational members see as distinct possibilities for themselves. An individual looks at others and imagines "there, but for the grace of God, go I." But more than simple human recognition is the entwining of fate. The community of fate identifies those the organizational members perceive as engaged in similar struggles for similar goals. Organizational members view their welfare as bound up with that of the community. It is a short jump to see how defining a community of fate has strong implications for the organization's scope of legitimate action. The community of fate may encompass only members of the organization, in which case its actions will be narrow and exclusively self-serving. But the community of fate could encompass unknown others for whom the members feel responsibility. These external others need not recognize or even know about the organization.

A community of fate requires recognition of common goals and enemies, and it is strengthened by interdependence. Social interactions, education, and the transmission of credible information by leadership shape common beliefs about what actions are possible for the organization and its members. Perceived interdependence is a function of immediate social, work, and residential networks, but it can also result from learning about distant events and connecting them to local possibilities.

Organizations successful at encouraging costly actions that transcend narrow self-interest are worthy of note in their own right. They also offer

---

[1] Levi and Olson believed they had invented the term but have since learned that other scholars have also employed the concept—albeit with somewhat different meanings. Possibly the closest usage to ours is Chang (1997), but he ties the awareness of a common goal to a shared legal framework. A related idea appears in arguments concerning how employers try to convince employees that the interdependence of their livelihoods should make workers willing to sacrifice for the firm. See, e.g., Cole (1979), Videla (2006). Baehr (2008) relies heavily on the concept of "community of fate" to describe a temporary phenomenon, ". . . a process of group formation under extreme 'disaster'" (140). He relates it to the contested German term *Schicksalsgemeinschaft*, which Weber also uses. Baehr distinguishes himself from Resnik (1999), who uses the concept in a medical context to refer to groups tied together by empathy.

insight into the processes that foster aggregate behavior and, possibly, changes in beliefs and preferences. An extensive literature exists on the factors affecting individual choice and the aggregation of individual preferences into collective outcomes. We build on that scholarship to understand the factors that encourage individuals to act in ways they may not have considered, let alone gone along with, prior to their engagement in a particular organization.

In attempting to explain the conditions under which organizational membership transforms individual action, altering aggregate behavior, we reframe the question that motivated Lenin in *What Is to Be Done?* (1963 [1902]). Lenin wanted workers to think beyond their own immediate needs, to imagine a society in which a different life was possible, and then to engage in revolution to achieve it. Workers are relatively easily persuaded to fight for improvements in wages, hours, and working conditions. For Lenin, such goals constitute "economism," a focus on the narrow economic interests bound up in the job. He wanted to transform the preferences, beliefs, and actions of the working class. His aim was to create class-conscious workers who understood their fate as bound up with each other across occupations and even borders, workers who realized their struggle had to be over far more than their working conditions and pay. Lenin held that only in this way could the proletariat become victorious, significantly improving their material well-being while also achieving a more equitable society.

Lenin proposed political education as the way to inspire workers. He advocated a workers' newspaper to convey information, and he encouraged other socialization processes to make workers aware of and sensitive to the salience of political projects near and dear to the revolutionaries' hearts.[2] His strategy, developed within an authoritarian and repressive context, also included the organization of the revolutionaries into cells, with very few individuals knowing each other. He was eager to prevent the regime from locating and jailing the Communist Party activists.

Predating Lenin and operating within a democratic framework, Frederick Engels argued that ballots might transform capitalism into socialism. However, confidence in electoral victories stumbled on the very problem Lenin identified: workers were more committed to achieving immediate material benefits than long-term changes that might come at a significant price (Przeworski 1985). The empirical reality is that middle-class

---

[2] Others who shared Lenin's commitment to revolutionary change offered other approaches. Rosa Luxemburg (1971 [1916]) argued for mass action and general strikes. Antonio Gramsci distinguished between democratic and non-democratic regimes and then suggested the most appropriate strategies for each (Gramsci and Buttigieg 1992).

and well-off proletariat voters reveal little interest in overturning the economic system (Przeworski and Sprague 1986; Ziblatt 2014).

Mobilizing the proletariat to engage in revolution is not what is at issue for us in this book, but we do care about the conditions that change individual beliefs and actions. While we can dismiss Lenin's model of revolution, we cannot so easily dismiss the central question he raises: What motivates members of organizations developed to serve the interests of their membership to choose to engage in actions on behalf of a larger whole? Nor can we easily dismiss some of Lenin's insights, namely the critical role of leadership, education, and information. Our research reinforces the importance of these factors in empowering members to act in ways they may not previously have thought viable.

Some scholars focus on structural factors and political opportunities that make it more or less likely for a group to act and to act in a certain way. The principal contemporary exemplar of this analytic tradition is the resource mobilization literature (Lipsky 1968; Tilly 1978; Zald and McCarthy 1979; Tarrow 1994) and its more recent contentious politics variant (McAdam, Tarrow, and Tilly 2001). While our approach shares much in common with the contentious politics perspective, our focus is more squarely on the micro-foundations of behavior and the strategic interactions between the leaders and followers and among the followers themselves. Consistent with recent work by Bueno de Mesquita (2010), we claim that leaders need to convince followers that they can succeed, which in turn requires a demonstration that enough others share the leaders' sentiments about appropriate actions and are willing to act when necessary.

One way to think about this set of issues, of course, is through models of collective action, particularly those that suggest the various dilemmas that exist for those deciding whether to cooperate or contribute (see, e.g., Lichbach 1995, 1997). Mancur Olson (1965), James Q. Wilson (1973), and many others emphasize selective incentives, largely material but also solidary and ideological. Selective incentives certainly play a role in accounting for certain kinds of contributions; indeed, Olson discussed union dues–paying as a primary example of how selective incentives work in practice. Others emphasized leadership as a means for providing and targeting selective incentives (Frohlich, Oppenheimer, and Young 1971). What selective incentives cannot adequately explain is how encompassing communities of fate are or how governance and norms influence group choice. Rational choice models, particularly the new economic institutionalism (North 1990; Ostrom 1990), get us a little further by considering how rules constrain or facilitate behavior. Behavioral economics provides even more clues with its focus on social preferences, such as ethical commitments and altruism. Considerations of when prosocial preferences are crowded out by material incentives (Bowles and Polanía-Reyes 2011) and the extent to which social context influences this process (Fehr and Hoff 2011) are related to the issues we raise here.

Our question and approach also have much in common with the large sociological literature on group mobilization and collective action.[3] Though we build on several insights in this literature, we differ in that our concern is not so much with cooperation in discrete, well-defined activities. Rather, we emphasize how groups already recognizing a mutual interest come to expand their scope of action to act on behalf of those outside the group. That is, we make endogenous the projects a group is willing to undertake. A central issue here—one that is less explored in the sociological literature—is how such commitments can be maintained and reproduced through time in the context of formal organizations.

Our approach is to identify the aggregate behaviors that result from interactions between leaders and followers, as mediated by organizational institutions. Although we rely on both game theory and economic models, ours is a highly contextual account emphasizing the beliefs of the leaders, the settings they create as well as inherit, and the beliefs, networks, and responses of the members. Unlike most of the work in the literatures from which we primarily draw, we do not presume that individuals already have clear preferences. We are open to the possibility that preferences change as a consequence of membership. At the least, preferences are clarified and, possibly, reordered as members come to believe that certain goals are actionable and potentially achievable.

Our Argument

We explore our puzzle in the context of labor unions, focusing on variation in unions' use of industrial power for political ends. A union's bargaining power ultimately lies in the members' ability to coordinate in withholding labor from employers.[4] Most unions maintain some contact with politicians and political authorities. Nevertheless there is variation across unions in both the extent of political mobilization and their industrial success. Most unions, not surprisingly, strike rarely and then only to promote the wages, hours, benefits, job security, and working conditions of members, or even specific subsets of members (Golden 1997). Many

---

[3] See Oliver and Myers (2002) for a review.

[4] Even when considering the seemingly straightforward situation of wage bargaining, there is considerable debate over how exactly to specify a union's maximand; see Dunlop (1944), Martin (1980), Oswald (1982), Blair and Crawford (1984), Mori and Tedeschi (1992), Booth (1995).

unions also lobby for protective legislation or forms of social insurance from which they will benefit. At the extreme end of both continua are unions that use their industrial power in the service of political ends having virtually nothing to do with their own conditions. They do not give up their social movement energy as Michels (1962 [1919]) predicted or displace their goals as Merton (1968 [1957]) observed.

But why do they behave this way and how do they sustain it? To state the main thesis of the first part of the book: sustained political mobilization requires an ideologically motivated founding leadership cohort who devises organizational rules that facilitate both industrial success and coordinated expectations about the leaders' political objectives. The result is contingent consent (Levi 1997): members will willingly, sometimes enthusiastically, go along with leadership demands as long as they are convinced that they are receiving the material benefits the organization promised them upon joining, that the leadership is accountable, and that enough other members are also going along. In the second half of the book, we explore the claim that members come to hold the belief (or at least act consistently with the belief) that their fate is intertwined not only with their associates in the organization but also with a larger population; by helping others, they are helping themselves. This may also require them to focus on long-term goals in addition to immediate aims. Interactions among the members, the capacity to challenge leadership arguments and demands, and attachments to the organizational traditions are the factors that produce both contingent consent with leadership and a more encompassing community of fate.

Figure 1.1 outlines schematically the first part of our argument, identifying the major actors, variables, and outcomes that we discuss in subsequent chapters. We begin at a moment of organizational founding or crisis. At such times a leader who devises tactical solutions to the threats confronting the organization has an outsized opportunity to design subsequent organizational governance institutions, defined as the formal rules and informal norms that delineate how decisions are taken, how the organization will respond to future events, and how and on what basis organizational members should evaluate the actions of leaders. But there is no guarantee that effective leaders will emerge. A persuasive leader could arise and drive the organization off a cliff with the wrong policies or weak governance institutions. Or perhaps the challenges facing the organization are simply insoluble. In these cases, the organization will fail.

All the leaders we investigate are asking members to act on behalf of material interests, but some are also asking members to act on behalf of political or ethical goals that have little or nothing to do with the reasons for joining the voluntary organization. Variation in leaders' political commitments is not the object of explanation here; we take the

Building an organization

Figure 1.1: The founding argument in schematic form

leaders' preferences as exogenous. Our explanation emphasizes the processes by which leadership earns the confidence of members and then succeeds in persuading them to act on behalf of goals the leadership argues are important. The leader attempts to convince members that their own fate hinges on achievement of ends that serve external others as well as themselves. Successful leaders effect their ends through a four-step process: (1) achievement of the economic goals of the union; (2) the announcement of principles the leaders pledge to uphold; (3) the creation of governance arrangements that allow leadership and members to effectively coordinate; and (4) processes and institutions that either induce consensual maintenance of the principles or compel members to act as if they consent. Numbers 2, 3, and 4 on this list are components of the organizational governance institutions.

Nearly all unions, indeed most organizations, have governance institutions in this sense. However, not all organizational governance institutions emphasize acting beyond material self-interest. That, we argue, requires leadership commitment to political causes. More generally we argue that leadership is costly and difficult. Those who undertake to lead do so not only for the benefit of the organization but also because they themselves have other desires and objectives—monetary, social, or political. Organizational members will be willing to contribute to the leader's "rents" so long as the leader continues to serve the members well. The founding leaders at these pivotal moments are in unique positions to establish the form and level of leadership rents. Where these founding leaders are politically motivated, the resulting leadership rents will be such that the leader is able to ask for member mobilization for political causes, up to a point.

We claim that these features—form and level of leadership rents, organizational principles, and governance institutions—form, loosely speaking, an equilibrium in which they are all self-reinforcing. Organizational principles coordinate member expectations about leader demands. Leader demands must be consistent with organizational principles.

In equilibrium we can observe stable organizational behavior, including action consistent with an encompassing community of fate when principles and governance institutions allow for it. Where leadership rents, governance institutions, principles, and behavior are out of equilibrium, the organization can fail. As an example, nominally Communist union leaders who engage in financial corruption while trying to suppress internal dissent act against their own stated principles; they are likely to precipitate a dramatic change in leadership and governance institutions.

If we understand the production of the organizational governance institutions as the result of a kind of contract between leadership and members, then there is also a question of how it is reproduced through time. Figure 1.2 presents a schematic representation of the dynamic part of our argument.

This dynamic part of the argument has two prongs. The first has to do with the endogenous effect of organizational governance, specifically leadership rents, on the types of individuals who are likely to come forward as potential leaders in the future. In an organization where leadership rents are mainly political in nature, the organization will tend to attract political activists as leaders over time. So long as the organization continues to perform well, this relationship will persist. Leaders will continue to demand political mobilization from members across leadership cohorts. The second prong involves the members' reasons for complying with the leader's calls to action. We suspect that the workers come to the job with beliefs about what is attainable through a union and what the union has a right to expect of them. Some of these beliefs are crystallized

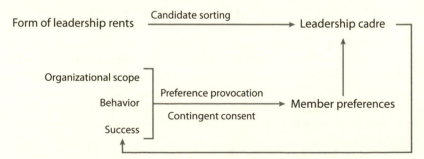

Figure 1.2: The dynamic argument in schematic form

before joining; others are evoked upon being asked to participate in political actions. As new members join, they will likely view the culture of the organization as so many norms of behavior. They will comply, i.e., engage in called-upon actions, provided there are sufficient numbers around them visibly engaging in that behavior. Initially, we expect that some combination of sanctions and expectations about others promotes compliance. Over time, however, the new recruits may come to reconsider their beliefs and preferences. By being asked to contribute—and initially doing so for simple rationalist reasons—members may come to update their beliefs about what is relevant and possible in the context of their union, a process we call preference provocation.

The first part of the book focuses on the issues outlined in figure 1.1. We consider what leaders do, given their particular aims and beliefs, to achieve their ends and engage members in that process. We imagine that, in these initial pivotal moments, members are in fact "economistic." Building on this basis we describe the nature of governance institutions required to elicit member compliance with requests for political activism, treating this activism as a benefit accruing only to the leader. In the second half of the book we turn the argument outlined in figure 1.2 to understand what members actually believe or prefer when it comes to political mobilization. This is more difficult to determine, and understanding change in those beliefs and preferences is harder still. Yet our investigation of how to achieve membership compliance also reveals some of the possible mechanisms by which beliefs might be formed or at least acted upon.

In addressing the issue of revealed organizational preferences, we build on economic theories of the firm, extending and modifying them to look at how organizations with different types of goals come about. In so doing, we present a basic framework for examining an organization's "culture."[5] Our focus is on the role of leaders in shaping and transmitting information to the membership through organizational rules and the leaders' actions. Members, for their part, come to accept the leaders' positions so long as the organization continues to deliver good basic outcomes. We will demonstrate that where there are costly actions exerted in support of causes that have no direct material benefit to union members; leadership abided by the principles established in the formative period; some members' beliefs were transformed by their participation in the organization; and leaders' demands were rewarded with membership's contingent consent.

---

[5] See Levi (2005) for an earlier version of this argument.

The Cases

The cases that particularly interest us are those organizations that ask individuals to engage in actions that require self-sacrifice, sometimes to the point of death, and where personal payoffs and selective incentives appear to be an insufficient explanation of behavior. In particular, we are fascinated by how organizations induce members to take costly personal actions that do not seem to have connection to the reasons people joined the organization initially. To understand these cases requires us to compare them with what the followers themselves are also likely to consider: cases where the organization survives without demanding similar actions.

Organizations that manage to expand their scope of action admittedly are not the norm, but neither are they unheard of. And whereas our discussion focuses on labor unions, the phenomenon that interests us is considerably broader. For example, McDaniel (2008) examines political mobilization among American black church congregations during the civil rights era. Some congregations mobilized at considerable risk and expense, while other congregations (and whole denominations) chose to eschew political causes as outside the purview of a religious community. He argues that preferences of the senior pastor along with organizational rules were pivotal in explaining which congregations mobilized and which did not.

Empirically we investigate a specific type of organization: labor unions in democratic countries. We choose four unions in the transport sector. Truckers and dockworkers occupy key positions in national and international supply chains. Their strikes stop trade. The considerable leverage their unions can exercise over the economy is certainly important in securing good contracts. It also means they could use industrial actions to political effect, even if basically symbolic. However, only some do. Among them are the International Longshore and Warehouse Union (ILWU) in the United States and the Waterside Workers Federation (WWF) in Australia (now merged into the Maritime Union of Australia, or MUA). In stark contrast are two other American unions, the International Brotherhood of Teamsters (IBT) and the International Longshore Union (ILA). Table 1.1 arrays the cases along the two dimensions we discussed earlier: degree of industrial success and the extent to which the members are politically mobilized.

The political mobilization dimension coincides with the business union/social movement union distinction made in the labor studies literature, with the IBT and ILA representing archetypical business unions, those whose commitments are to the welfare of members exclusively. But both business unions and social movement unions (those committed to the social welfare of members and the larger society) can vary in the extent to

TABLE 1.1: The cases organized by industrial
success and political mobilization

		Political mobilization	
		High	*Low*
	High	ILWU	Teamsters
Industrial success			
	Low	WWF/MUA	ILA

which they succeed in improving the material conditions of dues-payers.[6]
Almost all unions (and certainly those we examine) ask members to contribute personal time and money or approve organizational resources for
charitable purposes, electoral campaigns, and lobbying. Relatively few,
however, advocate political and social justice causes that seem unrelated
to the achievement of better wages or working conditions.

Another reason for examining unions is that they must recruit a large
number of workers in a firm or industry to effectively control the supply
of labor. This implies that unions cannot rely on strict rules and steep
demands on members to screen for only the most motivated—tools available to smaller groups with different objectives (Iannaccone 1992).[7]

All four of these unions have periodic elections, thus allowing us to
explore what leaders do to retain their positions and with what success.
In all of them we find examples of dissident behavior; how the leadership
deals with the members involved reveals something about the process of
institutionalizing acceptance of the leaders' beliefs.

Finally, these unions represent plausible counterfactuals of one another in the sense that all of these unions could use industrial action to
political advantage should they choose; they all occupy a critical niche in
international supply chains that permits them to exercise both economic
and political leverage unavailable to most unions. Any of these unions
could have followed the opposite path, and local branches within each
union often did.

We have selected unions that share certain features but whose governance institutions vary. The membership, at least at the beginning of

[6] The heading "social movement unions" is ambiguous, since some scholars use this
term to refer to organizing tactics (Voss and Sherman 2000) and others to refer to activist
unions with broad-based social commitments. When we use the term "social movement
unionism" we use it in the latter sense.

[7] But these unions do succeed in raising the cost of exit. We thank Ignacio Sanchez-
Cuenca for emphasizing these points.

the seventy-plus years we study, was largely drawn from a labor pool of casual, i.e., temporary, workers chosen more for their brawn than their brains. There is considerable evidence that the same workers sometimes were employed as truckers, sometimes as warehousemen, and sometimes as dockworkers. Yet, the workers also come from a diversity of religious, ethnic, and political backgrounds. Some have considerable exposure to and experience with radical unionism, and some have none. Our presumption is that the membership of the unions we investigate is heterogeneous in terms of the levels and even kind of political convictions they possess. Even when a union has a screening process before accepting a worker to full membership (as the ILWU does), whether the worker can do the job well and is a "good mate" are the most salient attributes. Even if unions expend a considerable amount of effort on socialization, political convictions appear to vary, albeit perhaps not by as much as prior to the socialization. Put another way, these unions are particularly interesting cases because people join them to find work on the waterfront, not because they want to join a political group.

The IBT and ILA exemplify unions that ask their members to act consistently with a relatively narrow concept of self-interest; the other two unions elicit from members not only effort to improve their own well-being but also sacrifices of time and money in support of social and political causes. The social movement/business union distinction is not meant to imply that business unions do not engage with politics. To the contrary, business unions routinely endorse and contribute to political parties and candidates and turn out to protest various public policies and government actions. Nevertheless, these political activities always surround policies and jurisdictions that are directly relevant to the members' interests and therefore lack the puzzling quality of the broader mobilizations we study.

The most dramatic—and risky—actions involve using the union's industrial strength and leverage to make political points on topics far from the direct interests of union members. The costs to the participants include loss of pay and threats of punitive action by employers and, sometimes, by government. These actions include work slowdowns, boycotts of ships, countries, or cargos, and even shutting down the ports. For example, on November 30, 1999, the ILWU closed the ports on the West Coast to protest the World Trade Organization (WTO) ministerial being held in Seattle. In his speech to the protest rally in Seattle, ILWU president Brian McWilliams declared, "That is why the ILWU is here today, with all of you—to tell the agents of global capital that we, the workers, those who care about social justice and protecting our rights and our planet, will not sit quietly by while they meet behind closed doors to carve up our world." He went on to refer to several similar events from the ILWU's history, including the following:

- The 1997 boycott of the *Neptune Jade* and the 1998 closure of the Port of Oakland to protest the ship loaded by strikebreakers in Liverpool. The ILWU boycott inspired subsequent refusals to work the ship in Vancouver, Yokohama, and Kobe.
- The 1989–92 boycott of coffee cargo from El Salvador in response to the killing of six Jesuit priests by U.S.-supported right-wing death squads
- The 1981 refusal to handle military cargo bound for El Salvador
- The sustained refusal of ILWU locals, especially Local 10 (Oakland/San Francisco), to handle cargo from Apartheid South Africa throughout the 1980s
- The 1980–81 boycott of Iranian shipping in response to the hostage crisis
- The 1974 boycott of Chilean cargo in response to the U.S.-backed Pinochet coup
- In 1939 the ILWU refused to load scrap iron heading for Japan in response to the Japanese invasion of Manchuria

The ILWU has simultaneously closed all West Coast ports in political protest on several occasions, including the 2008 May Day protest of the Iraq War; the 1999 WTO protest; the April 24, 1999 closure in solidarity with the national protest to free Mumia Abu-Jamal; the 1977 closure of the ports to all South African–flagged ships; 1968 port closures in mourning for Martin Luther King, Jr.

Similarly, the WWF has closed ports and banned certain commerce on a variety of occasions, including: the 1938 refusal to load scrap iron on ships bound for Japan; 1945–46 refusal to load Dutch ships bound for Indonesia; various closures in 1948–54 to protest the Australian Crimes Act, and especially the Menzies government's use of it against Communist activists. In the heated period of the 1960s through 1980s, the WWF instituted bans on South African shipping (not lifted until Mandela was freed) and on Indonesian cargo in support of the East Timorese. The Sydney branch repeatedly refused to handle cargo associated with involvement in the Vietnam conflict, including a 1973 ban on all U.S. military shipping in Sydney in response to U.S. bombing in Vietnam. The WWF also provided support for embattled trade unionists in Chile, Poland, Pakistan, and other parts of the world, often as part of a campaign initiated by the International Transport Federation (ITF).

High-profile port closures are only one indicator of costly political stands the union and its leadership have taken. The ILWU was among the most racially progressive unions in the United States, and the WWF promoted Australian Aboriginal equality early on. Both were among the earliest public opponents of the Vietnam War. The ILWU supported Henry

Wallace in the 1948 presidential election; 1950s WWF federal leaders supported the left candidates in the Australian Labor Party. The majority of the membership in both unions rallied around their leadership when they were under threat from national governments for political stands, even when those stands were not consonant with membership preferences. Both unions routinely raise and donate money to support striking and locked out workers but also to support humanitarian and political causes around the world. Contingents of ILWU activists routinely appear at major protest events, even those, such as the 2011 protests in Madison, Wisconsin, that are far from their industrial jurisdiction and homes.

The previous examples serve to emphasize two things. First, the dramatic political work stoppages are part of a larger pattern of organizational commitments and behavior. Second, there is an important distinction between the political mobilization we are examining here and political strikes more broadly. The activities of the ILWU and WWF are particularly noteworthy because the issues at hand did not directly affect their rank-and-file members; neither union was likely to effect change in government policy on its own.[8] This is in sharp distinction to large-scale labor mobilization and "strike waves" (Franzosi 1995) directed against governments in which there *is* an expectation that the unions' actions could force a change in policy or even bring down the government. Put another way, there is an analytic and qualitative difference between longshoremen striking to protest the Iraq War five years into the conflict and teachers, firefighters, and state workers protesting at the Wisconsin state capitol to influence legislation.

Our Data and Approach

Methodologically, we see our work as contributory to a growing research tradition that integrates interpretative perspectives with game theory (see, e.g., Ferejohn 1991; Bates, de Figueiredo, and Weingast 1998; Bates, Greif et al. 1998; de Figueiredo and Weingast 1999; Sanchez-Cuenca 2001; Chandra 2004; Brady, Ferejohn, and Pope 2005). We have immersed ourselves in the history and governance details of the organizations we study. This enables us to identify precisely how leadership builds a trustworthy reputation, the nature of the institutions and how they operate to constrain or enable behavior, the processes of socialization and education, the focal points for coordination, and the triggers for action. Formal models sensitize us to the dynamics of a given situation and allow us to derive testable propositions. The contextual and historical material provides the basis for interpreting the motivations of the actors and their beliefs.

[8] Although many unionists reported feeling that their actions had made a difference in the world, at least at the margin.

Our research relies throughout on the combination of multiple methods and developed theory (à la Poteete, Janssen, and Ostrom 2010). Statistical analyses of strike and survey data offer additional evidence for our claims. Recently developed tools for statistical matching even take us a good way toward showing that union membership can transform members' opinions and behavior. Our hard-won quantitative data, however, cannot provide the in-depth understanding of the organizations and the processes that our explanation demands. For a fuller account, we rely on the combination of our formal models and contextual detail. The end product, we hope, resonates with the experiences of the actors we describe as well as with our models.

We investigate the four unions over time so that we are able to identify the extent and nature of any belief change that takes place and the process by which it is reproduced, if it is, despite demographic and leadership changes within the union and technological, economic, and political changes affecting the industry. Our data come from records of union meetings and decisions, membership and electoral rolls, interviews, and oral histories that date from the 1920s through the early years of the twenty-first century. All the cases are considered at significant moments of transformation and growth.

At the pivotal moments, in the 1930s, our data allow us to determine whether the unions' members self-select for political or ideological reasons. They do not. As the unions develop over time and as the economic benefits of membership improve, there does appear to be a selection process at work. The motivation may be nepotism, or it may be political. The cause is of less import than the effect: It becomes relatively easy to reproduce the organizational equilibrium within the unions whose employers choose job applicants from among the family and neighbors of those already working there.

Alternative Accounts

Voluntary organizations exhibit tremendous variation in their expectations of adherents, and members differ in their willingness to comply with organizational demands. We argue that, in certain circumstances, organizational membership leads to actions on behalf of others or for a cause, actions that entail unrequited costs in time, lost income, and possible bodily harm. This seems to be what is happening within a subset of religious, political, and labor organizations.

We are hardly the first to observe that some unions and voluntary organizations sustain political, economic, or justice commitments that other similar organizations do not even consider. The easiest and most straightforward explanation is that the beliefs and preferences that seem to be shared by the group reflect a process of self-selection. Individuals join political parties, labor unions, churches, activist groups, and even soccer clubs in which the organizational expectations are consistent with their interests and leave those that make demands that are too onerous. This is an unlikely scenario for unions, however, whose membership is generally determined by employment opportunities or job preferences, not by political persuasions. Even so, we will explore any possible role of self-selection as we proceed.

In other cases, individuals fear ostracism if they deviate from the group norm and hope for social acceptance if they acquiesce. Selective incentives provide sufficient explanation for the collective actions produced by voluntary organizations relying on self-selection or social pressure. However, it is not always easy to tell if this is truly the case. Sometimes what appears to be shared norms is actually silence, as Timur Kuran (1995) has documented and as recent international events so well demonstrate. Organizations and governments often succeed in suppressing dissent. In the chapters that follow we will endeavor to show that preference falsification is not occurring in the most politically mobilized unions. Repression is most visible in the *non-mobilized* unions.

There is a long-standing and ongoing debate about the reasons why individuals adopt the norms of the organizations in which they find themselves a part or, less strongly, comply with the actions the organizations demand even when they do not fully agree with what is being demanded of them. One pole of the debate is represented by a social relational or network approach (Lawler, Thye, and Yoon 2009) that emphasizes the normative and affective commitments group membership elicits: "The strength of normative social commitments reflects the degree to which people perceive an affinity between themselves and a group's or organization's mission, values, and goals" (ibid., 24). The second is a rational choice account that emphasizes dependence on the organization or group (Hechter 1987). Individuals adhere to normative demands when there are no viable and preferable alternatives (also see Ensminger and Knight 1997). Relationships within the organization as well as dependence upon it are important factors in understanding group behavior, but more important, we argue, are the rents sought by the group's leadership and the institutional arrangements in which members operate.

Research specifically on union behavior has also generated some alternative explanations to ours. The first is that unions formed and initially led by Communists are the ones most likely to have broad political agendas (Stepan-Norris and Zeitlin 2002). It is indeed the case that radical leadership is a key to the beginnings of the ILWU and WWF, but a founding ideology in and of itself cannot account for why some of these unions maintain such commitments and others do not. Many of the unions founded or led by radical Communists in the 1930s–1950s did not mobilize politically, at least not to the extent we document here. Many have passed from the scene as their industries were transformed by technology and trade or because radical, ideologically driven leaders failed to ensure that the members' hard-won benefits were defended (Kimeldorf 1992). There are even examples, such as the British Electrical Trade Union, when radical leaders engaged in ballot-rigging, leading to their defeat at the hands of both internal and external foes and the wholesale reconstitution of the organization in the early 1960s.

A second alternative hypothesis concerning the role of leadership ideology comes from Robert Fishman (2004), who seeks to answer the question of why some unions engage in actions that link their specific struggles with larger national and international goals and some only engage in "defensive localism" (ibid., 62).[9] His answer emphasizes conversational ties that link socially recognized intellectuals with the leadership of local unions. Although links between leaders and parties certainly existed, we find little evidence of the deep linkages Fishman describes. Despite the existence of intellectuals eager to engage with unions in the periods on which we focus, hardly any such engagement took place. Perhaps this reflects the absence of a socialist party in the United States and the fraught relationship of the WWF with the Australian Labor Party. Nonetheless, Fishman's work alerts us to the possible influences the Communist Party may have exercised on several of the leaders we discuss.

Some scholars (e.g., Lipset 1994) argue that certain national cultures and religions are more likely than others to engender strong allegiance to democratic practices and social justice ends; progressive tendencies are more commonly attributed to Anglo-Saxon or Nordic Protestants, and conservative perspectives to Irish or Southern European Catholics. Howard Kimeldorf argues that the demographic differences between the largely Scandinavian Protestant dockworkers of the West Coast and the Italian Catholic dockworkers of the East Coast partially explain the distinctiveness of the ILWU relative to the corrupt and hierarchical International Longshoremen's Association (ILA), from which the ILWU splintered in 1937 (Kimeldorf 1988). An immediate reason to doubt this account is the fact that the Waterside Workers' Federation (WWF) of Australia shares the ILWU's political orientation but has a membership that is heavily Catholic and Irish.

Kimeldorf's primary explanation of the difference between the ILWU and the ILA is the degree of concentration and coordination among the employers of dock labor. His account resonates with others that

---

[9] The term "defensive localism" comes from Weir (1994).

emphasize government and employer initiatives in explaining the broad contours of labor power (Hall 1986; Swenson 1989; Western 1997; Iversen 1999; Ebbinghaus and Visser 2000; Wallerstein and Western 2000; Streeck 2002; Mares 2003). While they capture part of the story, they underplay the degree to which employer organizations are endogenous to labor power and vice versa. In the ILWU case, the coordination of employers was partly induced by the ability of the union to sustain a coast-wide strike.

Yet another explanation has to do with the nature of the work and the labor market. Maritime workers, including those in longshore, tend to be internationalist in perspective. They come into contact with individuals from many different countries, they are exposed to a wide range of ideologies and belief systems, and they recognize that they are part of a network of ports whose workers can make a big difference during job actions and contract disputes (Silver 2003; Gentile 2010). Moreover, the team nature of the work on the docks, particularly before containerization, made the workers interdependent in ways that should facilitate solidarity. These factors are important but do not account for the considerable variation in the militancy of longshore workers. The organizational governance institutions and aggregate behavior of the ILA are closer to that of the Teamsters than to that of the ILWU and WWF.

Finally, it might be the case that symbolic political action is actually an instance of instrumental action. By demonstrating solidarity and militancy around an issue that does not reflect attacks on wages, hours, benefits, and conditions of work, the union is in fact signaling how tough it will be if employers threaten union gains. We devote chapter 8 to examining this possibility.

The Chapters

We build our case in two parts. The first part of the book, consisting of chapters 2–5, focuses on the founding or pivotal moments of an organization when the major tactical and strategic innovations have enabled the union to overcome its fundamental collective action problems. Our first step, presented in chapter 2, is the development of a formal model that specifies the relationships between leaders and members. In the model we derive some key insights. Organizational leaders can develop reputations for effectiveness; this reputation makes possible leadership rents, which expand cooperation and compensate the leader when information acquisition and communication are costly. Members agree to contribute to the leader's compensation up to a point. The form these rents take, whether monetary or political, affects the scope of union activities. Since these outcomes are only a few of many possible, we introduce the concept of organizational governance institutions that embody the union's solution to the equilibrium selection problem. As in all formal models, particularly those intended as part of an analytic narrative (Bates, Greif, et al. 1998), the game lays out the paths not taken as well as the one followed. This allows us to derive alternative hypotheses and testable implications, which we then delve into with historical narrative and archival records as well as quantitative analysis of political and industrial work stoppages.

In chapters 3–5 we turn to the cases themselves, beginning with the two business unions, the IBT and ILA in chapter 3. Chapter 4 focuses on the two more politically committed unions, the ILWU and WWF. We identify the pivotal historical moments and leaders in these organizations and discuss their attitudes toward the appropriate scope of union activity and the type of rents they hoped to secure in exchange for taking up the costly and risky task of leading a labor organization in the 1930s–1970s. We identify the (usually) explicit set of organizational principles that formalize these beliefs about union scope of action and show how the organizational governance institutions are consistent with both the stated principles and the form of the leader's rents in ways anticipated by the model in chapter 2. In chapter 5 we begin the process of relaxing some of the assumptions in the theoretical model by examining how the national-level organizations manage internal heterogeneity across individual members as well as specific geographically defined subunits. We observe internal opposition to the dominant national leadership of the IBT, ILWU, and WWF. We compare specific locals within each union, to show the robustness of the larger organizational governance institutions to perturbation once in equilibrium and that, at the local level, workers did not sort in to unions for political or social reasons; rather, they joined where the economic opportunities first appeared. We find that the ILWU and WWF, the unions whose leaders ask member contributions to political projects, pursued active persuasion combined with tolerance, including leaders backing down from some controversial stances. The IBT, on the other hand, invested less in persuasion and employed screening and repression. This local heterogeneity and the strategies to manage it were unanticipated by the model in chapter 2, leading us to consider some model extensions in the second part of the book.

In chapters 6–9 we explore the anomalies and inconsistencies that our historical and statistical data have turned up, including ILWU and WWF members reporting profound transformations in their political thinking and behavior. In chapter 6 we revisit the theoretical argument, suggesting extensions and revisions of our basic theoretical framework. We argue that, while some people have specific and deeply held political commitments, most appear to hold only vague or ill-formed beliefs. People revise and act on them only when challenged to do so in particular contexts, and most have not had such an opportunity prior to joining the union. Presenting members with a specific demand to act jointly and coherently forces them to crystallize their preferences and generates information about their own political and industrial efficacy. We present interview and oral history evidence to document self-reported changes in political beliefs among the ILWU and WWF rank and file as a result of their union experiences.

In chapter 7 we extend the analysis to include an original survey of rank-and-file ILWU members. We begin with a specific puzzle: even though ILWU members clearly have benefited from increased international trade, the union has maintained a consistent stance opposing trade liberalization for several decades. Interviews with ILWU leaders show that the union's stance appears to be sincere, based on the belief that current international trade rules unfairly benefit multinational corporations while imposing costs on the workers and the environment in both rich and poor countries. Union leaders repeatedly justify their position in reference to the ILWU's stated organizational principles. We then turn to an original survey of both newly registered and long-term ILWU members in Los Angeles/Long Beach, Seattle, and Tacoma from 2006 to 2010. We compare ILWU members' attitudes toward trade with those of non-members with otherwise similar characteristics. We also compare new union members with older cohorts. We find that ILWU members are more likely to have strong political opinions; they are more likely to support trade restrictions and oppose NAFTA; and they are more likely to engage in politics, including turning out to vote, protest, and donate to political causes. All these relationships are stronger among those with a more intense exposure to the union, even accounting for age cohort effects. Taken together, these findings are difficult to explain with reference to union members' economic interests, but they are consistent with a process of preference provocation due to ILWU membership.

Chapter 8 seriously considers the possibility that political activism may yield an economic benefit to the union. To the extent that this is true, it further reinforces the rank-and-file confidence in the leadership and consequently the governance equilibrium leading to group-level political mobilization. Specifically we consider whether and how large-scale political actions by the ILWU and WWF/MUA could serve as signaling devices to employers when it comes time to bargain over wages. We lay out this logic and examine its implications using original data on ILWU and WWF political work stoppages. We find some evidence that the signaling explanation may be at play in the ILWU, but only after significant technological shocks to the industry and a softening of confidence in Harry Bridges' leadership. The WWF, operating in a far different institutional environment, displays no evidence that its political mobilizations are an attempt to signal solidarity or resolve to employers.

The final chapter represents our efforts to pull our findings together and extend the reasoning to other circumstances, including the future of the ILWU and WWF. We reflect on how organizational attempts to build (or restrict) a population's "community of fate" can have effects in state-building and in the politicization of ethnic or religious divisions. By uncovering the processes that account for why some unions go beyond economism when others do not, our intention is to offer a more general explanation of the observed diversity among religious, political, and even nationalist groups. Our first job, however, is to understand unions. It is to that task we now turn.

CHAPTER 2

Building an Encompassing Community of Fate and Winning Consent

In the last chapter we saw how some labor unions successfully and repeatedly mobilize in support of political causes that have little to do with the members' material interests or their reasons for joining the organization. This behavior presents a fourfold puzzle. First, why would the members of these organizations be willing to take these costly actions in the absence of any obvious benefit? One possible (although dissatisfying) explanation is simply that there are people in the world who hold certain political beliefs and moral commitments. Some organizations, including some unions, simply count a lot of those "types" as members and have somehow overcome the standard collective action problems. In subsequent chapters we detail how this selection story does not hold in the unions we study. But even if a significant proportion of a union's membership actually does possess larger political objectives, we still have the second puzzle: why pursue these political objectives through the union? Why not their church or political party or softball league? Why not form a new organization dedicated solely to those issues? Third, in the likely event that not all union members hold the political commitments of the leadership, why do they keep re-electing leaders who make additional demands on the members' resources beyond the leader of a traditional business union? Fourth, how does the organization maintain its commitments to broader goals across changes in leadership and membership?

In this chapter we present our most stripped-down theoretical framework focusing on the founding or pivotal moment for an organization in which a new leadership cadre has managed to effectively address fundamental existential challenges for the group. These existential challenges could include overcoming basic collective action problems at organizational founding, but they also encompass moments of upheaval such as major technological changes, economic depression, shifts in the political environment, or demographic pressures. What all these moments share in common is the necessity for an organizational response; failure to respond effectively could result in organizational failure. Leaders who are tactically successful in such situations have an outsized ability to affect the scope of the organizational activity and the organizational governance institutions that support it. We will show in subsequent chapters that this basic, rationalist model provides important leverage in understanding how some organizations can elicit group behavior beyond the members' immediate material interests. But we will also uncover evidence that points to a richer dynamic relationship between the objectives pursued by organizational leaders and the beliefs and revealed preferences of the rank and file. In chapter 6 we revisit the theoretical argument by relaxing some assumptions about the nature and stability of the members' preferences.

The abstract situation we consider here is one in which a group of individuals has organized to collectively generate some public or club good[1] through time. We take as given that the members of the organization agree on this common objective and recognize their dependence on one another in the production of this valued good. We are interested in considering how the group endogenously expands its scope of action to include projects that may not directly benefit the members.

The group is composed of a leader and the rank-and-file members. Leaders are individuals who hold a position of generalized salience for a group, that is, their statements and actions are widely observed by the members and the members are aware that the other members observe the same information. Furthermore, leadership is valuable because there is some uncertainty about the correct course of action for the organization. Leaders are thought to possess privileged and valuable information that enables the organization to function more successfully. For example, a union leader may have superior information about an employer's ability to withstand a strike. Or the leader may have a tactical or organizational innovation to implement. But while the leaders and members all share a common desire for the organization to be successful, the leader's valuable services are not free. Leaders have their own motivations: they may seek personal rents such as adulation and power, or more direct rents such as those garnered through a large pay package or side payments. Or they may have political or other social goals that the organization in question can help them achieve. Leaders thus face a credibility problem in making demands of the membership: members want to know that the leader isn't misleading or taking advantage of them. For their part, members must decide how much to contribute to the organization's mission(s) based on

---

[1] A public good is non-rival and non-excludable, while a club good is non-rival among some population but others can be excluded from enjoying the good. For our purposes here the distinction makes little difference.

their own preferences, on their beliefs about the actions of their fellows, and on the statements and credibility of the leader.

We will observe organizations taking actions consistent with an expanded community of fate only when a leader actually calls upon the membership to take concerted action in this regard. But simply asking is not enough. Echoing a long tradition of the theory of the firm (Kreps 1990; Miller 1992; Gibbons 1998; Hermalin 1998, 2001), we emphasize that it is essentially impossible for the leader and members to come up with some sort of formal incentive contract delineating the leader's role in all situations. Instead we focus on governance institutions—the combination of stated principles, organizational rules, and channels of information transmission—as the mechanism by which leadership can succeed in persuading the members of the leader's credibility. The set of principles articulated by the leader defines a causal model of the world—an ideology—that identifies and justifies the activities relevant to the organization. In a world of unforeseen contingencies and multiple plausible equilibria, this set of principles provides a way to coordinate expectations and a commonly understood benchmark by which to judge the leader's demands on the members. The organizational rules determine the process by which decisions are made and establish the rights of the rank and file vis-à-vis the leadership and one another. These formal rules thereby provide a public set of criteria by which to evaluate whether the decision to take an action (or refrain from doing so) is procedurally fair while also providing a way for the leadership to build a reputation consistent with their stated principles.

All this presupposes that the leader has not only successfully addressed the existential threat that opened the possibility for organizational change but that she also continues to preside over an organization that is able to deliver on the group's fundamental objectives. In order for the necessary subset of the members to go along with these demands, they must stand to lose more by replacing the leader with a new one than by going along with the leader's request. Both leadership credibility and the expected outcomes under a new leader are functions of governance institutions. We argue that the leader's ideological model and the governance of the organization will form an equilibrium; formal organizational rules and less formalized norms vary depending on the extent to which leaders make more activist demands of the membership.

The next section identifies key building blocks in the literature. The following section develops the argument. We attempt to minimize the technical demands on the reader, though we do explicitly build on formally proven results, especially those of Hermalin (1998, 2007). We do, on occasion, present mathematical expressions with the aim of making ideas as clear and specific as possible. We relegate some necessary mathematical manipulation to footnotes and the appendix. The concluding section summarizes the major implications and collects the empirical hypotheses that we take up in subsequent chapters.

Leaders, Governance, and Organizational Performance

Our argument has a highly contingent element: we argue that motivations that drive people to become leaders of organizations can, at certain moments and under certain conditions, have an outsized influence over the scope of the organization's actions through time.[2] This sort of model is unusual in the social sciences where explanations focusing on the strategic environment, information, structural conditions, and (assumed) exogenous institutions dominate. Reliance on historically contingent factors, much less the idiosyncratic attributes of specific individuals, is frowned upon as ad hoc and lacking in generalizability.[3] We sympathize with these criticisms. We are not arguing for "great men" or that the personal attributes of a few individuals are sufficient for explaining all our outcome of interest. But we do hope to convince readers that the content of organizational principles is important for understanding organizational behavior and performance. These principles, in turn, are intimately bound up in the motivations and objectives of the set of individuals who invested the resources and talent in solving a group's collective action problems at pivotal moments.

Titular leaders are part of virtually all organized political life. Some leaders appear able to elicit greater effort or sacrifice from their followers than others. Within the same industry, workers in some firms are demonstrably more productive and committed than in others. Some governments can raise armies and taxes with a minimum of coercion while others require considerable force and policing to gain even minimal compliance. Presidents and prime ministers vary in their success at generating a legislative record (Saiegh 2009). Members' activism and loyalty differ across political parties and voluntary organizations. Some social

---

[2] See Ahlquist and Levi (2011) for a more expansive review and assessment of the state of the art of social science work on organizational leadership. This section draws on that paper.

[3] However, the importance of historical contingency is enjoying a resurgence in some areas, as evidenced in Shapiro and Bedi (2007), Wood (2007), Acemoglu, Johnson, Robinson, and Yared (2008), and Acemoglu and Robinson (2012). This also resonates with the large body of work discussing "path dependence" and the importance of initial conditions, such as in Thelen (1999), Pierson (2000), Page (2006), as well as threshold models of collective action relying on the existence of a group of "low-threshold" agents. See, for example, Schelling (1978) and Marwell and Oliver (1993).

movements succeed while others fail miserably. Observers often lay credit or blame for these outcomes at the feet of organizational "leaders." Corporate executives (and even some city managers) routinely justify their high compensation packages by claiming credit for outcomes that are the culmination of the efforts of many thousands of others.[4]

The concepts of "leader" and "leadership" are inherently vague and contested. Journalists, polemicists, and scholars alike continue to appropriate the term "leadership" for a variety of purposes, maintaining a sterile debate over the meaning of the word. Nevertheless, in the last two decades a more refined and formalized discussion of what it means to be a "leader" is emerging. Recent contributions from political science and political economy reveal that studying pivotal and important individuals implicates virtually all of the thorniest issues confronting social scientists today, from instability and chaos in multidimensional voting situations to human cognition and the origins of preferences. In this literature there is actually considerable consensus that leadership is relational, asymmetric, salient, domain-specific, and instrumental. For the situations that concern us here, leadership has an additional characteristic: it occurs under the expectation of ongoing, repeated interaction between leaders and followers, often within durable organizations.

Leadership is *relational*; one cannot be a leader without followers. The dyadic (or multilateral) nature of leadership implies that we cannot understand the role of the leader unless we also have some ideas about the objectives and resources of the (potential) followers.

The leader-follower relationship is *asymmetric*. The leader enjoys attention and possibly loyalty and obedience from the membership, but the relationship need not work the other way around. Even if we consider a leader to be the "agent" of the membership (Fiorina and Shepsle 1989), the leader still possesses a position distinct from those on whose behalf she is acting. She may be the hub for information flows, the person to whom people turn for direction, or the one able to coordinate action. This asymmetry is reinforced if the leader also has the power to compel.

One form of this asymmetry can be made more specific: a leader is *salient*, that is, a leader commands her followers' attention. But more than that: part of the attraction of a leader is that the followers believe that other followers are paying attention to the same leader. Thus, *generalized salience* or common knowledge (Chwe 2001) is a necessary condition for being a leader of some population.

---

[4] "CEOs are paid what they are worth to their companies, and their high pay reflects the extraordinary value of their talent" (http://gregmankiw.blogspot.com/2006/10/gabaix-on -ceo-pay.html).

Leadership is *domain-specific*: an individual who commands the attention and respect of followers on certain matters may in fact be a follower in others. We can think of a CEO in relation to the principal at her children's school. The CEO may be the leader of a firm, but it is the principal who has the power to direct and coordinate the children's education as long as they attend that school; the principal also has the last word on who advances and who is expelled. This may draw too bright a line, however. High-salience individuals may find ways to expand the domains over which they attract attention. Prospective followers may attribute generalized knowledge or skill to a particular leader extending outside the domain of initial relevance.[5] Empirically, experimental subjects appear to attach status to individuals based on their superior performance on tasks irrelevant to the question at hand (Wilson and Rhodes 1997).

Fifth, a leader is *instrumental* in the sense that the leader is attempting to get the followers to do something. But while the notion of instrumentality is common in the literature on the topic, there are important differences in how authors conceive of leadership. We identify at least three different ways leaders act instrumentally. The first, and most common in the literature, builds on the foundation of coordination dilemmas. Agents are assumed to have the same objectives, know the structure of the game, and understand how their actions map directly into their individual and collective welfare. They just need some help moving in concert. To the extent there are multiple equilibria, leaders can tilt the group decision toward their preferred outcome. This is the approach we adopt in this chapter. Later, however, we take seriously the possibility that (potential) followers may be uncertain about the strategic situation in which they are embedded and the beliefs and likely actions of others. They may fail to recognize that there is a common purpose or agenda. Here the leader does even more: she provides a model of the world that enables followers to then impose some structure on their situation. Third, a leader may possess special characteristics—oratorical skill, a genuinely new idea, or perhaps "charisma"—such that the leader is able to transform the beliefs and possibly the preferences of the followers.

The political economy of leadership has emerged from two distinct modeling traditions: the spatial voting model with its corresponding "chaos" theorems and the economics of information, particularly models of the firm. In order to better organize current theoretical work, we refer to the former as *structural theories of leadership* and the latter as *informational theories*. In the former, the leader is someone who occupies a particularly

---

[5] See Kahneman (2011, 81) and passim on exaggerated emotional coherence or the "halo effect": "The tendency to like (or dislike) everything about a person—including things you have not observed . . .".

important position in some pre-defined institutional structure. By virtue of her position, the leader is salient. She also gains institutional (e.g., agenda-setting) and coercive powers to a greater or lesser degree. She can use her position to influence the organization in ways she prefers.

Informational theories of leadership emerge out of the game-theoretic analysis of coordination dilemmas with incomplete information. Players generally have aligned preferences but need help coordinating on the same action or strategy. In such a setup, agents can use commonly observed cheap-talk signals to coordinate on one equilibrium or another (Frohlich, Oppenheimer, and Young 1971). Relabeling this signal as "leader" then follows naturally. From this simple beginning, several intriguing models have emerged in recent years. Of course this distinction between information and structure breaks down rapidly once taken to the real world. Leaders generally occupy offices in pre-defined organizational structures and acquire and disseminate information by virtue of holding that office.

Modeling Organizational Scope and Governance

We develop our models in the context of specialized version of the collective action/public goods problem generally referred to as "moral hazard in teams." Members of a group contribute costly resources to some project. Each individual's contribution is unobservable and unverifiable, implying that it is impossible to write an enforceable contract stipulating how much each person will supply. Early work explored possible incentive schemes for eliciting optimal group effort. Holmstrom (1982) shows that there is no self-enforcing (Nash equilibrium) set of contracts that is both budget balancing[6] and Pareto efficient. The intuition behind this result is that individuals will only contribute to the group project up to the point that their *individual* marginal gain is equal to their *individual* marginal cost, even if their marginal cost of effort is far lower than the marginal team-level output, implying that the group could do better if they could induce members to work harder. The restriction that incentives must be paid out of total group output, however, prevents this from happening.

Suffice to say that the team production problem is a well-trod area of theoretical contract economics; the basic framework has been extended in many directions. Miller (1992: 198) summarizes the implications of his and other extensions with the dictum: "Information asymmetries . . . and production externalities make it impossible for managers to realize the full efficiency potential of team production processes through the manipulation

---

[6] The final output must be completely divided up, i.e., the sum of the payments to the team members cannot be more or less than total group production.

of short-term economic incentives alone." That pure incentive contracts alone fail to achieve the first-best group outcome implies that there can be performance variation across teams and scope for improvement.

Hermalin (1998, 2007) incorporates uncertainty and information transmission into the moral-hazard-in-teams problem, providing the information-based rationale for a group leader. The key attribute of a leader is her possession of useful knowledge about the state of the world that the average member does not have. As is standard in models of the firm, Hermalin presupposes that the task, production function, and objectives of all the team members are well-defined and common knowledge. The action in these games occurs as agents devise strategies for information transmission and learn dynamically; the scope of group activity and objectives are never in doubt. Existing models are generally silent on how the leader and followers coordinate on organizational objectives, leaving little room for the inspirational role leaders seem to play in the real world, where organizational goals, tactics, and the beliefs of others are frequently uncertain or even contested.

A key contribution of our work, then, is to begin the process of understanding how—and how much—a leader can affect an organization's scope of action. To that end, we develop an extension of the Hermalin models.

Suppose we have a union with N-1 members and a leader. Without loss of generality assume that $i=1$ is the leader. For now we assume N is "small" in the sense that each member's marginal contribution has noticeable impact on the group output.[7] The union is organized to produce a club good from which all members and the leader are assumed to benefit equally. The club good construction reflects how the union situation differs from the canonical principal-agent conception of production in a firm. Holmstrom, Hermalin, and others are interested in how some notional principal can allocate a perfectly divisible output to incentivize a team. The member-leader relationship in the union setting is less like the manager-employee relationship, more closely resembling that between legislators and a chief executive. Who is the "principal" and who is the "agent" in such a setting is not obvious (Fiorina and Shepsle 1989). The union leader cannot allocate wages directly to union members conditional on the quality of the union contract or their level of contributions to the union. The benefits of a union contract cannot be allocated to

---

[7] In this chapter we treat the members as homogenous and do not emphasize comparative statics on N. We could marginally simplify exposition by assuming a single "representative" member. In chapters 5 and 6 we revisit this model in the context of heterogeneous members and larger groups. To foreshadow this discussion and maintain consistency, we explicitly acknowledge the size of the group, N.

create any system of incentives for member contributions *to the union*. Rather the leader is, in some ways, the agent of the membership and must convince members to contribute through dues and, when necessary, picketing and striking.[8]

There is a random component, θ, that affects how much the union members get for their efforts.[9] The parameter θ summarizes the "state of the world," i.e., how auspicious the environment is for union activity. For example, strikes or other industrial action could have greater effect on the members' economic situation in certain periods and be riskier in others depending on the state of the economy, the political climate, the editorial stance of local newspapers, etc. Suppose the leader can learn the true value of θ.[10] Clearly such information is valuable to everyone, but effectively communicating it may not be so simple.

Formally, consider a simplified version of the Hermalin model. Each union member, i, derives club-good benefits, net of costly effort e_i:

$$V_i = \theta \left(e_i + \sum_{j=1}^{N-1} e_j \right) - \frac{e_i^2}{2} \tag{2.1}$$

where

$$\theta \in \{\theta_L, \theta_H\}, 0 < \theta_L < \theta_H$$
$$\bar{\theta} \equiv E[\theta] = p\theta_H + (1-p)\theta_L$$

The stage game, Γ, is defined as follows:

1. The value of θ is revealed to the leader.
2. The leader announces $\hat{\theta}$ which need not be the true value.
3. The rank and file update their beliefs about θ and then contribute their effort, along with the leader, non-cooperatively.
4. The true value of θ is revealed to all and output and payoffs are realized.

---

[8] The club good construction also avoids the possibility that the leader can play members off one another by differentially directing group output to some favored few. See Ferejohn (1986). We thank Scott Gehlbach for calling our attention to this.

[9] So long as N is small, treating team output as a club good has an analogue to an equal shares contract, which Holmstrom (1982) proves is optimal under the assumptions of non-negative shares, affine contracts (in θ), and common beliefs about θ. The more explicit public goods construction we pursue is also discussed in Hermalin (1998).

[10] We discuss costly leadership later. Whether the leader learns the true value with certainty or is simply better informed about its distribution makes no difference for the substantive interpretation of results.

Let $\tilde{\theta}_i$ denote i's beliefs about the value of θ. A union member's optimal effort as a function of her beliefs is simply $e_i^*(\tilde{\theta}_i) = \tilde{\theta}_i$. The strategic situation between the leader and followers arises because the leader has an incentive to misrepresent her knowledge. To see this, note that the leader's payoff is increasing in the efforts of all the $N-1$ followers.[11] Even when we are in the "bad" state $(\theta = \theta_L)$ the leader would still like convince followers that times are good $(\hat{\theta} = \theta_H)$ and they should contribute correspondingly more effort.[12] The followers, however, understand this and, in the one-shot game, rationally disregard any announcement by the leader. Absent any signaling ability, the leader's statement is uninformative and the members' beliefs about the state are simply the prior, implying that $\tilde{\theta} = \bar{\theta} \; \forall \; i > 1$. The stage game equilibrium is one in which the leader's announcement is ignored, the leader plays $e_1^*(\theta) = \theta$, and the rank and file play $e_i^*(\tilde{\theta} = \bar{\theta}) = \bar{\theta} \; \forall \; i > 1$.

Hermalin introduces two different ways that the leader can signal along with her announcement. He calls these signaling tactics "sacrifice" and "leadership by example," respectively. Under sacrifice, the leader can burn or distribute some fixed amount of resources before the members take their actions. Sacrifice is really just a mechanism design problem: can we come up with a contract that will induce the leader to tell the truth and that makes the leader better off than the situation in which her knowledge is not utilized? Hermalin (1998) proves that there is for the one-shot game while Hermalin (2007) does the same for the repeated game version of the model. The gist of the result is that the optimal contract stipulates that in the high-productivity state, the leader distributes some amount just big enough that a leader in the low-productivity state has no incentive to copy.

In the "lead by example" solution, Hermalin relaxes two assumptions of the standard team production game. First, the leader is allowed to expend her effort before the rest of the team decides how much effort to contribute. Second, he assumes that all other members of the union can observe the leader's effort (at no cost), but still no (enforceable) contract can be written based on effort levels. This is one way of modeling the leader's generalized salience. Since effort is costly, the leader can credibly signal to the team whether they are in a high- or low-productivity state simply by moving first; separating Bayesian equilibria exist.[13] The

---

[11] Symmetrically, all group members benefit from the effort of others.

[12] The leader's personal benefit to having all the members contribute θ_H compared to θ_L when the true state is θ_L is $\theta_L[(N-1)(\theta_H - \theta_L)]$, which is increasing in θ_L, the range of θ, and the size of the group.

[13] Hermalin (1998) assumes a divisible output. In this context, "leading by example" is superior, in welfare terms, to the "sacrifice" option since the leader's action (mimicked

transmission of information within the group, especially when leaders lead by example, is a critical component underlying Hermalin's solutions, echoing Arrow (1974).

THE REPEATED GAME

Now consider an indefinite repetition of Γ, with the game continuing to the next round with probability δ. We denote this game as Γ_δ. For the sake of simplicity we consider only a pure announcement game without signaling.[14] Following Hermalin, we assume that the leader is infinitely lived (with discount factor δ) while the followers each live only for one period yet know the complete history of the game to that point.[15] We assume that θ is drawn independently each period. Repeating the game through time allows for two results of particular interest for us: leaders can develop reputations for effectiveness and leaders can earn rents[16] for their expertise.

Reputation is an immediate consequence of valuing the future in repeated games. If the rank and file coordinate on a "trigger strategy" in which they punish the leader for lying, then the leader has an incentive to truthfully reveal the state of the world in every period so long as she values the future sufficiently. Formally, we can construct a set of equilibria in which the leader always announces the true state of the world $(\hat{\theta}_t = \theta_t,$ where t indexes time) and the rank and file believe the announcement $(\tilde{\theta}_t = \hat{\theta}_t)$ so long as the leader has told the truth in every previous period $(\tilde{\theta}_s = \hat{\theta}_s \; \forall \; s < t)$. If the leader lies $(\tilde{\theta}_t \neq \hat{\theta}_t)$, then the rank and file will ignore the leader's statements forever after, choosing their optimal effort based only on their prior beliefs.[17] This strategy profile is a (Perfect Bayesian Nash) equilibrium so long as $\delta \geq \bar{\delta}$ where

$$\bar{\delta} \equiv \frac{V_1(\hat{\theta}_t = \theta_H | \theta_t = \theta_L, \tilde{\theta}_t = \hat{\theta}_t) - V_1(\hat{\theta}_t = \theta_L | \theta_t = \theta_L, \tilde{\theta}_t = \hat{\theta}_t)}{E_\theta[V_1(\hat{\theta}_t = \theta, \tilde{\theta}_t = \hat{\theta}_t)] - E_\theta[V_1(\hat{\theta}_t = \theta, \tilde{\theta}_t = \bar{\theta})] + V_1(\hat{\theta}_t = \theta_H | \theta_t = \theta_L, \tilde{\theta}_t = \hat{\theta}_t) - V_1(\hat{\theta}_t = \theta_L | \theta_t = \theta_L, \tilde{\theta}_t = \hat{\theta}_t)} \quad (2.2)$$

by the other N-1 members) directly contributes to team production, whereas "sacrifice" contributes nothing to production.

[14] This follows Hermalin (2007). He also considers the effect of repetition on signaling behavior since continued signaling is no longer needed when the leader can develop a reputation for truthfully conveying her knowledge. He derives several interesting results about the amount of signaling in equilibrium and the degree to which it depends on p, the (prior) probability of being in the good state.

[15] This assumption, discussed in detail in Hermalin (2007), is driven largely by his technical concerns with the possible collusion among the followers to coordinate on higher effort levels and/or punishment strategies. Our assumption of a club good partially mitigates these problems. Collusion among followers does not eliminate the value of the leader's information.

[16] Hermalin (2007) refers to these rents as "tribute."

[17] In this context ignoring the leader and turning the leader out of office are equivalent. We discuss the role of elections and leadership selection below.

That is, the threshold level of patience required to sustain truth-telling in the repeated game is a ratio. The numerator is the leader's one-shot gain should she take advantage of her reputation by lying. The denominator is the sum of that quantity and the expected net gain associated with being believed (and telling the truth) compared with being ignored by her followers. Intuitively, as the value to the leader of being believed increases, the greater the range of discount factors that can support a truth-telling equilibrium. The value to the leader of the followers' trust increases in the prior uncertainty about the state of the world, p, and the difference between the states $(\theta_H - \theta_L)$.

LEADERSHIP 'RENTS'

Leadership positions are often sought after because leaders of organizations, including labor unions, frequently enjoy perks and even enhanced monetary compensation. We will refer to these extra benefits accruing to leaders as "leadership rents" in the sense that they are additional and sometimes costly resources directed to the leader because of her demonstrated knowledge and skill (i.e., her reputation). In the repeated game setting, leadership rents are a way for the membership to further incentivize the leader to truthfully reveal her information; losing office hurts more when the office has additional benefits associated with it.

If we suppose that acquiring information about θ is costly or that communicating with the membership entails additional effort, then we have an additional justification for rents. Leadership rents are incentives to take on this task or, equivalently, as compensation for these costs of leading. Including a cost of leadership along with possible rents is also attractive on substantive grounds: it models the notion that leadership is difficult; in order for someone to take on the mantle, she typically has other objectives in addition to those shared by the group she leads.

We can formalize this notion of leadership rents using an expanded utility function in which union members contribute (costly) resources to both the union project (e_{it}, as before) as well as the leader's compensation, denoted $r_{it}: U_{it} = V_{it} - \frac{r_{it}}{2} \forall i > 1$ while the leader receives payoff $U_{1t} = V_{1t} + \gamma_1 \sum_{j=2}^{N} r_{jt} - \xi$ where $\gamma_1 > 0$ captures how much the leader values rents and $\xi \geq 0$ represents these fixed costs of leading. We can then posit a modified version of Γ_δ in which the rank and file contribute r_{it} prior to the leader's announcement, $\hat{\theta}_t$. Rents can support a reputation for leadership effectiveness as part of a trigger strategy equilibrium in which the rank and file revert to the stage game equilibrium should the leader ever lie.[18]

---

[18] Hermalin (2007) refers to this as "enabling love," contrasted with "extorted love." In the latter the followers only revert to the punishment phase if the leader lies *after* receiving

To establish equilibrium we must identify the level of leadership rents the rank and file are willing to tolerate. The expected gain to each member for taking advantage of the leader's knowledge compared to the reversion point is given by

$$E_\theta[\Delta V_i] = p[V_i(e_i^* = \theta_H | \theta = \theta_H) - V_i(e_i^* = \bar{\theta} | \theta = \theta_H)]$$
$$+ (1-p)[V_i(e_i^* = \theta_L | \theta = \theta_L) - V_i(e_i^* = \bar{\theta} | \theta = \theta_L)] \quad (2.3)$$
$$= \left(N - \frac{3}{2}\right)(p\theta_H^2 + (1-p)\theta_L^2 - \bar{\theta}^2)$$

Equation (2.3) reaches its maximum at $p = 0.5$, i.e., the leader's knowledge is most valuable when times are most uncertain. The disutility for paying rents cannot exceed the value of the leader's knowledge to a member: $r_i \leq \sqrt{2E_\theta[\Delta V_i]}$. Total rents in each period, then, cannot exceed R_{max} where

$$R_{max} = (N-1)\sqrt{2E_\theta[\Delta V_i]} \quad (2.4)$$

Suppose we fix some rent level $R^* \leq R_{max}$ and assume that each member contributes equally such that $r_{jt}^* = \frac{R^*}{N-1}$. We also assume that the leader does not pay the costs of leadership in the punishment phase, should it occur. Then R^* is an equilibrium under the trigger strategy just defined so long as $\delta \geq \tilde{\delta}$, where

$$\tilde{\delta} \equiv \frac{V_1(\hat{\theta}_t = \theta_H | \theta_t = \theta_L, \tilde{\theta}_t = \hat{\theta}_t) - V_1(\hat{\theta}_t = \theta_L | \theta_t = \theta_L, \tilde{\theta}_t = \hat{\theta}_t)}{\gamma_1 R^* - \xi + E_\theta[V_1(\hat{\theta}_t = \theta, \tilde{\theta}_t = \hat{\theta}_t)] - E_\theta[V_1(\hat{\theta}_t = \theta, \tilde{\theta}_t = \bar{\theta})] + V_1(\hat{\theta}_t = \theta_H | \theta_t = \theta_L, \tilde{\theta}_t = \hat{\theta}_t) - V_1(\hat{\theta}_t = \theta_L | \theta_t = \theta_L, \tilde{\theta}_t = \hat{\theta}_t)} \quad (2.5)$$

Comparing $\bar{\delta}$ and $\tilde{\delta}$ yields a key insight: the availability of rents expands the set of discount factors that will support effective leadership in equilibrium. Including ξ as the fixed cost for learning (or communicating) the value of θ shrinks the equilibrium set, all else fixed.

We also see that the more the leader values rents (γ_1 larger), the more "effective" leadership rents become in the sense of expanding the set of truth-telling equilibria for a fixed contribution from members. Having a leader who highly values the rents of leadership makes it *cheaper* for the rank and file to induce the leader to behave in a trustworthy fashion and compensate her for the costs of acquiring and communicating valuable information. Setting $R^* = \frac{\xi}{\gamma_1}$ implies that total rents exactly offset the costs of leading, but $\frac{\xi}{\gamma_1}$ is not the minimum rents necessary to sustain good leadership in equilibrium since the leader also benefits from her

---

rents for that period. Both are supportable as equilibrium strategy profiles, conditional on the value of other parameters.

own truthfulness. Assuming $\delta > 0$, the minimum rents required for truth telling, $\underline{R}$, is given by

$$
\underline{R} = \frac{\xi}{\gamma_1} - \frac{E_\theta[V_1(\hat{\theta} = \theta, \tilde{\theta} = \hat{\theta}) - V_1(\tilde{\theta} = \bar{\theta})]}{\gamma_1}
$$
$$
+ \frac{(1-\delta)[V_1(\hat{\theta} = \theta_H \mid \theta = \theta_L, \tilde{\theta} = \hat{\theta}) - V_1(\hat{\theta} = \theta_L \mid \theta = \theta_L, \tilde{\theta} = \hat{\theta})]}{\delta \gamma_1}
$$

(2.6)

The second term on the right-hand side is the expected difference between the leader's public goods payoff under good leadership and under punishment. The third term is the weighted one-time benefit for misleading the rank and file. As $\delta \to 1$, the third term goes to 0, implying that the longer a leader's time horizons the "cheaper" she is to compensate. $\underline{R} < \frac{\xi}{\gamma_1}$ for sufficiently patient leaders; rents need not fully cover the costs of leadership.

To summarize: we have constructed a simplified, club goods version of the Hermalin leadership game. The model provides a rationale for a leader, namely incomplete information and the benefits accruing to all for adjusting the level of group effort in response to a changing external environment. The model highlights the strategic interaction between the leader and the rank and file, even when the union's overall objectives are commonly known and uncontested. Although there are possible strategies a leader can pursue in order to credibly communicate her knowledge in the one-shot game, we focused on the more realistic repeated situation. When the interaction is repeated, the leader can develop a reputation for effectiveness. Allowing the leader some perks of office further expands the set of equilibria in which the union can take advantage of the leader's knowledge. But there is a limit to the rents the rank and file will tolerate.

COMPETITION FOR LEADERSHIP

While we make a distinction between the leader and the followers, it seems hard to imagine that a well-informed individual simply appears on the scene, claims special knowledge, and the rank and file coordinate on an effective trigger strategy. More realistically, an emerging leader will have to attract the other members' attention and demonstrate her effectiveness by credibly signaling her valuable knowledge. This will likely require the leader to expend significant effort prior to seeing any of the perks of leadership. Moreover, it is not obvious how a leader can continue to extract rents over time. Under what conditions can a competitor supplant the incumbent by offering to provide leadership for some lower level of rents?

As a way of thinking through these issues we extend our leadership model (formal notation and equilibrium derivation are provided in the appendix). In this extension, leadership (learning and communicating important information) is again costly. Leaders can be compensated with rents, funded by the rank and file. But now suppose that the rank and file not only reward good leadership but they also have the opportunity to replace the leader with a challenger who attaches an unknown value to leadership rents.[19] The members want to select a leader who is more responsive to rents in order to minimize their own contributions while still enjoying good leadership.

Intuitively, we can imagine that the leader's ability to enjoy rents through time is a result of her demonstrated ability to cost-effectively learn about the world and communicate with the membership. Any challenger is a risk. So long as the incumbent continues to deliver good leadership (tell the truth), it is unlikely that the members will replace the leader. In the appendix we construct an equilibrium where the rank and file retain the incumbent if she is more responsive to rents than the challenger is expected to be; the members contribute to the leader's rents only if the incumbent has developed a reputation for good leadership. Similarly, the leader is willing to spend the effort to build a reputation for good leadership so long as the rents are forthcoming; she continues to deliver good leadership through time so long as she is rewarded. This arrangement is self-reinforcing and persists indefinitely since in this model there is no way for a challenger to credibly demonstrate that she can, in fact, provide good leadership more "cheaply."[20]

This sequencing has an important empirical implication: the leader extracts rents, whether monetary or political, only after her reputation for effectiveness is well-established.[21]

Clearly this model is highly stylized. Leaders can and do lose elections. More complicated and general models of election-induced accountability can be developed (Barro 1973; Ferejohn 1986, 1999; Ashworth 2005; Ashworth and Bueno de Mesquita 2008), including addressing the tension between using elections as tools of selection and punishment (Besley 2006; Ashworth, Bueno de Mesquita, and Freidenberg 2012). The model just outlined combines moral hazard with uncertainty about the leader's and challenger's types. What distinguishes this model from standard

---

[19] A key assumption of our model is that the members learn the leader's γ_1 once the leader pays the costs of leadership.

[20] Modifying the game to allow the challenger to propose some lower level of rents to the membership changes nothing since the loser's payoff is 0. Regardless of her γ_c, the challenger always has an incentive to propose a level of rents lower than the incumbent's. The membership will therefore rationally disregard any announcement.

[21] This echoes the result in Ashworth (2005) in which prior constituency service increases the likelihood that the incumbent will be retained for another term and will be able to devote more resources to his idiosyncratic policy projects. Also see Mayhew (1974).

models of accountability under elections is that the leader's actions and (sometimes) type are fully revealed to the membership. Rather than focus on the members' learning about the leader over time, we emphasize how the move to endogenous leadership rents allows us to separate accountability (using rents to reward good leadership) from the mechanism for selecting "better" types (elections).

THE FORM OF RENTS

Rents, as we have discussed them, are simply resources the membership is willing to turn over to the leader above and beyond contributions to club good production. Leadership rents can and do take several forms. Most obviously, rents can be monetary, including bonuses and higher salaries. In the Teamsters, for example, the leadership cadre, even at the local level, often earned significantly more than the rank and file (see chapter 3). Rents can include perks such as plush offices or travel to sunny locations.[22] Rents can also be simple adulation, deference, and respect. But, most interesting to us, rents can include the leeway to use generalized salience in one domain (collective bargaining) to extract rank-and-file resources for other projects. If the leader values political projects he can demand resources from the membership, *to a point*. From an equilibrium existence standpoint, what matters for generating effective leadership is that the level of acceptable rents is common knowledge.

Our assumption that rents are only available from the members also matters. Where others outside the organization (like the employer, the government, or the mob) can fund rents, we run the risk of a highly responsive leader selling out their membership. This seems most likely to happen when rents (and leadership desires) are monetary. In such a situation a leader sufficiently responsive to rents will tend to serve the interests of the rent-provider rather than the membership. If the leader is accepting cash or other financial benefits from those with interests opposed to the membership, the leader cannot expect to retain office by virtue of her credibility as a good leader. Rather, she will be forced to rely on some combination of patronage and coercion, both likely to be funded with the externally provided resources. Where the leaders seek political ends, things are more ambiguous. Leftist or populist political goals seem to require rank-and-file participation and contribution to the leader's projects. But if political goals are more self-aggrandizing, such as wanting to be treated as powerful and important by others—including other powerful

---

[22] Under Dave Beck, the Teamsters moved their headquarters to a custom-built building in Washington, DC. The 1954 profile of Beck in *Life* magazine reflected on his "penthouse" offices.

and important people—then some of the rents are contributed by those outside the organization.

This conception of leadership rents as the origin of political mobilization differs starkly from Lenin's solution to the problem of "economism." Whereas Lenin imagined that a successful leader will transform the members' "consciousness" such that they will come to share the leader's preferences, we argue that successful leaders can extract rents, but that these rents are limited and depend on the leader's continued ability to deliver good "economistic" outcomes. The leader may ask for member participation in political projects, but the leader's ability to pursue these goals is limited. Furthermore, *followers will tolerate a leader's rents, including activist demands, provided they do not conflict with the fundamental goals or undermine the successes of the union.* In other words, it is unlikely that union members will tolerate a leader that asks them to give up hard-won contract provisions in the name of a political goal. To this end, *leaders attempting to expand the union's "community of fate" will argue that their preferred political projects improve the union's prospects for industrial success.*

From Leadership Rents to Organizational Governance Institutions

As with most applications of repeated game theory, there are several important gaps in the model as described. The equilibria identified are but a subset of an infinitely large set. How do we end up settling on one? How do the trigger values and levels of leadership rents come to be common knowledge? Which rents are acceptable and which are not? How does the level and form of leader rents come to be decided and communicated? How do followers evaluate the leader's actions and effectiveness *ex post*, especially when rents are not strictly monetary?

If the leader-membership relationship is to be thought of as a contract specifying how the leader will deploy her informational advantage to make demands of the membership, it is most certainly an incomplete one, i.e., it is impossible to write a contract between the leader and the membership that covers every possible contingency. In addition, there are certain to be unforeseen events that require the leader and the membership to adapt. Without the ability to reasonably predict how his organization will respond to changing events, it is unlikely that a union member will be willing to commit substantial resources to his union or follow a particular leader.

We follow in a long line of scholars (Williamson 1993, 1996; Greif 2006) in arguing that organizational governance institutions—defined as the formal rules and informal norms that delineate how decisions are taken, how the organization will respond to future events, and how and on what basis organizational members should evaluate the actions of leaders—embody solutions to both the equilibrium selection and incomplete contracting problems.

This conception of organizational governance is directly inspired by Kreps's (1990) understanding of corporate culture in firms and Miller's (1992) argument about the role of management in equilibrium selection for instilling behavioral norms and common expectations within a firm.[23] Their rationale for corporate culture parallels ours: incomplete contracts, multiple equilibria, and unforeseen contingency in the context of group effort.[24] We cannot derive from first principles the exact "equilibrium" that organizational governance institutions will take, but we can use the logic of the model to make statements about the functional requirements that any set of governance institutions must satisfy in order to sustain the repeated game equilibria described above.

Explicitly stated principles delineating leadership rents perform the role of equilibrium selection in a context where multilateral trigger strategies are critical for supporting organizational performance. A corporate or organizational culture is, in part, a statement by the leadership (or prospective leaders) about how they will act when unforeseen contingencies arise, even if these actions are not in the immediate self-interest of the leaders.[25] If the organizational culture is to be effective, it must be clear and simple enough that both the membership and the leader know what should be done, and the principles must be widely communicated both inside and outside the organization (Kreps 1990). The actions of the leaders as they relate to decisions implicated in the organizational culture must be transparently observable to all.

Our model implies that the level and form of leadership rents are an integral part of organizational governance. Some leaders make the costly investment in skills or information acquisition because they have normative or political goals, while others may have more self-serving or materialistic objectives. With costly investment required to make an effective leader we should expect most leadership positions, at least in established organizations, to be associated with organizationally specific levels (and forms) of rents. The existence of these rents provides incentives for

[23] Our argument also bears a family resemblance to the "relational contracts" theories of the firm (Baker, Gibbons, and Murphy 2002).

[24] See Hermalin (2001) for an extensive treatment of corporate culture, including a discussion of the equilibrium selection versus incomplete contracts motivations for corporate culture. Also see Gibbons (2005).

[25] For example, mangers of a firm may promise to never lay off workers during a downturn provided workers commit to the firm.

individuals to come forward as leaders and perhaps even compete for the position. *We expect organizations to have formal and explicit policies and declarations delineating organizational scope and the levels of leadership compensation.*

The type of rents accruing to the leader is particularly important here because it has implications for other parts of organizational governance. Monetary rents are easy to agree upon and measure. They typically require the least-complex governance structure since it is relatively easy for the rank and file to evaluate the leader's performance and compensation.[26]

Leadership rents that are more difficult to measure and evaluate, such as allowing the leader some leeway to take on political projects, require governance institutions to be more complicated and explicit in both substantive and procedural dimensions. Specifically, *in organizations in which the leader successfully mobilizes the membership for expanded group action, we expect the organization to have explicit and widely disseminated statements delineating the substantive principles around which the leader will demand membership mobilization.* This is akin to Kreps's concern with "unforeseen contingencies," since it is not possible to specify all the issues or world events over which the leader wants to mobilize the union. Explicit "statements of principles" and the like allow the rank and file to form some expectations about when, how often, and over what the leader will ask them to contribute. As important, these principles allow the membership to coordinate on *ex post* evaluation of the leader's demands.

Similarly, allowing the leader additional leeway carries some additional risk. The leader may misinterpret her mandate by asking for too much from the rank and file. Or her political projects may put the organization at greater risk over an issue that does not directly serve the members' interests. These risks are hard to foresee. *We therefore expect organizations that allow leaders to make these additional demands of their members to have more extensive procedural controls, both* ex ante, *in deciding when to mobilize union resources and* ex post *in holding leaders accountable.* These procedural controls perform functions similar to those in Ferejohn's principal-agent model of politician control (Ferejohn 1999). Agents who accept greater monitoring of their actions and submit themselves to the possibility of punishment can, paradoxically, extract

---

[26] See chapters 3 and 5 where we discuss corruption and accounting irregularities in the Teamsters and ILA. In the Teamsters, the leadership made no serious attempt to hide the financial and other perks they were enjoying from the membership. Rather, the accounting shenanigans that eventually sent Dave Beck to prison seemed designed to avoid paying taxes. In Hoffa's case, he appeared to use Teamster pension funds to increase their political and industrial influence.

more resources from the principal.[27] Procedural "fairness" can also induce members whose political preferences diverge from the leadership to go along anyway (Levi 1997). Note here that organizational governance and procedures serve a functional role. In discussing such procedures empirically in the following chapters, we will link the *ex ante* controls with such governance institutions as larger executive boards and negotiating committees, requirements that policies and actions be put to a vote before the leadership acts, and the ability of the membership to confront the leader and demand that the leader publicly justify her actions. *Ex post* procedural controls will be linked with governance rules such as the direct election of national officers, the ease of recall of elected leaders, and the existence of open and detailed records of leadership debate and votes in executive bodies.

There is a constraint on the total amount of rents a leader can command ($\overline{R}$ in the formal notation). When this constraint binds, there is a trade-off between one sort of rents and another. If a leader extracts monetary rents there is correspondingly less willingness among the rank and file to tolerate additional rents of other sorts. *We expect organizations allowing their leaders to enjoy political rents to have restrictions, formal or otherwise, on the monetary compensation they enjoy.* These restrictions may, in fact, originate from the leader if the leader sufficiently values political rents. *Similarly, we expect organizations that compensate leaders with monetary rents and perks to explicitly eschew organizational involvement in any but a narrowly defined set of activities.*

Governance institutions are likely to affect who will become a leader in the future, inducing those with certain preferences to come forward as leaders. To be more specific, assume individuals vary in the value they place on a certain type of rents (relative to their valuation of the union's club goods). For example, one potential leader may hold strong normative or political commitments; she highly values "political rents." Another may have little interest in politics, per se, but does value monetary perks and the adulation of her co-unionists. The structure of the organization's incentive scheme will affect the relative willingness of these two individuals to invest in becoming a leader. Those who value monetary rewards are more likely to take on the challenges of leadership in organizations where the leader is rewarded in monetary terms. The same holds for political rents. The constitution of the organization arranges the benefits from leadership in ways that are likely to influence who will want to become a leader. *Organizational governance institutions that allow leadership*

---

[27] This also echoes the long literature on sovereign credibility and democratic institutions. Where the executive is constrained, they can borrow at better rates and tax more effectively (Levi 1988; North and Weingast 1989).

greater political leeway but restrict monetary compensation will tend to attract leaders with political commitments; organizations whose compensation is primarily monetary will not. Thus, leaders selected over time will hold commitments consistent with the formative organizational culture and will help maintain that culture over time. In this way the types of demands the leaders make of the rank and file through time are roughly similar, conditional on the organizational culture.

TRANSFORMING INFORMATION INTO REPUTATION:
THE EMERGENCE OF ORGANIZATIONAL GOVERNANCE

Governance institutions change slowly, but during pivotal moments—and with pivotal leaders—governance institutions may be built or radically altered. The most obvious such period is during organizational founding when foundational leaders manage to solve the fundamental collective action problems for some "latent group" (Olson 1965). Metaphorically (at least for Americans) the Philadelphia Constitutional Convention represents that kind of moment. There are also moments of existential threat to an existing organization, times when external events force the organization to react.[28] In the context of unions these are often periods of major technological upheaval in the industry or hard economic times. Empirically, we focus on leaders who emerge in pre-existing organizations. In the ILWU, Harry Bridges displaces the corrupt and ineffectual Joseph Ryan and breaks away to form the ILWU in the midst of the Great Depression, just as the right to organize is enshrined in American labor law. Dave Beck and Jimmy Hoffa emerge and consolidate their vision of the IBT by recognizing the importance of long-haul trucking as it emerges as a complement to (and often substitute for) railroads in the 1930s and 1940s.

In these pivotal periods leadership cadres have the rare opportunity to structure the organization's governance in ways that can imbue the organization with a set of attributes and likely behaviors that outlast the tenure of any individual leader. Leaders at these moments have the ability to formalize the level and type of rents they expect. Because greater valuation of leadership rents makes it cheaper for the rank and file to enjoy trustworthy leadership, the members have every incentive to go along. But the leader faces a tricky situation since there are limits on what the rank and file will tolerate. If the leader miscalculates or fails to allow for a governance structure congruent with her desired rents, she may lose office or the organization could fail. This, in turn, calls attention to founding organizational moments and "critical junctures." Pivotal leaders can expand the scope of activity of the organization by setting the terms of

[28] This is akin to the "constitutional quandaries" of Schofield (2006).

leadership rents, provided other governance institutions are consistent with the form of leadership rents. *Where founding leaders have strong normative and political commitments, they will try to promulgate organizational governance institutions that permit them to draw the organization into those activities. Where leaders' objectives are more self-seeking, we expect them to pursue monetary rents and other perks.*

Summary and Conclusions

In an effort to explain why some labor unions expand their activities to include those without obvious benefit to the members, we presented a theoretical account emphasizing the role of leaders and governance institutions. Lenin's "solution" to overcoming economism was built on the premise that all workers shared common interests, whether they recognized it or not. He called for a well-developed communication campaign to educate workers on the nature of their situation and the strategies for improvement, a secret network of activists, and vanguard cadre to lead the way. While we emphasize the role of leadership as a necessary condition, the rationalist model we develop here differs from Lenin's argument in profound ways. We emphasize that members become involved in a union precisely because they have expectations of economic gain. The ability of an organization to deliver the goods to the membership depends on the ability to coordinate group actions in ways appropriate to the circumstances. It is the job of organizational leaders to acquire the needed information and credibly communicate it to the group. Leadership is costly and members are willing to contribute to enjoy its benefits, but their economic interests place limits on what the leader can ask of the membership. Organizations that successfully build an expanded community of fate recognize these limits; they don't assume them away.

Borrowing from the political economy models of coordination under incomplete information (especially Hermalin 2007), we consider a public goods game in which there is a leadership cadre possessing better information about the world and generalized salience among the others in the group. It is possible for the leaders to credibly transmit their information to the members, both in a repeated game and in a single-shot situation. In a repeated game, however, leaders can develop reputations for effectively "delivering the goods." What's more, the repeated game introduces the possibility of leadership compensation or rents, which expands the set of cooperative equilibria and can be used to incentivize the emergence of a leader when information acquisition and/or communication is costly. We argue that leadership rents provide an opening for expanding the scope of union activities. Some union leaders have normative or political objectives. The members agree to contribute to these additional projects in the context of their union, up to a point.

These equilibrium outcomes are only a few of many possible and rely on trigger strategies and leaders with long time horizons. To explain how we might sustain such an outcome, we introduce the concept of organizational governance institutions that embody the union's solution to the equilibrium selection problem. For trigger strategies to work, all players must be aware of what to expect in equilibrium and when to revert to "punishment phases." They must be able to observe and evaluate the leader's actions and those of co-unionists. In our context, the organizational culture delineates the *level and type* of compensation the leader can expect, providing a focal point for the rank-and-file action and underpinning the equilibrium. The type of leadership rents has implications for organizational governance.

We argue that governance institutions are slow to change once established. Founding leadership cadres and those emerging in moments of organizational crisis are well-positioned, by virtue of their generalized salience, to set the terms of the leadership rents within the constraints of the equilibrium. Only when these leaders hold strong political convictions and believe the union is relevant to them will we see the emergence of organizational cultures that allow for leaders to extract "political rents." There is likely to be a path-dependent effect, as the governance institutions tend to stimulate the emergence of new leaders who value the types of rents the organization generates, simultaneously setting the expectations of the rank and file.

We can now return to our four questions from the beginning of the chapter. First, why would the members of these organizations be willing to take these costly actions in the absence of any obvious benefit? Our answer is that these members are simply paying the cost of having good leadership in one of several possible ways. They find the cost imposed by considering an expanded community of fate to be worth it. But beyond that, the members themselves, or some subset, may hold (or come to hold) normative commitments that their union enables them to express.

But even if some significant fraction of the union's membership actually has larger political objectives, we still have the second puzzle: why pursue these political objectives through the union? We respond that the members pursue broader objectives through their union *because they were asked to do so*. Having a leader who asks members to take specific actions in the context of an existing set of organizational rules is critical to our argument. We note, however, that contributing to political causes through the union in no way precludes individuals from also trying to mobilize other groups or set up a separate specialized organization.

Third, the rank and file are heterogeneous; not all union members hold the political commitments of the leadership. How do leaders who demand resources for an expanded scope of action keep getting re-elected? Our answer has four components. One, these members view the leader's extractive demands as equivalent to any other leadership rent; they are willing to pay so long as the benefits deriving from the leader's effectiveness in coordinating the union's industrial actions exceed the demands she makes on the membership and provided the organizational culture supports a trigger strategy that makes the leader's claims (and the effectiveness of a trigger strategy) credible. Two, union members engage in a form of contingent consent. Those who do not share the leader's political commitments nevertheless go along because they believe other members will go along; the organizational governance institutions and perhaps structural variables such as the nature of work (e.g., in teams) must make it easy for members to evaluate the procedural fairness of the decision and the likely behavior of his co-unionists. Three, the organizational institutions, including the level and type of rents that leaders can extract, also form expectations about what type of person will replace the current leader should she lose office. Those competing for office in an organization allowing leaders political rents typically are those who hold strong political or normative commitments. Finally, not all members support the leadership. All the organizations we study have vibrant, organized internal opposition groups. But as long as the current leadership cadre proves effective in coordinating industrial activity, the opposition remains just that.

These last points also form the basis for our answer to the fourth question, namely how the organization maintains its commitments to broader goals across changes in leadership and membership. Once organizational governance institutions are established, it structures the incentives for future leaders and expectations for the rank and file. So long as the current leadership is effective in delivering the goods that all members agree upon, they can also sustain a culture (and new leaders) that generates expanded political actions at the union level.

The model we've described generates several implications that we attempt to falsify in subsequent chapters. Table 2.1 presents them for ease of reference.

Appendix

Derivation of expression (2.2): For the equilibria to exist in Γ_δ, the short-term gain to the leader for lying cannot outweigh the discounted expected

TABLE 2.1: Summary of empirical hypotheses

H1	Membership organizations will have formal and explicit policies and declarations delineating organizational scope and the level of leadership compensation.
H2	A necessary but not sufficient condition for an activist union is a founding leadership cohort with strong normative and political commitments to expanding the community of fate.
H3	Politically activist unions will limit the pay of their leaders. Business unions will starkly limit the organization's scope of activity.
H4	Where leaders have more self-seeking objectives, we expect monetary rents and other perks.
H5	Where rents are contributed from those outside the organization, performance and responsiveness to the rank and file suffer.
H6	Followers will tolerate a leader's activist demands so long as they do not conflict with the fundamental goals or undermine the industrial successes of the union.
H7	We are unlikely to observe a leader attempting to extract rents or expand organizational scope until her reputation for effectiveness is well-established. Political demands will follow industrial success.
H8	Politically activist unions will have more extensive procedural controls, both ex ante, in deciding when to mobilize union resources, and ex post, in holding leaders accountable.
H9	Future leaders will tend to share similar commitments to those of the formative leadership cohort.

utility from playing the cooperative equilibrium. The leader only has an incentive to lie when $\theta_t = \theta_L$, so consider some period s in which this holds. Then

$$V_1(\hat{\theta}_s = \theta_H \mid \theta_s = \theta_L, \tilde{\theta}_s = \hat{\theta}_s) + \sum_{t=s+1}^{\infty} E_\theta[V_1(\tilde{\theta}_t = \bar{\theta})] \leq$$
$$V_1(\hat{\theta}_s = \theta_L \mid \theta_s = \theta_L, \tilde{\theta}_s = \hat{\theta}_s) + \sum_{t=s+1}^{\infty} E_\theta[V_1(\tilde{\theta}_t = \hat{\theta}_t, \hat{\theta}_t = \theta_t)]$$

$$\Updownarrow$$

$$V_1(\hat{\theta}_s = \theta_H \mid \theta_s = \theta_L, \tilde{\theta}_s = \hat{\theta}_s) + \frac{\delta}{1-\delta} E_\theta[V_1(\tilde{\theta}_t = \bar{\theta})] \leq$$
$$V_1(\hat{\theta}_s = \theta_L \mid \theta_s = \theta_L, \tilde{\theta}_s = \hat{\theta}_s) + \frac{\delta}{1-\delta} E_\theta[V_1(\tilde{\theta}_t = \hat{\theta}_t, \hat{\theta}_t = \theta_t)]$$

Solving for δ in the bottom inequality and simplifying yields the expression.

Derivation of expression (2.3): Note that the leader always contributes individually optimal effort, so we get the following expressions for V_i under different scenarios:

$$V_i(e_i^* = \theta_H \mid \theta = \theta_H) = \theta_H^2\left(N - \frac{1}{2}\right)$$

$$V_i(e_i^* = \bar{\theta} \mid \theta = \theta_H) = \theta_H[(N-1)\bar{\theta} + \theta_H] - \frac{\bar{\theta}^2}{2}$$

$$V_i(e_i^* = \theta_L \mid \theta = \theta_L) = \theta_L^2\left(N - \frac{1}{2}\right)$$

$$V_i(e_i^* = \bar{\theta} \mid \theta = \theta_L) = \theta_L[(N-1)\bar{\theta} + \theta_L] - \frac{\bar{\theta}^2}{2}$$

Substitution of these expressions into the first line of (2.3) and simplification yields the second line of equation (2.3).

Derivation of expressions (2.5) and (2.6): In deriving this expression we assume that the leader who deviates must pay leadership costs in that period but not in the subsequent punishment phases. Again, the leader only has an incentive to lie when $\theta_t = \theta_L$, so consider some period s in which this holds. To sustain truth-telling in equilibrium, the following must hold:

$$V_1(\hat{\theta}_s = \theta_H \mid \theta_s = \theta_L, \tilde{\theta}_s = \hat{\theta}_s) + \gamma_1 R^* - \xi_s + \sum_{t=s+1}^{\infty} E_\theta[V_1(\hat{\theta}_t = \bar{\theta})] \leq$$

$$V_1(\hat{\theta}_s = \theta_L \mid \theta_s = \theta_L, \tilde{\theta}_s = \hat{\theta}_s) + \gamma_1 R^* - \xi_s + \sum_{t=s+1}^{\infty} (E_\theta[V_1(\tilde{\theta}_t = \hat{\theta}_t, \hat{\theta}_t = \theta_t)] + \gamma_1 R^* - \xi_t)$$

$$\updownarrow$$

$$V_1(\hat{\theta}_s = \theta_H \mid \theta_s = \theta_L, \tilde{\theta}_s = \hat{\theta}_s) + \gamma_1 R^* - \xi_s + \frac{\delta}{1-\delta} E_\theta[V_1(\tilde{\theta}_t = \bar{\theta})] \leq$$

$$V_1(\hat{\theta}_s = \theta_L \mid \theta_s = \theta_L, \tilde{\theta}_s = \hat{\theta}_s) + \gamma_1 R^* - \xi_s + \frac{\delta}{1-\delta}(E_\theta[V_1(\tilde{\theta}_t = \hat{\theta}_t, \hat{\theta}_t = \theta_t)] + \gamma_1 R^* - \xi_s)$$

Solving for δ yields (2.5). Solving for R^* under the assumption that $\delta \neq 0$ yields (2.6).

FORMALIZING COMPETITION FOR LEADERSHIP AND CONSTRUCTING A PBNE OF THE GAME

In this extension we continue to have $N-1$ group members and an incumbent "leader." The extended game is played over an infinite horizon with leaders surviving indefinitely and followers surviving for one period but knowing the history from the last period of play. The stage game is played as follows:

1. Nature chooses a Challenger with γ_c. The γ_c are distributed according to known distribution F with mean $\bar{\gamma}_c$. At $t = 0$, Nature selects two challengers.
2. The Followers select[29] either the incumbent or the challenger (at $t = 0$ they choose between two challengers). The loser gets nothing.
3. Followers contribute $r_{it} \geq 0$ to leadership rents.[30]
4. Nature chooses θ_t as in the main text.
5. The Leader pays ξ to learn θ_t, announce $\hat{\theta}_t$, revealing γ_1 in the process, or pays nothing, learns nothing, and announces/reveals nothing.
6. Leader and Followers choose e_{it}.
7. Payoffs and the true state are revealed and the stage game ends.

We claim and then prove that the following strategy/beliefs profile is a Perfect Bayesian Nash equilibrium under the specified values of ξ and δ:

FOLLOWERS:

- At $t = 0$, choose challenger 1 with probability a and challenger 2 with probability $1 - a$ with $a \in [0,1]$.
- In each period t, re-elect the incumbent if $E[\gamma_1 | \hat{\theta}_{t-1}] > \bar{\gamma}_c$ where the conditioning argument also denotes whether the leader has ever previously revealed her type. Otherwise choose the challenger.
- Pay rents $r_i^*(\gamma_1)$ if and only if $\hat{\theta}_{t-1} = \theta_{t-1}$.
- If $\hat{\theta}_t = \varnothing$ (the incumbent makes no announcement about θ_t), hold beliefs that $\tilde{\theta}_t = \bar{\theta}$. If $\hat{\theta}_t = \varnothing$ and the current incumbent has never made a prior announcement, hold beliefs that $\Pr[\gamma_1 \leq \bar{\gamma}_c] = 1$. If $\hat{\theta} \neq \varnothing$ then there is no uncertainty, so the follower's beliefs are simply the value of γ_1. If $\hat{\theta}_t = \theta_L$ then $\tilde{\theta}_t = \hat{\theta}_t$. If $\hat{\theta}_t = \theta_H$ and $\gamma_1 > \bar{\gamma}_c$ then $\tilde{\theta}_t = \hat{\theta}_t$ otherwise $\tilde{\theta}_t = \theta_L$.
- Choose $e_{it}^* = \tilde{\theta}$ as above.

LEADER:

- If $\gamma_i \leq \bar{\gamma}_c$ then $\hat{\theta}_t = \varnothing$. If $\hat{\theta}_{t-1} = \theta_{t-1}$ and $R_t < (N-1)r_i^*(\gamma_1)$ then $\hat{\theta}_t = \varnothing$ otherwise if $\gamma_1 > \bar{\gamma}_c$ then $\hat{\theta}_t = \theta_t$.[31]
- If $\hat{\theta}_t \neq \varnothing$ choose $e_{1t}^* = \theta_t$, otherwise $e_{1t}^* = \bar{\theta}$.

---

[29] Since followers are all identical here, the decision rule is immaterial.

[30] In other words we allow the followers to set the level of rents.

[31] Note that the leader must pay the costs of leadership without earning any rents in his first period in office. This is how the model captures "building a reputation" for good leadership.

The rank-and-file choice at the beginning is arbitrary since the two challengers are equivalent in expectation.

Under the proposed equilibrium the incumbent will never lose office if $\gamma_1 > \bar{\gamma}_c$ so we first derive the minimum level of rents required for the incumbent to prefer delivering truthful, ongoing leadership. For this to happen rents must exceed (1) the benefit of lying when the opportunity arises and then paying to re-establish a reputation for good leadership; (2) lying once and then not leading thereafter; (3) not leading at all. The expression for the first condition is given by

$$\frac{\delta}{1-\delta}\left[E_\theta[V_1(\hat{\theta}_t = \theta_t, \tilde{\theta}_t = \hat{\theta}_t)] + \gamma_1 R - \xi\right] \geq V_1(\theta_t = \theta_L \mid \hat{\theta}_t = \theta_H, \tilde{\theta}_t = \hat{\theta}_t) + \gamma_1 R - \xi$$
$$+ \delta\left[E_\theta[V_1(\hat{\theta}_t = \theta_t, \tilde{\theta}_t = \hat{\theta}_t)] - \xi\right] \qquad (2.7)$$
$$+ \frac{\delta^2}{1-\delta}\left[E_\theta[V_1(\hat{\theta}_t = \theta_t, \tilde{\theta}_t = \hat{\theta}_t)] + \gamma_1 R - \xi\right]$$

Solving (2.7) for R yields

$$R \geq \frac{V_1(\theta_t = \theta_L \mid \hat{\theta}_t = \theta_H, \tilde{\theta}_t = \hat{\theta}_t) - E_\theta[V_1(\hat{\theta}_t = \theta_t, \tilde{\theta}_t = \hat{\theta}_t)]}{\delta\gamma_1} = R_1 \quad (2.8)$$

The expression for the second condition is

$$\frac{1}{1-\delta}\left[E_\theta[V_1(\hat{\theta}_t = \theta_t, \tilde{\theta}_t = \hat{\theta}_t)] + \gamma_1 R - \xi\right] \geq V_1(\theta_t = \theta_L \mid \hat{\theta}_t = \theta_H, \tilde{\theta}_t = \hat{\theta}_t) + \gamma_1 R - \xi$$
$$+ \frac{\delta}{1-\delta} E_\theta[V_1(\varnothing)] \qquad (2.9)$$

Solving (2.9) for R yields

$$R \geq \frac{\xi + E_\theta[V_1(\varnothing)]}{\gamma_1}$$
$$+ \frac{(1-\delta)V_1(\theta_t = \theta_L \mid \hat{\theta}_t = \theta_H, \tilde{\theta}_t = \hat{\theta}_t) - E_\theta[V_1(\hat{\theta}_t = \theta_t, \tilde{\theta}_t = \hat{\theta}_t)]}{\delta\gamma_1} = R_2 \qquad (2.10)$$

The expression for the third condition is

$$E_\theta[V_1(\hat{\theta}_t = \theta_t, \tilde{\theta}_t = \hat{\theta}_t)] + \gamma_1 R - \xi \geq E_\theta[V_1(\varnothing)] \qquad (2.11)$$

Solving (2.11) for R yields

$$R \geq \frac{E_\theta[V_1(\varnothing)] - E_\theta[V_1(\hat{\theta}_t = \theta_t, \tilde{\theta}_t = \hat{\theta}_t)] + \xi}{\gamma_1} = R_3 \qquad (2.12)$$

Denote by R_1, R_2, and R_3 the values of R at which (2.8), (2.10), and (2.12), respectively, hold with equality. By inspection we can see that R_3 is strictly less than R_1 or R_2. Comparing the other two, we can see that $R_2 > R_1$ if

$$\xi \geq V_1(\theta_t = \theta_L \mid \hat{\theta}_t = \theta_H, \tilde{\theta}_t = \hat{\theta}_t) - E_\theta[V_1(\varnothing)] \qquad (2.13)$$

That is, if the costs of leadership exceed the difference between the benefits of mis-leading and not leading at all, then leadership rents must be at least as great as R_2; otherwise rents must exceed R_1.

The rank and file will solve $\min[\max[R_1, R_2]]/(N-1)$ subject to the constraint that $R \leq R_{max}$, where R_{max} is given in (2.4). For ease of exposition we will assume an interior solution.[32] The interior solution also ensures that it is incentive-compatible for the members to pay rents r_i^* if they believe that the leader will refuse to lead otherwise.

We now examine the conditions under which it is rational for the leader to develop a reputation for good leadership[33] given $R(\gamma_1)$. There are two cases to consider:

Case 1: equation (2.13) does not hold; $R = R_1$. The following condition must then hold:

$$\frac{E_\theta[V_1(\hat{\theta}_t = \theta_t, \tilde{\theta}_t = \hat{\theta}_t)] + \xi}{1 - \delta} + \frac{\delta}{1 - \delta} \gamma_1 R_1 \geq E_\theta[V_1(\varnothing)] \qquad (2.14)$$

which is true for all values of γ_1 but requires that $\xi \leq V_1(\theta_t = \theta_L \mid \hat{\theta}_t = \theta_H, \tilde{\theta}_t = \hat{\theta}_t) - (1 - \delta) E_\theta[V_1(\varnothing)]$. This holds since, by inspection, the right-hand side of this expression is greater than the right-hand side of expression (2.13).

Case 2: equation (2.13) holds; $R = R_2$. The following condition must then hold:

$$\frac{E_\theta[V_1(\hat{\theta}_t = \theta_t, \tilde{\theta}_t = \hat{\theta}_t)] - \xi}{1 - \delta} + \frac{\delta}{1 - \delta} \gamma_1 R_2 \geq E_\theta[V_1(\varnothing)] \qquad (2.15)$$

---

[32] If the benefits (to the group) of leadership are sufficiently small or the costs of leadership are exorbitant, then there is no way the group can incentivize good leadership through time. Alternatively, N sufficiently large assures that the constraint does not bind, though this creates a tension with our earlier assumption that the group is small enough that an individual's marginal contribution is non-trivial. See chapter 6.

[33] That is, pay the cost of leadership in her first period in office when she knows she will not receive any rents.

which is again true for all values of γ_1 but requires that $\xi \leq V_1(\theta_t = \theta_L \mid \hat{\theta}_t = \theta_H, \tilde{\theta}_t = \hat{\theta}_t) - \frac{(1-2\delta)}{1-\delta} E_\theta[V_1(\varnothing)]$. This condition always holds given that that expression (2.13) holds.

We have now shown that $r_i^*(\gamma_1) = \frac{\min[\max[R_1, R_2]]}{N-1}$, subject to $R \leq R_{max}$. It is rational for all types of leaders to invest in a reputation were they to be re-elected indefinitely.

Since the members' contribution to leadership rents is decreasing in the leader's type, and since the leader's type is revealed once she leads, the voting rule is clear: elect the challenger in the next period only if the expected type of the challenger exceeds that of the leader. The rank and file will follow this strategy since, in expectation, they give up nothing, i.e., it is sequentially rational. Given that the rank and file will only re-elect leaders with $\gamma_1 \geq \bar{\gamma}_c$, any leader of a below average type will be willing to lead only if the costs of leadership are lower than the benefits of good leadership to her. In the absence of signaling, the only credible claim such a leader can make is $\hat{\theta}_t = \theta_L$ when in fact $\theta_t = \theta_L$. This implies that the below-average leader will only invest in leadership if

$$\xi \leq (1-p)(V_1(\theta_t = \theta_L \mid \hat{\theta}_t = \theta_L, \tilde{\theta}_t = \hat{\theta}_t) - V_1(\theta_t = \theta_L \mid \tilde{\theta}_t = \bar{\theta})) \quad (2.16)$$

Note that this expression does not depend on γ_1. Should an incumbent fail to lead, having never led before, the rank and file believe that $\gamma_1 < \bar{\gamma}_c$. No type of incumbent has any incentive to deviate, given these beliefs and the re-election strategy.

Finally we consider the incumbent's punishment decision should the members fail to deliver the expected rents. For the punishment to be sequentially rational, it must be forgoing good leadership for a period and then re-establishing her reputation yields a higher payoff than simply exercising good leadership in the absence of rents. Formally,

$$\frac{E_\theta[V_1(\hat{\theta}_t = \theta_t, \tilde{\theta}_t = \hat{\theta}_t)] - \xi}{1-\delta} \leq E_\theta[V_1(\varnothing)] + \delta(E_\theta[V_1(\hat{\theta}_t = \theta_t, \tilde{\theta}_t = \hat{\theta}_t)] - \xi)$$
$$+ \frac{\delta^2}{1-\delta}(E_\theta[V_1(\hat{\theta}_t = \theta_t, \tilde{\theta}_t = \hat{\theta}_t)] - \xi + \gamma_1 R^*) \quad (2.17)$$

We again have two cases to consider.

Case A: equation (2.13) does not hold; $R^* = R_1$. In this case, the leader's punishment if the rank and file fail to deliver rents is sequentially rational if

$$\xi \geq \frac{E_\theta[V_1(\hat{\theta}_t = \theta_t, \tilde{\theta}_t = \hat{\theta}_t)] - \delta V_1(\theta_t = \theta_L \mid \hat{\theta}_t = \theta_H, \tilde{\theta}_t = \hat{\theta}_t)}{1-\delta} - E_\theta V_1(\varnothing) \quad (2.18)$$

This will fail to hold only for extremely impatient incumbents. Specifically, expression (2.18) holds for all positive ξ so long as

$$\delta \geq \frac{E_\theta[V_1(\hat{\theta}_t = \theta_t, \tilde{\theta}_t = \hat{\theta}_t)] - E_\theta[V_1(\varnothing)]}{V_1(\theta_t = \theta_L \mid \hat{\theta}_t = \theta_H, \tilde{\theta}_t = \hat{\theta}_t) - E_\theta[V_1(\varnothing)]} \tag{2.19}$$

Case B: equation (2.13) holds; $R^* = R_2$. In this case, the leader's punishment if the rank and file fail to deliver rents is sequentially rational if

$$\xi > \frac{E_\theta[V_1(\hat{\theta}_t = \theta_t, \tilde{\theta}_t = \hat{\theta}_t)] - \delta(1-\delta)V_1(\theta_t = \theta_L \mid \hat{\theta}_t = \theta_H, \tilde{\theta}_t = \hat{\theta}_t)}{1 - \delta + \delta^2} \tag{2.20}$$

$$- E_\theta[V_1(\varnothing)]$$

Since expression (2.13) already holds by assumption, (2.20) must hold.

CHAPTER 3

Pork, Perks, and Predation

Most labor unions in Anglo-Saxon democracies are business unions, that is, the unions operate as businesses that offer bargaining, lobbying, and other services in return for dues. Their stated aim is to improve the economic and work situation of the membership, and many of them do just that. Unlike the leadership of activist unions, business union leaders believe that expanding the scope of the union's activities is costly, with few, if any, downstream benefits. If leaders provide sufficient selective incentives in services, patronage, or coercion, the members are likely to comply. If the leaders promote member welfare, the rank and file may actively support the leaders and the organizational governance institutions in which they are embedded. The system will then be stable unless government actions, technological innovations, or demographic shifts compel change.

Business unions differ from each other as well as from activist unions. Some, like the Teamsters, are legitimate unions whose leaders, while far less constrained and far better compensated than those in the ILWU, are nonetheless subject to regulation and re-election. Others, such as the ILA, are little more than a protection racket, whose leaders prey upon members and collaborate with employers and the mob. James and James (1965, passim) characterize corruption in the IBT as accounting irregularities accepted by the membership in the IBT, whereas the ILA leaders engaged in broader looting and general shenanigans.

The Teamsters are illustrative of a union whose leaders traditionally delivered the pork to members while doing well themselves in terms of both monetary compensation and national political influence. IBT leadership has understood that its effectiveness depends on the contingent consent of the members. Historically, they have used force as a tool of recruitment, dues-extraction, and suppression of dissidents, but they have also nourished membership support, which then enables leaders to employ credible threats against employers and to survive government attacks for links with racketeering. While the IBT leadership receives significant compensation, either through appropriation of member dues or via payoffs from corporations and organized crime, it also significantly improves the material condition of its members. They generally kept the bargain with members.

The ILA leadership, on the other hand, has tended to treat member benefits as secondary to leadership perks, power, and remuneration. They win some improvements for the members, or else they could not survive at all, but their modus operandi is often akin to a protection racket, expecting payment and using force when payment is not forthcoming. The union's organizational governance institutions privilege rent-seeking from employers, organized crime, and members.

In our business union cases, the Teamsters and the ILA, we explore several implications of the model developed in chapter 2. Our expectations are that there will be:

- Organizational governance institutions that are narrow in scope (H1)
- Few, if any, limits on the pay of leadership (H1)
- Relatively few extensive political controls, both ex ante in deciding when to mobilize union resources and ex post in holding leaders accountable (H8)
- A tension between responsiveness to the rank and file and to external groups when they are a source of some of the leader's rents (H5)
- Successive leaderships that uphold these organizational governance institutions (H9)

Most business unions, despite other differences among them, tend to have these characteristics, which means they also tend to be strongly hierarchical and, often, oligarchic. The union officers may be elected, but they are bosses[1] who are paid to wield power on behalf of the members. Deliberative processes, opportunities for challenge, even elections are circumscribed. Still, business unions are regulated by rules. In some unions, such as the Teamsters, these rules have normative and punitive force; the organizational governance institutions are constraining. In others, such as the ILA, the rules are whatever the leadership makes of them, and the organizational governance institutions thus appear incoherent and fragile.

---

[1] This is a term that, these days, tends to be used by conservative opponents of unions. However, in the 1940s, '50s, and '60s it was more of the common language, although it still tended to result in a caricature of a rather heavy-set white man smoking a cigar, not unlike the political or economic bosses. C. Wright Mills (1948, passim) talks about several types of labor leaders, and one type operates as a machine boss.

International Brotherhood of Teamsters (IBT)

> I run this office just like—just like an oil company or a
> railroad. Our business is selling labor. We use businesslike
> methods. Business people have confidence in us.
>
> Dave Beck, 1938[2]

> Running a union is just like running a business. We're in the
> business of selling labor. We're going to get the best price
> we can.
>
> Jimmy Hoffa, 1959[3]

The Teamsters exemplify a union that serves the material interests of its members well.[4] During the period dominated by the organizational innovations of Dave Beck and Jimmy Hoffa, wages for unionized truckers markedly increased (88% between 1939 and 1949), hours decreased, fringe benefits became generous, and levels of safety and security improved significantly (Gillingham 1956; Witwer 2003, 153–55). Between 1933 and 1961, the union itself grew from approximately 75,000 members to more than 1.5 million (Garnel 1972, 47). Beck's methods proved to be especially effective. By 1950, Oakland, San Francisco, and Seattle had the highest wage rates in the country; Spokane and Phoenix had the highest rates for smaller cities (Witwer 2003, 152). The leadership of the union has always committed to providing its members not just bread but pork chops (*The Herdsman* 1948), and they have been willing to do almost anything to achieve that goal. This mind-set, with modifications, was firmly in place from 1907 through the early 1970s, the period we are using for comparison with the ILA, ILWU, and WWF. After that the union began to undergo serious changes as a consequence of member pressures, governmental requirements, and leadership reforms.

Organizations of horse-and-wagon drivers have existed in the United States since the 1850s, when driver-owners began coming together to negotiate rates. With drivers becoming employees rather than owners, the Team Drivers' International Local (TDIL) formed in 1899 and registered with the American Federation of Labor (AFL). After a major schism in the union and with the encouragement of AFL president Samuel Gompers, the union re-emerged as the International Brotherhood of Teamsters (IBT) in 1903.

---

[2] From Neuberger (1938), 167.

[3] From Martin (1959), 27.

[4] This section draws heavily on material provided by Morgen Myrdal and by Barry Eidlin.

Cornelius P. Shea was elected the first president. Shea retained office following a corruption scandal in 1906, but a secession movement in the union led to his defeat in 1907 by Daniel Tobin. Tobin won by twelve votes in that first contest, but he went on to win many more elections, serving until 1952. Tobin's immediate successors were Dave Beck (1952–57) and James R. Hoffa (1957–71). In this period the organizational governance institutions went through several major revisions. Technological changes transformed an industry composed of horse-drawn carriages into an industry that was a lynchpin of U.S. commerce and transport. The regulatory demands on the industry produced an altered view of government's role; the traditional AFL aversion to state intervention gave way to a demand for legislation and its enforcement. Organizational strategies evolved in response. What changed hardly at all were leadership's expectations of members. The leadership asked them to be economistic. The occasional effort, most notably in Minneapolis in the 1930s and '40s, to raise other goals or to democratize the union were stifled. The leadership argued that working cooperatively with business could make everyone better off. The validity of leadership claims was reinforced by the improvements in the material well-being of and continued support by the dues-paying members.

The early Teamsters drove hacks and taxis, delivery wagons for products such as milk and laundry, and "trucks," hefty draft horse–drawn vehicles, to transport larger freight. Most worked for localized businesses, but some were employees of inter-city and national express companies, e.g., Wells Fargo or American Express (Witwer 2003, 8–13). Changes in technology, particularly from horse-drawn wagons to motorized trucks, led to a shift from a craft to an industrial orientation—although the leadership's rhetoric of a craft union lagged behind the reality. With the inclusion of over-the-road truckers, who use the interstate system to haul goods over long distances, the IBT gained the ability to disrupt the flow of goods nationally and enhanced the threat of a strike.

The Organizational Governance Institutions of the Teamsters

The union early on established its distinctive organizational governance institutions, which limit the scope of the organization (H1) and create political controls on and accountability of the leadership (H8).

The union's primary goal is to represent the workers in the sale of their labor in order to obtain for them both the highest possible material return from the employer and dignity and pride in being a member of the IBT. In return, the union demands dues, loyalty, and a willingness to engage in job actions the union deems necessary. While encouraging donations to charity by members and by the union as a whole, the IBT eschews any political actions or social justice commitments that fail to serve the direct interests of members.[5] The union fosters a symbiotic and positive partnership with business. It rejects the idea of class war and demands for the destruction of capitalism. The IBT lobbies for legislation and interacts with important governmental and political party officials, but these are generally activities in which leadership alone engages as part of its obligation to improve the material well-being of members.

In its earliest days, the IBT appears to have adhered fairly closely to the philosophy of Samuel Gompers, the first president of the AFL. His principle of "voluntarism" privileged economic over political action (Eidlin 2009, 251). Until the 1930s, the IBT opposed all state intervention in the relations between employers and unions. President Tobin and other officers supported—with reservations—the New Deal legislation, including the National Labor Relations Act (NLRA), but they insisted that there be no interference in the internal affairs of the union (ibid., 253–55). Subsequently Tobin and, most certainly his successors, Dave Beck and then Jimmy Hoffa, used the power of the state to their advantage, and they definitely engaged in partisan politics.

The Teamsters have a tradition of strong local autonomy (Romer 1962, 86, 92, 95; Garnel 1972; Dembo 1986; Witwer 2003). Increasingly, however, the union was centralized, and management was top down. The Joint Councils of unions in cities and states and then the conference system coordinated organizing and contract negotiation under the control of the International. The locals retained the powerful tool of secession, and its threat often evoked concessions—or repression—from the center. The International officers, for their part, strategically used the process of charter granting and the threats of trusteeship and charter revocation to keep recalcitrant locals in line. The general president even had the power to disapprove of local union bylaws. The rules in the constitution, largely dictated by the powerful executive committee, steadily enhanced International control over the locals (Romer 1962, chap. 7).

The occasional local encouraged rank-and-file democracy, but this was not the norm. The general membership has little voice in policymaking at any level. Until 1991, when federal trusteeship introduced the direct member vote over officers, the IBT chose its international leaders through indirect elections by the delegates who attend conventions where nominations are made. The selection and seating of delegates is the subject of extensive discussion in the Teamster constitutions and conventions. International officers and organizers were automatically delegates. In 1940, an appropriately eligible local (chartered for at least three months, in good

---

[5] One possible exception is involvement in the civil rights movement, which the Teamster website proudly trumpets.

standing, and up to date with its dues) would get one delegate for every 300 members; by 1961 it was one delegate for the first 1,000 members and an incremental delegate for every 750 members or majority fraction after that. This process remained largely unchanged through 1971.[6]

Leadership also tightly controlled contract negotiations. Traditionally, bargaining is relatively secret and closed. It was not until 1988 that members could reject a contract and authorize a strike with a simple majority rather than the two-thirds vote rule that had long been in place (A.P. 1988).

What principally distinguishes the organizational governance institutions of the IBT from the Gompers model of business unionism is the combination of its expansionist approach to organizing, its celebration of strong-arm tactics, and its links with organized crime. To some extent, these are intertwined. The leadership has a commitment to enriching its members and doing anything necessary in pursuit of that goal. Enlarging the union brings in more dues and more clout with employers and government. In the past, the willingness to use violence when necessary and acceptance of alliances with organized crime proved effective strategies for warding off competitors, gaining union recognition, and keeping both employers and resistant workers in line. Witwer (2000, 2003 passim, summarized on 237–38) argues that the perception of endemic Teamster corruption has two sources: its locus in economic sectors where employer collusion is the norm, and the anti-union sentiment that defined strong and successful unions as extortionists.

The original base of the Teamsters was in the transport sector, but since the 1940s its organizers have attempted to attract all kinds of workers, be they in the government, service, or industrial sectors. This tendency became even more pronounced after World War II. An expansionist policy is largely responsible for the size of the union, approximately 1.4 million members today and more than 2 million at its peak, at least according to IBT claims (IBT 2010), its maintenance as one of the largest and most diversified unions in the United States, and its relative wealth. Expansionism led to savage jurisdictional fights, most notably in the late 1930s with the West Coast longshore workers over who controlled the warehouses that served the docks (Neuberger 1938; Schwartz 1978) and in the 1970s with the United Farm Workers. But expansionism also promoted inclusiveness. The Teamsters actively recruited among traditionally female occupations, e.g., nurses and teachers, although integration and equity in pay and treatment were slow and incremental (Vosko and Witwer 2001). Since its early days, the Teamsters organized African Americans, despite the exclusionary practices of other AFL unions and the racist attitudes of much of the leadership (Witwer 2002, 15–16, 146–48). Several factors

---

[6] All information comes from the constitutions of the IBT.

contributed to the willingness of leadership to go against the times. The IBT had no apprentice program, the major mechanism of exclusion in craft unions, and it had a significant interest in winning recognition, bargaining power, and large numbers.

Historically, the Teamsters were renowned for violence directed internally to encourage reluctant recruits to join or to discipline the rebellious and violence directed externally against those with whom they were battling, e.g., employers or unionists who violated Teamster perceptions of jurisdictional boundaries. They had a reputation, seemingly well deserved, for busting arms, heads, and buildings. This was unofficial policy condoned and encouraged by leadership.

As with any large union, factions exist in the Teamsters and have throughout its history. There were radicals not unlike those in the ILWU, and there have always been voices demanding greater rank-and-file democracy and even political commitments. The choice of the Teamsters' particular organizational governance institutions and the continued maintenance of many of its norms and arrangements is contested today and has been since at least the 1930s. In the past, radical locals, notably in Minneapolis, had a vision of the Teamsters consistent with that of the ILWU. Yet, this was a path actively blocked and then destroyed by IBT international leadership in collaboration with government in 1941 (Eidlin 2009). The leadership has generally stifled dissent and competition. In later years, particularly in the aftermath of Hoffa's 1961 election, a number of reform groups emerged, ultimately leading to significant rule changes and even the election of a reformist president, Ron Carey.[7] The increasing importance of members engaged in work that did not involve long-haul trucking combined with government oversight of Teamster elections to facilitate serious electoral competition.

In the last decades, there has been a greater openness to rank-and-file participation, as indicated by the direct vote for officers and the defeat of the two-thirds rule for rejecting contracts and authorizing strikes. Nonetheless, from the 1930s until at least the imprisonment of Jimmy Hoffa, the Teamster organizational governance institutions, as described here, appeared strong and resilient. The clear delineation of organizational governance institutions, their relatively limited scope, and their maintenance by successive leaders fits with the expectations derived from the model in chapter 2. As we shall see below in the discussion of particular Teamster presidents, leaders regularly articulated their views of the

---

[7] Carey, who came from the ranks of the United Parcel Service (UPS) workers, became president in 1991 as a consequence of the first direct election in the union. However, his 1996 re-election was overturned because of illegal donations, and he was not allowed to run again.

mission of the union and ensured that the institutional arrangements of the union supported that mission, a mission quite distinct from that of a union whose leaders committed to political mobilization around social justice issues.

RENTS, PERFORMANCE, AND LEADERSHIP SUCCESSION

The Teamsters have stood accused of at least three kinds of corruption. First was the accusation of labor racketeering, resulting in restraint of trade and intimidation of employers. In many instances, this involved legal practices, and the charge was laid by those opposed to the growing power of the IBT (Witwer 2000, 2003). In other cases, it became a second kind of corruption, in which the Teamsters paid off the police and local officials or allied themselves with mobsters. Some Teamster leadership and, in particular Jimmy Hoffa, have a documented past connection with organized crime. The relationship may have enabled the union to increase the pie for all and to ensure relative labor peace, but it did involve illegal actions. Finally, there is a third kind of corruption, the larceny that lines the pocket of a union official. There is also documentation of this within the IBT. Dave Beck was the poster boy here. Interestingly, illegal corruption seems to have been largely tolerated by members unless it was at their expense.

In order to understand the extent to which pecuniary and status motivations influenced leadership behavior and trade-offs, we must investigate more closely three of the union's key presidents: Dan Tobin, Dave Beck, and Jimmy Hoffa. None of them asked members to expend effort beyond what would be individually and narrowly rational. All three improved the welfare of their members, were popular, and were in no fear of electoral defeat. In keeping with our expectations (H5), each used his position to advance individualist goals, sometimes at the expense of the membership. However, the IBT experience also reveals how well the Teamster leaders generally were able to use external rents to enhance, rather than undermine, their delivery of benefits to members. Balancing external rents with responsibility toward members may have been difficult at times, but it was nonetheless often achieved.

A review of Tobin, Beck, and Hoffa also confirms how successive leaders upheld the organizational governance institutions of the union (H9). Beck and Hoffa may have tweaked the arrangements they inherited, but they maintained the basic structure of the union and its identity.

DANIEL TOBIN

As president of the Teamsters, Tobin became one of the labor leaders C. Wright Mills characterized as "the new men of power" (Mills 1948). When Mills published his book, Tobin and the general secretary of the Teamsters were the highest paid labor leaders in the AFL at $30,000 a year, $10,000 more than the highest paid leader in the CIO (Mills 1948, 100). During Tobin's long reign, the Teamsters grew from 38,900 to more than a million members (Romer 1962, 8; Garnel 1972, 47). Tobin did well for his members, but he also did well for himself. Yet, there is little evidence he made any significant trade-offs to rank-and-file welfare in return for rents received from outside the membership.

Tobin established the organizational governance institutions of the Teamsters. He first tried to maintain a craft union orientation, later tried to resist a governmental role in employer-labor relations, and, as an active supporter of both Woodrow Wilson and Al Smith and then a good friend and confidant of Franklin Delano Roosevelt, most certainly engaged in partisan politics. He even chaired the Democratic Party's National Labor Committee (Leiter 1957, 41; Garnel 1972, 43–44). His own beliefs about the world and his model of how the Teamsters could best serve its members shifted with technological, economic, and political changes. But he always retained his commitment to top-down management, business unionism, and personal honesty. He had difficulties overcoming local prerogatives, practices, and corruption, but he kept himself and, to the extent he could, the International free of taint.

The IBT's mission was to serve its members; there were to be no other ideological goals. He and Beck even opposed sympathy strikes on behalf of other union campaigns. Both believed sympathy strikes were costly relative to the contractual and legal problems they created (Gillingham 1956, 62; Stier and Malone 2002, 66).

Tobin took over a union whose locals fiercely guarded their autonomy and, in some cases, corrupt practices. They used the threat of secession to maintain control. He faced an executive board composed of men who resisted centralized power, but he ultimately achieved his goal by changing rules and expanding the professional staff under his authority. He used the Constitutional Conventions to great advantage. He skillfully managed floor debate, proposals, and committees with the aid of his personal assistant. When he first took office the Convention met annually; by 1915 it began to meet every five years.

During his initial decade as president, Tobin faced considerable contention and resistance but also had significant victories. By 1908, the Constitution was amended to permit the General Executive Board to put locals into trusteeship if their leaders were incompetent, corrupt, or not serving members well. This broad writ gave the Executive Board a huge amount of discretion, and Tobin used it effectively. He resisted and dealt harshly with those who advocated any alternative to his vision of the Teamsters. In order to enforce the compliance of the locals, Tobin threatened trusteeship and, ultimately, charter revocation (Garnel 1972, 61; Witwer 2003, 68), as did Beck and Hoffa after him (Witwer 2003, 142).

Beck and Hoffa were Tobin's henchmen, and his granting to them the control of key districts gave them a degree of autonomous power and considerable influence to help mold the union and its organizational governance institutions. Both were brilliant organizers, who brought large numbers of new members into the IBT. Both were strongly committed to making the workers far better off than before, and both succeeded in doing so. Neither had time nor tolerance for notions of general class solidarity or social justice issues that did not directly serve IBT dues-payers. Both were hugely popular, but both used strong-arm tactics in jurisdictional battles, recruitment practices, and suppression of dissidents. They were oligarchs who treated those loyal to them well and the disobedient severely. Moreover, both lost power and even went to prison as a result of corruption charges. They did serve their members well but only those members who were willing to go along with politics and practices that promoted Beck and Hoffa's individual careers. They were perfectly willing to punish, expel, or worse those who did not toe their line.

DAVE BECK

David Daniel Beck, born in 1894, lived most of his life in Seattle, Washington. He dropped out of high school to help support his family (Morgan 1982, 216–17), and in 1917 Beck joined IBT Local 566, the Seattle Laundry and Dye Drivers Union. After returning from World War I, Beck resumed work as a laundry truck driver and eventually became business agent of Local 566. His antagonism to the Seattle General Strike of 1919, which he viewed as pointless and idealistic, influenced his perspective about how best to run a successful labor union (Morgan 1982, 218). In 1927 Tobin appointed Beck as a full-time organizer for the Teamsters. Throughout the 1930s, Beck established himself as an innovative and successful organizer on the West Coast. In the 1940s and '50s, he became a national figure in the union, the American labor movement more generally, and in national politics. He became general president of the IBT in 1952 but only served until 1957, when he was accused of grand larceny and then in 1959 of tax evasion, crimes that sent him to the McNeil Island Penitentiary in 1962.

Dave Beck spoke of an "industrial peace" that labor and capital could achieve if they learned to work together (Beck 1946, 1947). He encouraged employer trade associations in order to produce price stabilization and eliminate "unfair competition" (Garnel 1972, 69–72), and he prevented employer violation of the rules of the association with the credible threat of the refusal to load and haul their goods. If he thought there were too many firms in an industry, he would restrict further entry by refusing to sign a contract with a new employer, while at the same time squeezing the marginal firms out of the market.

In Beck's perspective, workers were analogous to customers, albeit of the union. They paid dues and received material benefits in improved wages, hours, and working conditions. To that end, Beck stated, "There is only one thing in Christ's world that 99% of our people have that's for sale: their labor. . . And that's what I'm representing—the sale of that labor" (Beck 1988). He claimed, "Everything else is incidental to wages, hours and improved working conditions for the Teamsters' membership. What are the men getting for what the men are paying?" (Beck 1957).

In the first of two times Beck appeared on the cover of *Time*, the reporter finds, "He wants his minions to prosper. . . He not only gets pork chops for his unions but disciplines them with an iron hand" (*The Herdsman* 1948). Beck assumed that regular union members neither understood nor cared about the complexity of union negotiations. He put important decision-making responsibilities in the hands of professionals who were paid sufficiently well to attract those who could run the union efficiently (Garnel 1972, 73; Witwer 2003, 139–40).

In theory, Beck believed that a union should be run much like a representative government (McCallum 1978, 241). "I am a firm believer," he said, "that the administration of a local union should be responsible to the members, but it should also have responsibility. It should be able to make decisions. . . Truck drivers can't do those jobs. But they can decide whether we are getting them what they want and re-elect the officials who do get them what they want" (Morgan 1982, 221). Thus, if high-level IBT leadership was not sufficiently "delivering the goods," there were mechanisms available to the membership to replace that leadership.

However, Beck gave the rank and file no real opportunities to decide which "goods" they wanted in the first place or otherwise express their opinions. When he assumed new jurisdictions, he integrated them into the union without giving a single thought as to what their unique preferences might be. Beck stated, "Unions are big business. Why should truck drivers and bottle washers be allowed to make big decisions affecting union policy? Would any corporation allow it?" (quoted in Witwer 2003, 139; also see Beck 1957, 6).

He also used trusteeship to advantage. Beck would allow the rank and file to choose their leadership and then personally judge its performance based on the union's growth and delivery. If the leadership was unsuccessful according to Beck's standards, he would put the local under trusteeship, giving a position of virtual dictatorship to a trustee (Romer 1962, 105; Witwer 2003, 140–42). This enabled Beck to guarantee competent leadership, keep internal conflict within a local from spreading, make locals finance their leadership, and control the locals through leaders he appointed (Garnel 1972, 164–67). Trusteeships proved an effective tool for suppressing opposition within the locals, according to those representing dissidents (Hass 1955, 7) as well as more objective observers (Romer 1962, 106). He used it to quash wildcat strikes, as in the case of the Seattle Taxi Drivers in 1944, and other unauthorized actions. Through a variety of governance processes and rules, Dave Beck further institutionalized the aspects of Teamster culture that made it virtually impossible for rank-and-file members to express, let alone develop, other than purely economistic preferences.

Beck may have quieted the voices of his rank and file, but he was not shy about advocating his own views through speeches and writing, using strong and repetitive rhetoric. He voiced opinions about the labor movement, foreign affairs, and politics, often claiming to represent the Teamsters Union as a whole and with no acknowledgment of dissenting perspectives within the union.

In a speech to the Western Conference of Teamsters in 1946, for example, Beck supported the free-enterprise system and the potential harmony between labor and capital, stating, "We are concerned with greater industrial development in the west because we know that our people and our Labor Movement cannot prosper and grow unless we have proportionate business advancement" (Beck 1946, 2). He continued, "We have no time for the various -isms, particularly communism, in the conduct of our affairs" (6). He believed that Communists "come in to destroy, to breed dissention, to create turmoil and misunderstanding" and did not "constitute a political party in the meaning of that term in America" (Beck 1949). On foreign affairs, he recognized the economic and political power of trade unions to "preserve democracy and advance the cause of social justice," and therefore donated Teamster funds to the cause of fighting communism in Europe (Beck 1957, 28–29).

Beck, perhaps more than anyone, was responsible for the ruthless expansionism that came to characterize the Teamsters. During his five years as general president, 1952–57, he reported that average yearly membership increased from 1,118,371 to 1,399,938, and organizing costs increased "tremendously" (Beck 1957, 5).

Beck's major organizational innovation was the area conference system. Beck formed the Western Conference of Teamsters in 1937 to overcome geographical obstacles, the increasingly regional/national nature of business, and, most important, a lack of adequate funding for his use and under his control (Garnel 1972, 180–81). The International leadership initially resisted the idea of the conference system; they were apprehensive about the effects that it would have on the union's traditionally craft-oriented structure. Beck was tireless and finally succeeded in 1947 (Romer 1962, 86). He was vice president by then and ensured that the general board had the power to force locals into an area conference if need be.

In 1947, Beck also achieved extension of Teamster jurisdiction to cover "other workers where the security of the bargaining position above the classification requires the organization of other such workers" (Romer 1962, 9). One labor leader is quoted as saying that Beck's idea of Teamster jurisdiction included ". . . anybody who sleeps on a bed with movable casters" (1957). There is little evidence, however, that casters were a prerequisite.

Beck's hunger for jurisdictional expansion was controversial within the larger labor movement. He used the CIO break from the AFL as an opportunity, defining as available for Teamster membership those whose unions were now affiliated with the CIO. He faced strenuous opposition on several occasions from unions who believed the Teamsters were poaching, among them the Brewery Workers International Union in the Northwest in the 1930s, the western conference of the ILA (before it broke off to become the ILWU) in 1936, and the International Association of Machinists (IAM) at Boeing in 1948. Beck's organizing drives involved strong-arm, often illegal tactics (Westine 1937, 39; Morgan 1982, 248; Witwer 2003, 135). He allegedly made it "unhealthy to drive anything for pay if you didn't wear a Teamster button" (Morgan 1982, 248). According to one report, Seattle taxicab drivers were encouraged to organize by being "rammed by automobiles with steel rails for bumpers" (*The Herdsman* 1948).

Jurisdictional battles often turned violent, as in the conflict over the "March Inland" in which the Teamsters and longshore fought over jurisdiction of the warehouses that served the ports (Schwartz 1978). Beck justified the use of violence by insisting that it was his opponents who "wrote the rulebook" (Beck 1988). If they wanted to negotiate peacefully, he would allow them to lose a fight with dignity, but he refused to take the blame if the fight got violent.

While threatened unions often greeted Beck with resistance, employers were more likely to willingly comply. Although employer preference was probably for no worker organization, many employers perceived Beck as the lesser of various evils. With Beck they avoided destruction of their business, labor unrest, and radicals on the left such as Harry Bridges. By showing them that he respected their desire to earn a profit, Beck gained the trust of the employers that was critical in allowing him to pursue his jurisdictional ambitions.

Employer respect also allowed him to pursue his reputational ambitions within his beloved city of Seattle. Charitable donations,[8] political

---

[8] Under the guidance of Beck, the union made considerable charitable donations to Seattle. According to the IBT Treasurer William Mullenholz (Mullenholz and Fitzgerald 1958), the Teamsters contributed a total of $59,800 in large donations to organizations

endorsements, and socializing with the business community were additional means to that end.

Beck commonly articulated his support for the war effort, but he paid special attention to the soldiers of Northwest. For instance, in 1941, Beck showed his support for servicemen by using $5,100 in Teamster funds to buy UW football tickets for soldiers and to buy them 8,000 free hot dogs (Anonymous 1941a, 1941b). He ran Washington's third war bond drive and used Teamster resources to buy football uniforms for soldiers at Fort Lewis and assist coordination between soldiers and their families (*The Herdsman* 1948).

Beck also provided significant political support to local officials. In 1936, he formed the Joint Council of Teamsters Promotion League, serving as an "advisory board" to influence the votes of union members and their families (Westine 1937, 21). Through the Joint Council 28's weekly newspaper, the *Washington Teamster*, Beck announced his endorsement of candidates to the Teamsters and explained why they would be beneficial to the Teamster cause. Beck defended this practice by stating that, because the ballot is secret, "You cannot tell your people how to vote" (Beck 1946, 20).

In 1947, Beck's efforts were rewarded with the kind of public recognition he appeared to seek and enjoy. He was appointed by Governor Mon Wallgren to the University of Washington Board of Regents, and he was promoted to president of the Board in 1950 (Morgan 1982, 221). He also served on committees such as the state parole board and the Seattle Civil Service Commission (McCallum 1978, 95).

Beck's world began to fall apart with increasing evidence of illegal actions involving political favors, personal expenditures, and questionable use of Teamster funds. Beck is credited with having misappropriated about $370,000 in Teamster funds between 1949 and 1954 to build a house and pay other expenses (Witwer 2003, 159). In 1957, when the U.S. Senate's McClellan Committee began investigating corruption in the labor movement, it found that Beck had spent $85,000 in union funds for "personal items." He would simply bill the union for his personal expenses. Beck also used more creative ways of acquiring union funds, such as directing his members to buy gas from stations he owned, or investing Teamster money in his own company (Morgan 1982, 270). Beck, of course, denied and rationalized misconduct (McCallum 1978, 110, 114),

---

such as The Good Neighbor Fund, Seattle University, Seattle Rebuilding Fund, Ballard General Hospital, Students' Association of the University of Washington, Seattle Rotary Club, and March of Dimes. He further notes the investments in Seattle that the Teamsters made under Beck, highlighting the transferal of a total of $7,771,000 in Teamster funds from Indianapolis banks to Seattle banks.

but he was nonetheless convicted in court and sent to McNeil Island Penitentiary in 1962.

Unlike Hoffa, Beck had no known connection to organized crime (Witwer 2003, 181), but he does appear to have bought influence, legally in some instances and perhaps not in others. He helped elect John F. Dore as mayor of Seattle in 1936 and expected favors in return. Consequently, when the IBT engaged in violent activities, the police would generally turn a blind eye (Morgan 1982, 246).

Beck was extremely competent at delivering measurable improvements to his membership, and this may help explain why so many Teamsters appear to have tolerated problematic aspects of Beck's leadership style. However, it is also worth considering—a la Hirshman (1970)—the extent to which this seeming tolerance was really a reflection of the suppression of voice and the high costs of exit.

Moreover, it is certainly possible that the organizational governance institutions Beck engendered may actually have reinforced members' economistic preferences. Beck elaborated his world review in what he said and did. The *Washington Teamster* includes many examples of Beck's (or, at least, the Beck machine's) attempts to convey his opinions and principles. Hearing his authoritative rhetoric so frequently may have convinced his audience to share his views and certainly signaled his expectations of them. At the least, it was part of his toolkit in coordinating action. His successful delivery of material benefits would have only further reinforced their acceptance of his credibility and his vision about the relationships of power and the points of leverage for influence.

Beck's message was not simple economism, however. Beck, via the *Washington Teamster* and his speeches and interviews, advised members about political issues and emphasized Teamster opposition to discrimination against minorities. In his 1957 general report to the Teamster convention, he demonstrated considerable concern with the plight of workers overseas. A closer read of Beck's report as general president reveals that he was mostly concerned with workers abroad because their welfare determined the welfare of American workers, which directly affected his constituency (Beck 1957). Indeed, all of these issues were bound up with member material well-being. The advice on politics was opportunistic, a means to gain influence and friends who would help the IBT. Beck proclaimed, "When I look at a candidate I ask myself, what would his election do to my relations with the men I do business with?" (Morgan 1982, 263). Beck's views about discrimination were perhaps more advanced than many of the time, but supporting minorities was also important for his expansionist recruiting (Witwer 2003, 144–46).

Despite efforts to convince members of a certain worldview and repress those who disagreed, there remains evidence of discord within the ranks. Not all agreed with the International's strict policy against sympathy strikes; locals often wanted to support other unions when they "felt that the dispute [was] bona fide and a strike morally justified" (Gillingham 1956, 81). One important West Coast example took place in San Francisco during the major waterfront strike of 1934. The rank and file refused their leadership's orders to cross the picket lines of the ILA. Indeed, the Teamster blockade of waterfront freight was of major help to the longshore action and a precipitant to violence when the employers organized alternative trucking arrangements (Dembo 1986, 30–32).

Direct and explicit accounts of whether or not the Teamster rank and file was happy with Beck are hard to find. In the Beck-approved hagiography, a member reports, "I've been a Teamster for 37 years and say what you want about Beck, he did more for the union than anyone we ever had" (McCallum 1978, 18). Even if the membership did not completely agree with Beck's principles, they are likely to have joined and remained in the Teamsters because of the material benefits and the few demands placed upon them beyond their dues. But there is also little doubt that through a variety of means, Beck made sure that the locals adopted his principles and participated in his idea of the American Labor Movement. He also made certain that if his members prospered, he prospered more.

JIMMY HOFFA

As a young warehouseman in the early 1930s, Hoffa had been innovative in his use of strikes and effective as an organizer. He learned from Minneapolis union leader Farrell Dobbs major new strategies for organizing long haul truckers and warehousemen (Moldea 1978, 28–30; Russell 2001, 33–47; Sloane 1991, 18–22). Hoffa used these techniques to great advantage, first in Detroit and then nationally. One of the most important lessons from Dobbs was the importance of overarching, multi-employer, multi-bargaining unit contracts. In 1964, as president of the IBT, he negotiated the first national Master Contract with the trucking companies.

Hoffa allied himself with organized crime, which helped him get good contracts for the men. Hoffa did not, however, ensure that all the rents of corruption went to his members. He did get a kickback, but many of his members believed—and most probably it is true—that they did better under these arrangements than without Hoffa's pact between organized labor and organized crime. Hoffa's strategy was a successful application of one developed by others. Instead of spending his time organizing potential members, he devoted most of his effort to organizing the industries themselves (Russell 2001; Sloane 1991). He did this by leap frogging, refusing to deliver or pick up from businesses that refused to sign union contracts, and he also used threats and protection rackets backed up by the Teamster's own thugs as well as the mafia's.

Hoffa abided by the fundamental principles of the Teamster organizational governance institutions as he understood them: improve the economic well-being and working conditions of the members; protect and expand the union; and govern through a top-down hierarchy. He used these principles to rationalize his relationship with the mafia, inhibit rank-and-file democratic participation or political activism within the union, and extend the power of the president. He ran something akin to a patronage machine (as did his predecessors), providing favors to and protecting the loyal and dealing harshly with those he defined as treacherous.

At the outset of the 1957 Convention (International Brotherhood of Teamsters 1957), Beck's last, anti-Hoffa groups challenged the seating of delegates. The opposition feared Hoffa would steal the election and that the AFL would then expel the Teamsters. Hoffa, who was easily elected, became not only general president but also chairman of the convention and chairman of the constitutional committee. The 1961 convention changed how delegates were selected locally and automatically conferred delegate status on all officers and elected business agents of the local as well as providing each Joint, State, and Area Council with one delegate. If the local was entitled to fewer delegates than the total of its officers, its executive board conferred delegate status. Elections among the members were only to occur if the local was entitled to more delegates than it had officers. If the union was under trusteeship, then the International appointed the local's delegates.

Under Hoffa, the IBT further centralized authority in the hands of the International at the expense of the rank-and-file delegates. Beginning with Tobin, the International became increasingly intrusive in the affairs of locals as to the form and manner of delegate selection, became more capricious about the exact timing of conventions, and steadily lowered the delegate-to-member ratio. Hoffa took the most extreme steps by preventing the rank and file from having any real access to the convention. The credentials committee reports from the 1957 and 1961 conventions show most locals with one or two delegates; few numbered over five (International Brotherhood of Teamsters 1957, 1961). Assuming any given local will have, at minimum, a president, vice president, treasurer, business agent, and several trustees, this rule effectively precluded the possibility of any insurgent rank-and-file movement from having access to the convention. By including delegates from area, state, and joint councils, the president could effectively counterbalance any insurgent delegates who managed to get through the hurdles.

Hoffa was a strong and tough leader, effectively expanding the union and improving the lot of the entire membership. He got things done, and he exuded confidence. He regularly articulated and acted on his mission: to do what it takes to improve the lot of dues-payers. He won the hearts and minds of a high proportion of the Teamsters (although hardly all) with his combination of success in winning material improvements for the whole and the patronage system he practiced. His door was open, and his telephone number available. He gave favors and aid often and easily.

When Hoffa agreed to lead the campaign against the dissident Minneapolis local (see chapter 5), he signaled what type of leader he was and his willingness to uphold the IBT governance institutions. The campaign required him to discredit his friend and mentor Farrell Dobbs even when it was against his personal preference—albeit arguably in his long-term interest. The fact that Jimmy Hoffa worked closely with organized crime when necessary also signaled his commitment to do whatever it took to improve the lot of the workers, or at least his workers. He engaged in actions that incurred great personal costs if it served the interests of his members.

Of course, while Hoffa was ensuring that the Teamster rank and file benefited from the relationship with organized crime, he did, too. He was convicted in 1964 of jury tampering and of fraud in handling of union benefits; in 1967 he began serving a thirteen-year prison sentence, which President Richard Nixon commuted in 1971 under the proviso that he not be active in the union until 1980.

Why would members prefer a leader who acted in such ways? Or, perhaps, the better question is "Did they?" He won re-election in 1957 during the height of the McClellan hearings and with the credible threat of expulsion of the IBT from the AFL-CIO should Hoffa be returned to office. A Gallup poll from September 1957 found that by 3 to 1, the rank and file—at least those who expressed an opinion—opposed Hoffa's election (Gallup 1957). Even if this survey and other observations of discontent captured the extent of disaffection, the fact is that the rank and file had no real voice and certainly no direct vote. Even so, there were strong oppositional candidates. Hoffa won handily, in large part because of the extent to which members and delegates appreciated Hoffa's contribution and were suspicious of the motives of both the McClellan Committee and the press (Witwer 2003, 7). More tellingly, in 1961, despite mounting government revelations about him, Hoffa insisted the union abide strictly by the Landrum-Griffin election requirements and handily won a very clean election—and was voted a tremendous raise (Russell 2001, 215).

Despite his conviction for raiding their pension funds, the membership allowed Hoffa to retain his union presidency until 1971, when the provisions of his sentence commutation required him to give it up. A. H. Raskin, who covered labor organizations for the *New York Times* and offered up regular criticism of Hoffa, conducted a non-scientific survey of the membership in 1971 and found that Hoffa, who was in prison at the time, was regarded as a hero and martyr (Raskin 1971b, 1971a; Russell 2001, 223–24). One quote sums up a common sentiment: "For what he did for the driver, I'd take a chance on him again. If he robbed a little, what the hell."

Hoffa's legal trials and convictions, especially those provoked by Robert Kennedy, were interpreted by many as a consequence of Hoffa's successes in bargaining and in challenging the power of employers and government (Sloane 1991; Russell 2001; Stier and Malone 2002, 146–47). Teamster power undoubtedly evoked antagonism from those who feared Big Labor and defined as labor racketeering any success by a union in restricting employer power over workers with threats of a strike, secondary boycotts, or other forms of workplace disruption. This was a major concern of the majority of the McClellan Committee, eager to institute stronger constraints on labor (Witwer 2000; 2003 passim and esp. chap. 9). The Landrum-Griffin Act of 1959 was the result.

In return for what he delivered, Hoffa required from his members their militancy as needed and their loyalty. There is little question that Hoffa, in the tradition of his predecessors, enforced the organizational governance institutions with strong-arm tactics. Nonetheless, the re-elections of Hoffa, the homage still associated with the Hoffa name (and skillfully employed by his son in his successful election campaigns), and the persistence of the kind of philosophy of unionism that Hoffa embodied are indicators of the extent to which members supported and continue to support the union governance institutions Hoffa represented. Jimmy Hoffa and his coterie would do all that was necessary to provide good contracts and to keep the Teamsters a strong, independent union, wealthy in numbers and money. In return, members re-elected them and seem to have accepted their way of doing things and the personal perks that were part of their payment.

The ILA

> [T]he ILA distinguished itself as one of the least effective unions in the country. Judged by even the minimal standards of business unionism, the ILA was an abject failure; it restricted neither the number of jobs nor the size of the labor force; it never established any system for equalizing or distributing employment opportunities; it tolerated cutthroat competition and conditions of chronic job insecurity. In sum, the ILA violated practically every tenet of job control unionism. (Kimeldorf 1988, 15)

The ILA governance institutions narrow the organization's scope and reinforce hierarchal power.[9] Top leadership expresses little or no interest in political action, and it was and continues to be self-serving at the expense of its membership. ILA leaders, as did the IBT's, benefitted from external

[9] This section draws heavily from Kelly (2009) and Kimeldorf (1988).

rents, but unlike the Teamster presidents, those who run the ILA have a relatively poor record of improving member welfare. It accepted large external rents and traded the well-being of the rank and file for its own pecuniary advancement. This begins to change, and then only marginally, after state and federal authorities intervene to transform the organizational governance institutions and to limit corruption.

The origin of the ILA was in 1892, when Daniel Keefe founded the International Longshore and Maritime Transit Association (ILMTA) to serve the Great Lakes region. By the early twentieth century the union expanded to both coasts and into the Gulf of Mexico. Soon after the union secured its first New York contract in 1916, New York became its headquarters.

By the 1920s, the ILA had fifty locals and covered a huge geographical area. The New York waterfront alone is hundreds of miles long and includes ports in Brooklyn, Manhattan, Staten Island, Newark, Hoboken, and Jersey City. Although the New York contract unofficially dictated wages in other Mid-Atlantic ports, South-Atlantic and Gulf Ports had significantly lower wages. Ports varied in hours, wage scales, and hiring schemes; no mechanism existed to produce uniform wages, benefits, or procedures. Several locals used steady gangs, groups of workers hired as a team and over some specified period. The majority relied on the shape-up, a method of recruitment that allowed the foreman or walking boss to choose workers arbitrarily among those who answered the call for immediate work and, often, day labor. The shape-up empowered the foreman to discriminate against those he did not like for personal and political reasons and on behalf of pals or those who paid a bribe.

Work was often scarce and the potential workforce large. Thus, initial struggles focused on wage gains, improvements in safety and work rules, and regulation of the labor supply.

Governance Institutions

The ILA constitution was silent on issues of leadership salary, benefits, and recall. Yet, salaries were high and remain high. The 2010 Labor Management Reporting and Disclosure Act (LMRDA) data reveal that Harold Daggett, ILA president, was the highest paid U.S. labor official in their database. Three other ILA officers were also among the top fifteen (Brenner 2010).[10] With little tradition of coming up through the ranks,

[10] According to Brenner's reading, Daggett's total gross salary was $646,621. Unionfacts.com, a strongly anti-union group, reports the total compensation of top union officials in 2010 as follows (www.unionfacts.com):

Richard Hughes, president, ILA: $479,829.00
Robert McEllrath, president, ILWU: $148,016.00
James R. Hoffa, general president, Teamsters: $368,000.00

some officers have never been dockworkers. This is in sharp contrast to the other three unions in our study.

Elections took place at International Conventions open only to select delegates; contracts required no membership vote. Joseph Ryan's election as international president at the 1929 convention consisted of a unanimous voice vote without an opposition candidate. Indeed, no contested elections for International Office took place until 1964, when two candidates ran for one of several second vice president positions. In 1943, a constitutional amendment allowed Ryan to be elected president for life (ILA). The ILA constitution remains virtually what it was in the 1940s.[11]

The ILA leadership made few efforts to win contingent consent. They used strong-arm tactics to enforce discipline and protect turf. They extracted dues but sometimes did not even seem to worry about that; their major compensation came from elsewhere. When members were finally allowed to vote on contracts, turnout was low and divided.[12] The task of convention participants was to ratify leadership proposals. Strike participation was often high, but most were wildcat strikes against ILA leadership.

As expected, the ILA has organizational governance institutions that are narrow in scope (H1), tolerate high officer salaries (H1), and provide almost no political controls on leadership (H8).

RENT EXTRACTION

Leaders supplemented their salaries with rents from corruption, and they regularly sacrificed the interests of workers to their own self-interest (H5). The international and several New York area locals collaborated with both the employers and the mafia. Dock work, like trucking, offers immense opportunities for pilfering from loads and for creating a protection racket. And that is exactly what Ryan promoted. As early as the 1930s, he was hiring strong ex-convicts to be union organizers, a practice that the employers seemed to like since these bosses ensured the men worked hard (Kimeldorf 1988, 121).

Even though the extortion and theft did have the consequence of raising insurance rates and making the New York port the most expensive in the world (Kimeldorf 1988, 121), Ryan remained close friends with members of the New York Shipping Association and would socialize with them frequently. Several were members of the Joseph P. Ryan Association,

[11] Kelly (2009) analyzed ILA convention proceedings and constitutions from the 1890s on, using original documents donated by the ILWU's research division to New York University's Tamiment Labor Library. This conclusion is based on his findings.

[12] The ILA does not report voter turnout rates, and ratification rates for many years are difficult to come by. Kelly (2009) documents that many contract ratification votes failed and others won by a very small majority.

a gentleman's club and political lobbying organization he founded in his own name. Ryan used membership dues and donations from the organization's "anti-Communist fund" to finance his lifestyle as well as to launder mafia money.

Local leaders constantly vied with each other and the International for power. Brooklyn leader Anthony Anastasia consolidated several locals and repeatedly threatened secession. Local leaders from Chelsea (Ryan's original local) often opposed both the International and the Anastasia locals. Leaders outside of New York had little influence on International affairs.

Failure to represent workers' interests generated rank-and-file resistance to the leadership. Antagonism was particularly strong on the West Coast, which rejected Ryan's leadership of the 1934 strike and in 1937 broke away from the ILA to form the ILWU. The 1934 West Coast insurgency inspired a new generation of rank-and-file ILA activists. In 1937, members from Chelsea testified to the New York Legislature about deplorable hiring conditions on the docks. Others circulated leaflets calling for better contracts and demanding union-controlled hiring. Brooklyn rank-and-file leader Pete Panto started a movement for democratic reforms and attracted thousands of longshoremen to his rallies.

The reaction was violent. Panto disappeared, and his body was found in a New Jersey lime pit. The Camarda crime family was probably responsible, but armed gunmen raided several Brooklyn locals and burned their files before the police had a chance to seize materials. Ryan responded by saying he would "clean up the docks" but did little more than relocate certain problematic leaders and members.

The rank-and-file membership tried again in 1945. Members in Chelsea and Brooklyn formed committees calling for dramatic raises and eliminating the evening shape-up. Ryan responded by negotiating a sweetheart deal with only a ten-cent raise. The committees called a seventeen-day strike against employers and their own leadership. Ryan wrote off the strike, labeling the organizers Communists, a common accusation in the 1940s–1960s. However, there is no reliable evidence that any of the wildcat actions were instigated by Communists (Jensen 1974; Kimeldorf 1988). The state intervened and sent the matter to arbitrators, who ultimately secured a contract with a 25-cent raise and a 40-hour workweek. The shape-up, which employers advocated, was retained but reduced to two per day (Larrowe 1955). Wildcat strikes against ILA leadership became a regular occurrence from this point on.

Leadership Succession

Successive leadership of the ILA upheld the organizational governance institutions of the union (H9). Ryan held office for twenty-seven years and was replaced by his chosen successor, "Captain" William Bradley, in 1953. The timely offer of continuing Bradley's salary under the title, president emeritus, avoided a messy election fight in 1963 (Toman 1994, 220) when the ILA International Convention delegates unanimously elected Teddy Gleason to international president, a position he held until retirement in 1987 at the age of eighty-seven. Both Bradley and Gleason were protégées of Joseph Ryan, and the two had reached an agreement as to the timing of their respective presidencies. Gleason sought to further centralize control of the union and maintained a rigid grip on its election machinery. In addition, Gleason's term saw the ILA engage in a host of illegal activities. During his administration, ILA officials received indictments for racketeering, extortion, and embezzlement (Toman 1994, 220–21).

The administration of the next president, John Bowers, was largely business as usual. Following a 2003 strike in several ILA ports, Bowers noted his preference to work with employers on industrial disputes, stating: "I haven't changed my attitude. I haven't turned radical overnight. I don't believe in strikes. I prefer to keep my people working" (Bonney 2003, 45). In the same discussion, Bowers also noted that the ILA had not engaged in a coast-wide work stoppage since 1977. In 2007, Bowers retired at age eighty-four and was elected president emeritus, which allowed him to stay on the union payroll with an annual salary of $219,764 (Union Facts 2011).

There were some stirrings of discontent from the membership. The 2004 vote on the ILA Nationwide Contract achieved only 56.5 percent of the popular vote, and several locals rejected the agreement (Bonney 2004, 16). During the election of Richard Hughes, Jr. as the next president in 2007, there were some rumblings from the rank and file and even threat of contestation for the position of assistant general organizer.[13]

The institutional governance did not change. At the 2007 International Convention, delegates resoundingly voted down a resolution aimed at revising the longstanding election system to direct membership voting. The vote was 389.2 to 31.8. International President Hughes spoke against the one man/one vote system, noting that the current system "maintained the organization's structure in a way that fairly and effectively represents the geographic distribution of its members" ("New Officers Elected at ILA International Convention" 2007). But there was a slight departure from the customary governance institutions; two amendments to the ILA Constitution in 2007 did succeed in reforming, albeit minimally, the salaries granted to ILA International and local officers. The first amendment

[13] See newsletter article, "New Officers Elected at ILA International Convention" (2007).

prevented elected officers in six executive positions from collecting more than one full-time salary from the ILA. The second amendment prohibited full-time local officers from receiving an additional salary as an officer from another local.

Hughes, Jr. did not seek an additional term in 2011, and at the age of seventy-seven he accepted the paid position of president emeritus. His chosen successor was the current ILA International president, Harold Daggett, who ran unopposed and was elected unanimously.

REFORM EFFORTS

The New York State Crime Commission started investigating Ryan and the ILA in the early 1950s. They ultimately brought twenty-seven counts against Ryan, ranging from racketeering and embezzlement to conspiracy to commit murder. The American Federation of Labor (AFL) convention overwhelmingly voted to eject the ILA from the federation and immediately create an alternative union, the International Brotherhood of Longshoremen (IBL).

Ryan, forced to leave office in 1953, was appointed president emeritus with a $10,000 a year stipend. ILA delegates passed various resolutions praising Ryan, criticizing the AFL and Crime Commission, and condemning corruption. Rank-and-file activists were outraged. Many left the ILA for the short-lived IBL (ILA Rank and File Committee 1945; Jensen 1974).

The state also created the Waterfront Commission to solve the longshore labor problem. In 1953, the commission created government-run hiring centers in Brooklyn, Manhattan, Staten Island, and New Jersey to assign work. The dispatchers permitted the formation of steady gangs, working for the same employer for long periods. For some, this was nothing but a "shape-up with a roof over its head" (Jensen 1974). Where the government centers did not exist, the shape-up continued, in some ports until the 1960s.

New York employers initially favored the corrupt ILA leadership, but they later preferred more standardized and predictable relationships. The New York Shipping Association (NYSA) and ILA leaders started discussing a master coastwide contract in the 1956–57 contract negotiations, but Anastasia objected and threatened to pull his locals out of the union if coastwide bargaining was enacted. This led to an informal Mid-Atlantic contract based on the existing New York-centered relationship but with little enforcement power.

ILA NOW

The ILA today still has more corruption than most unions and less democracy than many. In the ILA, elected officers receive considerably higher pay than their members—in contradistinction to both the ILWU and MUA. Alleged mafia connections remain. The union is frequently the subject of federal indictments and racketeering suits (Glaberson 1990; "Feds File Racketeering Lawsuit" 2005). There were 129 indictments for waterfront corruption charges between 1979 and 1981 alone, leading to 117 convictions. Of these, fifty-two were union officials, including Brooklyn ILA leaders and a future ILA national president ("Battling Corruption in the ILA" 2008). The membership still lacks some of the basic benefits of democracy, such as one-man, one-vote during international elections. Nor do they receive the quality of information, let alone the educational resources, of the ILWU or MUA.

Discussion

The historical evidence on the organizational governance institutions and leadership of the IBT and ILA is generally consistent with the hypotheses derived in chapter 2. Both had clear and widely disseminated statements of organizational principles describing the union's objectives and scope of action, though the ILA's were, in some sense, implicit. The formal governance rules of their organizations were designed to allow leaders to restrict organizational scope to economistic goals and to minimize dissent within the union. Leaders in both unions extracted substantial monetary rents and earned significantly more than the workers they were obliged to represent. Both sets of leaders benefited from rents funded by groups outside the organization itself, whether through hobnobbing with politicians and business leaders, as in the case of Beck and, to a lesser extent, Ryan, or from the mob, as with Hoffa and the ILA. Both unions also reproduced their organizational governance institutions over time by attracting and cultivating new generations of leaders who shared strong preferences for the sorts of rents the IBT and ILA directed to their leaders. Only external intervention by government was able to break this cycle.

Our expectation about the difficulties for leadership of balancing external rents and responsibilities to membership definitely fits the ILA leadership. It did a poor job of improving the conditions of the workers it represented and clearly advantaged itself. The IBT leadership seemed to have managed the balancing act fairly well. Although leaders varied in the extent to which they traded off member well-being for self-serving advantages, all appeared to have achieved industrial success and promoted the interests of the members.

The ILA leadership was more similar to personalistic feudal barons, interested primarily in personal gain and power. They made few efforts to attain optimal contracts. The guiding principle of leadership appears to have been maximization of income through predatory behavior. The use of coercion against members and the ability to extract rents without relying on members' active contributions—merely the buying off of a few and the submission of the rest sufficed—enabled the ILA's governance institutions to persist. It is an example of what can happen in the absence of a leadership embedded in organizational governance institutions that demand members' economic interests be served.

The IBT, on the other hand, is a union that sets the baseline for an effective union that is successful in winning benefits for its members. It does so with organizational governance institutions that centralize power in leadership with a stated mission to use that power to improve the material condition of those who pay their dues. Opposition to the dominant organizational governance institutions has long existed among the Teamsters, but there is also considerable evidence of contingent consent, even with international presidents shown to be corrupt. It may well be that the links with organized crime or the private benefits of the job help make the leadership more effective. The comparable effectiveness of the United Auto Workers or the needle trades unions suggests, however, that corruption is not a necessary condition. In addition, as the case study documents, Beck, Hoffa, and even Tobin considered the well-being only of those members who were willing to tolerate their methods and their personal gains; they expelled, suppressed, or cowed those who did not.

The behavior of the IBT appears consistent with Kremer and Olken's (2009) evolutionary model of unions in which leaders, insulated from the rank and file, devote more resources to organizing and/or sign less extractive contracts with employers. Unions with such insulated leadership are able to out-compete unions with leaders who are perfect agents of the members' economistic preferences. But the Kremer and Olken model fails to account for the other possibilities we investigate in this book, namely that, in the case of the ILA, leaders can simply predate on their members, earning rents from those outside the union, or that, in the cases of the ILWU and WWF, the leaders can in fact use their accountability to the rank and file to mobilize the membership to undertake additional costly political projects.

CHAPTER 4

An Injury to Anyone
Is an Injury to All

The International and Longshore Workers Union (ILWU) adopted as its own the slogan of the Industrial Workers of the World (IWW), the Wobblies: "An injury to one is an injury to all." The ILWU and the Waterside Workers Federation (WWF)[1] take this as a mantra and, as did the Wobblies, mean it to include any worker or exploited person, even if those being harmed are continents away. Their commitments go well beyond charitable giving and resolutions of support. They actually close down the ports, sacrificing their own income and time and sometimes liberty, for causes they believe in, causes that have little if anything to do with improving their own material well-being. They have a conception of their community of fate that extends well beyond the boundaries of the membership of their particular union.

Both unions refused to load ships taking scrap iron to Japan in protest of the killings in Nanking (1937–38) and refused to load ships from the Axis powers in the run-up to World War II. The Australians instituted a ban on Dutch shipping in 1945 in an effort to assist the rebels in Indonesia. In 1954, gangs in the Sydney branch would not load weapons for the French war in Indo-China, and in 1967 and 1969 would not load armaments in ships headed to Vietnam. The American longshore workers held work stoppages in relationship to South African apartheid, the war in Vietnam, and the war in Iraq, among others. In addition, both unions took many actions in support of workers in other industries seeking union recognition or engaging in strikes.

The ILWU and WWF leaders aimed to expand the community of fate beyond those who were members of the union and to advance economic or political goals requiring membership effort and contributions of time and resources beyond what is normally expected of union members. We find no evidence of corruption and little evidence of self-seeking motivations among these leaders in terms of pecuniary advantage, social

---

[1] The WWF amalgamated with the Seamen's Union in 1993 to become the Maritime Union of Australia (MUA) (Beasley 1996, 226).

prestige, or larger political ambitions. Certainly they relished the power and prestige derived from leadership of a major union, but their primary rents were derived from the opportunity to use the union to support political causes. The early leaders were all associated with left-wing organizations, which may, at times, have given them a dual loyalty and an external source of rents.

Given that these are activist unions, our model in chapter 2 leads us to expect that they will have:

- Leadership with strong normative and political commitments to expanding the community of fate (H2)
- Organizational governance institutions that are broad in scope (H1)
- Limits on the pay of leadership (H1)
- More extensive political controls than the IBT or ILA, both ex ante in deciding when to mobilize union resources and ex post in holding leaders accountable (H8)
- Problems for leadership in balancing performance and responsiveness to the rank and file when some of the leader's rents derive from an external political party (H5)
- Membership tolerance of leadership's activist demands so long as the demands do not undermine the industrial success of the union (H6)
- Political demands only after industrial success (H7)
- Successive leaderships that uphold these organizational governance institutions (H9)

After discussing the similarities between the ILWU and WWF, we explore the hypotheses listed above in more depth. Structural factors can provide only part of the explanation of why these two unions are so similar to each other and so different from the ILA and Teamsters; organizational governance institutions and leadership proclivities appear to matter more.

Commonalities Between the ILWU and WWF

> [T]he trade union seeks to combine within itself two extremely divergent types of social structure, that of an army and that of a democratic town meeting . . . the members constitute an army but an army that elects its own generals . . . (and) votes on the declaration of war and on the terms of armistice and peace . . . Imagine the conflict in the soul of a

> union official who must have the attitude and discharge the
> functions at one and the same time of both a general and a
> chairman of a debating society.[2]

A. J. Muste further notes how a union must also become an effective
business enterprise. The result is a nearly insoluble problem for union
leadership. If union members care about having a say, they will demand
results while also requiring consultation, something seldom expected of
generals, particularly in the heat of battle, or of CEOs, particularly those
in the midst of a major negotiation.

It is rare for a union or its leadership to realize a good balance of these
conflicting demands. Both the International Longshore and Warehouse
Union and the Waterside Workers Federation have. Both possess strong
and long-standing rank-and-file democracies, a demonstrated capacity for
winning good contracts that emphasize regulation of the labor supply as
well as working conditions and pay, a willingness to introduce new technology and improve the competitiveness of the ports, and a commitment
to solidarity with other workers and oppressed peoples. The workers and
their unions have developed a conception of their community of fate that
extends well beyond the boundaries of the membership of the particular union. Their organizational governance institutions are similar to the
Teamsters only in dedication to win the best possible contract and in the
capacity of the workers to act militantly and effectively.

The ILWU and WWF stand in marked contrast to the Teamsters and
even more so to the ILA in terms of their democratic practices, beliefs
about the appropriate role of unions, political commitments, and tendencies toward corruption. Criminal elements controlled but one Australian
union (Sheridan 1994, 262). Although it involved maritime workers who
cleaned and prepared the holds, ship painters and dockers, particularly in
Melbourne during the 1990s, it was not the wharfies. The West Coast and
East Coast longshore workers did have similar bouts with racketeering
prior to the 1934 strike, but that ended with the new leadership in the
west and persisted, even strengthened, with the old leadership in the east.

Longshore workers in the United States and their wharfie counterparts
in Australia have organized unions since the late nineteenth century, but
it was in the 1930s that their current organizational governance institutions were given firm grounding.[3] This was a pivotal period; the unions

---

[2] Muste (1928). This quote is attributed to various people, including J.B.S. Hardman,
in whose book Muste's piece appears. C. Wright Mills (1948, 3–7) makes a similar statement, paraphrasing Muste, who he credits in a footnote.

[3] The origins of the ILWU arrangements were in rules established for the Pacific Coast
Division of the ILA well before WWI when they were codified in a convention. According

existed but, until new national leadership took over, the unions lacked significant clout with employers. Harry Bridges took the helm of the Pacific Coast District of the International Longshoremen's Association after helping to lead the 1934 coast-wide strike. Lou Goldblatt was organizing the warehouse workers for the ILA, and he played a key role in the 1934 and subsequent 1936 strikes, which were key to the coalition of longshore and warehouse and to the "march inland," the unionization of terminals and storage facilities outside the ports. When Big Jim Healy became general secretary of the WWF in 1937 and when Ted Roach joined him in 1942 as assistant general secretary-organizer, they, too, rebuilt the organization they inherited and increased its power.

The similarities among these four leaders are striking. All four had strong left-wing political convictions and dedication to improving the material conditions of the workers they represented. They revealed the strength of their commitments by their willingness, if necessary, to arouse membership resistance and government punishments, including jail time. Bridges angered some of his members by opposing the Korean War, but most rallied to his defense when he was sent to jail for speaking out (see chapter 6). Most members certainly supported him during the many trials and threats of deportation as he tried to win citizenship and disprove prosecutorial claims of Communist Party membership. Goldblatt spent a night in custody in London in 1949 before being sent home as an "undesirable"; he had come from a meeting in Marseilles of the maritime conference of the World Federation of Trade Unions (WFTU) to meet with striking longshore workers (Ward 1978, 1979, 562–74). Both Healy and Roach were jailed for contempt of court during the coal strike in 1949 (Markey and Svensen 1996). Roach was jailed again in 1951 as he battled a judicial wage decision and was then held responsible for a cartoon published in the *Maritime Worker* that criticized the judge (Mallory 1997, 2005; Sheridan 2006, 115–16).

Australian and U.S. dockworkers had several things in common prior to containerization: the nature of the work with its reliance on casual labor and on teams (or gangs); fluctuations in employment; dangers on the job; and a syndicalist proclivity among the rank and file that produced resistance to arbitrary employer actions but also to authority of any kind, including that of their own leaders. The following list captures most of the key components of dockworker life and sentiment prior to containerization in Australia and the United States and perhaps, as the author claims, more universally (Miller 1969, 305):

---

to Vrana (2011), "In many ways the revolt against ILA national leadership in 1934 was a rising in defense of what had existed and the right to make them come alive in practice."

1. The casual nature of employment;
2. The exceptional arduousness, danger, and variability of work;
3. The lack of an occupationally stratified hierarchy and mobility outlets;
4. Lack of regular association with one employer;
5. Continuous contact with foreign goods, seamen, and ideas;
6. The necessity of living near the docks; and
7. The belief shared by longshore workers that others in the society consider them a low-status group.

Another shared characteristic was a high degree of assertiveness (Nelson 1957; Kimeldorf 1988; Nelson 1988; Sheridan 1994). To this day, the rank and file, particularly those in the ILWU, resist management by means of direct actions on the docks and quickie wildcat strikes, and they rebel against union leadership with noncompliance and electoral defeats. These are not the easily led sheep Michels believed compose the mass.

Despite multiple similarities, the workforces differed in ethnic and religious composition. Kimeldorf (1988, 42–46) argues that a key factor in ILWU membership receptivity to militancy and radicalism was the predominance of Northern Europeans and Protestants in the ports in the west, in contrast with the Catholic east. However, the ILA WWF members were also predominantly Irish Catholics in the period that produced the enduring organizational governance that we document. The wharfies were as radical as the West Coast longshore. There were differences, however, among the locals of the WWF that are partially explained by the greater influence of the Catholic Church in Melbourne than in Sydney, differences to be discussed in chapter 5.

Other potential explanatory factors for the willingness of members to support union activism also disappear upon closer investigation. The ILWU and WWF existed in significantly distinct legal and regulatory environments, but they faced similar kinds of concerted employer opposition (Nelson 1957; Kimeldorf 1988; Nelson 1988) to which they responded in similar ways. The ILWU and ILA existed in a common legal structure, yet behaved quite differently.

A major technological shock hit the industry in the late 1950s with the introduction of containerized shipping. Worldwide this led to a reduction in the numbers employed in dock work and, generally, to an increase in productivity. Dock work became more like routinized factory work (Finlay 1988). The transformation from manually handling cargo via gang work in a ship's hold to containers and crane operators drastically altered social relations in the ports and had consequences for the bargaining power of the unions. Yet, the governance institutions, crafted in the 1930s and 1940s, largely stayed in place, and political activism continued.

The founding fathers (men all) of the organizational governance institutions won the loyalty of membership, first and foremost through successful negotiations with employers. Only after they had improved the material well-being and enhanced the dignity of the rank and file did they have the opportunity to recommend significant changes in the rules and institutions of the union and, ultimately, request political activism. Industrial success enhanced the credibility of leadership claims about how the world worked and what organized workers could achieve. Not all members would come to share the beliefs of the leadership, and some would resist or even actively oppose their political positions. However, most members were at least willing to consider the strategies and interpretations of the world their leaders offered to them and join an expanded community of fate.

ILWU

BACKGROUND

The ILWU originated in 1937, when it broke off from the International Longshoremen's Association (ILA). Its historical roots lay in the ILA Pacific Coast District, founded in 1902 and in the many organizing efforts of waterfront workers and seamen that pre- and post-dated that founding. Both Wobbly and socialist influences were strong on the West Coast, and they inspired militant unionism, direct action, and demands for industrial democracy, i.e., that workers should share control of the workplace with the employers. The ideas inherited by the ILWU matched the experience and ideology of the workforce they represented (Nelson 1957; Kimeldorf 1988; Nelson 1988; Johnson 2000; Mallory 2005; Johnson 2008), but they were not institutionalized until after the 1934 "Big Strike."

Against the advice of the International and its president, Joe Ryan, all twenty West Coast ILA locals went out on May 9, 1934. The longshore workers protested unsafe working conditions, poor pay, the "blue book" or company union, and the dehumanizing shape-up system in which the "walking boss" arbitrarily assigned jobs. The strikers demanded a hiring hall, where work would be dispatched according to a fair and regularized process, and they demanded union recognition and collective bargaining rights for all longshore workers on the coast as well as a raise in wages and reduction of hours.

Employers refused to negotiate. On July 5—"Bloody Thursday"—two strikers were killed in San Francisco, precipitating a general strike in San

Francisco that involved almost all trades, including, quite crucially, the truckers. The California governor sent in the National Guard, and police and guardsmen were called out by governors and city officials all along the coast. During the strike, a total of six strikers were killed and hundreds injured as battles raged in the West Coast ports.

In the end, the union won. The workers gained recognition of the ILA as their union, coastwise bargaining in which one contract and negotiation served for all the covered ports, a substantial wage increase, an arbitration system, and a hiring hall, funded jointly by the employers and union with the dispatcher selected solely by the union. The warehouse workers, with Goldblatt among their leaders, won similar terms in 1936 when they went on strike.

In 1937, the West Coast locals (with the exception of Tacoma and two small Washington ports) disaffiliated from the ILA and American Federation of Labor (AFL) to become the International Longshoremen's and Warehousemen's Union (ILWU), affiliated with the new Committee of Industrial Organizations.[4] The ILWU was born, and Bridges became its first international president. In the decades that followed, the ILWU continued to win significant improvements in material benefits and control of work, transforming the "wharf rats into lords of the dock." The ILWU rarely engaged in strikes; the threat of a work stoppage was usually sufficient. It confirmed the union's control of the warehouses despite Teamster efforts to encompass those workers, and it expanded into Hawaii, where it organized field workers as well as port workers. The international officers demonstrated a continued commitment to racial justice and political mobilization around a variety of issues.

The ILWU, under Bridges' presidency, expanded during the 1930s through the 1960s by organizing warehouse and cannery workers along the West Coast, and, in Hawaii, sugar, pineapple, and "general trades" workers as well as those in the warehouses and on the docks. The union later organized hospitality and tourism workers across the islands. Consequently, the ILWU became a major force in Hawaiian politics and a leader in the movement for Hawaiian statehood. Local 142, based in Hawaii, is by far the largest in the union and the strongest non-longshore-dominated power broker in ILWU politics. In 1947, the longshore division alone had more than 63,000 members; by 2006 it was just above 42,000.[5]

---

[4] Both names changed subsequently. In the 1997 Convention, the ILWU officially dropped the "men" from Longshore and Warehouse. Upon its expulsion from the AFL in 1938, the CIO changed from Committee for Industrial Organization to Congress of Industrial Organizations.

[5] These figures are derived from the PMA website for 2003 and 2006 (December figures, same as in Annual Report); and from Per Capita Payments to International for 1945–1949.

The impetus for union expansion was in part to cement control of the docks; the march inland with its organization of warehouse workers (Schwartz 1978) in 1934–38 and the inclusion of the Inlandboatmen's Union of the Pacific in 1980 helped achieve this end. However, at least part of the motive for expansionism was racial justice. Commitment to an interracial labor movement influenced approval of cannery worker union affiliation with the ILWU in 1949–50 and the organization of Hawaiian workers in 1944–46 (Jung 2006).

The ILWU has a long history of membership involvement in social and political issues that have little bearing on their immediate economic interests. In 1938–39, rank-and-file ILWU members refused to load American shipments of scrap iron to Japan until forced to load by federal injunctions. The action began with a refusal to cross picket lines established by Chinese activists to protest against Japanese invasion of Manchuria, but the ILWU also wished to prevent the use of the iron by an enemy power in a likely future war. In the late 1940s, the ILWU rank and file voted to resist federal government attempts to use the Taft-Hartley Act to impose waterfront worker screening in West Coast ports in order to purge Communists. The union leadership had to go to court about this in 1951, and federal judges ultimately found the screenings unconstitutional. The ILWU still actively engages in national and international political and social conflicts. Some of those are on behalf of other workers, as in the refusal to load grapes that did not bear the United Farm Workers' seal and the 1997 worldwide boycott of the non-union loaded *Neptune Jade* ship and other solidarity actions for laid-off Liverpool dockworkers. However, it also closed ports on May 1, 1999 to protest the death sentence for Mumia Abu-Jamal and on November 30, 1999 during the demonstrations against the WTO Ministerial in Seattle. Most recently, the ILWU International has taken action against the war in Iraq, passing resolutions condemning the occupation and calling for immediate troop withdrawal. On May Day of 2008, thousands of ILWU members and community supporters shut down the ports to protest the war and call attention to workers' rights in the United States and Iraq.

Despite the long persistence of its governance institutions, generational shifts and technological change are taking their toll. The mechanics are now the fastest growing group in the union as automation of more of the jobs increases. The clerks, who used to clock the cargo in and out, now are often in buildings far from the docks, doing their work by computer. Young longshore workers fail to understand why a text message for job assignment cannot replace an early morning appearance at the hiring hall. Consequently and not surprisingly, all these factors combine to make it harder to maintain the high degree of participatory democracy and *esprit de corps* that once characterized the union.

Even so, in 2002, the union once again revealed its militant commitments to maintaining the hiring hall, the coastwise contract, and other union prerogatives, with the Longshore Caucus granting strike authorization over healthcare if contract negotiations failed.[6] Although striking was not seriously considered as a tactic by the ILWU leadership, the possibility prompted employer action nonetheless. Fearing a prolonged conflict, employers locked out union members before they could take action, and the Bush administration used a Taft-Hartley injunction to force them back to work—the first time a U.S. president has done so in the case of an employer lockout. Yet, the ILWU persisted and won most of what they fought for in this contract, and they continue to bargain hard and well while also continuing to mobilize politically against injuries to all.

THE NORMATIVE AND POLITICAL COMMITMENTS OF BRIDGES AND GOLDBLATT

The leaders during the pivotal period of the 1930s fit our expectations (H2, H7). They were ideologically on the left and envisioned a community of fate that encompassed the oppressed worldwide, but they saw as their first and most important task the improvement of the welfare of the workers. They became secure in their leadership only after attaining major gains, including relative job security, and they maintained their leadership positions by continuing to win better wages, hours, and benefits.

Harry Bridges was born into a lower-middle-class Australian Catholic family. He went to sea at seventeen and immigrated to the United States as a seaman. He had little formal education but a life-long love of learning. Louis Goldblatt came from an intellectual and left-wing Jewish family in New York. He came to the West Coast to attend graduate school after completing City College of New York. Their biographies differed, but Bridges and Goldblatt had similar underlying philosophies. Later in their collaboration, they disagreed over strategies and lost the camaraderie they once shared. Yet, both maintained unwavering commitment to improving the lot of the working class through successful negotiations with employers as well as through struggles to improve the world for all peoples. Within the union, this meant ensuring a relative equality of payment among the workers, a rank-and-file democracy, and racial justice. In terms of political actions it meant attempts to persuade their membership to join them in opposing national policies, including wars, that the leadership found questionable and supporting movements and activities the leadership believed to be progressive.

---

[6] Even though authorization was granted, the rank and file would have voted on the issue prior to striking. Personal communication (12/1/06) with former Coast Committeeman and member of the 2002 contract bargaining team Joe Wenzl.

Bridges and Goldblatt made themselves accessible to membership and actively communicated their views while energetically supporting the education of the members about their rights, their history, and their safety. They respected and, if need be, deferred to the workers' viewpoint; they recognized the limitations on their power. Goldblatt nicely sums up the approach:

> Unless you were awfully thick, what got to you was the whole business of timing, what issues could be effectively presented, a real consciousness of how the rank and file would react.
>
> It was not just a business of adopting a resolution; in many cases, this was the easiest thing in the world, particularly if you put it vaguely enough. The one thing that became most important was the measurement of any political action or position.
>
> How the thing could be bounced off the membership and to what degree they would support it? It was not a question of tailism, waiting for the workers to move before you start running to catch up.
>
> Leadership had with it certain obligations. The job of leadership meant that you would reflect as best you could the reservations, sometimes the reluctances, priorities, of the people you represented. This became a measure of leadership.
>
> It did not mean in any way compromising what I thought. An individual in my position, or any trade unionist, cannot over any long period of time make the price of his leadership the automatic support of the rank and file. You could not demand that price, but you could demand that you handle yourself with confidence and knowledge of the issue.
>
> What you could insist upon was that just because you had been elected a leader did not mean you had to give up any of your ideas. It was around this, for example, that we would fight things like redbaiting; and actually not so much the fight against redbaiting; the more correct way of appraising that would be, the right of a Red to retain his opinion when he was a union man. You began to put these things in a different equation; as a union we were not trying to change somebody's religious opinion; we were not trying to change their political registration. Neither was it anybody else's damn business how you as a leader felt about issues or political opinions or political registration. (Ward 1978, 1979, 243–44)

Members and leaders often disagreed over work rules and racial attitudes. They also disagreed over politics—and ultimately agreed to disagree.

GOVERNANCE INSTITUTIONS OF ACCOUNTABILITY

As hypothesized (H1, H8), the governance institutions limit the monetary returns to top officers, are broad in scope, and subject leadership to extensive political controls, both ex ante and ex post, that are far more extensive than those existing in the ILA or Teamsters.

Constitutionally (and effectively), the pay of the officers of the international is linked to that of the highest paid worker on the dock. The officers can secure a comfortable living, as can their members, but they cannot get rich off the union payroll.

In 1938, the new ILWU formalized its constitution, drawn from the ILA's existing Pacific Coast District constitution, which Bridges and others had crafted following the 1934 strike. Its clauses embody membership control as well as the broad scope of union activities. In 1953, these commitments were codified in the union's "Ten Guiding Principles" (see table 4.1).[7] They are embodied in the organizational governance institutions and practices of the ILWU.

In keeping with Principle I of its guiding principles, the ILWU developed a strong and participatory rank-and-file democracy, which the leadership respected even when the members disagreed with them (Levi et al. 2009). The constitution guaranteed the autonomy of locals, rank-and-file participation in local and international elections, one person-one vote in all contract and strike negotiations via a secret ballot, and a 15 percent threshold for recall referenda on elected officers. The bargaining committees are elected and inclusive, and the process is transparent to members. An active network of job stewards plays a key role in identifying workplace issues and representing the workers on the job.

The ILWU guarantees its membership multiple opportunities for participating electorally in its affairs. Members are periodically asked to vote on referenda over policy issues. Contract approval and strike authorization are conducted through elections. The selection of officers of the locals, their policies, and practices are subject to membership vote. The ILWU stands in sharp contrast to most American unions whose convention delegates select leadership; in the ILWU, members directly elect the union's international officers through one person, one vote. However, as a means of control of the supply of labor, the ILWU Longshore Division retains something of a craft union structure: workers first obtain status as identified casuals, eventually graduate to the B-list, and ultimately join the A-list and become full members, with rights to the pick of jobs and the full franchise. Those on the B-list can vote on the contract but not in elections for officers except, as of 1979, the Coast Labor Relations Committee. Casuals cannot vote at all.

The ILWU is composed of several divisions in its internal organization, including the longshore, the warehouse, and the inlandboatmen's divisions. All divisions in the ILWU are eligible to participate in the election

---

[7] http://www.ilwu19.com/history/the_ilwu_story/guiding_principles.htm, accessed August 15, 2011.

TABLE 4.1: Ten guiding principles of the ILWU

I.	**A Union is built on its members.** The strength, understanding, and unity of the membership can determine the union's course and its advancements. The members who work, who make up the union, and pay its dues can best determine their own destiny. If the facts are honestly presented to the members in the ranks, they will best judge what should be done and how it should be done. In brief, it is the membership of the union which is the best judge of its own welfare; not the officers, not the employers, not the politicians and the fair weather friends of labor. Above all, this approach is based on the conviction that, given the truth and an opportunity to determine their own course of action, the rank and file in 99 cases out of 100 will take the right path in their own interests and in the interests of all the people.
II.	**Labor unity is at all times the key for a successful economic advancement.** Anything that detracts from labor unity hurts all labor. Any group of workers that decides to put itself above other workers through craft unionism or through cozy deals at the expense of others will in the long run gain but little and inevitably will lose both its substance and its friends. No matter how difficult the going, a union must fight in every possible way to advance the principle of labor unity.
III.	**Workers are indivisible.** There can be no discrimination because of race, color, creed, national origin, religious or political belief. Any division among the workers can help no one but the employers. Discrimination of worker against worker is suicide. Discrimination is a weapon of the boss. Its entire history is proof that it has served no other purpose than to pit worker against worker to their own destruction.
IV.	**"To help any worker in distress" must be a daily guide in the life of every trade union and its individual members.** Labor solidarity means just that. Unions have to accept the fact that the solidarity of labor stands above all else, including even the so-called sanctity of the contract. We cannot adopt for ourselves the policies of union leaders who insist that because they have a contract, their members are compelled to perform work even behind a picket line. Every picket line must be respected as though it were our own.
V.	**Any union, if it is to fulfill its appointed task, must put aside all internal differences and issues to combine for the common cause of advancing the welfare of the membership.** No union can successfully fulfill its purpose in life if it allows itself to be distracted by any issue that causes division in its ranks and undermines the unity that all labor must have in the face of the employer.

(continued)

TABLE 4.1: (*continued*)

VI.	**The days are long gone when a union can consider dealing with single employers.** The powerful financial interests of the country are bound together in every conceivable type of united organization to promote their own welfare and to resist the demands of labor. Labor can no more win with the ancient weapons of taking on a single employer in industry than it can hope to win through the worn-out dream of withholding its skill until an employer sues for peace. The employers of this country are part of a well-organized, carefully coordinated, effective fighting machine. They can be met only on equal terms, which requires industry-wide bargaining and the most extensive economic strength of organized labor.
VII.	**Just as water flows to its lowest level, so do wages if the bulk of the workers are left unorganized.** The day of craft unionism—the aristocracy of labor—was over when mass production methods were introduced. To organize the unorganized must be a cardinal principle of any union worth its salt; and to accomplish this is not merely in the interest of the unorganized, it is for the benefit of the organized as well.
VIII.	**The basic aspirations and desires of the workers throughout the world are the same.** Workers are workers the world over. International solidarity, particularly to maritime workers, is essential to their protection and a guarantee of reserve economic power in times of strife.
IX.	**A new type of unionism is called for that does not confine its ambitions and demands only to wages.** Conditions of work, security of employment, and adequate provisions for the workers and their families in times of need are of equal, if not greater importance, than the hourly wage.
X.	**Jurisdictional warfare and jurisdictional raiding must be outlawed by labor itself.** Nothing can do as much damage to the ranks of labor and to the principle of labor unity and solidarity as jurisdictional bickering and raiding among unions. Both public support and strike victories are jeopardized by jurisdictional warfare.

of international officers, and all voting is, and always has been, conducted by secret ballot. Through debates and rule changes at its international conventions, the ILWU continues to evolve a system of elections aimed at promoting maximal participation. In 1994 it adopted the mail ballot and has used it since.

Going beyond the rules, we can document the actuality of rank-and-file democracy in the ILWU by investigation of electoral participation, effective member opposition to leadership demands, and effective local autonomy.

ELECTORAL PARTICIPATION

Analysis of voting tendencies and patterns in the selection of ILWU International officers from 1945 to 2006 reveals participation trends over time.[8] Longshore versus Non-Longshore members varied in rates of participation, and overall participation spikes when the union is challenged from without or experiencing internal leadership transitions, particularly over the past two decades.

The average turnout for the entire union is 45.7 percent, a participation level that exceeds most state and local voting rates in the United States, but in the Longshore Division, average yearly turnout increases to 60.5 percent. Particularly striking are the four identified periods when participation within the Longshore Division spikes at between 70 and 80 percent (see figure 4.1).

The non-Longshore members of the ILWU represent a highly heterogeneous division in the union, whose occupational categories include warehouse workers, seamen on inland waterways, Hawaiian pineapple and sugar cane and hotel workers, Alaska cannery workers, and Powell's Bookstore employees. The variation in their work environments and their category-specific struggles seems to reduce the probability of strong solidaristic ties among them. Although the turnout of other divisions is never as high as in the Longshore division, it is relatively close for the pre-1970s. Moreover, its spikes mirror those in the Longshore, with the 1971 strike period a notable exception. Only the 1991 election elicits an increase in participation; in subsequent contested elections, non-Longshore participation drops to 16.4 percent in 1994 and to just below 8 percent in 2006.

The Longshore Division has a much higher turnout than most American unions, although the comparison is a difficult one to make. Despite being public record, union voter turnout is rarely reported to the press and appears infrequently in academic writing. The little information accessible to scholars tends to come from rank-and-file movements for union democracy, such as the Teamster's for a Democratic Union (TDU), interested in publicizing the problems with the union they want to reform.

---

[8] We determined total membership figures from per capita payments to the International and from Convention voting strength records, while voting participation figures are found in validated election outcomes as reported in the union newspaper, *The Dispatcher*. Following PMA conventions, we consider Longshore division to include the clerks, foremen, and watchmen locals as well as the Longshore locals. The data presented do not take into account membership subtraction of non-voting locals. Thus, turnout figures will be slightly higher than reported here. For updated data, see project website at http://depts.washington.edu/ilwu/.

Membership voting rates in union elections

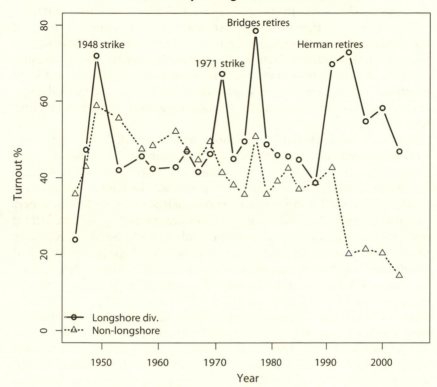

Figure 4.1: ILWU member turnout in union elections

The TDU reports Teamster rank-and-file turnout at 27.1 percent in 1991, 32 percent in 1996, 25.7 percent in 1998, 22.3 percent in 2001, and 19.3 percent in 2006.[9] These rates are consistently lower than the ILWU average and significantly lower than the Longshore Division. The spike in 1996 reflects interest in the election of Ron Carey, the first genuine democratic threat to oligarchic rule.

MEMBERSHIP OPPOSITION TO LEADERSHIP POLICY

Another way to assess the degree of democracy and the political control exercised over leadership is the extent to which members can successfully oppose leaders' advice. This was not rare in the ILWU, even

[9] IBT election data were compiled by Teamsters for a Democratic Union from IBT Election Officer reports. This information was secured by request. We thank Barry Eidlin for his help.

on major issues (Levi et al. 2009). Coding of all the Convention Proceedings of the ILWU from 1938 to 2000 reveals considerable debate and contention within the membership and with leaders.[10] Analysis of the summary of the Longshore Caucus Minutes on the same issues reveals additional information on leadership concerns, intra-leadership conflicts, and responses to membership initiatives.[11] Materials available in union publications and newspapers as well as in the general press supplement further confirm our finding of a lively and participatory membership.

Two examples will suffice (for more see Levi et al. 2009): one politically motivated and one pertaining to changes in work practices.

On October 3, 1945, the ILWU joined the World Federation of Trade Unions (WFTU) by virtue of its affiliation with the CIO. The formation of the WFTU was by national federations; neither rank-and-file members nor ILWU leadership had a role in its design or policy. In fact, little if any information was available to the rank and file on the issue; many members were not even aware of the decision. Subsequently, Bridges and Goldblatt both became involved in the maritime division. A few years later the CIO decided to withdraw from the WFTU because of its left-wing positions.

In 1950 the CIO expelled the ILWU, partly for failing to withdraw from the WFTU, partly due to Bridges' opposition to the Marshall Plan, but primarily for alleged communist leanings within the union. Following expulsion from the CIO, Bridges and Goldblatt both supported continued affiliation with the WFTU, but they soon confronted a groundswell of rank-and-file opposition. In August 1950, the elected representatives of the ILWU Caucus took up the issue in response to resolutions and letters emanating from the rank and file and local officers. The sentiment against maintaining WFTU affiliation became so heated that Bridges' own Local 10 in San Francisco demanded his resignation if he failed to withdraw from the WFTU. Bridges was, at the time, also an officer of Maritime Federation of the World, a WFTU subsidiary. Despite Bridges' pro-WFTU editorials in *The Dispatcher* between 1947 and 1950, membership remained firm in its opposition. On August 18, 1950, the ILWU Caucus voted 63 to 9 to sever relations with the WFTU, laying a politically divisive issue to rest. Membership conflicted with leadership, and membership prevailed.

---

[10] The coding and documentation are available on the website: http://depts.washington.edu/ilwu/.

[11] The Proceedings are public, but the summary of the Caucus Minutes required us to get extraordinary permissions from the officers of the Longshore Division, which they graciously extended to us.

In another highly charged issue, Bridges and Goldblatt supported containerization in the West Coast ports, realizing it was an inevitable development. The union signed "mechanization and modernization" (M&M) agreements in 1961 and again in 1966, wresting from employers concessions on work rules, procedures for reducing the workforce, and a $29 million payout to cover pensions and a wage guarantee (Ward 1978, 1979, 838 and passim). The M&M agreements fundamentally altered the nature of dock work. Between 1960 and 1980, the number of registered longshore workers declined from 13,941 to 8,389, and by 1994, at its lowest point, the number was 6,049.[12] Simultaneously, between 1960 and 1980, ". . . productivity, measured in tons per hour, increased from .837 to 5.498, and the cost per ton decreased from $4.94 to $3.60 despite a fourfold increase in the longshore hourly wage rate" (Finlay 1988, 5).

From the employers' perspective, the M&M agreements offered increased productivity and declining labor costs. Dock work became more like routinized factory work (Finlay 1988). The transformation from manually handling cargo via gang work in a ship's hold to containers and crane operators drastically altered social relations. In some ports, most notably San Pedro, and for some kinds of work the practice of "rotation on the job" yielded to "the steady man" working a single job type, often for the same employer.

The membership was far from unanimous in support of these changes. In 1971, contention in the ranks about changes in work and the mistaken belief by some that Bridges was collaborating with the employers led to rejection of the employer's plan and, against Bridges' counsel, a vote to go on strike. The strike lasted 134 days but failed to achieve many of the contract provisions the rank and file desired.

EFFECTIVE LOCAL AUTONOMY

Locals have always possessed autonomy, including over aspects of the electoral process. As it does in the IBT, autonomy ensures leadership power bases independent of the International, and, as in the IBT, the International reserves the right to put into trusteeship any local that violates the basic principles or code of conduct of the union. In the IBT, trusteeship is used often as both threat and action; in the ILWU it is used hardly at all.

The effect of local autonomy in the ILWU is significant variation in term limits for officers, meeting attendance requirements, and even political orientations. For example, term limits differ across locals for union officers and job dispatchers. Local 19 in Seattle lacks term limits for its local officials, while Local 10 in San Francisco has term limits of two

[12] These numbers were compiled from Pacific Maritime Association Annual Reports.

years on and one year off for all full-time elected positions. In addition, autonomy permits policies contrary to the prevalent norms and rules of the union, as when Local 13, in San Pedro, decided to adopt the steady man, despite the opposition of Bridges and others in the leadership.

Local autonomy also facilitates decisions that expand the community of fate. San Francisco has always been a particularly active port in relationship to political issues, and this quote from a National Farm Workers Association (NFWA) organizer from 1965 reveals how local leadership can make and implement decisions independently of the national decision process.

> We went there as the grapes were being loaded onto ships to Japan . . . and I'm standing out there with a little cardboard, with a picket [sign], "Don't eat grapes." Then some of the longshoremen asked, "Is this a labor dispute?" And I [was nervous and didn't know whether we were legally allowed to use the term, so I] said, "No, no, no labor dispute." So they would walk in. Jimmy Herman came over and asked me, "What the hell you doing?" And I told him we were striking. He knew about the strike but wanted to know, "what are you asking for?" And I was telling him, and then he says, "Come with me." He took me to his office; he was president of the clerks [a Longshoremen's Union local]. He took me to his office and he got on his hands and knees, Jimmy Herman, and he made picket signs. And he told me, "You go back there and don't tell nobody about who gave you this. But you just stand there. [You] don't [have to] say a goddamned thing." The sign said, "Farm Workers on Strike." And everybody walked out of that fucking place, man! That's the first time I felt like I was 10 feet tall, man! Everybody walked out. So then they asked what's happening and we were telling them, and Jesus Christ, man, I never seen anything like it. There were trucks all the way up to the bridge, man! So they stopped and Jimmy says, "You're gonna get an injunction as soon as the people find out what's happening. In the meantime you got to stop them. You go ahead and do it. They ain't gonna do nothing to you. Can't do a thing to you, but they're gonna go after . . . Harry Bridges [the Longshoremen's Union president, who] will have no choice but to ask you to leave, because if they get an injunction, they'll get fined. So you do it until that happens." (Ganz 2009, 140–41)

Each local makes its own determination of whether or not to engage in the political mobilizations the International Executive Board (IEB) endorses, and sometimes the locals initiate the action. The boycott of South African cargo as a protest against apartheid is a case in point. In 1976, in response to a proposal from San Francisco Local 10, the IEB polled the locals for support of a referendum for a boycott; eighteen locals responded in the affirmative, six against, and thirty-nine did not respond. The IEB issued a letter in 1977 advising that there was an official boycott of all cargo to and from South Africa, but they did not do much to enforce it. In 1984, for eleven days San Francisco longshore workers refused to unload South African cargo from the *Nedlloyd Kimberley* until the arbitrator determined it was an illegal work stoppage and the local was threatened with a $10,000 daily fine. According to *International Labour Reports* (1984), "250 dockworkers had refused to work this cargo each losing an average of $200 as a result of their action." Many, but hardly all, locals followed suit in 1985–86 with demonstrations or actual boycotts.

GOVERNANCE INSTITUTIONS ENSURING
WORKER WELFARE, DIGNITY, AND RIGHTS

Leadership can make political demands, we argue, only once they develop a reputation and capacity for improving the well-being of the workers. The pivotal strikes and negotiations of the 1930s resulted in greater job security, increased worker safety, better wages, fewer hours, more benefits, greater worker power, and elimination of degrading employer practices. Particular union governance institutions were crucial to winning and sustaining these victories, among them the hiring hall, instant arbitration, and industry-wide bargaining.

HIRING HALL

One of the great victories of the 1934 strike was the elimination of the shape-up and, in its place, the establishment of a regularized dispatch system in the union-controlled hiring hall. In sharp contrast to the pre-1934 conditions, workers receive their assignments at a pre-determined time and away from the elements. In that pre-Starbucks period, the hiring hall provided the rare place where workers could get warm, drink coffee, read the newspaper, and interact off the job with other workers and union officers. They could talk politics and raise questions about the union and their officers. Dispatch of jobs was and is still done (at least for some jobs and in some ports) through the "low-man-out" system in which those who work the least number of hours get the first pick of available work. The practice of "rotation on the job" equalized earnings and increased worker control of their work life by permitting them to take time off (albeit with loss of pay) when they chose.[13] For many workers, "the ILWU is the hiring hall" (Wellman 1995, 60).

---

[13] Larry Hansen, president of Local 19 on several occasions during the 1990s and 2000s, both worked on the docks and earned a PhD in Asian Studies from Berkeley. He would take

Other unions, e.g., the International Typographical Workers (ITU), had similar institutions that played similar roles, including producing a relatively flat income range (Lipset, Trow, and Coleman 1956). The longshore of the 1930s generally lacked the high education levels of the printers, nor did the job require educational qualifications. Yet, the hard manual labor of loading and unloading cargo required not only coordination and cooperation but also the capacity to engage in a variety of highly technical tasks involved in tying and moving break-bulk cargo. The job was intense, difficult, and dangerous. Workers had to depend on each other if they were to be both productive and safe. The slogan, "An injury to one is an injury to all," had a very practical implication. This clear sense of an occupational community was enhanced by the importance of family and neighborhood connections among workers (discussed in chapter 5), common social activities, debate and discussion in the hiring hall, and union meetings and communications.

The combination of a space for interaction and the necessity of teamwork on the docks reinforced the development of a strong social network and the norm of cooperation (also see McGinn 2006). It is enduring evidence of the capacity and commitment of the pivotal leadership to make the workers better off.

The ILWU possesses governance institutions meant to enhance the power of the ILWU with employers. Some of these address processes of direct action through arbitration. Others focus on contract negotiations. These institutions, which the pivotal leadership helped craft, have the further advantage of helping leaders build a reputation for industrial effectiveness. Only once that reputation is established, we maintain, can leaders begin to make political demands of the rank and file (H7).

DIRECT ACTION—AND ARBITRATION

Principle IV endorses the right of members to promote labor solidarity even when it violates their contract or the advice of their leaders. ILWU members have long taken matters into their own hands. In the two years immediately following the "Big Strike," there were more than 500 "quickies," short and non-authorized work stoppages, mostly aimed at ridding the docks of "scab bosses" and at reducing sling load limits (Kimeldorf 1988, 112–13; also, see Kagel in Schwartz 2009, 37). Quickies and other work stoppages continue to occur but not at such a rate, largely because of a change in procedure following this significant outbreak in 1934–36.

---

months off at a time to go to Asia for fieldwork. Hansen is an extreme case, given that most workers just take time off for a short respite or vacation, but he is idolized by his local for having achieved an education, maintained his research, and, simultaneously, proved himself an able worker and a trustworthy and respected leader, particularly at contract time.

President Franklin Roosevelt established the National Longshore-men's Board in 1934 to mediate and later arbitrate the strike. According to Bridges, the union ". . . fought arbitration all the way down the line . . . but the San Francisco general strike was settled with arbitration . . . and the decision came down on October 12, which was a big resounding victory" (Schwartz 2009, 28–29). It provided for the hiring hall, union selection of the dispatcher, and, as it turned out, "insulated the longshoremen from conventional forms of industrial discipline" by reducing the punishment for an on-site job action to a temporary loss of pay (Kimeldorf 1988, 112). The employers had no power to deregister a worker.

The Award also provided for a continuing arbitration system, and the Secretary of Labor selected the arbitrators. Not surprisingly, the employers turned to it in order to control the quickies. The arbitrator found in favor of the employers, but this seems to have had no effect on worker behavior. Bridges first advised the men to comply with the arbitrator's decisions and then took it to a membership vote. The rank and file agreed to observe the new decrees, particularly since the employers had effectively reduced the sling load limits (Kagel in Schwartz 2009, 37).

In 1948, there was another major strike, and the employers tried to get rid of the union-controlled hiring hall and industry-wide bargaining, goals they continue to pursue. In the aftermath, the employers created the Pacific Maritime Association (PMA) as their bargaining agent, and the PMA and ILWU together agreed on a new arbitration process for grievances.[14] Four area arbitrators (San Pedro, northern California, Oregon, and Washington), two picked by the union and two by the employers, would engage in "instant arbitration." The area arbitrator is on 24-hour call to intercede whenever and wherever longshore stops work because of a safety issue. If the arbitrator finds there was a safety violation, those who stopped work get stand-by pay and the employer is ordered to correct the situation. If the arbitrator finds no violation, there is no stand-by pay. The workers who stand by over safety do lose pay for that period as well but, if found to have acted in "good faith belief," are subject to no additional penalty or disciplinary action. All area arbitrator decisions can be appealed to the Coast arbitrator, jointly appointed by the ILWU and PMA.

The system was reinforced in 1961 when the mix of traditional and new mechanical methods created problems with the sling load limits.

[14] The information on the arbitration system comes mainly from Sam Kagel, Coast Arbitrator, 1948–2002—Kagel (1999), Project (2009), Schwartz (2009), 55–59, and from a presentation by Washington Area Arbitrator, Herald Ugles, to Margaret Levi's labor studies class at the University of Washington on February 2, 2011. Also see the interview by Herb Mills, a former officer of San Francisco Local 10 in Schwartz (2009), 59–62.

Given that longshore has a strong norm to "meet the hook," that is, pick up the load whatever the weight, the contract includes a provision that workers can stop work until an arbitrator arrives if they assess the job as "onerous" (Ward 1978, 1979, 843–44).

Instant arbitration survives until this day. It enables the union leadership to permit the direct job actions they could not otherwise stop, and it permits the employer to get issues resolved quickly so that work can proceed. Both the ILWU and the PMA benefit from the increased productivity that results. However, increasingly some workers have turned to the courts rather than the grievance machinery; they file class action lawsuits. While this may have been a necessity to correct racial and gender imbalances, at least one former ILWU International president, Dave Arian, expressed concern about the long-term effects on arbitration and grievance processes.

For the ILWU, arbitration provided a complement rather than a substitute for collective bargaining and the weapon of the strike. When Congress considered imposing compulsory arbitration to end the 1971 strike, Bridges and the union resisted. Kagel, appointed as mediator, aided the ILWU and PMA to reach a settlement that ended the strike and avoided compulsory arbitration.

An illustration of how the union membership used arbitration to good effect is the case of asbestos found in a ship's hold in San Francisco in 1975 (Schwartz 2009, 59–62). Herb Mills, who previously had been an officer in Local 10 and was back on the docks as a steward, tried to correct the situation by first going to the PMA safety officer and then to OSHA, with no effect. After work stoppages and arbitration all along the Coast, the union resolved the issue with the PMA. However, when Mills and his compatriots realized that the effects of asbestos were long term, they engaged in two additional actions: systematic education of the membership and litigation against the manufacturers. Mills concludes his oral account, "My point is that we got a longshore contract that says, 'Damn it, you stop work when it's unsafe'" (Schwartz 2009, 62).

When asked by the Senate Labor Relations Committee what made the ILWU a left-wing union, Harry Bridges' first response was, "It's a union that's willing to arbitrate . . ." (Minolt 1992, part I; Cherney 1994, 1; Harry Bridges Center for Labor Studies 2009–2010b). This provoked laughter in the room, but unquestionably arbitration in the ILWU facilitates direct action, a left-wing and syndicalist impulse. Bridges went on to say:

> It's also a union that believes in a lot of rank and file democracy and control . . . It's a union that believes that its officers should be easy to remove and . . . [that] their wages and expenses [should be] no more than the . . . highest paid worker that's a member of the

union. It's also a union that recognizes that, from time to time, it's got to stand up and fight for . . . civil liberties, racial equality, and things like that.

INDUSTRY-WIDE BARGAINING

One of the major wins for the longshore in 1934 and for the warehouse in 1936 was the coastwise (the ILWU terminology) contract, and the union later embodied its commitment to coordinated bargaining in its Principle VI. Bridges and the union fought hard to maintain industry-wide bargaining, something the employers are still attempting to end, but so far with no success.

SCOPE OF UNION COMMITMENTS

The ILWU has a broad definition of action by its members on behalf of social justice and political causes. The membership sometimes conflicts with the leadership concerning when and whether to engage in political mobilization. Yet, the evidence of tolerance of these leadership and organizational commitments is overwhelming but only once political controls are in place and industrial success has been achieved (H6).

NON-DISCRIMINATION

Bridges and Goldblatt were firmly committed to racial justice, embodied in Principle III, but racism nonetheless persisted in the union. Some rank and file and local leadership expressed a strong concern that the activist demands of the leadership for racial justice would undermine industrial success. As expected, following H6, the tolerance of political activism (at least on this issue) was consequently reduced among these members.

The tensions became particularly clear in the period immediately following World War II. A surplus of workers on the docks included many African Americans hired during the war effort. San Pedro evoked a seniority rule and created the "unemployed 500." In 1945, at a stop work meeting, San Francisco's Local 10, which had become one-third black, debated what to do. When his views were demanded, Bridges made his famous statement that if only two jobs were left on the docks, one should go to a black worker. Cleophas Williams, an African American who began as a longshore worker in 1944, was present. He found Bridges' statement

> . . . very shocking to me because there was no political gain for him by making this statement. There was no gain even among blacks at that particular time because many of the blacks were still on probation, so they couldn't vote. I considered it a statement of conviction. I was shocked. I had read and been exposed to some of the left-wing forces, but I had never heard anyone put his neck

on the chopping block by making a public statement of this kind. (Kimeldorf 1988, 148)

That same year the leadership suspended the charter of the Stockton unit of Warehouse Local 6 when members refused to work with a Japanese American recently returned from the camps (Schwartz 1980).

By 1946 11,000 (22%) out of approximately 50,000 members of the ILWU were black (Nelson 1998, 159). The inclusion of Hawaiian pineapple, sugar, and hotel workers made the ILWU a very multiracial union. Goldblatt and the others centrally involved in the strikes against the Big Five sugar companies in Hawaii demonstrated with their actions and contractual demands ILWU commitment to an interracial union movement and an end to discrimination (Ward 1978, 1979 passim; Jung 2006, 191).

However, even for these very principled leaders, principles could come into contradiction with each other. The values of seniority and local autonomy trumped racial justice in at least two important instances (Nelson 1998, 162–84; also see interview with Walter Williams in Schwartz 2009, 80–86). The first was Portland, where Local 8 excluded African Americans until the 1960s, despite efforts by Bridges and many others to change their policy. Fear of the ILA, waiting in the wings, may have been one reason the International did not expel Local 8, but equally important was the desire to retain the coastwise contract, which would have been threatened. In San Pedro the docks were integrated during the war, but racial tension and segregation were high. After the war, Local 13 decided to deregister the 500 workers lowest in seniority, and it received International approval to proceed given the inviolability of the seniority principle. About half of the "unemployed 500," as they came to be called, were African American. But Local 13 went further and broke its promise to hire first from the list of 500 and in order of seniority; instead, it privileged whites over blacks. In 1947, Bridges offered a possible solution, which was rejected by Local 13. In 1965, when twenty-four of the black "unemployed 500" filed a grievance against the employers to have their full seniority reinstated, the ILWU filed in support of the grievants. The claim was twice rejected, largely because it was the union, not the employers, who had made deregistration and rehiring decisions.

San Pedro is now a multicultural local, one of the most diversified in the ILWU. Portland's history of racial discrimination is behind it. But in the 1980s another form of discrimination came to the fore: discrimination in the recruitment, hiring, and assignment of women. The court cases to rectify the treatment of women, combined with the increased dissatisfaction with nepotism, led to new hiring practices throughout the industry. No longer is the route into the union only through fathers, brothers, neighbors, and friends; it is now also through advertisement and competition, a process we shall discuss in chapter 7.

INTERNATIONAL SOLIDARITY

The ILWU retains a strong commitment to international solidarity, instantiated in Principle VIII. Some of the port closures already mentioned reflect this commitment, as do involvement in international organizations such as the WFTU and, currently, the International Transport Federation (ITF), which involves the union in the campaign against flags of convenience and other such actions. We provide additional documentation of ILWU internationalism in chapter 7.

WWF

BACKGROUND

Australian maritime workers have a long history of struggle against employers and political mobilization. Some accounts emphasize how the wharfies treat all industrial action as class warfare and are uncompromising to the point of engaging in disastrous strikes (Australian Stevedoring Industry Board 1950). Others emphasize wharfie actions in support of improved conditions for themselves and other workers and in opposition to imperialist and fascist wars (Nelson 1957; Lockwood 1990; Mallory 2005).

Certainly conditions on the docks were abysmal. The "bull system," the Australian variant of the shape-up, prevailed, with a short reprieve, until the early 1940s. Whether or not it was as corrupt as the American version (Waterfront Commission of New York Harbor 1954, 32), it most definitely victimized militants, favored friends of the boss, and dehumanized the worker. The work was unhealthy, with almost no facilities for washing, eating, or resting made available. Heavy sling loads and old equipment created serious safety hazards. Much of the time, too many workers were available for too few jobs, keeping wages low and work irregular.[15]

Documented periodic work stoppages date from the mid-nineteenth century, and so do politically motivated actions—in opposition to transportation of slaves and in aid of political prisoners from the French Commune. Although the burgeoning union movement suffered a serious setback in the general strike of 1890, within a few years several branches reorganized and then amalgamated in 1902, a year after Australia gained independence. The Waterside Workers Federation was born. The secretary

---

[15] These conditions are documented in a series of government reports.

of the Sydney branch and future Prime Minister, W. M. "Billy" Hughes, was its first general secretary. Hughes was already a federal member of Parliament, and with one exception all those on the original governing body were politicians (Beasley 1996, 21–22).

The WWF had at least three strong ideological influences as it evolved in the first half of the twentieth century. The first was syndicalist (Williams 1975, 32; Lockwood 1990, 129, 170–71; Burgmann 1995; Macintyre 1998, 16–18, 26, 46–47; Burgmann 2005; Mallory 2005, 25 and chap. 7). Tom Nelson, a strong Communist and many-time Sydney branch secretary, praised the Wobblies for their actions against the bull system, leadership in the fight against conscription, and for their role in the 1917 strike, but he excoriated them for their divisiveness, contempt of the reformist unions, and lack of sophistication about the class nature of the state (Nelson 1957, 31–34). Suppressed by the Hughes government and blacklisted by the ship owners, they were never again much of a force after World War I. In a last hurrah, the IWW was present at the unity conference called by the Australian Socialist Party in 1920.

The Communist Party of Australia (CPA) was more directly and clearly influential. Much of the WWF leadership belonged to the CPA. However, on more than one occasion, Healy and Roach and others broke from the Party line in favor of pragmatism and union-building (Macintyre 1998, 334–36).

The Australian Labor Party (ALP) was the third influence. Hughes and many of the early WWF leaders were active in the ALP, and they supported government regulation of the stevedoring industry and arbitration under the Commonwealth Court of Conciliation and Arbitration (Australia Commonwealth Court 1908–1956). The link between the ALP and the WWF remained strong throughout most of the century, albeit with some serious ups and downs. Not surprisingly, the CPA and the ALP were not always in agreement. A split within the ALP between its anti-communist right and its left wings was mirrored within the WWF. The ALP's Industrial Group, known as the "Groupers," was composed of anti-communists whose program derived from the conservatives B. A. Santamaria and Archbishop Daniel Mannix, both of Melbourne. The Groupers dominated the Melbourne branch of the WWF and conflicted regularly with the federal leadership over policy in the late 1940s through the early 1960s (Sheridan 1997). When the Victoria ALP itself split in 1954, this also had implications for intra-union debate.

Hughes appears to have worked hard to obtain the first arbitration award in 1914–15, which won general approval from the locals (Beasley 1996, 36–40). The Higgins Award required the registration of workers and improvements in pay as part of an effort to standardize conditions across ports. The judge recognized that having to appear at the wharf gates and stand idle, sometimes for days, awaiting an assignment was time that should be compensated. In justifying appearance money, he famously stated, "They also serve who only stand and wait" (Croke 2011, 24). Justice Higgins was a social reformer; he also authored the 1907 Harvester decision, which established a family wage based on the male breadwinner and proved ". . . a landmark of Australian social democracy" (Macintyre 2004, 63).

Meanwhile, Billy Hughes, while still maintaining his position as general secretary of the WWF, became prime minister in 1915, serving until 1923. In 1916, Hughes was expelled from the ALP and WWF because of his advocacy of conscription. Hughes shifted to the Nationalist Party in 1916 and won re-election as prime minister, despite two defeats of referenda for conscription that he introduced (Levi 1997, 121–23). He successfully exerted pressure for the Court to consider cases brought by striking unions and then, in 1917, applied to the Court for deregistration of the WWF. Higgins agreed on the first but not the second (Macintyre 2004, 63), but Higgins resigned in 1918 when the High Court found that the Arbitration Court had no power to enforce its decisions (ibid., 71). During the next decades, the Court became far more conservative than it had been under Higgins.

A failed strike in 1917 set the stage for more concerted employer opposition to labor's demands. In 1928 the union struck again in repudiation of the Beeby Award, which reinstated a second pick-up, reduced overtime, and otherwise reduced the power and conditions of the workers. The ship owners hired "volunteers" as replacement workers, and the government subsequently recognized them as the Permanent and Casual Wharf Labourers' Union (PCWLU) in the Transport Act of 1928. To the WWF the P&C's were scabs. The Act not only ended the preferential hiring of registered WWF's, it permitted the continuation of the "bull system" with free selection at the port gate. The "Dog Collar" Act, as the wharfies called the 1928 legislation, required the wharfies to have licenses, which were subject to forfeit if the licensee did not obey the rules and awards established by the Court and by the law. The law made the union accountable for strikes called by its branches or for unauthorized stoppages by members. It became an ". . . offence to prevent any person from working in accordance with an award, and the Court was given a general power to punish contempt" (Macintyre 2004).

By the early 1930s, the WWF was as weak as it had ever been.

THE NORMATIVE AND POLITICAL COMMITMENTS OF HEALY AND ROACH

It was at this point that both Big Jim Healy (1898–1961) and Ted Roach (1909–1971) emerged as a new generation of leaders. Like their counterparts in the ILWU, they had strong commitments to the workers' welfare and to a participatory union democracy, and both held left-wing ideologies—indeed, they were active members of the Communist Party of Australia (CPA).

Jim Healy immigrated with his young family from Manchester, England to Mackay, Queensland in 1925. He had served and been wounded in action in World War I but then had trouble finding employment. He began working on the wharves in 1927; by 1929, he was branch president of the WWF. He was active in the ALP but also became attracted to communism after he went on a union-sponsored trip to the Soviet Union in 1934. He was a committed Communist from then until his death and served on the central committee of the CPA. In 1937, within a year of moving to Sydney, he was elected general secretary of the WWF. The first-past-the-post system allowed him to defeat his three opponents, including the incumbent, with less than one-third of the votes. Given the lack of a clear majority, the disarray of the union under the Transport Workers' Act, and his own experience, he started ". . . from well behind the scratch" (Lockwood 1990, 341–42).

But he came on fast and strong. He immediately initiated a campaign against the "Dog Collar Act," documenting the injuries that it permitted and the harassment of the Vigilant Officers who attempted to enforce safety standards on the docks (Lockwood 1990, 342–43). One of his first acts was to create a union-wide newspaper, the *Maritime Worker* (Noel Butlin Archives 1937, 33–35, 38). Despite regular and often hotly contested elections, he served as general secretary until his death in 1961.

Healy was an extraordinarily effective union leader (Williams 1975; Markey and Svensen 1996). One of his guiding principles was the promotion of unity among the membership. To this end, he pushed forward the re-absorption of the Permanent and Casuals into the WWF, which he finally accomplished in 1942. He always ran on a Unity ticket, which included the Communists but also the left wing of the ALP and other leftists. He was also, by all accounts, an extremely personable man. "Dutchy" Young, once a Grouper and always affiliated with the ALP, didn't buy the Communist line but worked closely with Healy. He recounts (1986, 157–58), "His humour was profound. He was a tremendous individual. An entertainer that . . . couldn't be excelled. And at any rowdy or bawdy party Jim would get up and he'd sing that Irish songs that would finish up, the most hardened fellow would be in tears . . . And yet he wasn't born Irishman, he was a Manchester man. And . . . he had such capacity to make friends and most importantly a man of his word." With the exception of dyed in the wool Groupers, most cannot say enough in Healy's praise.

Ted Roach was Australian born and bred, but otherwise his history is somewhat similar to Healy's. He began work in the coalfields, and early on he became an organizer. By the early 1930s he had been active in movements on behalf of the unemployed and union actions by coalminers. He became a member of the Communist Party in 1931, and in 1934 was accepted into the Newcastle branch of the WWF. In 1936, he transferred to the South branch at Port Kembla and immediately began to engage in militant action there to combat the bull system and other abuses. By 1938 he was branch secretary. One of his first acts was to prevent the loading of the *Dalfram* and initiate the pig-iron dispute. His strategic thinking and militancy subsequently helped him secure the new position of assistant general secretary of the WWF in 1942, a position he held until 1967 (Lockwood 1990; Griffith 1997; Mallory 1997).

While both of these men were committed to a fundamental transformation of the economy and society, they appear always to have put the interests of the workers they represented before all else. They fought tirelessly to end the "bull system," to create centralized and regularized pickups, to repeal the Transport Workers Act, and to improve wages, benefits, and safety on the wharves. They wanted a pension system that would enable older workers to retire—and retire comfortably—and allow younger workers to have jobs. And they succeeded in almost every goal they set for making the wharfies better off. Militant and political as they were, both, but especially Healy, endured considerable criticism from even more militant members on both the left and the right. They opposed the arbitration system but worked with it. They encouraged support of others on strike, and both were indicted and served jail time as a result of their actions to aid the coalminers in 1949. They continued to mobilize around political actions, as the list of political work stoppages suggests, but they were even more hamstrung than their ILWU colleagues by the legal system in which they operated.

Political Control

The WWF established governance institutions that gave the members extensive control over the leadership (H8), including limiting their pay (H1). Among the rules, adopted under Healy, were the easy recall of officers and the limits on salary, the same rules that applied in the ILWU. Electoral procedures were improved, and general membership conventions and Federal Committee of Management (FCOM) meetings regularized in terms of timing and composition. Healy centralized more power in the Federation but never at the expense of branch and member input. The WWF's vibrant rank-and-file democracy, as measured by its electoral system and participation in branch and stop work meetings, ensured effective ex ante and ex post constraints on leadership.

Its electoral system appears to have been above board. Although a few elections were challenged, it was as likely because of a close vote count as a suspicion of fraud. Norm Phillips, a veteran of the union, described the process in an interview:

> The dominant executive was they called them the Unity Group, which consisted of Communists, Labor Party and other individuals who belonged to a particular party. I myself, as a returning officer, I was a member of the Labor Party myself. Most of those that opposed Unity were the Industrial Group mob and others influenced by mostly right-wingers. Everyone had the chance, the opportunity, to stand for a position for the executive. I was very proud of the way the elections were conducted... As a returning officer, I stood for election. As a returning officer, I was never ever opposed. I was a returning officer for 12 years. Before that I was assistant returning officer for a few years... I was never opposed by any faction at all. Most of the men, I'd say 99%, had complete confidence in the way the elections were run in a democratic manner. Might I say that the way we run the elections was even stricter than the way they run state or federal elections. No member at all was denied the right to vote. We used to have to produce financial metal card to show that we were a genuine waterside worker entitled to vote... We had the election on one day. If a chap were to turn up and had forgot his metal number, he'd have to make a statutory declaration, and all of these would go into a sealed envelope... Then we checked all the polls to see if they had voted anywhere else... All votes by secret ballot He went into a booth we got from state electorate body. Vote went into a sealed ballot box, and those ballot boxes were collected at the end of the day and were taken up to the Commonwealth Bank, main office, and lodged in a sealed vault. Next morning at 7 o'clock, all the poll clerks, returning officer and scrutineers... We carried the boxes down to Sussex Street union rooms, and everything was counted under the supervision of a scrutineer. Any candidate at all was allowed to have a scrutineer. Cost a bit of money but to make sure it was run correctly. Were never ever doubted, no complaints from any newspaper or publication. (Waterside Workers of Australia 2006b)[16]

Although Healy won re-election until his death in 1961, he did not win all the elections handily. Nor did Roach. For example, in 1943, after winning significant gains for the union, Healy still faced considerable opposition; he won with 8,095 votes to his opponent's 3,934. By

---

[16] In response to questions from Levi and Ahlquist, Phillips attested that this was the process used in all the branches; it was federal policy.

1949, when the Groupers and anti-communism had gathered momentum, Healy defeated one of the Grouper leaders, Gus Alford, in a closer election, 11,812 to 9,486, and Roach defeated another 10,040 to 9,063 (Beasley 1996, 139).

The governing body of the WWF was the Federal Committee of Management (FCOM), which included the national officers but also representatives elected by the membership. In addition, there was an active system of job delegates and gang leaders (Waterside Workers of Australia 2006a; Sheridan 2006). The Job Delegate Association (JDA) sponsored classes and organizing actions. They were kept actively informed of Federation policy discussions and their opinions were often solicited (Heidtman 2006).

Debate was always lively within the Committee of Management, but the influence of the Groupers in the late 1940s intensified it. They were resistant to almost every change in work rules or governance that Healy and Roach proposed, and they most definitely opposed "political" issues. Their strongest base was in the Melbourne branch, which exercised its local autonomy regularly and vigorously. They started their own newspaper, the *Watersider*, arguing that the *Maritime Worker* was being used as communistic propaganda (which it arguably was). For his part, Healy felt the *Watersider* was propagandistic. In the heated 1950 Biennial National Conference, he noted in his general report: ". . . the Board, Court, and employers know that the leaders of the so-called A.L.P. Industrial Groups will come out in full cry in opposition to any move which involves a stoppage or a threat of a stoppage, even when such a move may be supported by some of its members in the Branch concerned. And if delegates are in any doubt about my allegation on this particular point, I suggest they have only to read the *Watersider*. . . " (Noel Butlin Archives Centre 1950, 56).

The refusal of the Melbourne groupers in 1951 to go along with Federal policy concerning overtime bans and then in regard to the New Zealand waterfront strike won them praise from the press and the government and may well have been ammunition in support of the use of the Crimes Act against the WWF. Their efforts appear to have backfired, even in their own branch. On more than one occasion, the members voted against the Groupers at a stop work meeting, particularly when Healy flew down to provide an alternative view. At the end of 1953, the discovery that branch secretary and Grouper Bert Clarke had embezzled a large sum of money seriously diminished their influence. Gus Alford continued to be active, however, and in 1961 claimed the position of general secretary was his when Healy died while the votes were still being counted, but a new election was held. The non-Communist Charlie Fitzgibbon succeeded Healy (Sheridan 1997).

CONTROL OVER THE WORK AND ITS DISTRIBUTION

Industrial successes in the WWF revolved around achieving improved recruitment and working conditions, which in turn often required legislative reform and effective lobbying.[17] Healy and Roach succeeded at both, thus making it possible for them to demand political action (H7).

The WWF shared with the ILWU the goal of worker control over the jobs and equity in the distribution of work. It also facilitated the building of a strong social network among the rank and file and with the leadership, but its processes were different than the ILWU's and, as it turns out, not as durable, an issue to which we return in chapter 5. Both the ILWU and WWF relied on arbitration systems, but they varied significantly; the system had a far greater dampening effect on strikes and direct action in Australia.

DISPATCH AND ON-THE-JOB CONTROL

Not long after Healy and Roach attained their leadership positions in the union, they also began to win significant improvements in the way workers were assigned work. Without question, the importance of the wharves for the war effort enabled them to persuade the Commonwealth government to make long-demanded changes. In response to numerous reports of problems with discipline, health, and safety on the waterfront (Australia Commonwealth Court 1908–1956; Australia Commission 1945–1946) and eager to make the ports more productive, ALP Prime Minister John Curtin established the Australian Stevedoring Industry Commission (ASIC) in 1942. The Chief Judge of the Conciliation and Arbitration Court chaired; Healy and two other WWF officers represented the union on the Commission, which also included employer representatives. The Commission required the registration of waterside workers, obliged the workers to attend the increasingly centralized pick-up, and abolished the bull system (Beasley 1996, 115).

The hiring hall, one of the ILWU's defining features, is absent in the WWF. What they had instead were pick-up centers, and ports varied in how many there were. Initially, employers controlled the centers, but control shifted in the 1940s to the Commission. The WWF advocated a single morning pick-up, which it achieved in 1942. After 1956, the pick-up process was exclusively by press and radio; it was incumbent on the workers to learn if and where they were rostered, i.e., put on the work list, and then report at the specified time and place. Those not allocated jobs were required to attend the Bureau on that day, where they would

[17] Most of this discussion derives from the work of research assistant, Chris Croke (2011).

receive attendance money or be allocated to work that had been requisi-
tioned late. With the advent of permanent employment in the late 1960s,
the workers received notification of jobs for the next day on site and via
dedicated telephone lines.

WWF members also achieved priority-hiring preference, a battle that
had been hard-fought since the Beeby Award in 1928. Equally important
was the institution of the rotary gang system. Men became members of
gangs that were then picked on a rotation basis for available work. If a
gang had not been employed the day before, they would then be top of
the list to be allocated the next day. If gangs had work the day before,
their place on the next day's roster would be determined by the "time of
finish"; the earlier they finished, the higher they would be on the next
day's roster.

ARBITRATION, STRIKES, AND DIRECT ACTION

In 1947, the Transport Workers Act was finally repealed. The Stevedoring
Act of 1947 established a new Stevedoring Industry Commission, still to
be chaired by the chief judge of the Court of Conciliation and Arbitration. In 1949, the chairman suggested that Healy and Roach, now also a
member of the Commission, should be replaced due to their support of a
work stoppage. It became a battle over the right to strike. The chairman
terminated their positions, the union refused to nominate replacements,
and the effectiveness of the Commission was at an end. The Stevedoring
Act of 1949 abolished it and established the Australian Stevedoring Industry Board (ASIB) to administer the industry and relegated other powers to the Conciliation and Arbitration Court (Beasley 1996, 136–37;
Sheridan 1997, 276–77).

The arbitration process often led to gains for the workers, but it also
inhibited collective bargaining and made direct action difficult. Arbitration for the WWF is a very different process than that in the ILWU. The
union has to develop a log of claims to initiate a judgment. Complaints
are adjudicated on the basis of submissions from all relevant parties, and
judges of the court make awards. It is often a costly and time-consuming
process. Moreover, the only form of union appeal is protest or illegal
work stoppages. There is no membership vote on the award, although
there is often considerable membership input into the log of claims.

The arbitration system and Commonwealth regulation did not deter
all actions, however. In the 1950s, Healy and his allies fought hard to
gain some direct bargaining power. In 1954, the WWF struck to protect
their right to control recruitment via membership in the union; the ship
owners claimed there were not enough workers on the wharves, and they
wanted the right to hire on their own, an issue that is reprised even to
this day. The employers won the right in principle but never exercised

it. Healy provided 1,000 names for registration three days after the end of the strike, and the credible threat of further WWF actions backed up by secondary strikes supported by Australian Confederation of Trade Unions (ACTU) was an additional deterrent to the employers changing recruitment practice. A new agreement, negotiated by Harold Holt, then Minister for Labour and the National Service, with the ship owners, ACTU, and WWF recognized the right of the WWF to recruit labor. The film unit's *November Victory* documents the case (also, see Beasley 1996, 168–75). In 1956, there was another strike, this one over "margins," i.e., pay and cost-of-living adjustments. It ended with threats of troop involvement by Holt and a call by the ACTU for the WWF to return to work and apply to the Arbitration Court (which led to protests against the ACTU). Not long after, wharfies received a significant increase in pay, and Healy helped secure a reform of the way the ACTU executive made decisions (Beasley 1996, 175–82).

Strikes were not the only tool in the WWF toolkit. In other instances, wharfies protested against increased sling loads and other work rule changes with informal slowdowns, by simply working according to the safety regulations (Beasley 1996, 185; Waterside Workers of Australia 2006a, b).

The effect of government regulation via Commonwealth-established commissions, boards, and arbitration courts was to reduce the capacity of the WWF members to engage in direct action and strikes. It increased the barriers to political mobilization by making most such work stoppages illegal. Even so, the rank and file maintained a reputation for job militancy and political action and continued to engage in on-the-job stoppages. According to Sheridan (1994, 260), other than coal the waterside workers have the most disputatious history in labor in Australia.

Principles of the WWF

The leadership and the organizational governing institutions of the WWF affirmed the union's commitments to both racial justice and international solidarity. The scope of the union was broad (H1) and the members generally tolerant of the leadership's political demands, given their demonstrated industrial success (H6).

Racial Justice

In its earlier, pre-Healy days, there had been institutional racism within the union. Specifically, the rules excluded "Asiatics" ("Federal Rules, Questions to be Submitted" 1938). By 1938, this clause no longer appeared in the Federal rules, but it was still in the Melbourne branch rules at least until 1949 (Noel Butlin Archives 1949a). At least in its institutionalized forms, racism did not exist in the WWF by the 1950s.

The WWF long supported the civil rights demands of Australia's aboriginal people. In the 1950s, its film unit proposed a series of twenty-five films on "Land of Australia—Aboriginal Culture." Roach saw the films serving "a two-fold purpose, to satisfy a huge demand for Australian Aboriginal Art and Culture overseas, and by doing so provide the finance for films portraying the problems of the Australian working class, exposure of monopolies, etc., which in turn can command a market in the Socialist world" (Noel Butlin Archives 1958, 26, 28–29). In the 1960s and 1970s the union made contributions to support indigenous businesses and political actions. It also supported its own members in their mobilization for Aboriginal rights. Chicka Dixon, a leading Aboriginal rights activist and a member of the WWF, recalls his first political exposure when he worked in Port Kembla as a casual immediately after the pig iron dispute (Dixon 1995). He joined the WWF on the Sydney waterfront in 1963 and was active with a group of black wharfies in the burgeoning civil rights movement led by Charles Perkins. He claims to have been both influenced by and supported by the left-wing leadership of his local.

INTERNATIONAL SOLIDARITY

The WWF's commitments to international solidarity were evident in the variety of political actions, including the pig iron dispute, black bans, and anti–Vietnam War mobilizations. It also had links with unions throughout the world. Healy not only had strong ties with the Soviet Union but with socialist labor organizations more generally. In 1971, under Charles Fitzgibbon, the WWF decided to extend those links and joined the International Transport Federation (Fitzgibbon 1986, CF: 2: 2/1).

Tension between Political and Industrial Commitments

Leaders who derive rents from alliance with an external political group may, under some circumstances, sacrifice performance and responsiveness to the rank and file (H5). When national leadership plays "off the path," violating organizational principles, it can destabilize the existing equilibrium.

Bridges came close to destabilizing the ILWU's governance institutions when he adhered too closely to the Communist Party line in demanding total commitment to the war effort during World War II (after the German invasion of the USSR) (Kimeldorf 1988, 130–38; 1992). However, responsiveness to membership displeasure with this policy trumped any rents he may have received from the Party in the form of ideological approval and political goals.

"A Plan for Maximum Production of Maritime Transport of War Materials or Supplies," otherwise known as the "Bridges Plan," advocated sacrifices by the workers and suspension of hard-won work rules all in the name of faster production for the war effort. Supervision of the plan was by a tripartite committee composed of representatives from the waterfront workers, their employers, and government. With no dissent, San Francisco approved the plan in a stop work meeting soon after Pearl Harbor. Seattle, however, was not so keen, and the members withheld their endorsement for three months and continued to raise questions throughout the process. Despite rationalizations of the industry and seeming concessions by the ILWU, the chair of the supervisory Board, Paul Eliel concluded:

> I have gone over the Orders issued by this Board, one by one and I fail to see how any of them, without exception, can be considered as entailing a real sacrifice on the part of the Union or of the longshore-men. It is true that some of them have been directed toward practices which have accumulated over the years but which no one can defend. In these instances . . . [union leaders] have merely carried out what the Union was already obligated to carry out under the terms of its contract with the employers. (quoted in Kimeldorf 1992, 258–59)

Assessment of wartime productivity rates bear out Eliel's claim (Kimeldorf 1992, 261–62).

Bridges and the other leaders, although sympathetic to the Communist demands, demonstrated considerable flexibility in their enforcement of productivity when the membership objected, as it often did. When war-time requirements conflicted with union control over the job, the second took precedence. If the leaders veered too far in promoting productivity, they were reprimanded with electoral defeats of key supporters and slow-downs in the ports.

Bridges skirted the edge during the War, but in the WWF, Healy, an avowed member of the Communist Party, always put workers' interests above wartime productivity and speed-ups. He gave verbal support to the CP position but not to the point of risking the stability of his union's organizational governance institution. He recognized that if he asked the members to sacrifice their industrial gains beyond a point, he would lose the ability to credibly call upon the membership in the future; he might even lose his job.

Continuity Over Time

Since Healy's death and Bridges' retirement, generational, political, eco-nomic, fiscal, legal, and leadership shifts have all taken place. Yet the unions' officers—and members—continue to uphold the fundamental organizational governance institutions established in the 1930s and 1940s (H9). There have been changes, of course, but they are generally the tweaks and improvements necessary to adapt to the times while upholding the commitments of the past and the identity the unions worked so hard to establish.

ILWU

Virtually all the international presidents who followed Bridges have proudly maintained arrangements that ensured limits on their compensation, local autonomy, and a willingness to act on behalf of an extended community of fate. The pay of the ILWU international officers continues to be linked to that of the members, and the easy recall provisions remain in place. Several former international presidents have been given the title president emeritus, but this is not a salaried position, as it is in the ILA.

The founders improved their credibility and more general trustworthiness by recommending constitutional limits on their salaries; they traded monetary compensation for ideological influence. Their successors make much of the fact that the officers maintain an economic status similar to those they serve, and it is customary for those defeated for office in the ILWU to return to the docks as rank-and-file workers. Recent examples include International Presidents David Arian and Brian McWilliams in 1994 and 2000, respectively; Coast Committeeman Joe Wenzl in 2006; and Local 13 (Tacoma) President Conrad Spell in 2010. International President James Spinosa completed two terms in 2006, stepped down, and then became president of Local 63 (clerks) in San Pedro until his retirement from the union in 2011.

Changes in organizational governance institutions have nonetheless taken place as the union itself evolved. During most of Bridges' presidency the union had neither term limits nor an official retirement age for either its local or International officers. By the early 1970s, several locals had adopted term limits for local officers, and the majority of locals today have set rules governing term limits. An amendment to the ILWU Constitution in 1975 instigated mandatory age limits for candidates for International Executive Board positions, including the international presidency (ILWU 1938, Article 6, Section 4). The amendment required that candidates be under the age of sixty-five in order to run for these positions. Bridges himself abided by the new rule and retired from the presidency in the election cycle following the constitutional amendment. More recently, in 2006, his age prevented James "Spinner" Spinosa from seeking a third term.

While many of its governance institutions survive, rank-and-file democracy is not as vibrant as it once was. The ILWU never gave the full vote to the casuals or to those on the B-list, and it still does not. A Melbourne Branch leader, observing the contrast with the MUA, believes limitations on suffrage reduce the commitment of ILWU workers to the union (Bracken 2006). Even among the A-list members, there is some evidence of a decline in meeting participation, particularly those not focused on contractual negotiations. During focus group sessions we ran at the 2007 LEAD Institute, participants expressed unease about the drop-off in active participation at all levels in the union and were keen to correct the problem.

Even taking account of these concerns, the ILWU remains a democratic union both procedurally and substantively with considerable levels of solidarity and class-consciousness (Finlay 1988; Wellman 1995; Levi et al. 2009). The ILWU carries into the present day the lessons learned from the hard-won struggles of the 1930s and the 1950s, when employers and governments did all in their power to blunt union power. Democratic, militant, and proud, the ILWU confirms the possibility of combining a commitment to democratic practice and militant actions in the economic and political spheres. It retains its hiring hall, coast-wide bargaining, tradition of political mobilizing, and rank-and-file democracy. The longshore workers of the West Coast maintain their commitment to a very wide community of fate.

WWF/MUA

Several of the general secretaries of the WWF who followed Jim Healy distanced themselves from his communism, but everyone perpetuated as best they could the organizational governance institutions that Healy and Roach set in motion.

After Healy's death in 1961, Charlie Fitzgibbon beat the CPA candidate and Healy affiliate, Tom Nelson. Even those on the losing side came to support this change in leadership. One Melbourne Branch rank and filer and CPA member recounts: "Tom Nelson, the Secretary of the Sydney Branch and a Communist, stood on a unity ticket of the Left, and we Communists worked for him very hard and very loyally, but it must be conceded that Fitzgibbon was the man for the job" (Lowenstein and Hills 1982, 162).

Fitzgibbon demonstrated his commitment to the union's organizational governance institutions by deferring to local autonomy in several important instances. In 1964, the Melbourne Branch indicated they were preparing to protest the Victorian state government's attempt to reintroduce an income tax. Fitzgibbon initially moved a resolution directing the Melbourne Branch not to hold a stoppage; the Melbourne Branch leadership issued a statement in opposition. Fitzgibbon's conference respected the Melbourne Branch's position without endorsing a unilateral stoppage (Noel Butlin Archives 1964, September 14). Fitzgibbon and the leadership tolerated several other instances of local actions that were in contradistinction to Federal advice, e.g., the Sydney, Melbourne, and Port Kembla protest stoppages over the war in Vietnam in 1965 (Lowenstein and Hills 1982, 168; Beasley 1996, 212–13).

Norm Docker, who served as assistant general secretary, succeeded Fitzgibbon as general secretary in 1983 but had to resign for health reasons approximately a year later. His successor, Tas Bull, a former CPA member, endeavored to uphold the organizational governance institutions in the face of massive legal and technological changes. He presided over the amalgamation of the WWF and Seamen's Union of Australia to form the Maritime Union of Australia (MUA) in 1993. Slightly less than 70 percent of those eligible in both unions voted on the measure, and 95 percent of those who voted did so in favor of the amalgamation (Beasley 1996, 284).

The MUA remains a decentralized organization; its structure is based on port branches controlled by locally elected committees, but directly linked to the national office. The MUA's elections and finances are generally transparent. The union publishes its financial audits online. It is also still one of the few unions in Australia to have rank-and-file members administer local and Federation elections, which they do under the scrutiny and regulation of the Australian Electoral Commission (Crumlin 2011). In addition, the MUA's acceptance of new enterprise bargaining agreements (EBA) is still voted on by the workers that are affected by that agreement. In the 2011 dispute with Patrick, Stevedores members in MUA branches around the country rejected the company EBA offer (Maritime Union of Australia 2011b).

There are, however, some signs of discontent among MUA rank and filers with the union's current governance. The main story in the 2011 Autumn/Winter *Maritime Workers' Journal* addressed the issue that some branch-level candidates had been using social media sites to accuse the current leadership of using union funds for perks and campaign resources. Indeed, several rank-and-file bulletins have been making these accusations about Federal officers for the past several years. The *Journal* also noted the historically low voter turnout in the most recent election. Even though voting is mandatory in the MUA (as it was in the WWF), only 45 percent of members voted in the most recent 2011 election, compared to 56.7 percent in 2007 and 63.5 percent in 2003. The article urged members to vote, stating: "The employers may well read into a lower participation rate as a lack of commitment or interest by the members" (Byrne 2011).

The WWF/MUA tradition of political mobilization has not survived as well as that of the ILWU (Smith and Reynolds 2009). Yet it
is still there. On the home page of the MUA website (Maritime Union
of Australia 2011a), it describes the union's efforts in support of Occupy Sydney and states: "As a key affiliate of the International Transport Workers' Federation, the union also helps represent 320,000 of the
world's seafarers fighting for wage justice and protection against human
rights abuses."

Conclusion

We find that political mobilization on behalf of issues of social justice and
foreign policy was explicit in the missions of crucial leadership cadres in
both unions, and those leaders embedded their visions in organizational
governance institutions quite distinct from and far more demanding of
members than that established by the Teamsters. Although they, too, defined the union's core mission as improving member welfare, they had
a very different view of governance. They asked members to participate
actively in a rank-and-file democracy, and they opened themselves to considerable monitoring and political accountability. The Teamster leaders
communicated to members from the top down; the ILWU and WWF
leaders interacted with members in a wider variety of ways.

The behavior of the leadership that created the organizational governance institutions of the ILWU and WWF fits with our predictions. They
most definitely possessed strong political and activist objectives, which
they promoted only after successfully attaining industrial success through
improvements in wages, hours, working conditions, and benefits. They
traded off monetary compensation for ideological influence.

Where the unions differed, and differed significantly, was in the form
their work institutions took. The hiring hall and union job control undoubtedly contribute to the ILWU organizational governance institutions
and may well be largely responsible for its greater capacity for continu-
ity over time. However, as the WWF case reveals, the hiring hall is not a
necessary condition for political mobilization. The government-imposed
institutions and constraints on the WWF and certainly the MUA further
distinguished it from the ILWU.

What both unions and sets of leaders shared was a vibrant rank-
and-file democracy, a high degree of local autonomy, and a membership
steeped in traditions of militancy. These ingredients combined with an
ideologically committed leadership to foster enthusiasm for or at least
compliance with political demands. In a period where the political causes

of the 1930s and the anti-Communism of the 1950s are a distant memory, their successors in the leadership and membership have managed to maintain those organizational governance institutions and political commitments that make the ILWU and WWF/MUA still capable of an expanded community of fate.

CHAPTER 5

Managing Heterogeneity

National-level unions succeeded in imposing (ILA, Teamsters) or winning consent with (ILWU and WWF) their formal and explicit policies, including those delineating organizational scope. This is what our model anticipates, but it does not anticipate the challenges to national organizational governance institutions created by heterogeneity among the members and across the locals. Almost all members were militant on behalf of their pocketbooks, but some held strong political convictions while others were not at all keen to be politically mobilized. Within the ILWU and WWF, many opposed Communism in principle even if they liked their union leaders. Many members were welcoming of all colors and creeds, but strong racist elements also existed within the workforce. Within the Teamsters and the ILA, there were those who, despite leadership antagonism, were strong partisans of communism, socialism, and syndicalism.

In the model elaborated in chapter 2 we make the simplifying assumption that the rank and file are similar in their political views and that they are largely indifferent to politics. In reality we recognize that there is diversity in the range and intensity of political perspectives within the populations from which the unions draw, but we document that no simple individual sorting or self-selection takes place. With a closer investigation of the cases, more complicated sorting and selection processes emerge. At the organizational level, locals can be quite distinctive from the national governance institutions and remain so even in the face of leadership efforts at persuasion and inducement. The national leadership has several legal means to screen out recalcitrant locals, including putting locals under trusteeship, a procedure the IBT used regularly and the WWF and ILWU almost never did. The Teamsters and ILA were notorious for resorting to illegal persuasion, including violence against dissidents. The ILWU and WWF, on the other hand, tend to tolerate local dissent, at least as long as it does not violate fundamental principles of the union such as non-discrimination on the basis of race, religion, or political persuasion.

Unions also possess means for managing individual heterogeneity and dissent. Business unions tend to provide members with few avenues for expression of disagreement with the leadership. In activist unions, we observe significant investments in preservation of their history, news-papers and newsletters, and educational and training programs. These and other communicative strategies seem intended to create a common base of political knowledge and, from the leadership's perspective, an appropriate definition of the community of fate. Further, we discovered processes endogenous to activist union membership that involve the cre-ation of social networks, largely through residence patterns, that might reinforce support for the organizational governance institutions. Social networks may be quite important in the willingness of reluctant members to go along with union political actions. We document the communi-cative strategies and endogenous processes in this chapter; in the next chapter we revise our theory to incorporate heterogeneity and the devices for managing it.

Managing the Heterogeneity of Locals

By comparing locals, we can demonstrate the expected variation in how business and activist unions handle dissidents. We suspect that business unions will rely more heavily on trusteeship and other forms of suppres-sion, whereas activist unions will be more tolerant of difference even to the point of living with secession. We investigate paired locals within the Teamsters, the West Coast longshore, and the WWF. In each pair one con-tested the national-level governance institutions, especially the form of leadership rents, and the other supported it. We also contrast the Seattle ILWU with the Teamsters in the same city. Both union locals drew from the identical population of workers, but the workers' subsequent behav-ior differed markedly as a result, we argue, of the distinct governance institutions and processes for managing heterogeneity.

The historical material reveals not only local variation but also the difficulty in establishing an alternative to the existing national organi-zation so long as organizational leaders continue to deliver sufficiently good economic outcomes. In the ILWU and WWF, dissident leaders claimed legitimacy derived from key aspects of the organizational gover-nance institutions: militant action that benefits their members, honesty, and rank-and-file democracy. In the Teamsters, the Minneapolis local claimed consistency with these same organizational governance institu-tions, which were not those of the IBT generally. The dissident local was able to survive only as long as it upheld these institutions, achieved in-dustrial success, and escaped national union suppression. When the ILA in Tacoma lagged behind the ILWU locals in pay and pensions, when a dissident Melbourne leader was caught with his hand in the cookie jar and with little to show in the way of industrial success, and when

Minneapolis Teamsters succumbed to IBT executive suppression, the locals (or branches) perturbing the "dominant" governance institutions were ultimately pulled back into equilibrium. The Teamsters did this by uprooting the dissident local. The ILWU and WWF waited it out.

MINNEAPOLIS: TEAMSTERS WHO ACT LIKE THE ILWU

The Teamster local in Minneapolis in the 1930s and 1940s had marked similarities to many of the ILWU locals.[1] It was left wing in orientation and democratic and egalitarian in constitution. It engaged in militant industrial action, even when the International preferred it not to. Whereas the Teamster community of fate was limited to those who paid their dues to the IBT, leaders of the Minneapolis local advocated for a more encompassing community of fate, similar to the ILWU's. Again, the story is one of a committed and ideological leadership, in this instance Trotskyists, confronting major external challenges to the union. As in the ILWU, in return for extracting political rents, they submitted to procedural controls on their decision-making, invested heavily in communicating with members, and were industrially successful. Addressing the twin challenges of the Great Depression and the expansion of long-haul trucking, they improved the material well-being of members. In the process, the leadership achieved significant contingent consent as evidenced by the votes and actions of the members.

What ultimately destroyed Local 544 was what had also been their strength: their deviation from the dominant Teamster organizational governance institutions. The IBT attempted to undermine the leadership soon after the "Teamster Rebellion" (Dobbs 1972), the successful 1934 strike in Minneapolis, while also absorbing some of the tactical and organizational innovations that had enabled the local leaders to earn a base of support. But it was not until the mid-1940s, and then only with government assistance, that the IBT was able to oust the upstart local leaders and transform the Minneapolis local.

The Teamster strategy of charter revocation had a notable failure in the 1930s when Tobin tried to purge Local 574 of the Trotskyists, Farrell Dobbs, Carl Skoglund, and the Dunne brothers (Ray, Grant, and Miles), who ran the local and the strike. He revoked the local's charter but he was stymied by the combination of membership protest through letters and statements with the ineffectiveness of the replacement local he established (Eidlin 2009, 252–53). After negotiations with those he had tried to remove from office, Tobin ultimately merged the replacement local with the old 574 into a new 544 with Dobbs and the Dunnes once more in charge.

---

[1] This account of the events in Minneapolis draws largely from the original research of graduate student research assistant Barry Eidlin, some of it now published (Eidlin 2009).

Dobbs then went on to organize interstate over-the-road truckers, who he perceived—as did Beck at about the same time—as the future of the union.[2] Both he and Beck recognized the importance of multistate organizations and used innovative strategies such as leap frogging.[3] They also used the secondary boycott to good effect. Nor was Dobbs afraid to use strikes. Their joint organizing efforts gained considerable momentum in the late 1930s. By 1938, Dobbs had achieved "a master agreement involving 175 locals and signed by 1700 trucking companies, covering an estimated 125,000 workers" in eleven Central states (Eidlin 2009, 253). In 1939, Tobin offered him a job as one of the union's general organizers (Dobbs 1973–74), and Hoffa recognized him as a mentor (Moldea 1978, 28–30; Sloane 1991, 18–22; Russell 2001, 33–47). Indeed, Hoffa's blurb on the back of *Teamster Power* reads:

I wouldn't agree with Farrell Dobbs's political philosophy or his economic ideology, but that man had a vision that was enormously beneficial to the labor movement. Beyond any doubt, he was the master architect of the Teamsters' over-the-road operations. (Dobbs 1973)

The Minneapolis local continued to pose a threat to the dominant Teamster governance institutions even as it significantly expanded the membership of the IBT. When Local 544 actively opposed the United States' entry into World War II and succeeded in getting the Minneapolis Central Labor Council to follow suit, Tobin saw his opportunity. In 1941 he used a suit filed by dissident members within Local 544 as the basis for investigating the leadership, and he relied on an FBI report on the local as a basis for imposing trusteeship. Once again, the Dunne brothers and their allies outmaneuvered Tobin. They obtained a charter to become a CIO affiliate as the Motor Transport and Allied Workers Industrial Union, and they won a clear majority vote for secession.

Tobin ordered Dave Beck to go to Minneapolis to win the members back, but it was Hoffa who masterminded and ran the ensuing campaign and literal battle in the city's streets (Sloane 1991, 28–31; Russell 2001, 79–82). The conflict ended as a result of a federal action combined with state action under the new Minnesota Labor Relations Act (MLRA), a law that permitted intervention in the internal affairs of the union. A

[2] Dobbs claims that he and those working with him originated the idea of the area conference and some of the organizing techniques, that Beck "sought to emulate our aggressiveness, using tactics of his own kind" (Eidlin 2009). Also, see Dobbs (1973), 238.

[3] Unionized truckers and intercity haulers with union contracts would leap frog companies that refused to unionize, bypassing them and refusing to do business with them (Romer 1962, 85).

district judge subsequently awarded what was now the CIO local headquarters and its contents to the AFL local, and the Minnesota State Labor
Conciliator unilaterally decided that AFL Local 544 was the sole and
legitimate bargaining agent for all trucking industry employees in the
state. Almost simultaneously, a federal grand jury indicted twenty-nine
of the 544 activists under the Smith Act on charges of sedition and conspiracy to overthrow the government, and key members of the Minneapolis leadership, including Dobbs, were convicted and jailed. Four of the
leaders were also indicted for embezzlement and grand larceny.

And what did the general members of Minneapolis CIO Local 544
want? That remains unclear. There were enough opponents to cause serious trouble for the local leadership, but, still, the leadership got the votes
it needed for its own elections to office and for the secession to the CIO.
A Teamster organizer in Minneapolis argued that "these fellows are like
a pendulum on a clock which swings back and forth–CIO–AFL–CIO–
AFL" (cited in Eidlin 2009, 257). Dobbs argued that many (but hardly
all) had become convinced that class warfare was the way to think about
their relationship with employers (also see Dobbs 1973, 243–44; Dobbs
1977, 76–77, 120). This is a hard claim to establish, but the election and
re-election of the local leadership is strong evidence that members approved organizational governance institutions distinct from those offered
by Tobin and the IBT.

Minneapolis strained the national union's respect for local autonomy.
The IBT managed political heterogeneity by using its twin powers of
charter revocation and trusteeship, resorting to violence, and, finally, invoking the power of the state to imprison dissident voices.

SEATTLE: TEAMSTERS WHO FOUGHT THE ILWU

A closer look at the IBT in Seattle provides more insight into the tools
Teamster leadership used to ensure that locals did not deviate too much.[4]
According to our model, IBT leadership rents were monetary and de-
pended on the combination of an increase in dues-payers and industrial
success. However, once signed up, leadership was far from keen to encourage political participation and organized political activism. Such behavior
raised problems for leadership control and threatened their personal rents.

Beck's organizational strategies in various Seattle industries included
sending "spotters" to Produce Row in Seattle to look for non-union
workers and illegally investigating truckers to see if they were union
members (Westine 1937, 50). Jurisdictional battles often turned violent,
as in the notorious case of the Brewery Workers International Union

---

[4] This section draws heavily on research work provided by Morgan Myrdal, when she
was an undergraduate research assistant. Undergraduate research assistant Angeli Bhatt
also provided useful input.

(Gillingham 1956, 41–54; McCallum 1978, 71). During the jurisdictional battles with the ILWU in the 1930s, one report claims:

> Beck's teamsters also gathered a force of "goons"—hefty, beer-guzzling musclemen who wore heavy shoes for kicks to the groin and fought with baseball bats, fists, rocks or whatever other weapons came to hand.
>
> Said one ex-goon, reminiscing last week about the teamsters' battles to contain Harry Bridges' inland march into uptown Seattle warehouses: "We always used indoor bats with about four inches sawed off so we could hide them in the sleeves of our coats. We had to use bats because the longshoremen fought with their cargo hooks. Sailors used a two-foot length of tracer chain, or wrapped window-sash chain around their fists. (*The Herdsman* 1948)

Beck's claim that violent acts were few and far between appears to have some merit (McCallum 1978), but so, too, does the documentation of the violence he condoned (Garnel 1972, 71).

While Beck may not have resorted to violence frequently, he certainly had little tolerance for dissent. In 1944 taxi cab drivers staged a wildcat strike (Myrdal 2007). The strikers felt the leadership had long ignored their grievances, and they feared retaliation by goon squads (Cooper 1944). They were suppressed, their local put into trusteeship, and their voices stifled.

As we have already noted, Beck had no tolerance for political radicalism, and he saw virtually no place for political mobilization in the labor movement. His idea of the Teamster community of fate, whether at the national or local level, was restricted to those who were in the IBT. Nor did he seek a particularly well-developed community of fate even among the membership. He discouraged actions that emanated from below. Rather, his interest was in soldiers who would do his bidding in the wars he chose to fight.

SEATTLE AND TACOMA LONGSHORE

We can learn more about variations in the management of local heterogeneity and the role of leadership by looking at conflict within the Puget Sound longshore union locals.[5] Both the Seattle and Tacoma ILA locals were quite similar to each other in many ways. They lived in the

---

[5] Much of the account of the Seattle and Tacoma locals is drawn from the work of historian Ronald Magden (Magden and Martinson 1982; Magden 1991b, 1991a; also see Harry Bridges Center for Labor Studies 2009–2010a). In addition, there is the useful perspective on the period provided by Ottilie Markholt (1998). We have also relied heavily on an excellent paper prepared by Bamberger (2005), when Bamberger was an undergraduate research assistant for the project, and on interviews with and oral histories of pensioners in both locals.

same corner of the world with the same radical and labor influences, had similar ethnic and religious backgrounds, and faced the same set of companies and employer organization. The Wobblies infiltrated both locals during World War I, and a significant part of the membership of each sympathized with or actually belonged to the Communist Party during the 1930s through 1950s. Both locals had strong traditions of rank-and-file democracy and direct action, evidenced through "quickies" (short individually- or small group-initiated strikes, usually over safety issues). Nor did the locals differ much in their willingness to engage in political actions.

The contrast between the Pacific Northwest longshore and IBT locals is sharp. Yet, both drew from the same labor pool of poorly educated, relatively low-skilled men (and men they all were) who relied more on brawn than human capital and who took the jobs available. Both unions had their beginnings in the nineteenth century and felt the impact of the same wars and depressions, but they varied significantly in their leadership and in their governance and work rules. The explanation for the differences appears to lie less in self-selection of members than in the ability of leaders, with different sources of rents and embedded in distinctive organizational governance institutions, to evoke a different set of behaviors.[6]

But what then explains the distinctive choices of the two longshore locals? In 1937, Seattle became ILWU Local 19, CIO (Congress of Industrial Organization), while Tacoma remained in the ILA and the AFL as Local 38-97. It is possible that a structural difference in their ports and an age difference among their members may have contributed. According to Selig Perlman (1928, 24), Seattle tended to handle general cargo and Tacoma raw materials and commodities, commodities that were more likely to be "penalty cargo," that is dangerous (Gillingham 1970, 90). At the time of the 1937 split, the average age of the Tacoma workforce was fifty-five, with a high proportion of family men; in Seattle it was thirty-five, with a larger proportion of single men who seemed to fit the stereotype of hard-living, often rowdy, itinerants (Gillingham 1970, 16; Bamberger 2005, 34, 75–77). By some accounts, Tacoma men were less willing to travel to other ports for work, whereas the Seattle longshore would go up and down the coast as needed. Perhaps differences in skill sets, age, and family status affected local bargaining relationships with employers.

---

[6] It may be the case that the different union reactions to the Red Scare of the late 1940s and 1950s may account for some sorting into the ILWU by those with strong radical bona fides. We have some suggestive evidence of this. We also have some suggestive evidence that ILWU contract terms that required drivers to be certified prior to driving provided an opportunity to Teamsters, who retired from the IBT, got their pensions, and then took an ILWU A-level job. See Ugles (2012).

But the key differences between the two were in organizational governance institutions and leadership approaches. From their beginnings the longshore workers, in Tacoma as well as Seattle, fought to win control over the allocation and equalization of work. Tacoma succeeded by the end of World War I. Seattle was not successful until 1934. Tacoma's organizational governance institutions enhanced its capacity to win benefits prior to the "Big Strike." Moreover, its leaders were antagonist to what they perceived as the anti-democratic and centralizing tendencies of Harry Bridges, CIO President John L. Lewis, and the "Communist bloc."[7]

The contingency in this story reinforces our argument that when an organization faces an existential threat, the possibility arises for a new set of leaders to supplant the old, constructing new governance institutions in the process. The existing leadership in Tacoma prior to Bridges and the 1934 strike already had many of the contractual rights and protections the other locals won only in the aftermath of the 1934 strike. Their members faced less of an existential threat and had leadership whose strategies produced industrial success, in contradistinction to many other ILA locals on the West Coast. Their pivotal moment was during World War I, when Tacoma union leaders and members decided to work with the city and the employers to build a strong and competitive port in Commencement Bay (Magden 1991a, 93–95). They turned out voters in support of the proposition to create the Port, and, in the process, won a position on the new Port Commission. A militant union that refused to buckle to the employers' efforts to dismantle their rights, they were also a cooperative union when it served their interests. This strategy continued to pay off, even during and in the aftermath of the 1934 strike.

Tacoma also had a somewhat different history than Seattle in its relationship with the Maritime Federation and with the Teamsters. It was a stronger supporter of the first and more collaborative with the second. Indeed, it was one of the few ports that did not participate in the March Inland (Magden 1991a, 160).

The Seattle and Tacoma locals reacted quite differently to the CIO split. Tacoma leadership saw the CIO as a threat to labor unity and, certainly, to Tacoma local autonomy. They perceived Bridges as a tool of the Communist Party and particularly resented his role, as they understood it, in undermining the Maritime Federation. The anti-CP faction, which labeled itself "progressive," included the Trotskyists, socialists, and others on the left who opposed the "Party's conspiratorial secrecy" (Markholt 1998, 325). Many were also concerned that the CIO appointed rather than elected leadership, had no constitution, and had yet to call a

---

[7] This is the term Markholt (1998, passim) uses to describe the Communist Party members and their sympathizers.

convention. They profoundly distrusted Lewis as dictatorial and believed he was stifling labor progress. They said as much in a letter explaining their reasons for not joining the CIO (Editorial 1937):

> Dear Brother Bridges,
>
> We don't believe the time has come YET when you will refuse to answer the honest questions of rank and filers who believe that perhaps you, too, don't quite see the danger of the Lewis-CIO movement, and what it is leading us into . . . The United Mine Workers/ John L. Lewis regime has thrown hundreds of thousands of (UMW) members and their families into the depths of poverty and destitution. Election stealing, convention packing, and slugging of delegates have reduced the old-time democracy of the union to a ghastly farce.

In their later testimony to the NLRB, they expressed similar concerns about Bridges (Magden 1991a, 168–69).

The perception of Bridges and the CIO marked a major difference between the Seattle and Tacoma locals. Paddy Morris, a leader of the 1934 strike, an international officer of the ILA and later the president of ILA Tacoma Local 38-97, opposed Bridges and the CIO early on. Seattle's *Waterfront Worker* responded by labeling him a "labor faker" and Bridges called him one of the "old reactionary leaders" (Magden 1991a, 156). The vitriol against Morris seems to have reinforced Tacoma local membership beliefs about the dangers of Bridges' leadership. Although there was some support for the ILWU in Tacoma,[8] most members preferred to stay in the ILA and opted out of the Coast consensus to form the ILWU.

Seattle ILA Local 38-12 proved distinctive from its Tacoma counterpart in a variety of ways. The local suffered badly in the aftermath of the General Strike of 1919, was a major battlefield during the "Big Strike" in 1934 and during the March Inland jurisdictional fight with the Teamsters, and was a strong supporter of Bridges and CIO affiliation. As in Tacoma, there was dissent in the ranks, but the majority vote was for affiliation.

Seattle's governance institutions and leadership approach were broadly similar to Tacoma's but distinctive enough to make a difference in the behavior of the membership. Leaders of the local had long sought rents from political action, and its members responded. In 1918, they

---

[8] A particularly notable supporter was Ernie Tanner, who had been the sole black worker on the 1934 Northwest Joint Strike Committee Phill Lelli interview (Schwartz 2009, 132).

walked out of work to protest the execution of Tom Mooney and even condemned those who voted otherwise (Magden 1991a, 118). After some heated internal debate, they engaged actively in the Seattle General Strike of 1919: "The men had made their choice. It was more important to be part of Seattle's labor movement than to honor their agreement with the employers" (ibid., 120). They even sent delegates to Tacoma to persuade the General Cargo local there to change its vote against supporting the Strike—and convinced them. Not long after the strike, Seattle longshore refused to load ships for General Kolchak's White Russians (Magden 1991a, 136–38). During the same period, black workers in the local won reaffirmation of the 1917 non-discrimination statement from ILA Pacific Coast Division convention (144).

As in Tacoma, the men fought hard for the closed shop, union-run hiring hall, and rotary dispatch system, which they briefly won and then lost. In the 1920s, a decasualization of longshore work commenced, initiated by the WEA and managed by Frank Foisie (Foisie 1934; Jones 1957; Gillingham 1970; Magden 1991a, chap. 9). Foisie introduced an employment bureau whose dispatch was run by the employers and reduced the number of registered workers and steady men, i.e., those who worked regularly for a particular employer. From the workers' perspective, the union was experiencing industrial failure, which made them more open to a new national leadership, even a new union, that could help them achieve greater industrial success through coordinated and not just local action. The evidence is the intensity of Seattle involvement in the Big Strike of 1934 and in the 1937 vote to split from the ILA, which many of them condemned, and to join the new ILWU, CIO. Local 19, ILWU, represented the longshore workers of Seattle. Other ILWU locals represented the walking bosses, warehouse workers, and clerks.

Further distinguishing the Seattle and Tacoma locals may have been the kind of rank-and-file democracy leaders encouraged. Some pensioners, particularly those who had experiences with both locals, describe Tacoma as more top-down in its governance than Seattle. They felt that Paddy Morris and, later, Phil Lelli controlled the Tacoma local far more than any of their many counterparts in Seattle controlled Local 19 (ILWU Pensioners 2007a,b). According to Martin Jugum, who held multiple offices in Seattle, Local 19 had strong "bottom-up democracy" (Jugum 1994).

Despite the fact that Tacoma was in the ILA and Seattle in the ILWU from 1937 until 1958, and despite some differences in the structures of their ports and the trade in which they engage, the locals turned out not to be that different. This was particularly the case in the aftermath of the 1934 strike, once Seattle had secured the hiring hall and union-controlled dispatch Tacoma already enjoyed. Tacoma leadership made two key strategic decisions that further distinguished the locals. The first was promoting the construction and management of the Tacoma Port after WWI. The second was the decision to stay in the ILA when every other major West Coast local joined the ILWU.

Tacoma ultimately reversed its position and joined the ILWU in 1958 to secure the pension program and other superior benefits enjoyed by ILWU affiliates. Some differences between Local 19 and 23 persist, nonetheless. Local 23 includes the clerks, and in Seattle they have their own separate local. Until the relatively recent past there was also a real distinction in the attitude of the members toward Bridges. Indicative of this is a story historian Ron Magden tells: At the banquet to celebrate the Tacoma local's one hundredth birthday, there was first debate over whether to even invite Bridges and then consternation where to seat him. Magden himself ended up being at Bridges' table, as he was one of the few to be counted on to be polite.

WWF

The interesting contrast in the WWF is between the Sydney and Melbourne branches, particularly during the period in which Jim Healy served as general secretary, 1937–1960. In these years, the Melbourne branch was often the major opposition to Healy and Roach. Melbourne activists ran against the international officers and were often the source of serious opposition to policies and decisions made at the federal level. In fact, as in the Seattle and Tacoma cases, the differences between the branches were relatively minor. Militant unionists dominated both, and both experienced difficulties in their efforts to win worker protection and rights. However, the difference in the labor politics of their two regions led to election of branch officers with distinctive programs and ideologies. Conflict between the oppositional local and the national leadership was evident in votes on federal policies and in responses to call for action, both industrial and political. In marked contrast to the Teamster reaction to opposition, the WWF leadership neither threatened charter revocation nor trusteeship, and they encouraged neither union nor government violence. They fought with words and policies. In effect, they tolerated—if bitterly—the differences.

The Sydney branch shared many similarities with the Seattle local of the ILWU. While there was considerable rotation of leadership in both, there was always a strong commitment to the national union leadership and to progressive causes. If anything, the Sydney branch, particularly under the leadership of Tom Nelson, a Communist, was even more innovative in the development of tools and processes for creating worker solidarity, for expanding the community of fate beyond the membership of the union. The film unit originated in the Sydney branch, and so did much of the emphasis on international issues (Heidtman 2006).

Melbourne waterside workers were renowned for their militancy throughout the late nineteenth and early twentieth centuries. As early as the 1880s, the predecessor of the Melbourne branch, the Port Phillip Stevedores' Association (PPSA), ". . . insisted that members be picked up for work at its own clubrooms and not in the street. The union also insisted that the foremen become members of the union to obviate bribery and ensure a fairer distribution of work" (Lockwood 1990, 74–79; Beasley 1996, 8).

Melbourne suffered badly in the 1928 strike. It stayed on strike when Sydney went back to work. The PPSA was destroyed. The Permanents and Casuals (P&C), the union formed of those who had collaborated with employers during the 1928 strike, had a stronger presence in Melbourne than in Sydney; they were awarded preference by most employers and even attempted to replace the WWF as the primary union (Lockwood 1990, passim). The pick-up process in Melbourne was also particularly humiliating and discriminatory (Lawson 1939; Australia Committee of Inquiry1957, 37).

The major distinction between Melbourne and Sydney, however, particularly from the late 1940s through the early 1960s, was the importance of the Australian Labor Party (ALP) Industrial Group members, known as "Groupers," in the former and their relative insignificance in the latter.[9] Most of the Groupers were Catholic and right wing by Australian labor standards, and they opposed the left-wing political mobilization advocated by Healy and Roach. In one of the kinder interpretations, one Melbourne veteran claimed that the Groupers were strongly opposed to political action, for they feared it would be the "bosses' politics" (Maritime Union of Australia 2006). Some Groupers were part of The Movement, an anti-Communist Catholic lay organization initiated in Victoria and led by B. A. Santamaria, with the support of Daniel Mannix, the Archbishop of Melbourne (Murray 1970). The Groupers became so strong and fractious in Victoria that their actions precipitated a split in the ALP in 1955, considered by many to be a major reason why the ALP could not win a federal election until 1972.

The Grouper domination of the branch office in Melbourne lasted from 1947 through 1954, when the larceny of the Grouper branch secretary was detected and prosecuted. In the aftermath of a stop work meeting that included a two-hour speech by Healy, the branch members demanded the resignation of the current secretary, the executive, and

---

[9] Research assistant Chris Croke (2011) provided the background memo which included discussion of the Groupers. On their role in the WWF, especially in Victoria, see the work by Tom Sheridan (1997). For more general histories of the "Split," see Campbell (1962), Murray (1970), and Costar et al. (2005).

trustees and then held a special election (Lowenstein and Hills 1982, 132; Beasley 1996, 165). Charlie Young, a Communist Party member, became the new Melbourne Branch secretary. However, Groupers continued to hold positions of influence and to run, sometimes successfully, for both branch and federal office. Gus Alford continued to oppose Healy even after Healy's death, when he claimed that he, as second in the recent and not yet fully validated election, should become the general secretary.

There were three factors influencing the Grouper animosity toward Healy in Melbourne. The first was most certainly anti-Communism and fear of the Party's influence on the union. The second was the support of the Catholic Church. It was not so much the proportion of the Catholics in the two branches, which appears to have been similar. It was the difference in the attitude of the leadership in the dioceses. Sydney Auxiliary Bishop James Carroll was not as keen on Santamaria as was Melbourne's Archbishop Mannix. Indeed, the Sydney bishops sought to limit Church involvement in The Movement (Croke 2001). The third had to do with the way the ALP and Groupers organized themselves in different states. According to several observers, differences in regional trade union rules made it easier for the Groupers in Melbourne to infiltrate the WWF and to influence the Melbourne Trades Hall (Campbell 1962; Brigden 2005).

Over time the Groupers discredited themselves. According to our model, leaders must first be industrially successful. They then face a trade-off between higher monetary compensation to themselves and the extraction of political rents. The revelation of embezzlement by the Melbourne Branch secretary, a Grouper, in 1953, followed by his conviction and imprisonment was one major precipitant to the downfall of the Groupers in the Branch. He was most definitely exacting monetary rents while attempting to score political points.

The industrial strategy of the Groupers also came under increasing scrutiny by the rank and file. According to Lowenstein and Hills,

> the conditions won by the Federal leadership and by other States were not always won by the Melbourne Branch. There were still only six men to a gang below hatch, compared with eight in Sydney. Men were forced to load whatever the foreman decided, however unsafe. (1982, 126)

Hills himself states, "some of the leadership we had in the Union, we knew it was useless sending for a bloody VO [Vigilance Officer]" (126).

Still, there might be some truth to Sheridan's claim:

> While the Melbourne groupers opposed WWF policy on "political" issues and could seldom be accused of enthusiastically promoting

anything originating from Healy's federal office, their fervent opposition on "industrial" issues like the P & C, shorter shifts and
weekend work rested on genuine rank and file sentiment in Melbourne. (2006, 80)

Certainly this describes Melbourne Branch resistance to absorbing the
Permanent and Casuals (P&Cs) even after Sydney finally did in 1950 and
even after the Federal Council transformed them into a part of the WWF
as No. 2 Melbourne Branch. More hotly contested was the Grouper
stance in relationship to the 1950/51 dispute over the Arbitration Court's
calculation of a wage increase. Melbourne refused to go along with the
overtime ban, which the WWF Federal Council (with dissenting votes by
only two Melbourne Groupers) approved as a means to win the full wage
increase. Indeed, Melbourne leadership campaigned against the overtime
ban both at its own stop work meetings and in stop work meetings at
other ports (also see Noel Butlin Archives 1950; Sheridan 2006, 116–17).
The Melbourne leadership survived a charge of disloyalty by the Federal
Council and, at a Melbourne stop work meeting, they won a 1044 to 883
vote (Sheridan 2006, 121).

There is evidence that some Melbourne members began to have real
doubts about the commitment of the branch leadership to industrial action. As one veteran recalls:

They would come out of the gate with you. . . There was an unwritten policy amongst the officials of . . . the majority of the capital branches around Australia that if the workers in the port went
through a pay day without pay the officials had to go through without theirs . . . the Grouper faction didn't have to follow that policy
because they didn't have any strikes! (Waterside Workers of Australia 2006a)

Not surprisingly, Jim Healy was even stronger in his condemnation:

If we stop a moment and carefully examine our present position we
find that on every action some well needed militant action is taken
by the Federation—no matter who or by what authority it may be
decided upon—somebody considers it their business to dispose of
it and the Board, Court, and employers know that the leaders of
the so-called A.L.P. Industrial Groups will come out in full cry in
opposition to any move which involves a stoppage or a threat of
stoppage, even though such a move may be supported by some of
its members in the Branch concerned. (General Secretary's Report,
Noel Butlin Archives 1950, vol. I, 56)

The Groupers attempted to articulate an alternative set of organizational principles for the union, asking for members' contributions to anti-Communist activities both inside the union and more broadly, while claiming to be able to lead the union to industrial successes equal to Healy's. They were, in short, extracting a political rent, forcing a trade-off with personal, monetary compensation. Not only did they fail to deliver clear industrial success, but the larceny of the branch secretary violated the implied understanding about leadership rents.[10]

There is also evidence that the Groupers were attempting to alter branch-level governance rules (or undermine existing ones) to reduce ex-post accountability to the membership. The Grouper reliance on the autonomy of branches was used to reveal irregularities in the way they held and contested elections. The Federal Returning Officer, in his 1954 report to the Federal Council (Noel Butlin Archives 1954, 1–9), reflected on the special election to replace the dismissed Melbourne Branch secretary, H. E. Clarke:

> The Ballot developed into one of the most keenly contested in the Federation's history, and attracted the close interest of the whole membership . . . The election later became notable as being the second occasion on which certain members had attempted to interfere with the democratic processes of this Federation and destroy its independence by placing its ballots in the hands of the Arbitration Court. This attempt met with the same fate as the earlier attempt in Sydney in 1950. It was rejected and condemned by almost the whole membership and was finally totally defeated. (1)

He went into some detail about irregularities in past Melbourne elections and how the Federal Office attempted to correct them. He decried the Industrial Group members' efforts to create problems by going to court to challenge procedures, compelling the WWF to spend money that could have been better spent. He goes on to say:

> The Court challenge revealed that there are still some few members of the Federation prepared to sell out the independence of our organization and to seek interference by outside authorities in our affairs in order to serve their own selfish interests and to frustrate the decisions and will of the membership. (Noel Butlin Archives 1954, 8–9)

---

[10] This also resonates with the model Greif (2012) offers on the unravelling of moral authority.

It should be noted that the Federal Returning Officer was one of the Communist Party members for whom Healy had helped secure a major position with the union. However, it should also be noted that he enjoyed considerable support from the membership at large, who continued to elect him to office and who eventually promoted him first to assistant general secretary and then to general secretary in 1983.

Several of the veterans from that period, all of them ALP, most of them Catholic, and many of them former Communists as well, expressed strong antipathy to the Groupers, who they perceived as right-wing and anti-unity (Waterside Workers of Australia 2006a, b, c). We see the Grouper faction in Melbourne failing to deliver acceptable economic outcomes, attempting to extract both political and monetary rents from the membership while undermining the governance institutions that might support an equilibrium in which there is political mobilization. As our model anticipates, the Groupers failed and were forced out of leadership roles.

Once the Groupers no longer controlled the Melbourne Branch, Healy and his cohort helped further strengthen its participatory culture as part of their effort to bring the branch membership fully into the fold. To promote local leadership and voice, they supported the creation of the Job Delegates and Gang Leaders Association. In 1955, the Federal leadership finally achieved a long-held goal, one that the Groupers had strongly opposed: the Melbourne Branch fully absorbed the remaining members of the "scab" union, and No. 2 Melbourne Branch existed no longer.

EFFECTS OF INTERNAL CHALLENGES

The comparisons among locals show how different organizational governance institutions led to different treatment of internal dissidents by the leadership. Unions, whose leadership rents are political and thus ask for significant member contributions to larger political projects, maintained more open, accountable democratic governance and tolerated dissent, even to the point of leaders backing down from some controversial stances. The combination of dissent and local autonomy are part of the fabric of activist unions. These two features are among the kind of extensive political controls on the national leadership that are consistent with our model. In the business unions dissent was suppressed, and the political control of local autonomy proved negligible.

Managing Individual Heterogeneity

Most union leaders have to manage individual heterogeneity to the extent it threatens the dominant governance institutions, but union leaders whose rents derive from political action must also find ways to create a consensus around a project that is neither centrally related to industrial success nor necessarily consistent with the political persuasions of all the membership. While we are able to demonstrate in chapter 4 how the activist union leadership makes political demands which members act upon, we consider as explanations only factors that have to do with the combination of governance rules and industrial success.

The case studies suggest that at least two other processes may also play a role: communicative strategies and residency patterns. The information the union provides might make political issues and causes more salient, creating knowledge about events in the world and stimulating normative responses. A vast literature on political knowledge suggests this could be the case (see, e.g., Norris 2000; Galston 2001). In addition, as we have already noted, interdependencies on the job create social networks, sources of information, and pressures to conform, and so, too, can participatory democratic governance practices. What we now consider are interactions and social networks outside of work and union life. The institutionalization of nepotistic recruitment patterns, especially if combined with residential concentration, is likely to help confirm what it means to be a member of the union and to encourage willingness to go along with political actions the majority supports.

Communicative Strategies

The leadership cadre and organizers of the ILWU have always engaged in considerable communication with the rank and file, using newspapers and meetings for purposes of both information transmittal and stimulus to action. Bridges himself regularly attended local meetings, conventions, and stop work meetings in which a significant percentage of the membership, particularly those on the A-list, participated. The *Waterfront Worker*, whose first issue appeared in 1932, was "the unofficial voice of the Pacific Coast Division of the International Labor Association" until 1936 (Harry Bridges Center for Labor Studies 2009–2010b). Historian Bruce Nelson, concerned to put to rest skepticism about the extent to which the paper actually reflected the perspectives and concerns of most rank-and-file workers, notes, ". . . longshoremen demonstrated their commitment to this journal by avidly reading it, raising money on the docks to keep it alive, and endorsing its program" (1988, 4–5). In 1942, the ILWU's official newspaper, *The Dispatcher*, appeared as a means of communication with and education of ILWU members and the larger labor movement. In "On the Beam," his column in *The Dispatcher*, Bridges discussed issues of workplace radicalism, union democracy, and racial equality. Goldblatt notes that during the 1971 strike "On the Beam" kept "the membership informed as to where we were going and how we were trying to get there" (Ward 1978, 1979, 1033).

The column provided Bridges with a means of informing but also of educating and persuading. He offered his perspective on causes on which he felt the ILWU should act. Sometimes he focused on foreign policy: in 1948 he published several pieces expressing his opposition to the Marshall Plan, and in 1966 (and after) regularly attacked President Johnson and the War in Vietnam. Other times he focused on issues being debated within the union. For example, in 1971–72 (1988, 4–5) Bridges used the column to push for merger with the Teamsters or ILA and to criticize those who opposed his views.

Bridges and Goldblatt were strong advocates of worker education and labor schools, which were on offer from early on. Many workers describe them as formative experiences (see chapter 6). When the ILWU was less than a decade old, it established a library to preserve its records and also collect reference material useful to the union. The union currently houses this library and employs a full-time archivist/historian at its international office in San Francisco. The ILWU's Research and Education Department, established in 1945, develops and provides union education materials directly to members and for dissemination by locals, which almost universally have their own local education committees. The pivotal leadership promoted these agencies and processes in order to improve the capacity of members to organize and act strategically in their own interests but also as a way to influence how members come to think about what they should and can do about the larger world in which they live.

The ILWU continues its long tradition of transmitting information to members through its newspapers and in educational programs. The ILWU library holds an oral history collection, which employs a curator who has documented dozens of oral histories of its notable members (Schwartz 2009). The union also actively works with labor studies centers at various universities in maintaining its historical material and with the libraries of the California State University at Northridge and the University of Washington to preserve and, when appropriate, digitize historical union material, such as the *Waterfront Worker*, the rank-and-file bulletin during the 1934 strike. When the University of Washington's Harry Bridges Center for Labor Studies proposed the creation of the Labor Archives of Washington State (LAWS) and the hiring of a full-time labor archivist, the Longshore Caucus voted to contribute $150,000 in support of the project. LAWS is now well established, and the ILWU lauds it as an important example of the extent to which the union understands ". . . the power of its own history in shaping and informing its actions and policies" (Walker 2011).

In addition to the formal department devoted to research and education, local education committees are also prevalent. They offer safety, contractual rights, and leadership training, and they run local membership education events, organizing local and regional conferences on the history and traditions of the ILWU, and providing and distributing articles in the *Dispatcher* on union history. They help keep alive and salient the history of the union and the norms that have enabled the ILWU to endure. Exemplary is the weeklong Leadership, Education and Development (LEAD) conference, in which ILWU officials and members of the rank and file discuss leadership strategies.

The WWF/MUA has a similar set of communicative strategies. Both Healy and Roach actively sought to influence and educate members about the issues, both union and political, that most concerned them. Their public and available reports at the biennial conferences, the Federal Committee of Management (FCOM), and other governing bodies are long and information-packed. They regularly made speeches at stop work, branch, and other meetings.

The WWF established its first union newspaper, the *Waterside Worker's Gazette*, in 1903. The WWF's first president, Billy Hughes, wrote and produced most of the paper himself. The paper, which always ran at a loss, carried information and reports on arbitration, disputes, conferences, and rule changes as well as articles about the hardships of working on the docks (Beasley 1996, 24). Its successor, the *Maritime Worker*, continues to be a major means of communication from leaders to members and among the members. The WWF hired an effective editor in Communist Rupert Lockwood, and its pages were filled with material on work disputes but also political causes.

In the 1950s, the union commissioned filmmakers and artists to document life on the waterfront. During this time, the WWF film unit produced the documentary, *The Hungry Mile*, which is still widely circulated among MUA members. Its documentaries and newsreels were designed to educate members and persuade the general public about the value of union actions. Roach reports on the unit's success to the Sixth Biennial National Conference, ". . . it is disclosed that no where else in the history of the working class movement of the world has a trade union film production unit been established. It is true unions in other countries have produced pictures, but they have them made by commercial firms" (Noel Butlin Archives 1958, Assistant General Secretary's Report, 23). He goes on to address the demands they are receiving for the films and the hiring of the unit by other unions (23–25).

The MUA also invests considerably in communicating with members, educating them, and retaining its history. In 2004 it reestablished the WWF film unit, which continues to commission its members to document current and historical union issues. The MUA film unit currently uses social media sites to educate members, most notably through maintaining a YouTube channel. Finally, for the past twenty-five years the union has employed a full-time Media and Projects Officer, whose task is to document WWF/MUA involvement in the community, as well as its commitment to international causes.

All unions have newspapers, newsletters, and, these days, web pages to inform members of a bit of history and of the current rules, officers, and negotiations. The Teamsters most certainly do. Moreover, as we saw in chapter 3, Beck often used his speeches and articles to promote a particular view of world politics. Teamster leadership did not, however, attempt to mobilize political actions on behalf of others. What clearly distinguishes the ILWU and WWF/MUA from the IBT and ILA is the amount of investment in information that might encourage political activism and in preserving and making available historical documents, including detailed records of union governance, including conventions and meetings. The combination of passing on history and maintaining transparency provides signals to the members and the wider public of what kinds of unions the ILWU and WWF/MUA are and the nature of the traditions they seek to instill and uphold.

RECRUITMENT AND SELECTION PRACTICES

Whereas both the ILA and MUA have very little control over recruitment,[11] the ILWU has always had and continues to have considerable influence over who works on the docks. Actual membership in the union and thus registered status on the waterfront required sponsorship by a union member—not unusually a family member. Nepotistic procedures facilitated the maintenance and reproduction of ILWU organizational governance institutions; those who joined the union were often well socialized in the union norms before even beginning work on the docks.

Nearly all the workers were friends, neighbors, or relatives of ILWU members, and they were also almost all male. Women began to secure jobs in the 1970s. They too were often family members. Some received employment because of the long-respected legacy norm (formalized contractually): When a longshore worker was killed on the job, one of his children got the job in order to support the family. This did not always mean, however, that their fellow workers treated the legacy women well or equitably.

In the late 1980s, the combination of litigation with regard to nepotism and a judicial finding of gender bias motivated the union and employers to seek a different recruitment strategy. In the first years of the

---

[11] In the MUA, the individual companies do all their own recruitment. Right after the establishment of the Waterfront Industry Reform Authority (discussed in chapter 8), many companies tried to hire people that they thought would not fit in to the wharfie culture. They recruited, for example, women and college students, thinking that these groups would become loyal to the company and not to the union. According to the MUA, however, the union has been able to accept these new workers into their organization with very little friction.

millennium, several ports determined to use a "two pool" system: half of new casuals would come from applicants who had answered an advertisement and half from those who held industry cards, provided by employers or union members. Longshore jobs are keenly sought-after, given the quality of pay and benefits for those on the A and even B lists. In 2004–5, when San Pedro needed to take on 5,000 new workers, the administrators of the San Pedro lottery stopped counting the public applicant pool after the number reached 150,000. The estimated pool was 350,000–500,000. Tacoma and Seattle both engaged in job lotteries in 2006, and San Pedro had a second lottery a few years later.[12]

When the lottery system commenced, the ports were booming. Trade from China and the Far East was high. The recession of 2008 killed the flow of imports, and trade was only just beginning to pick up again in 2011 (PMA 2011). If the boom had continued, the effect of "two pools" on the ILWU organizational governance institutions may have been significant. Instead, those who recognized the long-term benefits of staying with port work, even if there was little to be had immediately, were disproportionately from ILWU backgrounds.

RESIDENCE PATTERNS

Union rules and governance institutions can have consequences for other aspects of members' lives that can mitigate heterogeneity across members.[13] Where work opportunities, hiring, and dispatch are spatially concentrated, workers have a strong incentive to live near their jobs. Living in close proximity creates a high likelihood of repeated interaction and the development of dense network ties through which union members exchange information, and in some instances, exert social pressure. Other research has demonstrated a strong propensity for political opinions and behavior to cluster in space and, perhaps, for individuals to be influenced by those living around them (Stovel 2001; Cho, Gimpel, and Dyck 2006; Rodden 2010; Ward, Stovel, and Sacks 2011). We find that members of the ILWU continue to live in close proximity to each other and to the hiring hall. For the MUA, proximity to the union hall, which is not a hiring hall, has taken on less salience for workers' choice of residence over time, and even residential concentration of the workers has declined over time. Proximity to the union hall and to other union members appears to have no effect on Teamsters' choice of residence.

[12] The lottery process and the possibility of leveraging a "natural experiment" is what led us to field the survey that we use in chapter 7. See the detailed online appendix at http://depts.washington.edu/ilwu/ that describes the lottery process, our survey procedures, and the challenges that we encountered.

[13] This is based on research done by Amanda Clayton (2011), based on her 2010 master's thesis at the University of Washington. The maps are reprinted with her permission.

Initially, the geographic specificity and requirements of dock work fostered the growth of dockworker neighborhoods around the gates of many ports. With technological changes, demographic changes, improvements in transportation, and industrial success, the tendency to residential concentration is likely to decrease. On the other hand, reliance on the hiring hall as the source of work assignments may counteract these pushes.

We map the residence patterns of the ILWU and the WWF during their formative periods in the 1940s and the current patterns of the ILWU, the MUA, and the IBT.[14] Unfortunately we do not have membership residence data for the ILA. The maps show the percentage of the total number of union members out of the entire local membership that live in each postal code. Given these percentages, the maps identify clusters with values similar in magnitude as well as spatial outliers. Spatial correlations are described using Moran's I. In constructing the spatial weights matrix we use squared distance from the postal code centroids. We also measure distance in city blocks between them, which is appropriate in urban areas in which union members must commute through city streets to work.[15]

Each of the maps displayed in figures 5.1 through 5.4 shows Local Moran's I values, which produce a Z score, a p-value, and a color code representing the cluster type for each zip code. The Z score and p-value represent the statistical significance of the cluster. A positive Moran's I value indicates that the zip code is surrounded by zip codes with similar values, which are indicated by darker shading on the maps. A negative Moran's I value indicates that the zip code is surrounded by zip codes with dissimilar values, which are represented by light gray.[16] The p-values indicate the probability of observing such a clustering pattern if residency patterns were actually distributed randomly in space.

---

[14] To examine residential patterns among these unions we use current and historic membership lists. The 1940 data from the ILWU Seattle Local comes from the union's original membership list. The Tacoma Local did not leave the ILA to join the ILWU until 1958; therefore the Tacoma 1940 data are from the original ILA membership list. The 2006 data from all three locals are from the ILWU *Dispatcher* mailing list, and include both active members (Class-B and Class-A members) as well as retirees in the longshore division. The historic MUA data are also from the original membership for both the Melbourne and Sydney Branches in 1945 and 1949 respectively. The 2009 MUA data are from the union's current membership list and include active members in the longshore division. The Teamster data from Seattle and Long Beach are from the current membership lists for all short-haul and long-haul truck drivers. This is the first time these original data have been recorded and used for academic purposes.

[15] The distance between two points is measured along axes at right angles and then calculated by summing the absolute difference between point coordinates.

[16] The zip codes that were not included in the analysis do not have any shading. Bodies of water are shown in white.

As a limitation of this analysis, these patterns only reveal the "statistical significance" of the spatial autocorrelation without taking into account other neighborhood characteristics that might influence where an individual chooses to live. Comparing ILWU and IBT membership in similar cities, however, partially mitigates the impact of potential confounders, such as median home value, racial composition, and crime rates that might also affect where union members choose to live.

Figures 5.1–5.4 display residential patterns in Seattle (1940 and 2006) and Tacoma (1940 and 2006). In the Seattle area we see that dockworkers concentrate in a small number of areas. Even more startling, longshore workers followed the hiring hall, moving away from the downtown docks to the more isolated area of West Seattle as the center of Seattle shipping and the hiring hall moved south. Indeed, there is no clustering of residences in any other area of the city, despite the fact that their incomes and the transportation infrastructure would allow them to easily live elsewhere. The Tacoma local even more clearly reveals the pull of the hiring hall. The union members clustered around the docks in the 1940s but actually moved farther away from the Port of Tacoma to live near the local headquarters and dispatch.

Figure 5.5 shows residential concentration of ILWU members in Long Beach in 2006. Despite the large size of the local, there is still a high clustering around the hiring hall. Bobby Olvera, Jr., current vice president of the Long Beach Local, speaks to this trend:

> Look, I'm the exception that proves the rule. I'm the only Local 13 official who did not spend his whole life growing up in 'Pedro. When my father got elected to the International, I was seven and we moved from here up to San Francisco. Even though I moved back and have been a Local 13 member for the past 20 years, a lot of guys still call me as 'Frisco. Most of our officials are known either as "'Pedro guys" or "Wilmington guys" and count on getting a majority of their support from their locality. We're extremely close-knit here. The three major freeways (I-405, I-710, and I-110) around the Port of Los Angeles create a bubble that not many of the dockworkers tend to get out of. (Olvera 2011)

Figures 5.6–5.9 display the WWF/MUA residential patterns in Melbourne (1945 and 2009) and Sydney (1949 and 2009), revealing less residential cohesion than for the ILWU. Locals had neither a hiring hall nor union control of dispatch, but in the 1940s members resided primarily around the docks. This is still largely true of the Melbourne Branch, although its members are somewhat more dispersed than their ILWU counterparts in Seattle, Tacoma, or San Pedro. The Sydney Branch's

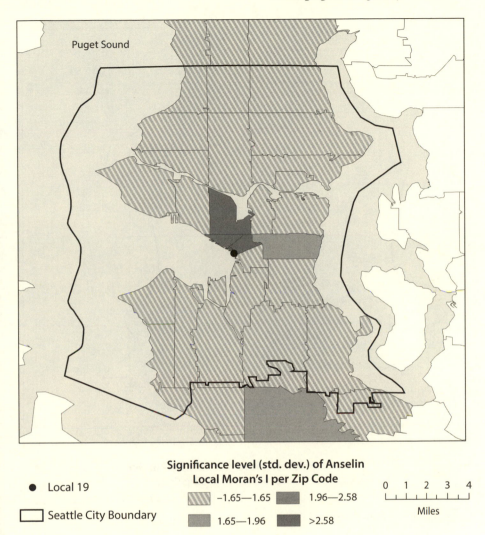

Figure 5.1: Seattle ILWU residential density 1940

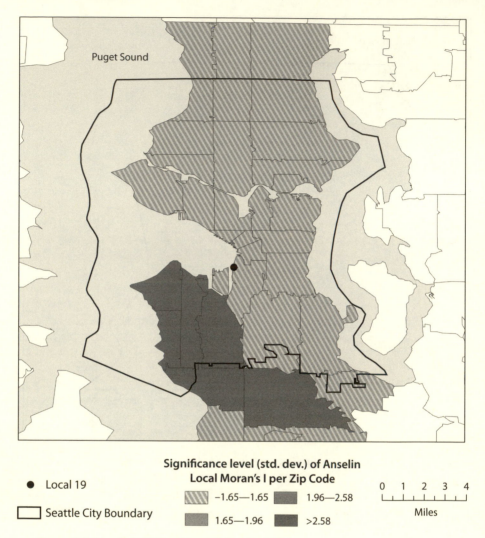

Figure 5.2: Seattle ILWU residential density 2006

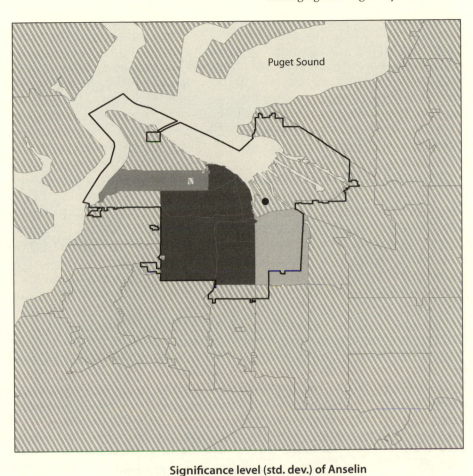

Puget Sound

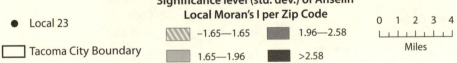

● Local 23

□ Tacoma City Boundary

**Significance level (std. dev.) of Anselin
Local Moran's I per Zip Code**

▨ −1.65—1.65   ▪ 1.96—2.58

▪ 1.65—1.96   ▪ >2.58

0 1 2 3 4
Miles

Figure 5.3: Tacoma ILWU residential density 1940

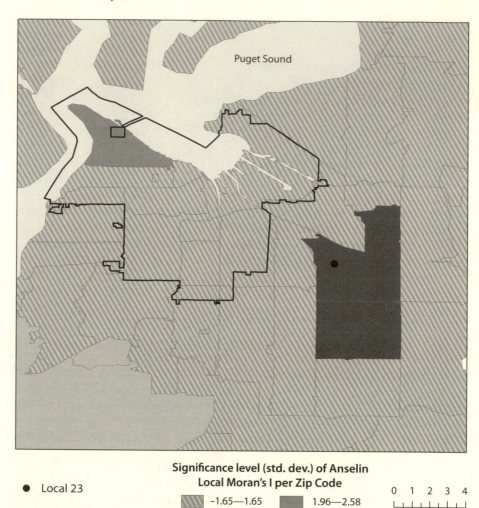

Puget Sound

**Significance level (std. dev.) of Anselin
Local Moran's I per Zip Code**

● Local 23

□ Tacoma City Boundary

▨ −1.65—1.65   ▩ 1.96—2.58

▨ 1.65—1.96   ■ >2.58

0 1 2 3 4
Miles

Figure 5.4: Tacoma ILWU residential density 2006

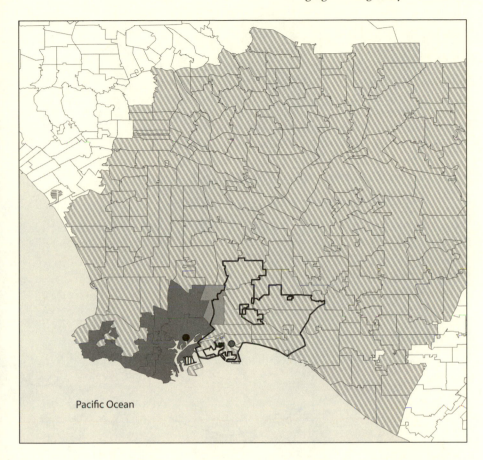

Pacific Ocean

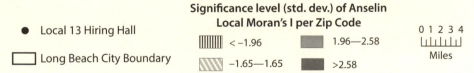

● Local 13 Hiring Hall

☐ Long Beach City Boundary

Significance level (std. dev.) of Anselin Local Moran's I per Zip Code

▓ < −1.96   ▓ 1.96—2.58

▓ −1.65—1.65   ▓ >2.58

0 1 2 3 4
Miles

Figure 5.5: ILWU Long Beach/San Pedro residential density 2006

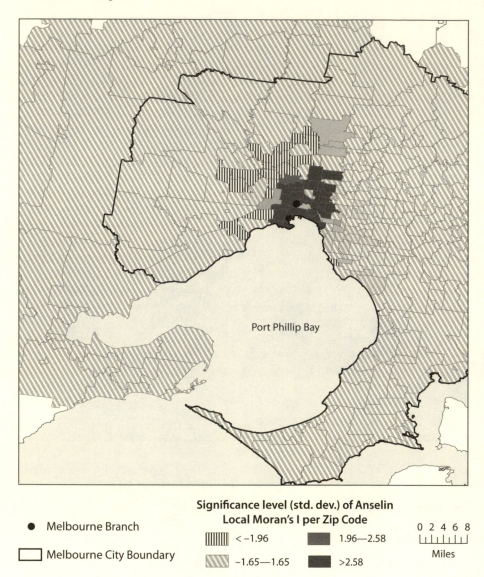

Port Phillip Bay

Significance level (std. dev.) of Anselin Local Moran's I per Zip Code

● Melbourne Branch

☐ Melbourne City Boundary

|||||| < −1.96   ▓▓ 1.96—2.58

▨ −1.65—1.65   ▓▓ >2.58

0 2 4 6 8
Miles

Figure 5.6: WWF Melbourne residential density 1945

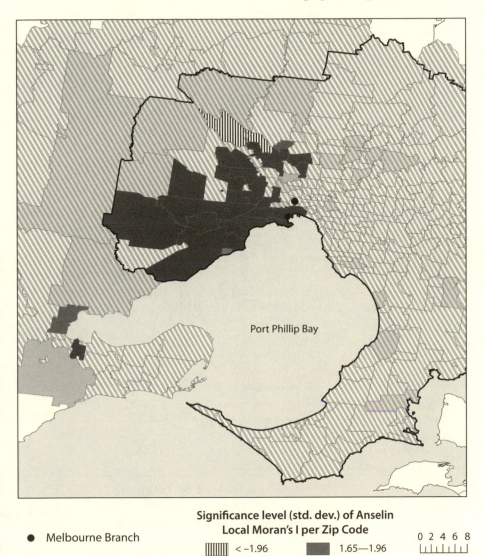

● Melbourne Branch

☐ Melbourne City Boundary

Significance level (std. dev.) of Anselin Local Moran's I per Zip Code

▥ < −1.96   ▨ 1.65—1.96

▨ −1.65—1.65   ■ >2.58

0 2 4 6 8
Miles

Figure 5.7: WWF Melbourne residential density 2009

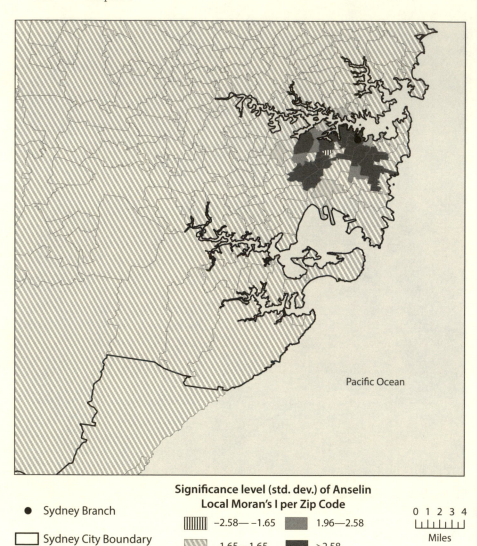

Pacific Ocean

**Significance level (std. dev.) of Anselin
Local Moran's I per Zip Code**

• Sydney Branch

☐ Sydney City Boundary

|||||| −2.58— −1.65   ▓ 1.96—2.58

▨ −1.65—1.65   ■ >2.58

0 1 2 3 4
Miles

Figure 5.8: WWF Sydney residential density 1945

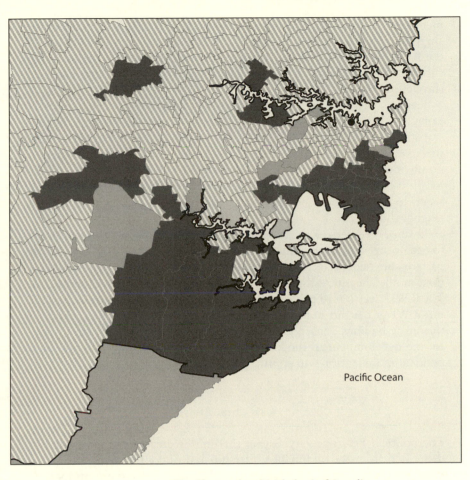

Pacific Ocean

● Sydney Branch

☐ Sydney City Boundary

**Significance level (std. dev.) of Anselin
Local Moran's I per Zip Code**

▨ −1.65—1.65   ▨ 1.96—2.58

▨ 1.65—1.96   ■ >2.58

0 1 2 3 4
Miles

Figure 5.9: WWF Sydney residential density 2009

membership, however, does not reveal a clear trend. The majority of shipping cargo in Sydney goes through Botany Bay, which is south of the Branch's offices. This in part explains the clustering in the southern suburbs. Nevertheless, we see a worker population essentially dispersed throughout the city.

Figures 5.10 and 5.11 display the IBT residence concentrations in Long Beach and Seattle, respectively. Although there are clusters that are statistically significant, LA/Long Beach members are dispersed around the greater Long Beach, San Pedro, and Covina area. In Seattle there is no obvious relationship between Teamsters' residential patterns and the location of the IBT union offices. However, a slight racial concentration seems to occur in the Central District, the historically African American neighborhood.

In sum, members of the three ILWU locals still live in close proximity to each other and to the union dispatch hall. The MUA displays weaker patterns of residential concentration over time and the Teamsters, almost none at all. The interesting contrast here is between the ILWU and MUA. The ILWU decision to privilege union-controlled dispatch was something the WWF/MUA did not do. The evidence suggests that the existence of the hiring hall has consequences for residential patterns and, we suspect, for the development of the kinds of social networks that facilitate both political mobilization and contingent consent.

Conclusion

The political heterogeneity within the unions creates the possibility of dissension from the dominant leadership and of conflict over the appropriate union governance arrangements. How the different unions manage such heterogeneity reveals how they sustain and reproduce the scope of union activity the founding leadership preferred. In the business unions, to the extent there is an investment in ensuring that members do what leaders ask, it takes the form of repression and suppression of dissent. For the activist unions with a commitment to rank-and-file democracy, the strategy is twofold: tolerance of difference and positive efforts to create contingent consent. Achieving contingent consent involves investments in efforts to convince individuals that political mobilization is appropriate through information provision, discussion, and education. It also requires establishing an environment in which the dissidents prefer to remain part of the group and cooperate with each other, even if in disagreement over a particular action. Building tight social networks through work and residence is one way to achieve this, but so is democratic practice, in which losers can one day win.

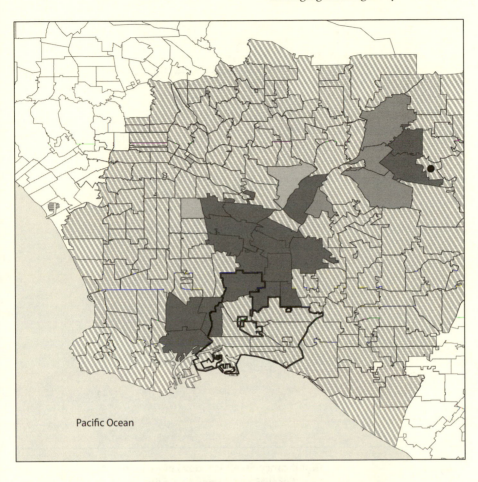

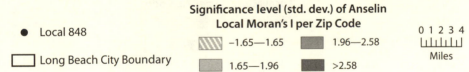

Figure 5.10: Long Beach IBT residential density 2009

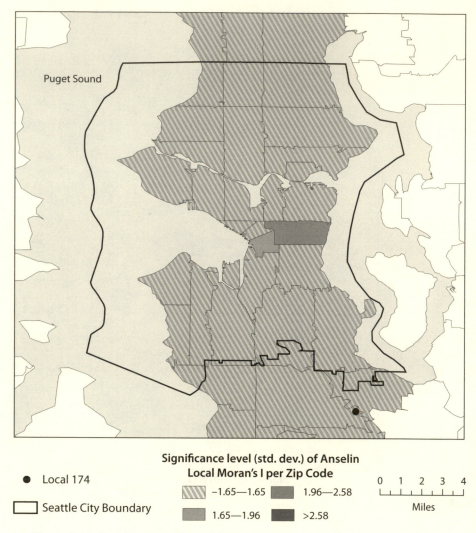

Figure 5.11: Seattle IBT residential density 2009

CHAPTER 6

Provoking Preferences

The basic theory discussed in chapter 2 treats members' willingness to go along with a leader's political project as a purely instrumental one; the members benefit sufficiently from the leader's knowledge and coordination abilities that they are willing to tolerate various forms of rents in order to induce the leader to be reliable through time and make the costly investments needed to acquire the necessary information. Rents can take multiple forms, including allowing leaders to take on political projects. We argue that leadership cohorts at pivotal moments can shape the nature of rents an organization directs to its leaders. The union's governance institutions resolve the informational, coordination, and contractual incompleteness problems that can degrade organizational performance and make collective action more difficult and fragile. The organization's form and level of leadership rents, decision procedures, and monitoring rules all reinforce one another. We compared the ILWU and WWF, two unions that built and sustained more encompassing "communities of fate," with the Teamsters and ILA, two unions that remained resolutely economistic and restricted their "communities of fate" to only those in the union (if that). We showed how the governance and historical behavior of these unions are consistent with our model.

The models from chapter 2 focused on pivotal or founding moments, having less to say about the dynamic functioning of the organization over time. The discussion in chapter 2 left little room for the inspirational role some leaders seem to play or the emotional responses some unions evoke from their members. More troubling is that the theory fails to anticipate several aspects of organizational governance and behavior that we uncovered in the historical record, in interviews with unionists, and in a survey of ILWU members.

First, union leaders in the ILWU and WWF spent considerable resources communicating with the rank and file. They established union newspapers, film units, member education committees, and leadership training. They traveled frequently to local and regional union meetings, attempting to persuade members of the relevance of politics to the union's activities and the correctness of the leaders' political stances. Leaders subjected themselves to intense questioning from members, including those most opposed to them. If political projects are simply rents the members rationally tolerate, it is not obvious why the leadership would do any of these things. As to be expected, the IBT invested much less in education and persuasion and the ILA, almost nothing.

Second, we documented the heterogeneity in members' attitudes toward the unions' political projects; there were vocal dissenters in all the unions we studied. The ILWU and WWF tolerated political mobilization contrary to the leaders' goals, and the IBT and ILA actively suppressed dissent. Our initial model ignored member heterogeneity and leadership reaction to dissent, again considering political mobilization as a form of leadership compensation.

Third, we see consistent evidence that ILWU and WWF members believed the union procedures produced decisions that were legitimate and worthy of their active support; we encountered virtually no evidence of anyone actively claiming that the governance institutions were illegitimate or unfair. This appears to be true even among those who were indifferent to or disagreed with industrial or political actions the leaders demanded. Our initial model predicts rational compliance, not the active contingent consent we observe.

More profoundly—and controversially (at least in traditional social science)—we also find that participation in activist unions seems to have transformed the beliefs and, possibly, the interests of some rank-and-file unionists. They engaged in activities and expressed concern about causes and peoples that, we have reason to believe, many had not even thought about prior to becoming part of the union. Some, of course, came to the union with strong left-wing commitments, others were indifferent to political action and remained so even if they went along, and for some proportion the unions provoked preferences of which the members were not previously aware. The union expanded members' community of fate and developed their sense of efficacy around a broad range of issues.

The explanations for what we observe are not obvious, certainly not in the literature on unions. However, recent developments in social psychology, behavioral economics, and network analysis offer more guidance.

In this chapter we suggest extensions and revisions of our basic theoretical framework that can help us account for the observed transformation of some members. We argue that, while some people have specific and deeply held political commitments, most appear to hold only vague or ill-formed beliefs. People revise and act on them only when challenged to do so in particular contexts and most have not had such an opportunity prior to joining the union. Presenting members with a specific demand that they act jointly and coherently forces them to crystallize their preferences and generates information about their own political and industrial efficacy (Rosenstone and Hansen 1993). Allowing leaders to make activist demands on the members may transform some subset of the members, inducing them to reconsider the activities they consider relevant to the union, making them aware of previously unconsidered political preferences, and providing the emotional benefits associated with some large, coordinated group actions for a cause (Chong 1991; Petersen 2002).

We turn to oral histories and interview data to document self-reported changes in political beliefs among the ILWU and WWF rank and file. We take these as demonstrations of existence. In the next chapter we use original survey data to compare the political beliefs and actions of ILWU members to otherwise similar non-members to provide some evidence of prevalence. We contend that members' policy preferences, at least at the margin, are affected by the decisions and information that ILWU and WWF membership implies. In the ILWU, members talk about these issues in the hiring halls where they meet almost daily to pick up shifts. In both unions they communicate in quite open and participatory union meetings and in interactions at and around the docks. They are recurrently asked to ratify union decisions to contribute time and resources to support the union's political projects. Repeated demands for active decisions on the part of the members implies crystallization and, possibly, shifts in members' opinions on the relevant topics.

The Literature

UNIONS, PUBLIC OPINION, AND PUBLIC PARTICIPATION

An enormous literature, going back over six decades in the United States (Masters and Delaney 1987), considers the "effect" of unionization on public opinion and voter behavior. American unions are held to be particularly interesting organizations since workers end up as union members for reasons of employment; there is little evidence that workers sort into unions for political reasons.[1] Early contributions to this literature relied on interviews and, occasionally, surveys of members of specific unions[2] in order to describe the political opinions and activities of union members. But these studies never constructed compelling, rigorous comparisons with non-unionists. Later studies (Nagler and Leighley 2007) relied on large-scale public opinion surveys to compare the political opinions

---

[1] This is clearly not the case in some European countries (e.g., Italy, Spain, Belgium, the Netherlands) in which unions directly affiliate with specific political parties or sectarian interests and often compete to represent the same class of workers.

[2] The United Auto Workers was a particularly well-studied union in the 1950–60s. Also, see the seminal British study Goldthorpe, Lockwood, Bechhofer, and Platt (1968), and Goldthorpe, Lockwood, Bechhofer, and Platt (1969).

and behavior of those claiming union membership against non-members. While we have developed better estimates of unionization's "effect" on voter turnout in the United States (Radcliff 2001; Nagler and Leighley 2007; Rosenfeld 2010) and other democracies (Radcliff and Davis 2000), these studies have a different problem: we have no information on which unions the respondents belonged to or their level of exposure to politics. After more than sixty years of research on American unions, we still lack convincing evidence of whether or how union membership affects political attitudes.

Similarly, the mechanisms through which unionization affects opinions and (to a lesser extent) behavior are still underspecified. In addition to the literature on the relationship between union membership and voter turnout, there is also work on the effect of union membership on political participation more broadly (Verba, Schlozman, and Brady 1995; Kerrissey and Schofer 2010). There is less work studying unionization and preference formation and virtually none looking at how unions might differ in their effects on members' beliefs and opinions.[3] Our interviews and oral histories reveal that the type of union makes a difference.

It is, of course, possible that members are also simply responding to the discourse of salient elites (union leaders) with whom they already agree on some issues (Zaller 1992). This is likely the case for new organizational members, who view the organization's activities and rules as so many norms of behavior. But we believe that this explanation is insufficient in the cases of the ILWU and WWF. Their elites were elected by the membership and, as we show in the next chapter, they continue espousing some positions that can be construed as contrary to the members' short-term economic interests. If simple parroting of recent elite discourse were what was happening in the ILWU and WWF, then we are hard-pressed to explain why those with longer tenure in the union are also the most "affected" by the union.

Some help comes from recent research in behavioral economics, network analysis, and social psychology. There are emotional benefits and personal commitments derived from the combination of repeated interaction and being part of a group (Lawler, Thye, and Yoon 2009). The workers in the unions we examine are engaged in the successful joint production of a collective good that improves their economic situation; they depend on each other and their leaders for industrial success. Moreover, longshore work involves teams and interdependencies, albeit less so than in the past. The regular interactions with each other and their leaders produce attachments, and the efficacy of their economic actions has the

---

[3] One partial exception is the investigation by Rosenfeld (2010) of sectoral variation in the United States.

further effect of inducing considerable pride in their organization and in themselves, which in turn encourages both loyalty and further investment in the unions.

While pride and other positive emotions clearly contribute to solidarity and may help reinforce the group's norms (Wood 2001, 2003), pride is not enough to account for the provocation of preferences we observe. The Teamsters appear to be equally proud unionists but are not asked to reconsider their beliefs nor engage in political action. The ILWU and WWF, like the Teamsters, were industrially successful, which enhanced the credibility of leadership. In the ILWU and the WWF, the leaders or, in some instances, other members, asked the rank and file to participate in specific and clearly defined political activities. The union's internal discussion of these issues was the first many members had heard about them. The union's broader industrial success reinforced the members' willingness to listen to arguments about politics and entertain demands that they mobilize in non-industrial actions. The arrangements for assigning work and making collective union decisions created opportunities to debate, challenge, and learn while the unions' educational opportunities helped socialize members into the norms of the organization.

BELIEFS AND ENDOGENOUS PREFERENCES

Preferences and beliefs are two of the fundamental building blocks of any model based on individual decision-making. They are generally considered to be quite distinct. The former are typically taken to be primitives, simple logical objects. The latter are either objects of interest, in the case of models of learning or games of incomplete/imperfect information, or irrelevant. This is surely an analytical convenience, easily sustained since it is impossible to directly observe a preference. Nevertheless we now have a substantial body of work that takes seriously the possibility that preferences and beliefs are not so easily separable. The process of learning and forming beliefs can have profound effects on revealed preferences that are not easily interpretable as the result of simple Bayesian updating.

Preferences and beliefs vary among groups and individuals. Some theorists attribute this variation to individual difference (Fisman, Kariv, and Markovits 2005) and others to the kind of interactive setting, network, or social structure in which individuals are embedded (Huckfeldt and Sprague 1987, 1988; Hagan 1991; Bowles 1998; Bawn 1999; Druckman and Lupia 2000; Bowles and Gintis 2002; Henrich et al. 2004; Lawler et al. 2009). Some have begun to consider and model evolutionary processes (Ostrom 1998; Gintis 2003; Kurzban 2003; Bicchieri 2006) and others the role of cognitive functioning, framing, and information-processing (Jones 2001; Kahneman 2003; North 2005; Chong and Druckman 2007; Kahneman 2011). Historical institutionalists (Thelen 1999; Katznelson

2006) and cultural theorists (Wildavsky 1987) claim that macro struc- tures and institutions generate and sustain preferences. Recent work suggests that belief updating leads to a transformation of preference or- dering (Brady, Ferejohn, and Pope 2005; Bicchieri 2006). It is that line of reasoning we follow here, but we are as concerned with how belief updating takes place as with its consequences for revealed preferences. We recognize individual differences, but, in our model, the organizational setting and the kinds of institutions that govern it are even more impor- tant in transforming beliefs.

The terminology and concepts can prove thorny. The most straightfor- ward term is "beliefs," which we continue to use in the conventional de- cision/game theoretic sense: as a subjective probability distribution that is updated (via Bayes' Rule) as new information becomes available. To link beliefs and preferences, we propose a framework in which empiri- cally observable behavior ("revealed preference") is the result of three objects. First, we posit that agents posses what we term *primitive prefer- ences*, which are defined as a binary relation between two objects, pos- sibly conditional on some state of the world, that the agent would choose *if the agent were to be presented with a choice over these two objects*. We are agnostic as to the origin of these preferences. Next, there is the *universal set*. This is the set of all possible objects (and states) over which agents could possibly have primitive preferences. This set is massive. A full ordering of primitive preferences over this set is impossible for any agent to undertake in finite time. It is also difficult to imagine that an agent has a well-defined preference over an action or experience she has never experienced or about which she is ignorant. Thus, agents hold a belief as to what constitutes the *feasible set of outcomes*. This set is a strict subset of the universal set and contains the states of the world and outcomes that the agent deems to be relevant and possible. Agents then have traditional preference orderings over the elements of the feasible set. We assume that the revealed behavior (and even stated preferences of the agents themselves) are the result of the agent's choice of optimal strategy (in the utility maximization sense) given (1) their feasible set, (2) the state of the world or the agent's beliefs about the state of the world, (3) the actions of other players, and (4) the information about the other players available to the agent.

We argue for a specific type of bounded rationality, namely that hu- mans cannot realistically consider all possible worlds but rather they hold, in North's terminology, "mental models" (North 1990; Denzau and North 1994). These mental models are meta-beliefs representing an individual's understanding of what is possible or relevant in a given situation and how her actions interact with those of others and the environment to yield dif- ferent outcomes, some of which she prefers to others. In a game theoretic sense, these mental models describe the agent's beliefs about the game she is playing. In a strategic setting they must also include beliefs about the models used by others, or at least their likely actions.[4] From here it is easy to see how the development of common knowledge becomes important.

These mental models need not correspond to the "true" way in which the world functions, if such a thing is even knowable. Individuals revise their models of the world based on their own experience as well as the claims of others. A revision in an individual's mental model can induce a change in the actions and outcomes she deems relevant, which can lead to a change in revealed preference. Altering what players consider relevant and possible could have dramatic effects on agents' observable behavior.

This notion of agents with strongly defined, situationally contingent preferences over some activities but ill-considered preferences over others is consistent with other theorists (Brady et al. 2005; Weingast 2005; Bicchieri 2006). Bicchieri (2006, 6–7) says that "the default rules that we automatically follow are accompanied and supported by beliefs and desires that we become aware of only when challenged. Surprise in this case breeds awareness of our underlying motives." It is also in line with Kreps's (1990) thinking about modeling unforeseen contingencies:

> [I]f there are unforeseen contingencies and if individuals attempt at any point to make provision for them, then one might better regard the state space of an individual's model as part of the subjective inputs the individual provides . . . in a model with unforeseen contingencies might subjective choice behavior reveal the individual's conception of what the future might hold. In such a model it would then become important to speak of how the individual's state space (and probability assessments and utility function) evolves through time. (118)

Our argument is perhaps most consistent with the "active decision hypothesis" of Stutzer, Goette, and Zehnder (2011; also see Fehr and Hoff 2011). They argue that

> [e]ngaging uninformed individuals in an active decision to contribute or not contribute to a public good induces them to reflect and form a subjective value for the prosocial activity. If their value is sufficiently high, they will contribute. Indeed, it is often argued that only slight nudges are sufficient to engage individuals in deliberations that substantially affect their behavior. (Stutzer et al. 477)

Participation in certain types of social interactions, especially in formally structured organizations in which leaders are consistently engaging

---

[4] See Dickson (2006) for an interesting discussion on optimal learning when others use different learning rules.

the membership in active group political decisions, is likely to induce agents to reconsider the set of relevant actions, with implications for individual action and group-level outcomes. Many people have political commitments of varying intensities, but it is not always obvious how or when to act on them. Some actions may also entail risk or require a large group; individuals may be unwilling to act if they do not believe that a sufficient number of others will also. Having a leader ask an organized group to act changes all this. For example, an individual may hold vague ideas that people facing tough circumstances should be aided, but his current way of thinking does not link his activities on the job as longshoreman to his normative commitments; he may not even be aware of situations about which he might otherwise feel normatively implicated. Asking an individual to take specific action can provoke preferences from some members by forcing them to consider a course of action they may not have considered relevant before. Suddenly his actions on the job *are* relevant to politics and possibly the welfare of others. What's more, he gains the previously unrecognized "utility" for taking efficacious action consistent with his normative goals.

Preference Provocation

Theorists have developed several ways of formalizing "endogenous preferences" (Bowles 1998; Bowles and Polanía-Reyes 2011). Here we simply extend the notation of the model developed in chapter 2 to incorporate the realistic possibility that members are not neutral with respect to the leader's activist projects, nor are they indifferent to the activities of their fellows. These extensions do not alter the basic results from chapter 2 but they provide added nuance and flexibility.

Recall the strategic setting outlined earlier: We have a group of union members and a "leader." In the notation developed in chapter 2, an individual's payoffs, net of costly effort contributed to the group's core project, is $V_i = \theta(e_i + \sum_{j=2}^{N} e_j) - \frac{e_i^2}{2}$. The parameter θ governs group productivity and is assumed stochastic. The leader knows (or expends effort, ξ, to learn and communicate) the value of θ. But the leader has an incentive to misrepresent the truth, telling the rank and file that times are good when in fact they are not. In a repeated game situation, the leader can develop a reputation for honestly communicating her knowledge; this behavior is supported by the threat that the rank and file will ignore the leader in all subsequent periods if the leader should mislead them.

We also showed that allowing the leader to earn rents expands the set of truth-telling equilibria. The members each contributed some costly resources, r_i, to the leader's compensation; member payoffs are $V_i - \frac{r_i}{2}$.

Leaders received payoffs $V_1 - \xi + \gamma_1 R$, where $R = \sum_{j=2}^{N} r_j$. Leaders who are "extreme" in the sense of valuing these rents a great deal are cheaper to compensate from the members' perspective. Further, credibly promising rents conditional on past behavior enables the members to select leaders who are relatively "cheap" to compensate while also providing incentives for leaders to pay the costs of building a reputation for good leadership and delivering on it. We argued that the ability to call on the union for political activism is one form of leadership rents—one that has particular implications for organizational governance.

We initially assumed all members were identical and the group was small enough that an individual's marginal contribution was non-negligible. We relax both these assumptions. First we allow for heterogeneity in members' preferences over their contributions to the leader's rents. In other words, union members might also benefit from their contributions to the leader's rents if they share (or come to share) the leader's preferences and if the leader's rents also generate spillovers or other group benefit.[5] These additional benefits develop dynamically as part of organizational membership; they are "provoked."

Specifically, leaders who ask the rank and file to contribute to political projects face the possibility that some of the rank and file might share her commitments and likewise derive benefits from the union's expanded scope of action. These benefits could be psychic, in the sense of acting in accordance with one's principles, or it could be the feeling of efficacy gained through group action, what Wood calls "the pleasure of agency" (Wood 2001, 2003).[6] Or the union may succeed in affecting an external situation, changing policy, or altering an election outcome in ways that coincide with some members' primitive preferences. Suppose each individual's valuation for the proposed political activities, net of the costs of participation, is given by

$$K_i = \gamma_i R - \frac{r_i^2}{2} \qquad (6.1)$$

[5] If leadership rents are purely monetary, then it seems unlikely that any of the members gain "spillover" utility from contributing to the leader's compensation. Formally we might extend the model to consider rent-specific γ_i and different production functions. We avoid introducing these additional complications here. Rather, we proceed assuming political rents that have some sort of public goods quality to them while monetary rents are assumed to be alienable.

[6] Wood describes the motivating emotions of insurgents in El Salvador as beginning with a desire to assert agency and express their humanity by "acting to act." As they become more involved in the movement, they also began to feel a "deepening pride—and indeed pleasure—in their exercise of agency in the realization of their interests" (Wood 2001, 243).

where γ_i is analogous to the leader's γ_1; it describes how much the member enjoys the union's political mobilization.[7] The γ parameter captures something like "intrinsic" or "expressive" utility for participating in certain causes. But the form of equation (6.1) implies an important difference: the extent to which others also participate in the political actions affects i's utility. Thus it is closer to the "pleasure of agency" (Wood 2003) than simple expressive motivation. γ_i also describes an individual's political inclinations. Leaders with intense normative, political commitments have large γ_i. Members with $\gamma_i > 0$ have political goals aligned with the leader's, while those with $\gamma_i < 0$ are opposed. The quantity $|\gamma_i|$ describes how "politicized" an individual is, with larger values representing more political motivation. A member with $\gamma_i = 0$ is purely "economistic." When $\gamma_i = 0 \forall i$, we have the basic Hermalin model that we built upon earlier. Someone with a large and positive γ_i derives enormous benefits from a relatively small mobilization by the union (since everyone else's participation makes this person happier).

We assume that the value of γ_i is initially unknown to each i. This makes more sense than appears at first: γ_i governs the utility to each individual not just for expending effort, *but for expending effort in the context of the organization*, i.e., along with his co-unionists. Protesting by yourself seems much less satisfying (and much less likely to be efficacious) than protesting in a large group with economic leverage.[8] It stands to reason that a union member cannot know with certainty how he values this activity when he has never experienced it. A leadership cohort that has earned the limited ability to mobilize members for political projects (as described in chapter 2) can induce members to contribute those resources for purely instrumental reasons.[9] Once the rank and file have contributed their r_i, however, their private benefit for political activism is revealed, perhaps altering their (revealed) preferences over the objectives in the organization and their role in it.

The distribution of γ_i among organizational members then becomes an object of interest with implications depending on organizational

---

[7] It is easy to show that, independent of the strategic effect on leadership performance, each individual's utility-maximizing r_i is given by $r_i^* = \gamma_i$. In the case where $\gamma_i < 0$ we can either assume that agents are restricted to non-negative r_i, in which case $r_i^* = \max(0, \gamma_i)$ or we can interpret $r_i^* < 0$ to be effort spent opposing the leader's activities. For the moment we assume $r_i \geq 0$.

[8] We can view this as a particular form of the threshold model of collective action in which an individual's contribution depends on the contributions of others (Granovetter 1978); those with bigger γ_i have lower thresholds.

[9] Formally we could assume prior beliefs that $E[\gamma_i] = 0$. More broadly, any activity or outcome about which the agent is ignorant or has excluded from her feasible set would receive zero weight in her utility function for that decision.

governance institutions, specifically voting rules for selecting leaders.[10] For example, if leaders are selected by simple majority and the r^* that the members are initially asked to contribute as part of the organizational equilibrium turns out to be less than the median γ_i, revealed after members participate, then there is substantial intrinsic organizational support for the leader's expanded scope of action going beyond the instrumental need to provide leadership rents. What's more, the majority would actually prefer to do *more* political activity *in the context of the organization* than what r^* prescribes. In such circumstance we may observe political initiatives emerging directly from the rank and file and garnering wide support. Leaders valuing such projects will benefit all the more.

There is no reason to believe that all members will come to value political projects. Asking members to contribute to political projects will surely reveal heterogeneity. Some support the leader's political projects to some degree while others derive additional disutility from the political action above and beyond their costly contributions. Allowing political rents can have the consequence of revealing distinct polarization among the membership. This underscores two points made earlier: leaders with political rents are "cheaper" to compensate, all the more so if a portion of the rank and file hold (or come to hold) political preferences aligned with the leader. But there are limits to what the leader can ask for. The more demands the leader makes, the higher the cost to members and the more she risks alienating those who do not share her preferences. The extent to which the level of disaffection threatens the organization again depends on the distribution of γ_i. If a majority has $\gamma_i < 0$ then the existing equilibrium r^* may become unstable. There is a risk to both the leader and the rank and file of allowing the leader to earn political rents.

If members are ex ante uncertain about their γ_i then we also have an additional interpretation for ex post controls (recall provisions, referenda, etc.) that we observed as part of the ILWU's and WWF's governance institutions: they are a form of insurance for the rank and file. Members who are unsure about the effects of or their private valuation for political participation but do know what they are being asked to give up can try to remove the incumbent if they are disappointed. Since the benefits (perhaps emotional or psychological) vary across individuals and are more difficult to measure and evaluate than simple monetary dues, ex post governance arrangements provide a way for the leader to "tie her hands" in a way that enables her to extract more from the rank and file (Ferejohn 1999).

---

[10] This does not necessarily affect the equilibria we identified in chapter 2, but it may affect the level of equilibrium political activism that we observe.

NETWORK EFFECTS, GOVERNANCE, AND CONTINGENT CONSENT

In order to focus on the member-leader game and organizational governance, we began by assuming that the union had solved its basic collective action problems. But as Olson (1965) recognized long ago, it is unlikely that any one member's dues payment or shift on the picket line will make a noticeable difference in union-employer bargaining, problematizing even the most basic contribution to the union. All these unions do manage to elicit significant contributions from the membership. In the ILWU and WWF we documented repeated cases in which those in the union who did not share the leaders' political objectives nevertheless assented to the group's decision, once taken. Why would those opposing the leader's project go along and remain in the organization?

We argue for three mechanisms. First, the value of the leader's knowledge (and the economic benefits derived from being a member) could be so great that it outweighs the cost of tolerating (and perhaps even contributing to) the leader's political objectives. Indeed, this is the entire justification for leadership rents in the initial model.

Second, it is easier to tolerate a decision against your preferences if you believe that you retain the ability to affect policy in the future (Przeworski 1991) and the decision was made according to appropriate procedural rules (Tyler 1990; Levi 1997). Governance institutions in which the leader must justify her positions and persuade the rank and file provide members with the opportunity to influence organizational action through debate and votes. Ultimately, the leader can be replaced if there are sufficient numbers of dissatisfied members.

Third, union members want to coordinate; no one wants to be too far away from what others are doing. This "desire to coordinate" underpins broader collective action in larger groups. It could be the result of a variety of factors including a simple desire to conform (Gould 1993; Cialdini and Goldstein 2004; Rilling and Sanfey 2011), fear of sanction or disapproval from one's fellows (Hechter 1987; Heckathorn 1990; Heckathorn 1993; Kim and Bearman 1997; Abrams, Iverson, and Soskice 2010), and fear that failing to support the union even when an individual disagrees with the organization's stance could degrade its effectiveness in industrial negotiations (see chapter 8). Put another way, members, on some level, want to go along but they don't want to be the only ones contributing. This is akin to Levi's (1997) notion of contingent consent in which followers go along with extractive demands so long as they feel that the decision was taken "fairly," they will get the promised returns for their compliance, and that others are going along as well.

We can formalize this idea by considering a particular type of "network game" described in the utility function

$$U_i = V_i + K_i - \alpha_i[(e_i - \bar{e})^2 + (r_i - \bar{r})^2] \qquad (6.2)$$

where $\bar{e}$ and $\bar{r}$ represent the mean contribution levels to the union's project and to leadership rents, respectively, and α_i describes how sensitive an individual is to deviations from the group. Akin to the problem studied in Dewan and Myatt (2008), members must anticipate the contribution levels of others in order to minimize their deviation from the group.[11] Both the nature of communication within the group and organizational governance serve an important function in coordinating beliefs and expectations and therefore sustaining equilibria.[12] The formal rules generate common knowledge about the level and types of effort demanded of the rank and file. They outline how decisions should be taken, allowing members to determine the "fairness" of the leader's demands, but they also support the equilibrium in which leadership announcements about θ are informative, enabling coordination on the optimal level of effort. Regular communication with other members, whether on the job, in hiring halls, or in union meetings provide information on how others are likely to behave. Leaders have an incentive to make sure that all the members hold (and see that their co-unionists hold) the same information to minimize concern that others know something you do not.

IMPLICATIONS

If preference provocation and contingent consent are significant in situations where leaders attempt to extract rank-and-file resources for political mobilization, then we should observe a variety of things that make no sense if members already have completely formulated, stable preferences, even if these preferences are more than purely "economistic." First, and most obviously, we should be able to record, at least qualitatively, some degree of transformation in the thinking of the members. More specifically, the longer a member is exposed to the union, the more crystalized her preferences will become, at least on issues discussed by the union. Union members will be more likely to express opinions on these topics when asked. Second, the leadership has an incentive to communicate with the members not only to "frame" her proposals and attempt to persuade the members that her course of action is correct, but also to provide a venue in which members observe one another. Third, we should see evidence of sustained but loyal opposition to the leader. While they may

---

[11] Also, see Gould (1993) in which agents dynamically and retrospectively adapt their contribution levels to minimize deviation from the group average, settling on stable equilibrium outcomes.

[12] We can also expect to observe heterogeneity across individuals in their contribution levels, sustainable in equilibrium so long as the aggregate rents provided to the leader are consistent with R^*.

oppose the leader on some issues they abide by the group's decisions, so long as they are procedurally transparent.

The notion of preference provocation in organizations helps us account for the presence of things like the ILWU's Educational Committee and its LEAD Institute as well as the WWF's renowned Film Unit. We also note that the incoming Communist and politically radical leadership also founded the major union papers, the *Dispatcher* and the *Wharfie*. Bridges, Healy, and their successors regularly wrote columns, many of which discussed political or social issues far removed from the members' immediate economic situation. Teamster leadership—and many other union leaders—also write columns for union publications and make speeches that lay out their worldviews. However, in contrast with the ILWU and WWF/MUA, most unions invest relatively little in education, communication, or persuasion. In particular, the Teamsters and, especially, the ILA, made almost no demands of the membership other than that they pay their dues, come out on strike when called, and tolerate leadership rents that mostly took the form of perks and salary.

In the remainder of the chapter we document the existence of preference provocation and active contingent consent, relying mainly on self-reports by members of the ILWU and WWF. In chapter 7, we explore the effect of the union on preferences about international trade policy.

Evidence of Preference Provocation

During and after their formative periods under Bridges and Healy, respectively, the ILWU and the WWF made extensive demands of the rank and file. We provide evidence that there were, in fact, individuals who revised their beliefs about the role the union could play, the appropriate scope of union action, the existence of specific events or issues, and their normative beliefs about them as a direct result of their experiences as members of these organizations. We also provide evidence that some of them appear to have altered their preferences about taking part in political action.

To make our case, we draw on numerous oral histories and archives maintained by both the ILWU and the WWF/MUA. We have combed the archives and read the minutes of meetings at federal and local levels of the ILWU and WWF/MUA. We have coded debates about political issues in convention proceedings, and we have followed these debates in the *Dispatcher, Wharfie,* and the *Maritime Worker.* We have read numerous oral histories for evidence of the practices and effects of the union. Howard Kimeldorf gave us access to his interviews for *Reds and Rackets,* and we undertook original interviews of our own. For the WWF we relied on the union's pensioner (retiree) organizations in Sydney and Melbourne to put us in contact with the interviewees. In the ILWU we interviewed pensioners in Tacoma and Seattle and casuals, active members, and officers in the three locals (13, 19, and 23) in which we conducted our survey. We also interviewed international officers, both past and present. In addition, we ran more than twelve hours of focus groups at the ILWU's Leadership, Education and Development (LEAD) Institute in September 2005 prior to constructing the final version of the survey.

We emphasize that the Teamsters and the ILA differ significantly from the ILWU and WWF/MUA in the extent and quality of their historical recordkeeping. Both the ILWU and WWF/MUA preserve their histories with extensive union archives, including having a full-time archivist/historian on staff. Neither the IBT nor ILA maintains the same quality of historical records, particularly at the rank-and-file level, despite the fact that both unions are considerably older than the ILWU. Records that do exist, particularly convention and meeting minutes, are substantially sparser, with fewer direct or paraphrased quotations of speakers and fewer records of who cast what vote.

Unfortunately it is impossible to reconstruct a random sample of members and evaluate retrospectively the degree to which members in general altered their beliefs about the world. Our interview subjects have maintained their union affiliation for many decades, even in to retirement. Interview subjects and those providing oral histories necessarily represent those who were most strongly affected by their unions.

TRANSFORMATION

The first transformation had to do with the workers' realization that they could exercise control over their lives. This is summed up in the claim, made endlessly and correctly by ILWU members, that the union transformed them from "wharf rats to lords of the dock." Moreover, they realized that they could act on their own behalf; they discovered the "pleasure of agency."

Early in the history of all these unions, dockworkers and even many of the drivers were drawn from pools of casual labor, often men with little formal education or skills. The histories and interviews reveal that many of the workers who populated the waterfront had never thought a better life was possible, that change could be achieved—until their unions succeeded in winning collective bargaining and decent contracts. Thus, it is hardly surprising that the workers, particularly those who had the lowest expectations, expressed such pride in their union.

While we find similar quotes among white workers, some of the most moving are from people of color with backgrounds in grinding poverty and racist discrimination.

Joe Uranga, a Mexican American worker and '34 man, was a member of Local 13 in San Pedro/Los Angeles:

The struggle in '34 was something worth fighting for. I remembered the conditions of my dad. He didn't say much, but you could see them by going down to the fink hall and standing around. . . What made me so loyal? Love for the people, for the organization, and my background of being poor, never having anything, and then going back to work and making some money and working with guys. After the strike three of us bought brand-new cars in 1937. Hey, this was it, man. This was just like throwing up new avenues and living. (Schwartz 2009, 75)

Cleophas Williams, born in Arkansas in 1923, was the son of school-teachers and the victim of segregation. He began to work on the docks in the San Francisco Bay Area in 1944 and became the first black president of Local 10. He sums up his experience:

The union was the greatest thing in my life, other than my family. In terms of economics and social growth, this union was a platform on which I made my stand and found a place in the sun. I was political and became president, but when I was out of office and working, I was even more proud. I had the most prized thing on the waterfront, a longshore registration, and I didn't mind working. Some called this arrogance, but it wasn't arrogance. It was pride. (Schwartz 2009, 51)

In the ILWU, union control of the jobs gave the workers control over their work, in a way few had hoped to achieve and few other unions have been able to attain or maintain:
Pete Grassi, a '34 man from Local 13, says:

That union dispatch hall was the greatest thing that ever happened. If I didn't want to go to work, I replaced myself for one day. I didn't have to ask the boss. Before the union he'd say, "You can't take off. If you don't show up, somebody else'll be in your place." (Schwartz 2009, 69)

Members of the WWF expressed similar sentiments. For example, Manny Calleja, a Maltese who migrated to Australia after World War II, began work on the waterfront in 1949:

God bless the union today that we have somebody who fights for us, struggles, because the boss, he gets his cargo out and you're just a rabbit in the paddock, there's one dies and the other one just born, and he doesn't care, you're only a number. (Lowenstein and Hills 1982, 121–22)

The level of commitment to the unions was and remains strong. The film, *The Eye of the Storm*, produced by the ILWU in the aftermath of the 2002 lockout to prepare the membership for the 2008 contract negotiations, repeatedly reveals this. Most moving is when Coast Committeeman Joe Wenzl says, "'one of the things I used to tell the employers in side bar: 'Would you die for your organization?' 'Not a chance!' 'Lot of people on my side of the table would'" (Williams 2007).

The second kind of transformation is in political thinking. We earlier cited the MUA veteran who followed us out of a meeting in Sydney and reported how he got involved in political action. He was at a lunchtime stop work when he first heard about the Dutch ships planning to come to Sydney to load arms to put down the Indonesian revolution. By admission, he was not particularly political, had little sympathy with Communism, and had never given a thought to the Indonesian rebellion. As soon as he learned of the Dutch ship, he was immediately convinced that these ships should not be loaded. The Dutch were violating his sense of fairness: "What they were doing was not fair dinkum" (Maritime Union of Australia 2006). Similar stories were repeated to us over and over again by members of both the ILWU and WWF/MUA spanning numerous political and social causes.

In some cases, members simply come to accept as valid a range of political opinions. Marvin Ricks, a veteran of the 1934 strike in Portland, a strong unionist but in no sense a political radical, came to appreciate what the leftists brought to the waterfront:

I used to be against the idea of Wobblies, and against Communism, but now I think they did more for the union and getting organized than anyone. . . I think nearly all our early top leadership was a little bit on the Wobbly side, whether you could prove it or not. Now I don't know about Harry Bridges, but it takes someone like him to get out and do the job. (Schwartz 2009, 108)

We find the same kind of sentiment in the WWF:

They [the Communists] kept winning elections because they were doing a good job, but there was a hell of a lot of opposition. (Levinson 2006)

In the late 1940s and 1950s, during the "Red Scare," many members of the ILWU, including some of the local leadership, were anti-Communist.

In a paper drawing on a detailed reading of International records, the *Dispatcher*, the minutes and archives of Local 19, and government records, it appears that leaders of three locals, including Seattle, were complicit with the Navy's screening process on the docks and with the blacklisting of suspected Communist members (Robertson 2007). Both Locals 19 and 10 initially adopted the voluntary compliance program proposed by the Navy. Within the International, Bridges and other officers strongly opposed screening and blacklisting and urged noncompliance with the Navy's program at meetings and in the *Dispatcher*. Bridges argued:

> It's as plain as the nose on my face that any longshoreman, ship-sclerk or waterfront worker who doesn't vote to approve the caucus recommendation on screening is voting to return to the fink halls, the Blue Book days, and all the abuses we removed from the waterfront forever after 1934. (quoted in Robertson 2007, 1)

The rank and file was initially divided on the issue, but extensive debate and discussions ensued. The behavior of the government in expanding the screening and intervening on the docks confirmed Bridges' predictions. Over time the rank and file came to strongly oppose the screening program. To achieve this transformation in members' understanding of the issues, the leaders had to respect rank-and-file reluctance while engaging in hard work trying to convert mild support of screening into passionate antagonism. In the words of Bill Gettings, Northwest regional director of the ILWU:

> I have spent a lot of time and effort on this, but cannot fight it unless the membership is behind it. Because if they are not, the fight is lost. If I could have won it alone, I would have done so long ago; but I was powerless to move until the membership of 19 gave their approval. I am convinced that when the membership knows what we want, and understands it, they will go along with it.[13] (Robertson 2007)

Randal Hicks, a member of Local 19 who was screened, agreed with Gettings' perspective:

> there was misinformation and lack of understanding among the union members. One of the important things to be accomplished

---

[13] Bill Gettings, Minutes, Northwest Conference on Blacklisting, March 18, 1951, p. 2. SMP 16/16, p. 12.

was getting the right information to the unions to get support and unity.[14] (Robertson 2007)

In a series of referenda in the early 1950s, the rank and file rejected screening and blacklisting. What ultimately changed their perspective was the combination of information provided by the leadership about the importance of solidarity, the unfairness of the procedures, and the threat the screening process posed to the union's prerogatives by ceding to employers increased control over the hiring process. The members had come to realize how "an injury to one," in this case their fellow workers suspected of being Communist, could in fact turn into "an injury to all."

In some instances, members come to care about issues that the union made them aware of. The boycott against apartheid, the embargo against coffee shipped from El Salvador, and other such political projects started with a few intensely political leaders and members. Reading the debates in the Conventions, in the minutes of the International Executive Board and the Caucus, and the discussions in the *Dispatcher* makes this clear but also reveals how members came to change their views over time. By using the combination of debate, information dissemination, and, most importantly, the democratic decision-making processes of the union, partisans were able to introduce other members to new causes, win their acceptance, and even make some of them activists on those issues.[15]

The WWF operated in a similar fashion (Beasley 1996, passim). An example is the embargo on loading ships for the Dutch Armada in 1945 (Lockwood 1975). The Communist Party of Australia initiated the call for bans on the Dutch to protest treatment of deserters and to register support of the Indonesian Revolution. Brisbane unions, including the WWF branch, were among the first to take action, and the Sydney branch, with a far more vocal call, was not far behind. Other branches, including Melbourne, soon joined in. Indeed, for a time, the left, right, and center of the WWF were united. Moreover, the WWF, in collaboration with a wide range of other unions, engaged in significant efforts to educate their membership about the issues. Lockwood estimates that the blockades succeeded in holding up 559 Dutch vessels in the four years of the bans, 1945–49. All of the interviews and minutes confirm that many WWF members were uninformed about, some even indifferent to, the Indonesian Revolution prior to the campaign but became enthusiastic supporters of the black bans.

---

[14] Minutes, Northwest Conference on Blacklisting, March 18, 1951, p. 2. SMP 16/16, p. 12.

[15] Another student research project provides detailed evidence (Sachse 2007).

Chicka Dixon, a famous Aboriginal activist, reports how his political views were developed during his ten years as a Sydney wharfie, beginning in 1963:

> [I]t was the greatest political experience of my life. I learnt to care about other people. We walk off the ships on Greek political prisoners, South African cargo, the Vietnam War. We refused to load the japaret and bomb somebody's kids. That was a learning exercise.
>
> You see, up to that point of time most Kooris[16] were in a sort of a shell; well, I was. I thought we were the only people in the world discriminated against, and never went beyond that. So I started to look at Greek political prisoners. I started to look at other issues and mainly the Vietnam War because it wasn't just a local issue; it was world-wide. They were saying, you know, "Let my people go", and it was exciting time. (Dixon 1995, 7)

ON THE CREDIBILITY OF LEADERSHIP

We argued that calls to action by the leadership will only be effective if the leaders are viewed as credible and trustworthy. Demonstration of leadership commitment to the membership and union principles lies first and foremost in industrial success. That is the necessary and backdrop condition for extensive demands. However, to gain cooperation with political action further requires the combination of leadership willingness to back down in the face of rank-and-file opposition and arguments framed in terms of union norms of fairness.

What we kept hearing were statements like these:

> I found that it has always been traditional for people, working people, particularly unionists, to give to underprivileged. They've always been very generous to the underprivileged. . . And that extended not only to the underprivileged but to underdogs, too, anyone who seemed to be oppressed. That mentality ran through the wharfies . . . And I think we had that much confidence in our officials that if the officials said "Look over in South Africa. They're the underdogs over there," or "they're underprivileged," we were nearly all there . . . There's always been blokes who were only interested in their pay and their working hours but the majority of blokes were only too happy to stick their hands in their pockets and give to somebody who the officials recommended required some assistance. (Waterside Workers of Australia 2006a)

---

[16] Kooris are Australian Aboriginal people.

In the mid-1960s there was a civil rights drive on the hotel industry in San Francisco. The goal was to end employment discrimination. There was a demonstration at the Sheraton Palace Hotel. The ILWU endorsed it. That was all I needed. I went over there with some other Local 10 guys. We picketed, then entered the building and sat down on the floor. Four or five of us longshoremen linked arms. The cops arrested us, but the union lawyer got us acquitted. (Whitey Kelm in Schwartz 2009, 55)

The transformation of some members may relax the budget constraint in leadership rents, tempting the leader to extract more. To the extent monetary compensation crowds out other types of motivation (Bowles and Polanía-Reyes 2011), intensely political leaders would appear insincere if they took advantage of this situation by accepting increased monetary compensation. Formal organizational rules linking compensation to membership pay achieves this in the ILWU. In the WWF we see the leadership actively refusing raises offered them by the membership. For example, the 1950 WWF conference voted to give Healy and Roach raises. Delegates from Sydney branch moved to increase the size of the raise. The motion carried but Healy refused to accept it, resulting in an overwhelming vote of support for Healy by the conference delegates, but no raise (Noel Butlin Archives 1950, 110–12). This example is consistent with reports of WWF norms that functioned more broadly. As one interviewee told us, "There was an unwritten policy amongst the officials of . . . the majority of the capital branches that if the workers in the port went through a pay day without pay [due to a work stoppage] the officials had to go through without theirs." He went on to note that the branch officials from the Grouper faction "didn't have to follow that policy because they didn't lead any strikes!" (Waterside Workers of Australia 2006a).

The governance institutions undergird the credibility of leaders. In recent discussions with leadership in ILWU Locals 19 (Seattle) and 23 (Tacoma),[17] we repeatedly heard how the final decision about political actions lay with the Longshore Caucus. When the Caucus called for a port closure to protest the death sentence of Mumia, the membership acquiesced—even though few even knew what the issue was. It was the Caucus that passed the resolution calling for action on May Day 2008, and it was the fact that the ILWU Longshore Caucus did not support the Occupy Oakland call for a coast-wide port shutdown on December 12, 2011, signaling publicly that this protest was not an ILWU event.

---

[17] John Ahlquist and Margaret Levi met with Cam Williams, president of Local 19, on Monday, January 9, 2012 and with Scott Mason, president of Local 23, Carl Rendell, vice president, and Holly Hulscher, Education Committee, on Wednesday, January 11, 2012.

INFORMATION EXPOSURE AND MEMBER EDUCATION

Both the ILWU and MUA commit substantial resources to developing member education on the history of the union, issues relating to struggles of the working class, and questions of social justice more broadly. We encountered many unionists who reflected on the education they felt they received in the union and on the job. During much of the period under study here, dock work was organized and allocated in gangs—groups of four or eight (though work rules varied by union, cargo, and ship type). Much of what they reported learning was communicated in these dense, close groups of co-workers. As one WWF retiree put it, "[Working in the holds with other unionists] was like being at school everyday. School on the waterside" (Waterside Workers of Australia 2006a).

Tom Hills, born in 1904 and a former Communist, participated in the 1928 strike and subsequently was denied his "dog collar" or license, that is, the official government registration that gave him the right to seek work (see chapter 4). Once he got it back he became extremely active in the Melbourne branch. He notes:

> Rank-and-file activity in the Union meant that people like myself and hundreds of other workers were encouraged to take part in our Union activities. It's been our education. . . . It had an immense effect on morale. Instead of sitting home and reading the paper, listening to the radio talk about the wicked wharfies, and getting demoralized, people developed their talents. People could do posters, could write, could do a variety of technical work. There is tremendous talent among the working class and we developed it. It gave them self-confidence, and it made them inquisitive. If you start to take an interest in your Union, you see how politics is affecting the Union, how they are affecting you. (Lowenstein and Hills 1982, 172)

Several of the veterans we interviewed in both the Melbourne and Sydney branches emphasized the importance of the discussions at both the stop work meetings and the Job Delegate Association (JDA) meetings. They found the discussions informative and enlightening about politics largely because they were democratic, had real arguments and debates, and both raised and solved problems.

> We had an hour for dinner. A lot of fellows would put an hour in at the pub but we had meetings in the union rooms. We had a film group that used to sometimes put on films, or we would have a speaker, might have a little bit of a concert . . . At the meetings the idea of social justice and questions like that were brought

up. Enlivened discussion on it. Yes. I would say we were educated on the waterfront, politically educated. Not intimated or that but educated politically on the waterfront, . . . You had time in those days. Because of the hour for lunch, you had time to invite one of people down on any political struggle going on, be it South Africa, Spain, or whatever. You could invite them down, and they could tell you what's going on. Gave you a good platform for the next general meeting at Town Hall. You could tell people let's do something about this, help me. (Waterside Workers of Australia 2006b)

From stop work to stop work meeting, you would have different meetings in this Job Delegates association. Would involve all different groups and all different sides. And they would discuss what went on in the job, what went on in politics, in the world at that time. There were some terrific discussions. Then we'd pass those resolutions up to the committee. If they needed to be acted on, they acted on them. It was really sensational. . . . That was the best part of being on the wharf. . . . Some of them were really like scientists . . . the guy who talked about fluoride. Really, really good meetings.

Not only did the information come in, but the information and solutions went out.

JDA would carry out the policy of the union. They were the leaders on that ship, on that job. Would be elected from rank and file. . . . A lot of leaders came from the delegates and became officers and good officers. (Waterside Workers of Australia 2006a)

Ruben Negrete, Local 13, a Mexican American, came to the waterfront in 1944 during World War II:

Being in this union was a big education. I never had the opportunity of being in anything. All I do was mule train before—really work hard. After I joined here, a few years later I started getting active. The ILWU made life a lot easier and more interesting. You get to meet people from different places. Once they know you belong to the ILWU, they look up to it, all over the world. I was an ILWU overseas delegate to the Philippine Islands in 1975. Harry was looked up to. The ILWU was looked up to. People knew it wasn't a corrupt union, that it was a straight, working-stiff union. (Schwartz 2009, 79–80)

In addition to what was learned on the job, members and even casuals were encouraged and sometimes required to attend the formal educational programs. Information about these programs remains prominently featured in ILWU hiring halls and the WWF/MUA union halls.

Abba Ramos, of Filippino background and son of a Hawaiian field worker, ultimately became an ILWU organizer in California:

By 1948 I ventured out from the Big Island. I went to Oahu to live with my uncle, who was a longshoreman. In Honolulu I was influenced by the ILWU education department under Dave Thompson and Ah Quon McElrath. Ah Quon encouraged me to read. I spent hours at the ILWU library with the transcripts of the Harry Bridges hearings. I met Anne Rand—the International's archivist, not the conservative writer—who set up the library in Hawaii. These people answered my questions and opened my view politically. I got most of my education from them. (Schwartz 2009, 271)

Cleophas Williams, the same man who was so surprised and pleased by Bridges' commitment to racial equity, recalls:

[I]n the mid-'40s, I attended the California Labor School (CLS). The ILWU backed it, and many of its teachers were identified with the Left. The first time, I went in order to get my union book. I was forced to go then. Later on, I chose to go. I took history, sociology, and economics. These classes expanded my mind. This was the first time I had ever gone to an integrated school. I was curious. I wanted to know. And what I wanted to know, the CLS taught. (Schwartz 2009, 48)

COMPARING UNION EXPERIENCES

We only have interview, oral historical, and archival data for the cases in which we expect to observe rank-and-file members updating their preferences, presenting a methodological challenge in establishing a link between a union's "community of fate" and preference provocation. Demonstrating that preference provocation did not happen in other unions, e.g., the Teamsters, is nearly impossible. Such belief updating may also be occurring in the Teamsters, and we simply don't observe it.

We nonetheless have reason to believe that we are not simply "selecting on the dependent variable." As we document in chapter 3, traditional "business unions" explicitly refuse to ask their members to engage in broader political causes.[18] Their communities of fate are bound by the union's jurisdiction. But more to the point, many individuals who came

---

[18] This brings up the interesting possibility that members of business unions also alter their beliefs about what is possible to accomplish through their union, just in the opposite direction from members of more activist organizations.

to work on the docks, ending up as members of the ILWU or WWF, had been members of other unions in the past. For example, sailors frequently moved on to dock work.[19] As we note in chapter 5, workers in the transport industry often moved back and forth between work on the docks and work in warehouses, trucking, and railroads.

In both interviews and oral histories, unionists repeatedly compared their experiences in the ILWU or WWF to their experiences in other organizations. For example, one former sailor energetically compared his experience in the WWF to that in the Seamen's Union:

> It was like a breath of fresh air when I joined . . . You found you had rights that you'd never heard of on other ships . . . couldn't believe it. Beautiful. And these campaigns. Once they were on and the die cast, you were eager to join in on them like. Because you were proud of your union and what you was doing . . . It's a really good feeling. I'm still a proud member of the Vets. (Maritime Union of Australia 2006)

Tony Adcock came from the Fire Brigade Union, which he characterized as "a good union" and joined the Port Kembla branch of the WWF; he "couldn't believe the democracy that existed in our union. From the day I joined until the day I die so proud to be a member" (Maritime Union of Australia 2006).

The ILWU members had similar reactions. Billie Roberts Hendricks participated in the San Francisco warehouse organizing campaigns during the march inland, and she was an active member of the ILWU Local 6 from 1936 to 1951, when she left to take a restaurant job and joined the waitress union, AFL.

> They were a very so-so outfit. You didn't have to go to union meetings. In early Local 6 days, we couldn't wait for out two meetings a month . . .The waitresses, too, always worked for tips and were jealous of each other. There wasn't that comradeship like we had in the ILWU, where you knew that you belonged . . . I love the ILWU. I'm so proud of it. I don't know what life would have been for me without the union. (Schwartz 2009, 193)

In the late 1930s, Lou Sherman helped organize a dissident movement in a truck drivers local of the IBT in Los Angeles. "The Teamster

---

[19] Indeed the ILWU absorbed the Inland Boatman's Union in 1980 after a major Washington State Ferry strike and later the cannery workers. The WWF and the Seamen's Union of Australia merged in 1993 to become the MUA.

International moved in and took away our autonomy. They threw out the officers and appointed International representatives." He was on their "shit list" and so left to work as an organizer for the ILWU and then as a warehouseman. He was an officer of Local 26 (Schwartz 2009, 195).

In our interviews among the pensioners of Local 19, Seattle, we heard stories like these:

> I started a little late here in life. Came into the pool in 67. Stayed in the pool for seven or eight years. A long one. Made a good living. Got into the local in 1975 or 76 . . . Great place to work and really a boon to the working stiff. Prior to being registered I went to sea and also worked as a Teamster . . .This is by far the best. The most democratic. Great structure because run from the bottom up. Bridges philosophy is one which is a model, has been proven as such . . . of labor organization and rights of people and workers.
>
> When I got out of high school in 1946, I went to sea. So you get the indoctrination of the waterfront from that era. From then on you have that to start with. And I drove a truck. I was a Teamster for years. You look at the structure, and you see it's a good deal, and I got a good a pay check. You go to meetings and you say "aye" and that's the end of that . . .The Teamsters and Tacoma, the ILA, was run from the top down . . . Jimmy Hoffa and Beck did a good job. They got good working conditions and good wages for the guys working for the labor force. So you didn't criticize them much. If you did have some critical things, you didn't say anything. Why rock the boat? But the ILWU thing is democratic and, if I may use the word, communistic. Day and night difference . . . Teamsters a different ballgame. If you want to go talk socialistic or anything else contrary to the establishment, that didn't work. Brother, you're out. They controlled the jobs. Had good jobs but came out of the hall. You could be the best worker in town but if you were a little radical they could put the thumb on you and get rid of you . . . In the first opportunity, when they were taking a pool in the 60s, I quit a good Teamster job.[20] (ILWU Pensioners 2007a)

[20] This quotation seems to contradict our claim that workers did not sort in to the ILWU and IBT based on politics. Rather than individuals sorting themselves based on pre-existing political convictions, we take this as further evidence of the IBT actively suppressing dissenting political opinions, whereas the ILWU tolerates a variety of political voices within the union. We uncovered no evidence of someone leaving the ILWU for political reasons. See below for a discussion of the WWF actively retaining those with dissenting political positions.

Evidence of Contingent Consent

In chapter 4 we document how members of both unions went along with decisions made through democratic processes, even if they had strongly opposed the position.

This form of contingent consent was most apparent in the ILWU during the debate over the Mechanization and Modernization (M&M) agreement. Over and over again, at meeting after meeting, Bridges reiterated, "You can't stop progress." He faced considerable hostility for his advocacy of the M&M. Some of the Seattle pensioners remembered how old timers really went after Bridges at their local meetings, yelling, "Sell out artist! You sold out cheap!" (ILWU Pensioners 2007a,b). These same pensioners noted that many of them thought the M&M was a bad idea but felt that "Harry knew what he was talking about and went along." By the time of the 1971 strike, however, they had come to believe that, despite Bridges' best efforts, the employers had not given them enough. Many noted that Bridges opposed the 1971 strike but managed it as well as anyone could. The consensus on this and on his leadership of the strike was far from universal, however. Many of those interviewed by Kimeldorf in Portland and San Francisco had mixed to hostile feelings about the M&M agreement. Indeed, some lost confidence in Bridges as a result and came to believe (or felt this proved) he was more allied with the bosses than the men. The way he ran the strike further confirmed their already negative perceptions. For them his "halo effect" had worn off, or, more accurately, everything Bridges did confirmed how dirty his wings had become. Yet, despite the increasing division over Bridges within the ILWU, he continued to win the active contingent consent of the majority. The evidence is in his continued electoral support and capacity to influence policy (Levi et al. 2009).

A particularly stark and large-scale example of contingent consent in the WWF came in 1949. The WWF's Federal Council voted (10 to 9) to call a work stoppage to protest the Australian government's imprisonment of several Communist activists under the Crimes Act.[21] The leadership of both the Melbourne and Hobart locals was part of the anti-Communist, anti-Healy faction of the union; they refused to take the issue to a membership vote.[22] In Brisbane the branch executive was conflicted over the call, but they nonetheless gave the rank and file a vote on the issue. Consequently, the branch passed a resolution expressing

---

[21] The 1948 WWF conference issued a resolution condemning the Crimes Act and calling on the Federal Council to take actions to actively oppose it.

[22] The Melbourne Mechanical Branch telegrammed Healy separately, saying they "disassociated themselves with the actions of the [Melbourne Branch] executive" on this matter.

disagreement with the Federal Council's action but acquiescence with the work stoppage, given their assessment that Council's decision was in compliance with WWF procedures (Noel Butlin Archives Centre 1949a).

The call for a work stoppage also generated conflict within the Sydney branch, which counted among its leadership some of Healy's strongest supporters and several Federal Councilors. The arbitration judge responsible for handling WWF industrial awards issued a public statement asking the WWF membership to ignore the call for a stoppage. Most of the 7,000 Sydney branch members nonetheless stopped work, but ninety-seven continued throughout the stoppage. At the subsequent Sydney stop work meeting there was a motion from the floor to expel the ninety-seven "Kirby scabs."[23] The branch leaders opposed the expulsion but lost by around one hundred votes. The vote was later recommitted, and the branch leadership was able to swing enough people to the softer stance of just citing the "scabs" rather than expelling them. In this instance, we observe rank-and-file members punishing one another for showing disloyalty. But we also see the leadership of the Sydney branch actively endeavoring to keep supporters of their political opponents from being expelled by rank-and-file vote. Their vision of union democracy and norms required tolerance of strong dissent and efforts to bring the actively non-compliant back into the fold.

The refusal of the Hobart and Melbourne branches to abide by the Federal Council's call for a work stoppage led to a serious rift in the union and a special session of the Federal Council. The minority anti-Communist faction of the Council claimed that the Council's decision was purely political, beyond the scope of legitimate union activity. Healy delivered an impassioned defense of his position in the Federal Council, explicitly linking the union's political positions and activities with its industrial success. He justifies the extractive demands by tying these demands directly to the interests of all members:

Stoppages must always be an action of strong protest and what it costs the members must also be considered. A lot of people rush around saying "you are going to stop us another day, we will lose a day's pay." I have been General Secretary of the Federation since 1937.... I would say this and challenge anybody to disprove it ... that there have been less (sic) man-hours lost through stoppages since I have been General Secretary than prior, and that has to be considered when somebody says "you are going to stop us for a day" ...Yet when the Federation calls for a stoppage of a particular

---

[23] Kirby was the arbitration judge who called for the members to defy the union leadership.

kind, two hours in the first instance, 24 hours in the second, which moans the loss of 2 hours on the first day and a full shift at best on the second, somebody squeals about the cost, not realizing that the solidarity shown while the stoppage is on is of the utmost value when dealing with other matters. (Noel Butlin Archives 1949b, 20)

Healy then promises (subsequently fulfilled) to personally go to the major locals to make his case on the issue:

I am not going to be satisfied with this matter being dealt with here [as a Council resolution], irrespective of how the vote goes, I am going to suggest this matter be taken down to the Branches and that it be thoroughly thrashed out. That is how anxious I am that this matter be cleared up and the unity of the Federation maintained. (Noel Butlin Archives 1949b, 127–28)

The Council proceeds to pass a three-part resolution: (1) affirms that the decision taken by the Federal Council to call a stoppage was in accordance with the resolution at the biennial conference and since endorsed by all branches; (2) condemns the actions of the executives of Melbourne and Hobart branches for defiance of Council authority; and (3) declares that Council decisions are binding on all Branches and can only be upset by a referendum of the rank and file. The first two parts passed 12–6; part 3 passed unanimously.

Conclusions

In this chapter we extended our basic theoretical framework to better account for some findings we uncovered in the course of our research, including extensive efforts at member communication and education as well as passionate reports from union members about the effect the union had on their thinking. We argue that many individuals either have ill-formed preferences or have not been presented with an opportunity to act in ways consistent with their political commitments. Presenting members with an organized opportunity to act jointly and coherently forces them to solidify their preferences and presents them with information about their own efficacy. We translate these into our modeling framework from chapter 2 by allowing for members themselves to benefit from their contributions to the leader's political projects. Members' preferences for political actions in the context of the union differ across individuals and are learned through participation. Once there is industrial success and social commitment to the union, leaders are able to make extensive demands for political action. Their capacity to achieve contingent consent with these demands depends on: leadership credibility and trustworthiness; governance arrangements that enable debate, challenge, and even rejection of the leadership demands; and processes for conveying information about the relevant causes, for persuading members of their importance, and for appealing to (and demonstrating consistency with) the norms that define the organization.

Unions do more than simply offer their members the necessary resources, both intellectual and organizational, for becoming more politically engaged. Relying on historical records and original interviews, we show that the act of direct political mobilization and the issues around which the leaders seek to mobilize the membership can profoundly transform the beliefs and revealed political preferences of at least some of the rank and file.

CHAPTER 7

Political Attitudes and Behavior among ILWU Members

With Amanda B. Clayton

If any group of American workers has benefitted from the growth of trade, it is the unionized dockworkers along the U.S. West Coast. It is estimated that more than 40 percent of U.S. imports pass through the Los Angeles/ Long Beach port alone (Bonacich and Wilson 2008). Container shipping volumes through West Coast ports tripled between 1990 and 2007, growing at an average annual rate of almost 5.4 percent between 1990 and 2010. Over the same period the total value of U.S. international trade grew at an average annual rate of 7 percent while annual GDP growth averaged 2.5 percent. Employment, hours worked, and real compensation for West Coast dockworkers grew in tandem. The collapse of work on the docks in 2008–2009 dispelled any doubts these workers may have had regarding the connection between their livelihoods and international trade activity. During the near-meltdown of the world economy in 2008–2009, the value of U.S. trade showed a 20 percent decline and West Coast shipping volumes dropped 15 percent (American Association of Port Authorities 2011; U.S. Bureau of Economic Analysis 2011).[1]

While international trade and the "logistics revolution" may have abetted the offshoring of manufacturing jobs and the decline of unionization more broadly (Bonacich and Wilson 2008), most external observers would expect dockworkers to support freer trade. Nevertheless, the ILWU has vigorously opposed trade liberalization for several decades (Turnbull 2000).[2] The union was vehemently opposed to the North

---

[1] Material in this chapter draws on work first reported in Ahlquist, Clayton, and Levi (forthcoming).

[2] While this chapter focuses on the ILWU, we note that the WWF has also long maintained a stance on trade that seems inconsistent with the immediate material interests of members. For example, former WWF General Secretary Fitzgibbon said the following in an oral history in which he reflects on Australian (ALP) Prime Minister Whitlam's decision to drastically cut tariffs in the early 1970s: "I disagreed violently with the Whitlam decision to cut tariffs 25% across the board. I disagreed violently with it for two basic reasons: (a) there

American Free Trade Agreement (NAFTA), shut down all West Coast ports in 1999 to protest the World Trade Organization (WTO) ministerial in Seattle, and has voiced strong opposition to the Free Trade Area of the Americas (FTAA) as well as new bilateral free trade agreements with South Korea and several Central American countries. To add to the puzzle, dockworkers on the U.S. East Coast, organized into a different union, the International Longshoremen's Association (ILA), have no history of taking public stands on trade issues one way or another.

The ILWU couches its position in terms of "fair trade." While the advocacy for fair trade policies by other labor groups has been criticized as "shadow protectionism," the ILWU's stance on international trade is noteworthy in its stark opposition to what would appear to be the members' material interests. But it is one of many political commitments the ILWU maintains as consistent with its organizing principle that "an injury to one is an injury to all." In this chapter we use original survey data that allow us to compare the political attitudes and behavior of ILWU members with that of otherwise similar non-members. We develop a better picture of how and the extent to which ILWU membership provoked preferences.

We initially focus on trade policy, for this is an issue in which the union's stance is so contrary to what an external observer would expect and difficult to explain coherently using traditional trade theory. We trace the union's position on trade over several decades. In the most recent period we rely on interviews with several union leaders in addition to a survey of both newly registered and long-term ILWU members in Los Angeles/Long Beach, Seattle, and Tacoma from 2006 to 2011. We then examine the extent to which ILWU members' opinions coincide with the union's positions, relative to comparable non-members. We also compare new union members with older cohorts. The union's stance appears consistent with the ideological commitments of its founders and difficult to justify otherwise. It appears to be conveyed through an educational and information sharing process taking place within the union. Consequently, union members with longer tenure tend to be more likely to have an

---

had been no discussion with the trade union movement at all . . . The second objection I had is that you can't do any such thing, because if you cut things like that without any consideration of the particular requirements of a particular segment of industry, then you're going to damage that very, very badly indeed." He goes on to talk about creating "a flood of imports in to this country that its infrastructure couldn't handle, its balance of payments couldn't handle, and it would create enormous, growing inflation . . . We had to put a thousand extra men into the Waterside Workers' Federation at a time when we didn't want anyone, in order to handle that flow of imports, because it was blocking the wharves . . ." Fitzgibbon (1986), CF: 2: 1/10–11.

opinion about trade policy, to favor restrictions on trade, and to oppose NAFTA when compared to similar non-union members.

We then turn to whether the union's political mobilization carries over to individual members' self-reported political behavior. We find that ILWU members with extensive exposure to the organization (A-class members) are significantly more likely to vote, contribute to campaigns, and participate in public protests than otherwise similar non-members. Newer ILWU affiliates (identified casuals) are indistinguishable from non-members. This ILWU "effect" does not appear to be the result of any increased interest in politics generated by the union; ILWU members and non-members report similar levels of political discussion and interest in politics. Rather, our findings appear consistent with our broader finding that extended exposure to a politically mobilized union influences members' feelings of efficacy in political action. The ILWU provokes preferences and behavior from its members.

The next section establishes the extent to which ILWU members have benefitted from the growth in international trade by documenting the expansion of shipping through the West Coast ports in recent years along with growth in real wages and employment for dockworkers. In the following section we briefly review the literature on trade and public opinion, identifying how our focus on one union can add nuance to our understanding of attitude formation. We document the ILWU's official stance on international trade over a period of six decades, and then examine the difference in self-reported political behavior—voting, contributing to campaigns, protesting—between ILWU members and non-members. The final section concludes. We collect details on the survey instrument and matching procedures in the appendix.

Employment, Compensation, and Shipping Volumes on the U.S. West Coast

Dock work is notoriously variable, oscillating rapidly between periods of slack and very high demand. Stevedoring companies therefore require a large pool of labor that can be called upon at short notice in periods of high demand. For their part, dockworkers would prefer some predictability. To address these competing demands, the ILWU and employers have developed a system of tiered worker classifications and job rotation that we described in chapter 4. Worker classifications are based on job type (clerk, foreman, "walking boss," mechanic, etc.) and seniority. The most senior longshore workers, enjoying full ILWU membership rights and first dibs on work shifts, are referred to as "Class-A." The less senior ILWU members are "Class-B." The "Casual" pool is called upon in high demand periods. Among the Casuals, the so-called Identified Casuals are those with an ongoing relationship with the ILWU; as they accrue more work-hours they become eligible to become Class-B members. "Unidentified Casuals" are individuals who might work just a few shifts on the docks.

Figure 7.1 displays the relevant data on U.S. trade and longshore work. In the upper left panel we display basic indicators about U.S. trade exposure: U.S. trade volumes have increased while average applied tariff rates have fallen. The upper right panel plots shipping volume, measured in millions of twenty-foot equivalent units (TEUs), and total hours of paid longshore work (for all tiers of longshore workers). Both show impressive, sustained increases from 1995 to 2007 reflecting the expansion of U.S. trade in the Pacific Rim, especially with China. The financial crisis and ensuing recession of 2008–9 induced a pronounced decline in trade and

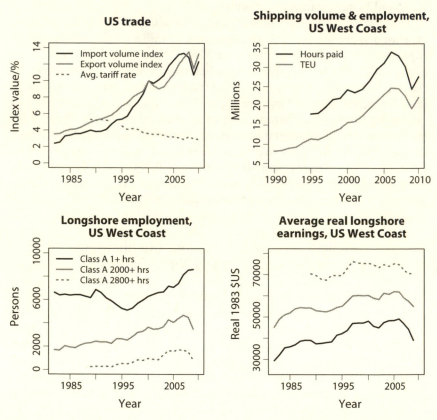

Figure 7.1: Shipping volumes, longshore employment, and longshore earnings for the U.S. West Coast have all increased substantially in recent decades, along with overall U.S. trade

shipping volumes, but hours worked by West Coast longshore workers decreased even more sharply. While the compensation data discussed below are partially the result of wage rates negotiated by the ILWU and the employers, the volume of trade reflects structural demand for stevedoring services. Demand for dock labor is clearly tied directly to trade volumes.

The bottom-left panel gives us one picture of the expansion of ILWU membership (and available work) over the last twenty-five years. The solid black line displays the number of active Class-A workers, i.e., those working at least one hour in that year. This value remained essentially flat through the 1980s, declined in the early 1990s, and then expanded systematically from 1995 onward. The two lighter lines represent the number of Class-A individuals working full time or better (at least 2,000 hours/year) and those getting consistent overtime work (at least 2,800 hours/year). Both of these values show sustained increases; an expanded workforce and increasing hours complemented growth in trade. As a demonstration of the ILWU's commitment to equalization of work opportunity, note that the collapse in trade and work opportunities at the end of the 2000s does not show up in the size of the active Class-A workforce, though the proportion of Class-A workers putting in full-time hours or better declined markedly. Rather than push workers off the rolls, ILWU members shared the pain.

The bottom-right panel displays the average real earnings for Class-A workers over time by the same hours-worked divisions just described. These data indicate that compensation grew *along with* the size of the workforce, opportunities to work, and international trade. The union's strategic position in the American economy clearly enables it to maintain high wages, but the growing demand for the workers it represents underpins its position. The amount of annual pay ultimately depends on the number of hours worked, and those hours fluctuate with the volume of trade. Thus, earnings go up with increased trade. So, too, do the number of workers. This growth in real earnings is even more remarkable when we consider that median real wages for American male blue-collar workers have been stagnant since the 1980s. By virtually any measure, ILWU members have benefitted from expanded U.S. trade. It seems unlikely that ILWU members would expect future trade to harm them given the union's continued strength and long-term contracts with the PMA.

International Trade and Public Opinion

Since the Great Depression, policymakers and scholars have viewed public acquiescence to free trade policies, especially in the rich democracies, as important for maintaining a stable and growing world economy.

Establishing the distribution of public opinion about trade policy and the extent to which individual attributes, cultural characteristics, and various public policies can affect voters' opinions on trade remains a vigorous and contested area of research.

Early work used either the sector-based (Ricardo-Viner) or factor-based (Hecksher-Ohlin) models of trade to derive workers' preferences over trade policy. Under the former, capital and, possibly, workers are assumed "fixed" in their respective industry or sector.[3] Expressed preferences over trade exposure should vary systematically with industry of employment and the extent to which that industry benefits from trade. The shipping and distribution industries, such as stevedoring, longshore, and warehousing, clearly stand to benefit from more trade. In the case of U.S. dockworkers, union representation is an important industry-specific consideration, especially in an era of rapidly eroding private sector unionization. And since longshore unions on both the East and West Coasts have succeeded in keeping wages relatively high, we argue that, from the perspective of Ricardo-Viner, we should consider labor to be a fixed factor in this situation. The Ricardo-Viner model then predicts longshore workers and employers should have homogenously pro-trade policy preferences. Furthermore, if, in the event of a trade slump, less senior union members face a greater risk of being forced out of the industry into less lucrative employment, they should also be more vocally pro-trade than the more senior union members.

Under the Hecksher/Ohlin-Stolper/Samuelson model, the benefits of increased trade accrue to the owners of productive "factors" in which a country is relatively well endowed while the owners of relatively scarce factors see their incomes decline. Rich industrial nations are held to be relatively well-endowed in capital and skilled labor; capital owners and high-skill workers stand to benefit from more trade while unskilled workers run the risk of lower wages and deteriorating employment prospects. Empirical work consistently turns up evidence that more educated individuals tend to favor lower trade barriers (Scheve and Slaughter 2001; Mayda and Rodrick 2005), a finding frequently interpreted as consistent with the Hecksher-Ohlin model. If this factor-based model holds, then we should see longshore workers behaving like other similarly skilled workers. If they are "low-skilled" then they will oppose trade liberalization while their employers support it.

The dominant trade theories share one empirical implication in common, namely that unions organizing similar groups of workers in the

---

[3] More nuanced interpretations treat Ricardo-Viner as a "short-run" model whereas Hecksher-Ohlin describes long-term equilibrium. See Alt and Gilligan (1994), Alt, Frieden et al. (1996).

same country should take similar policy positions over trade. But the two models make differing predictions about what those positions will be. We also note that it is unclear what the appropriate skill categorization for longshore workers should be. On the one hand, longshore work has become more capital-intensive and requires greater skill than in the past. On the other, incoming longshore workers are not required to have any particular level of skill training; virtually all training on the West Coast docks happens on the job or through the union and employer. Many of these skills are not portable to other industrial settings.

Arguments about whether an individual's opinion about trade policy derive from how they earn their income (factor-based) versus the industry in which they are employed (sector-based) have given way to more nuanced claims involving sociotropism (Mansfield and Mutz 2009), preferences for fairness (Ehrlich 2010), exposure to economic ideas during college education (Hainmueller and Hiscox 2006), risk exposure (Walter 2010), individual risk tolerance (Ehrlich and Maestas 2010), and survey framing effects (Hiscox 2006). Directly germane to this paper, there is no consistent evidence that unionization has any relationship with trade opinions one way or another.[4] Taken together, these papers indicate that, at minimum, trade policy preferences may not be easily reducible to the expected income effects anticipated under the classical macroeconomic trade models. Our findings strengthen this conclusion.

A criticism that can be leveled at all these studies, however, is the reliance on the standard national-level survey instruments. While surveys can be powerful tools, it is not always clear what we are tapping with our questions, all the more so when asking respondents to conjure opinions on topics about which they may be ill informed. When asking about trade protection, tariffs, and various international treaties, it stands to reason that many survey respondents have little knowledge of these issues.[5] Examining the ANES question commonly used to measure American attitudes on trade (e.g., in Scheve and Slaughter 2001) we see that "haven't thought much about it" is the modal response.[6] And even if they are aware of these issues there is little evidence that voters consider them salient or important. For example, the Gallup "most important problem" question, a widely used measure of issue salience, records a negligible number of respondents mentioning trade or the trade deficit as among the most important problems facing the United States in 2011,

---

[4] Interestingly, Ehrlich (2010) finds a null relationship between unionization and reported support for "fair trade."

[5] Hiscox (2006) shows that negative framing effects are largest among the less educated.

[6] For example, in the 2004 ANES, 44% of respondents reported not having thought much about trade issues (Survey 2004).

a period in which economic issues, broadly, are extraordinarily salient (Gallup 2012).

The ILWU, then, presents an interesting case. For dockworkers, international trade is, objectively, intensely salient; their earnings prospects are directly bound up with the volume of international trade, especially in the Pacific Rim. They are already employed and their likelihood of remaining so depends positively on shipping volumes. They tend to live near the docks in the cosmopolitan and outward-facing areas like Los Angeles/Long Beach, Portland, Seattle/Tacoma, and San Francisco/Oakland.[7] The level of skill needed to work on the docks has also increased over the years, especially since the advent of containerization in the late 1960s and computerized dispatch and tracking in the 1990s and 2000s. But these workers are also nearly completely unionized in one of the most powerful, militant, and socially activist unions in the United States. We now document how the union translated this social justice orientation into positions on international trade.

The ILWU's Organizational Principles and International Trade

ILWU LEADERSHIP AND TRADE POLICY

For much of its early history, the union supported low trade barriers, but the rationale expressed by union leaders was not one of classical comparative advantage, nor was it one of myopic ILWU self-interest. Rather, the ILWU's trade stance reflected the leadership's express commitment to broad labor solidarity and support for the Communist and Socialist regimes in Asia and Eastern Europe. After the union's initial leadership (and Communism) had passed from the scene, the ILWU's trade stance evolved in ways consistent with both the broader American labor movement and the leaders' reading of the 10 Guiding Principles. Specifically, the union reacted to the changes in the economy in which world trade enabled the offshoring of American manufacturing, often to countries with weak labor protections.

During his forty-year term as president, Harry Bridges often spoke of trade as a way to increase cultural contact with other nations, particularly with the Soviet Union, China, and Eastern Europe. Between 1955

---

[7] Scheve and Slaughter (2001) show that support of trade declines among homeowners in counties that are negatively affected by trade. Los Angeles/Long Beach, Portland, Seattle/Tacoma, and the San Francisco Bay Area have all had very robust real estate markets over the last 20 years, recent declines notwithstanding.

and 1973, the union passed several resolutions to this effect.[8] In his column "On the Beam" in the ILWU's official newspaper, the *Dispatcher*, Bridges occasionally commented on this issue. In 1955, he wrote:

> As things shape up now probably the next most important step in the improving relations between the United States and the socialist countries of the world will come about in the field of expanded East-West trade. Foreign trade and more of it has always been the lifeblood of the ILWU. (Bridges 1955, 2)

In 1965, in opposition to the AFL-CIO's position to prohibit increased trade with China, Bridges wrote:

> Any student of history knows that expansion of world trade has always strengthened the cause of peace. It may be true that many wars have broken out in the past over a division of world markets, but even in these cases the aims were to increase trade for one country over another. No reasonable nation ever assumed its capacity to grow and prosper without trade. (ibid.)

Bridges' position is clearly informed by his pro-Communist political stance. Gene Vrana, the ILWU's former Associate Director of Education and archivist, notes: "Bridges supported these policies due to his political convictions and it was easy for the rank and file to get behind him out of self-interest" (Vrana 2011).

In a 1968 statement before the U.S. House of Representatives' Committee on Ways and Means, the ILWU Washington Representative summarized the union's position, noting: "The ILWU supports free trade and urges the opening of markets in Eastern Europe and China as a means of improving our trade balance and helping world peace." And "Recognizing the frustrating problems in working out agreements, we believe that negotiations, such as those being conducted through GATT, are the answer" (Lannon 1968).

The ILWU's policy shift to an anti-liberalization stance did *not* parallel that in the larger U.S. labor movement. The AFL-CIO began taking protectionist stances as early as 1969 when it opposed the Trade Act of 1969. The ILWU supported this act, saying in congressional testimony

---

[8] See ILWU, *Proceedings of the Biennial Convention* (San Francisco), Resolution 15: "On World Trade" (1955). Resolution 2: "On World Trade" (1957). Resolution 9: "On Trade with China" (1959). Resolutions 41 and 42: "China Trade and China Policy" and "On World Trade" (1963). Resolution 28: "Free Trade" (1965). Resolution 3: "Foreign Trade" (1973).

that it was "a modest, but vital, step in the direction of freer, expanding trade" (Lannon 1970). However, the ILWU did support the AFL-CIO's position about curbing the incentives for multinational corporations to invest overseas. The ILWU, in contrast to the AFL-CIO, also supported the Trade Act of 1974, which established "fast track" trade negotiating authority for the U.S. president.

The ILWU's opposition to trade liberalization emerged in the early 1980s. It appears to be driven not so much by trade but rather by the increasing prospect of *capital mobility* and the resulting offshoring of American manufacturing. The union's 1988 Statement of Policy says "tariffs, and quotas are among the least significant factors in international trade. The underlying cases of the [trade imbalance] crisis have yet to receive the public attention they deserve, and tinkering with formal import restrictions by itself will do nothing to resolve this problem. About 30% of the trade imbalance has resulted from the US corporations moving their operations to other countries, manufacturing products there, and importing them to the US." Around this time the union formally voiced its concern to Congress on a number of trade issues. For example, the union wrote to the Senate Finance Committee in 1987 expressing support for a bill that would define denial of workers' rights as an unfair trade practice (Lewis 1987). The letter states,

> For the ILWU the current trade imbalance only confirms what we have long known: that American workers' own well being is inseparably bound up with the progress of our fellow workers abroad. But self-interest is not our only motivation. Just as we reject the callous assumption by some that economic recovery in the United States will require the steady erosion of domestic labor costs . . . we reject the common assumption that labor rights must be trampled on as they are in many countries for the sake of what is euphemistically called "initial capital formation." (ibid.,190–91)

We note that even in this letter the ILWU's conception of "self-interest" seems to encompass all American workers, not simply ILWU members. Concerns about labor injustices associated with freer trade generally emerged after Bridges' time, but his thinking clearly shapes current ILWU policy. Joe Wenzl, a former member of the ILWU's Coast Labor Relations Committee, states:[9] "The union's position [on trade] is right in line with Bridges' type of thinking. It flows directly from our 10 Guiding Principles" (Wenzl 2011).

[9] The Coast Committee is the executive body for the union's dominant longshore division (International Longshore & Warehouse Union 2006).

The current opposition to trade liberalization became particularly pronounced around NAFTA. In April 1991, the International Executive Board issued a Statement of Policy on the North American Free Trade Zone raising concerns about "the maquiladora pattern"—or the likelihood that these agreements would give companies unfettered access to easily exploitable populations of workers and resources. In the same month, ILWU International President Dave Arian made a speech to the union's Coast Committee, referencing government abuses of the Stevedores Union in Veracruz, Mexico and linking free trade to the attenuated power of organized labor in liberalizing economies.

In the run-up to NAFTA ratification, the union issued several statements opposing the agreement and launched an educational campaign to inform its members of the deleterious effects of free trade on workers' rights, both American and foreign. The union utilized its District Councils, Regional Organizing Committees, and International Representatives to disseminate information on NAFTA. The educational material, entitled *"No on NAFTA" Petition; Fair Trade, Free Trade, and the ILWU*, involved an effort to raise 10,000 signatures to send to American, Canadian, and Mexican government officials in opposition to the trade agreement.

Joe Wenzl states: "The vast majority of the ILWU opposes NAFTA and CAFTA. You'll be hard pressed to find a dissenting opinion. NAFTA has become a dirty word to the average longshoremen, same as 'employer'" (Wenzl 2011). Gene Vrana confirms, "You won't be able to find any officer who is going to sidetrack this issue. We have a consistent policy of 20 years by the union against free trade and an even longer history of being in favor of worker solidarity internationally" (Vrana 2011).

It is important to note that though certain members might articulate protectionist reasoning in their opposition to NAFTA, the union has never espoused overt protectionism. David Arian emphasized this stance in a speech during U.S. negotiations leading up to NAFTA: "First I would like to point out that our Union has always supported free and fair trade, but the agreement that is being negotiated is neither free nor fair. . . " (Arian 1992). Instead, the International leadership has condoned apparent worker-friendly international trade programs, such as the European Community codifying worker rights in its design and certain AFL-CIO trade proposals.

The high-profile WTO Ministerial meeting in Seattle again brought the issue of U.S. trade policy to the union's attention. In August 1999, in a Statement of Policy on the World Trade Organization, the International Executive Board detailed the union's plans to demonstrate against the WTO meeting in Seattle. In support of the protests, the union stopped work for eight hours on November 30, 1999 at all locals along the West

Coast. During a speech on the first day of protests, ILWU International president Brian McWilliams stated the union's position:[10]

> And let us be clear. Let's not allow the free traders to paint us as isolationist anti-traders. We are for trade. Don't ever forget—it is the labor of working people that produces all the wealth. When we say we demand fair trade policies we mean we demand a world in which trade brings dignity and fair treatment to all workers, with its benefits shared fairly and equally, a world in which the interconnectedness of trade promotes peace and encourages healthy and environmentally sound and sustainable development, a world which promotes economic justice and social justice and environmental sanity. The free traders promote economic injustice, social injustice and environmental insanity. (McWilliams 1999)

More recently, in December 2010, ILWU president Robert McEllrath sent a letter to then-House Speaker Nancy Pelosi expressing the ILWU's opposition to the South Korean Trade agreement. Reiterating the union's position on these matters, McEllrath states:

> By all accounts, the Korea-United States Free Trade Agreement (KORUS FTA) will increase trade between South Korea and the United States, which will result in an increase in cargo movement between the two countries. An increase in cargo movement is good for dockworkers. However, this fact alone is insufficient to overcome the vast deficiencies of the KORUS FTA.
>
> The KORUS FTA will cost jobs, lower environmental, labor, food and product quality standards, and empower corporations from the United States and South Korea to challenge public interests in both countries. The labor standards provision of the agreement only provides that each country enforce its own laws to adhere to the core labor standards identified by the International Labor Organization. The United States and South Korea's laws and enforcement in this area are completely inadequate and must be amended prior to the implementation of the agreement. (McEllrath 2012)

Although official statements and resolutions put forward by the International largely express these issues in terms of global worker solidarity, local opposition can take a form more protectionist of the American

---

[10] The continued hostility the union feels toward the WTO and similar organizations is available to ILWU members on Local 19's website: http://www.ilwu19.com/history/wto/wto.htm.

worker. Scott Mason, President of Local 23 in Tacoma, elaborates his position:

> If imports rise faster than exports, American workers lose. A net balance that results in a trade deficit affects the whole country. We ship a lot of empty containers and longshore workers are not okay with this. We benefit from both imports and exports and we even benefit from shipping empties, but we're only happy when the balance helps the American worker. We realize that shipping away all of our jobs is not smart in the long run. In Tacoma at the local level, we support Obama's mission to double exports, but not by shipping out empty containers. Of course we are not against all forms of trade, but only when the net effect means we're losing more than gaining. (Mason 2011)

In interviews with several former and current ILWU leaders, not one reported a change in the position of the union leadership or the rank and file with the collapse of trade in recent years. In the several conventions and International Executive Board meetings since the onset of the financial crisis, the union has not changed its stance on this issue.

DISCUSSION

Across the years, ILWU leaders clearly believe that trade issues are relevant to the union's mission. The leadership regularly invokes the declared principles of the union to justify and explain their stance. Interestingly, however, these positions, especially since the 1980s, seem to conflict with the immediate, short-term material interests of the members and, perhaps, the leaders as well.

It may be argued that the ILWU position on trade is the result of a political compromise within a union whose constituency includes more than dockworkers. The union, itself, recognizes this:

> Because the ILWU's membership includes longshore workers who rely on international commerce for employment, sugar workers in Hawaii who need legislative protection from sugar imports, warehouse workers who handle both domestic and international products, and hotel workers whose livelihood rests on a growing global economy, the union has sought to develop a solution to the trade problem that answers all members' concerns. (ILWU n.d.)

Nevertheless, the union's Longshore Division remains the heart of the union; all ILWU presidents have come from Longshore. Our survey data below look only at Longshore workers, which means we cannot assess whether Hawaiian sugar workers are more protectionist than the Long-shore division. However, we will show that long-term ILWU members are considerably more skeptical about trade than similar non-members.

The ILWU's position is clearly contrary to what we anticipate in Ricardo-Viner world. Looking at the positions taken by longshore employers makes a Ricardo-Viner story even less tenable: the ILWU's and employers' trade policy positions were diametrically opposed on NAFTA (Johnson 1993). The American Association of Port Authorities (AAPA), the port operators' industry association, repeatedly filed public testimony with both the U.S. Trade Representative and Senate Finance Committee strongly supporting the FTAs with all three countries (American Association of Port Authorities 2011). Hanjin Shipping, a Korean conglomerate and PMA member with a large trans-Pacific container shipping business, filed a separate comment with the USTR in support of the KORUS FTA. APL, another major trans-Pacific shipper and PMA member, was signatory to the U.S. Chamber of Commerce's U.S.-Korea FTA Business Coalition pro-KORUS public letter to the U.S. Congress (U.S. Korea FTA Business Coalition 2008). We found no evidence of any shipping or stevedoring company opposing any recent U.S. trade agreement.

We might consider the ILWU's position as consistent with the Stolper-Samuelson logic except for the fact that the ILWU's shift in trade policy came much later than the AFL-CIO's. The ILWU has generally not supported increased tariffs or quotas. Its opposition to FTAs has been focused on their catalytic effect on the offshoring of domestic production, often to countries with weak labor protections.

Comparing east coast (ILA) and west coast dockworker's unions makes it even more difficult to explain away the ILWU's position either as myopic economic self-interest or as consistent with standard trade theory. Both the sector- and factor-based models expected unions of dockworkers to take similar policy positions on trade. Extensive searches in the secondary literature, primary source archives, and the public record turned up no record of the ILA ever taking formal positions on trade policy one way or another.[11] They certainly were not advocating "fair trade" positions in the *Congressional Record* or calling work stoppages to protest the WTO. Whether preferences are industrially derived

---

[11] A search on OpenSecrets.org revealed several lobbying reports on trade assigned to the ILA. For the years in which the actual reports were available (2006–12) the reports are mis-categorized. They actually refer to lobbying by the ILWU. Of the visible reports on trade issues, *none* were from the ILA. We also looked for evidence of ILA support of the Panamanian FTA, given that it enhances the attractiveness of shipping from Asia directly through the Panama Canal rather than shipping to the West Coast and then transferring cargo to rail and truck. Nevertheless, the ILA has taken no discernable position on this FTA.

or class-based we would expect both unions to take similar positions in roughly equal intensity; they do not.

ILWU Members' and Affiliates' Attitudes Toward Trade

To what extent do their opinions track those stated by the leadership? Are ILWU members systematically different from otherwise similar non-members? We measure attitudes toward trade through individual-level survey data of ILWU members and registered casuals (both groups subsequently referred to collectively as affiliates) in the locals of Seattle, Tacoma, and Los Angeles/Long Beach. The survey was conducted from 2006 to 2011.[12] Surveys were administered in a variety of formats. Early surveys were administered over the phone. After some in the union objected to phone surveys, subsequent survey administration occurred on site at the union hall during meetings using pencil-and-paper survey instruments. As a final method, we also conducted a web-based survey for members in the LA/Long Beach Local. Members were encouraged to participate via a raffle of local college football tickets. Over the same period we generated a sample of non-union members by administering a similar survey using random digit dialing (RDD) into the area codes with geographic coverage containing the most common union member residence areas in each local. In total, we surveyed 675 ILWU affiliates and 604 non-affiliates. Exhaustive details of the survey administration procedures and events are detailed in the online supplementary materials housed at http://depts.washington.edu/ilwu/ .

Some internal union opposition, the 2008 contract negotiations, and the dramatic effect of the global economic crisis on dock work availability stymied our efforts to generate either a longitudinal or simple random sample of the union affiliate population. We ended up with a set of respondents that selected in to our study.[13] For this reason we rely heavily on ex-post matching techniques to construct defensible comparisons of ILWU affiliates with non-affiliates.

---

[12] The union's requirement that we repeatedly gain permission of the local leadership to conduct the survey and their prohibition of the survey during the contract year of 2008 account for the extended survey time frame.

[13] Specifically, the national leadership permitted the survey but required us to secure the permission of local leadership as well. Local leaders varied in their willingness to allow outsiders to access the membership, inducing delays, gaps, and an inability to reliably construct a random sample of the membership. See the online survey appendix that outlines in detail the survey procedures, the challenges we encountered, and response rates. More information is available at http://depts.washington.edu/ilwu/.

MATCHING

Since ILWU membership cannot be considered randomly assigned, we follow the strategy proposed in Ho, Imai, King, and Stuart (2007) and use a matching step to "preprocess" our data, selecting a subset of ILWU and RDD respondents that are as balanced as possible on observable "pre-treatment" covariates. By discarding observations that do not fit in the range of a balanced distribution of covariates, we eliminate approximately 28 percent of our observations but achieve ILWU and non-ILWU groups that are closely blanaced on observables.

By matching prior to implementing standard parametric models we reduce the model dependence of our estimated average "treatement effect" of ILWU membership on trade attitudes. We put the term "effect" in quotation marks for two reasons: First, we do not observe the "pre-treatment" attitudes of ILWU members. Second, as with any matching procedure, we cannot unambiguously rule out the possibility that workers select in to the ILWU for unmeasured reasons that may be correlated with their political attitudes. That said, we have shown in earlier chapters that survey respondents (and ILWU members more generally) are not self-selecting in to the ILWU for political reasons, nor are they exiting the union when the union takes political stands with which they might disagree.

In some sense the ideal "control" group would be West Coast dockworkers who are not members of the ILWU. There are none; virtually every West Coast dockworker is somehow affiliated with the ILWU. Similarly, we might like to survey those ultimately chosen to work on the docks with those not selected. Gaining access to ILWU affiliates was quite difficult; gaining access to the latter population proved impossible. That said, based on the data in figure 7.1 we would naively expect that dockworkers would be more pro-trade than otherwise similar individuals. Matching, in this case, lets us construct the most defensible set of comparisons even if we are not able to claim to have perfectly estimated the causal effect of ILWU membership.

Because we have several covariates and a limited number of potential matches, one-to-one exact matching is not feasible. Instead we use the genetic matching technique described in Abadie and Imbens (2011) and Diamond and Sekhon (forthcoming). Up to two RDD observations can be assigned to each ILWU observation. We discard observations for which there are no effective matches in both the treatment and control groups. Pre-treatment matching covariates are the age, sex, ethnicity (white, Hispanic, and others), education level, geographic location, and the date the survey was conducted. To avoid problems with post-treatment bias, we do not match on the respondents' political party identification or income category as these are arguably effects of increased ILWU tenure. Similarly we do not include covariates for the mode of survey administration (paper/pencil, phone, web) in either the matching or parametric model since the RDD sample was surveyed exclusively by phone. Balance diagnostics are reported in the appendix to this chapter.

Although the rate of missingness is low (between 0 and 10 percent for most of our covariates) we impute missing values rather than list-wise delete entire observations (King, Honaker, Joseph, and Scheve 2001). We use Amelia II for R to perform the multiple imputations.

If we perform the matching exercise seperately on each imputed dataset we end up with slightly different sets of matched observations with different weightings. Since the underlying sets of observations then differ, we cannot use the standard algorithm for combining parameter estimates and uncertainty for models fit across multiply imputed pre-processed datasets. We therefore took three approaches. First, we constructed twenty imputed datasets and then averaged across them to generate a single complete dataset.[14] We then performed the matching pre-processing and subsequent modeling using this single complete dataset. The results presented here use this strategy, which obviously fails to fully account for imputation-based uncertainty. To address this we took five of the imputed datasets and performed the matching exercise on each seperately and combined results using standard rules (Little and Rubin 2002). Third, we analyzed only the complete cases. Across all three strategies our broad substantive conclusions remain unchanged, though the specific estimates, of course, differ.

Attitudes on U.S. Trade Barriers

The first relevant survey question asks respondents their opinion on the U.S. government limitations on imports. Our survey uses the same wording as the ANES question commonly used in other studies. The question reads:

> "Some people have suggested placing new limits on foreign imports in order to protect American jobs. Others say that such limits would raise consumer prices and hurt American exports. Do you favor or oppose placing new limits on imports, or haven't you thought much about this?"

The respondents were allowed to answer "Favor," "Oppose," or "Haven't thought much about it."[15] Figure 7.2 displays the frequency

[14] Specifically continuous variables were averaged. We took the modal value across imputations for categorical variables.

[15] The possible response "Don't know/refuse to answer" was also included on our survey, but only 7% of ILWU respondents chose this answer and 3% of RDD respondents, so we exclude it from analysis.

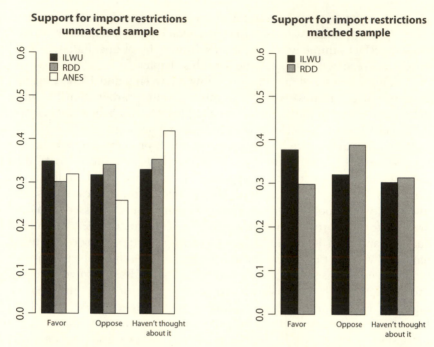

Figure 7.2: Distribution of responses to whether the U.S. government should place new limits on imports

distribution of ILWU and RDD responses to this question for both the raw data and the matched set of observations. As a point of comparison we include the ANES 2004 responses as well.

Figure 7.2 reveals that in the raw data, a similar number of ILWU and RDD respondents report holding an overall opinion on this issue in either direction (67% and 64% respectively). However, conditional on having an opinion, 53 percent of ILWU respondents said they favored new restrictions on imports, whereas 47 percent of RDD respondents chose this category.[16] In the matched data, of those that reported an opinion (approximately 68% RDD respondents and 70% of ILWU respondents), 43 percent of RDD and 54 percent of ILWU respondents reported favoring increased restrictions (a difference of 11 percentage points as opposed to 6

---

[16] In addition, our survey asked respondents the follow-up questions: "If you favor/oppose, do you strongly favor/oppose or just favor/oppose placing new limits on imports?" Though we do not include the follow-up question here, it is interesting to note that among ILWU respondents, 48% said they strongly favored new limits and 35% strongly opposed, whereas among RDD respondents, 42% strongly favored new limits and 64% strongly opposed.

TABLE 7.1: Multinomial logistic regression results on attidues toward trade barriers using imputed and matched data

	Favor Restrictions/ No Opinion	Oppose Restrictions/ No Opinion	Favor Restrictions/ Oppose Restrictions
	$\hat{\beta}$ (SE)		
Intercept	−1.48 (1.14)	**−4.30 (1.29)**	**2.81 (1.26)**
ILWU affiliate	−0.05 (0.25)	−0.30 (0.26)	0.35 (0.25)
ILWU * Class A	**0.52 (0.26)**	0.52 (0.28)	0.00 (0.25)
ILWU * Class B	**−0.57 (0.29)**	0.11 (0.29)	**−0.68 (0.30)**
White	0.04 (0.24)	−0.24 (0.24)	0.28 (0.21)
Hispanic	**−0.79 (0.34)**	**−0.81 (0.35)**	0.02 (0.32)
Female	**−0.52 (0.26)**	**−0.80 (0.29)**	0.28 (0.30)
Seattle	−0.04 (0.31)	0.50 (0.31)	**−0.55 (0.27)**
Tacoma	−0.52 (0.31)	0.03 (0.31)	**−0.55 (0.27)**
Age	0.06 (0.05)	**0.10 (0.05)**	−0.05 (0.05)
Age2	−0.00 (0.00)	−0.00 (0.00)	0.00 (0.00)
Education	0.03 (0.07)	**0.27 (0.07)**	**−0.24 (0.07)**
Survey date	0.00 (0.00)	0.00 (0.00)	−0.00 (0.00)

N = 892
AIC 1879

Note: Coefficients with *p*-values ≤ 0.05 are indicated in bold. Reference category for geographic area is Los Angeles/Long Beach. Reference category for race includes Asian Americans, African Americans, Pacific Islanders, and those that self-identified as "other."

points in the unmatched data). All groups in our survey are more likely to have an opinion on trade restrictions and to be more likely to oppose trade restrictions than the ANES 2004 sample, though the difference in time and regional specificity of our survey make this comparison less illuminating.

We take the three possible response categories, "favor," "oppose," and "haven't thought much about it," to construct the dependent variable for our multinomial logistic model. Table 7.1 displays results, with "haven't thought about it" as the reference category. We model union tenure using indicators for union rank.[17] The ILWU indicator takes a value of "1"

---

[17] While we also have data on self-reported length of time a respondent has "worked on the docks," we prefer the union rank indicator as a measure of union tenure and exposure since hours worked on the docks determines rank. It is possible to have worked on the docks infrequently but over a long stretch of calendar time.

for all affiliates, while the Class-A and Class-B take on a value of "1" for affiliates self-reporting those ranks. As such, these indicators are the same as interaction terms and reflect the *additional* "effect" of increased union seniority on the (log odds) of the two choices relative to reporting "haven't thought about it."

Our results indicate that ILWU affiliates are distinguishable from otherwise similar workers, contrary to expectations derived from a Stolper-Samuelson model of trade. Consistent with our argument about preference provocation, those with the greatest union exposure, Class-A members, are significantly more likely to favor increased restrictions on imports compared to not having an opinion. Holding covariate values at sample means/modes, a Class-A ILWU respondent is 32 percent more likely to favor import restrictions than an RDD respondent. Nevertheless, Class-B respondents are significantly less likely to favor import restrictions, perhaps reflecting an increased sensitivity to work opportunities on the docks. We discuss this further below.

We note that our findings are consistent with other previous studies: women are more likely to support restrictions on imports and more educated respondents are more likely to oppose restrictions on imports. Nevertheless, conditioning on education we still uncover a union seniority effect. We see modest regional variation in trade opinions along the West Coast, with those in the Pacific Northwest less likely to favor import restrictions compared to Southern California.

The presence of interaction terms makes interpretation of results somewhat complicated. To that end, figure 7.3 presents a ternary plot displaying each respondent's predicted probability for each possible response. Light triangles represent ILWU respondents while dark circles depict RDD respondents. The predicted probabilities for RDD respondents do cluster away from favoring import restrictions. ILWU affiliates appear more likely to report favoring increased trade barriers, though there is considerable overlap between the groups in this figure.

This overlap become easier to understand, however, when we consider ILWU affiliates by status. Figure 7.4 highlights the union tenure effect by comparing the predicted response probabilities of Class-A members (solid triangles), Class-B members (crosses), and casuals as (open circles). Class-A members are clearly separated from other affiliates: they are more likely to have opinions and more likely to favor new restrictions on imports than either Class-B or casuals. Much of the overlap between the RRD and ILWU affiliate responses in figure 7.3 comes from the most junior ILWU affiliates.

Since union seniority and age are correlated, it may be that we are simply picking up an age cohort effect (even though we condition on age in the model). To test for this we conducted a separate matching exercise in

**Predicted probabilities
ILWU/RDD attitudes on placing limits on imports**

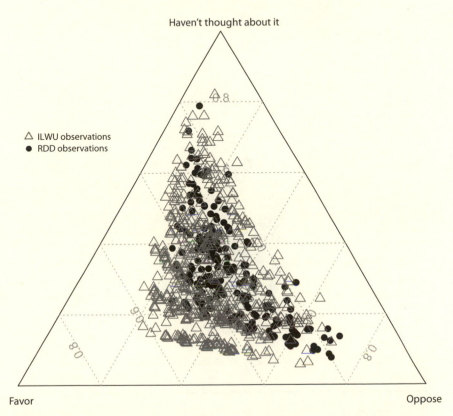

Figure 7.3: Predicted probabilities for all respondents in the matched dataset, by ILWU affiliation status

which we matched ILWU union members (Class-A and Class-B members) on age and then examined the differences between them. The frequency distribution is reported in the left-hand panel in figure 7.5. Even among those of similar age, union exposure, as measured by rank, affects attitudes toward import restrictions. We also matched Class-A and Class-B members on the number of years they report being a registered member of the union (highly correlated with age) and report the distribution frequencies in the right-hand panel of figure 7.5. Class-B members who have been in the union as long as Class-A members, but have not logged enough hours of work to achieve A-status, are much less likely to have an opinion on foreign imports as well as less likely to favor increased restrictions.

**Predicted probabilities
A/B/Casuals' attitudes on placing limits on imports**

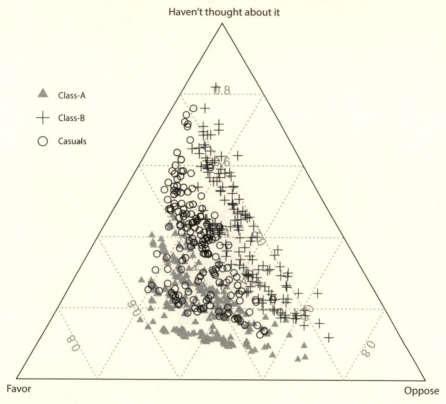

Figure 7.4: Predicted probabilities for all ILWU respondents, by seniority status

One plausible interpretation of our findings involves the relative risks of having to find other work. Perhaps ILWU affiliates are insecure in their employment status, particularly as trade volumes in the ports collapsed in 2008–9. Their stance reflects their fear that they may be forced to look for work elsewhere in the economy where their earnings prospects might be harmed by trade openness.[18] In our survey we ask whether respondents have other paying employment, how much of their income they earn from their port-related job ("almost all," "most," "about half," "some," "not much," or "don't know") and whether they

[18] Even if it were the case that ILWU members felt insecure in their jobs, it is not obvious that a more protectionist stance should follow; they would have an incentive to actively try to *increase* the volume of shipping through West Coast ports so as to prevent job loss.

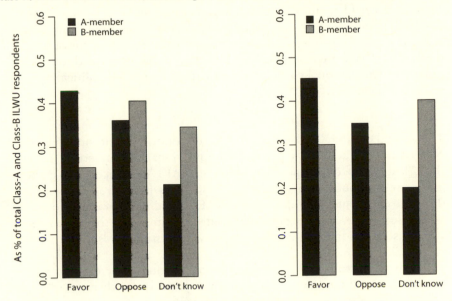

Figure 7.5: Comparing trade attitudes among union members by union tenure, matching on age

are "very," "somewhat," or "not worried" about losing their port-related job.[19] There is some evidence that those more worried about their port job were more protectionist: 46 percent of those "very worried" favored import restrictions, while 33 percent of those who were "not worried" favored restrictions. Looking by union rank, however, we see a different picture. Casuals, whose job status is, by definition, more precarious, were almost twice as likely as Class-A members to report being "very worried" (26% against 14%). But of those claiming to be "very worried," 57 percent (24/42) of Class-A members favored import restrictions against 43 percent of Casuals (19/44). Of those claiming to be "not worried," 44 percent (47/108) of the Class-A members favored import restrictions against only 25 percent (13/54) of the Casuals. Regardless of the extent to which ILWU affiliates feared losing their port-related jobs, those with greater union tenure were more anti-liberalization than newer recruits.

[19] While the job security question was also asked of the RDD sample, the fact that we referred to a "port-related" job" limits our ability to generate a meaningful comparison between ILWU affiliates and non-affiliates.

Class-A members are more likely than Casuals to have thought about whether the U.S. government should place new limits on foreign imports. They are more likely to have an opinion on this issue in either direction but tend to significantly favor increasing import restrictions. Similarly situated respondents in the broader population are less protectionist than their ILWU Class-A counterparts. This pattern is consistent with the notion that organizational participation can affect individual political preferences dynamically.

Attitudes Toward NAFTA

The second trade-related question asks respondents their opinion on NAFTA. This question is particularly important for our study since ILWU leadership took a specific position on NAFTA, as opposed to making vague pronouncements about trade or tariffs in general. We would therefore expect member opinions on NAFTA to differ from the broader population more dramatically compared to findings for the "trade restrictions" question just analyzed. The survey question reads:

> "I am going to name a number of organizations. For each one, could you tell me how much confidence you have in them: is it a great deal of confidence, quite a lot of confidence, not very much confidence or none at all? – NAFTA."

Unfortunately, the wording of this question, taken from the U.S. version of the World Values Survey, is vague. Leaving aside the fact that NAFTA is not an organization, the respondent may be unclear if the question is asking him/her to state their level of confidence in whether NAFTA signatories will uphold the treaty or whether they are confident that NAFTA is a good policy. Based on conversations with unionists, we believe the most common interpretation of the question is the latter. In any event, we have no reason to believe that ILWU affiliates would be systematically more or less confused by the question's wording than RDD respondents.

The response distribution based on raw data displayed in figure 7.6 makes clear that ILWU affiliates are much more likely than RDD respondents to have "no confidence at all" in NAFTA. The 2006 WVS response distribution ($n = 1117$) is included here for comparison.

We use the four possible survey responses to construct an ordered dependent variable with larger values representing *less* confidence in NAFTA. Table 7.2 displays results from our ordered probit models fit to the matched data.

The coefficient estimates imply that all ILWU affiliates are significantly less likely to express confidence in NAFTA. As we go up the seniority ladder we see a marked and significant increase in this anti-NAFTA

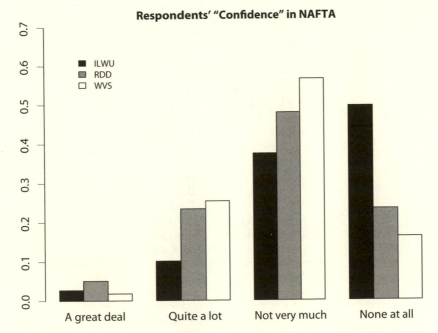

Figure 7.6: Distribution of respondents' level of confidence in NAFTA for RDD, ILWU, and 2006 World Values Survey

sentiment. To visualize the scale and uncertainty around this implication, figure 7.7 plots the difference in the predicted probabilities of having "no confidence at all" in NAFTA for ILWU Class-A member versus a non-affiliate (solid curve) and for a Class-A member versus a Casual (broken curve). All other covariates are held at their appropriate central tendencies. That is, the simulation describes the difference between a Class-A and an RDD (Casual) respondent who are both forty-six-year-old white males from Long Beach with college degrees, and taking the survey on August 7, 2009. The densities reflect our uncertainty in these differences. As an odds-ratio, the ILWU Class-A member is 74 percent more likely than an RDD respondent and 53 percent more likely than a Casual to express no confidence at all in NAFTA.

DISCUSSION

Findings from our survey uncover several interesting features about the ILWU membership, largely consistent with our argument about organizational principles and the notion that organizational participation can provoke members into having more clearly formulated preferences. First,

TABLE 7.2: Ordered probit regression results on confidence in NAFTA using matched and imputed data (higher values imply less confidence)

	$\hat{\beta}$ (SE)
ILWU affiliate	**0.22** (0.06)
ILWU * Class A	**0.51** (0.07)
ILWU * Class B	**0.14** (0.07)
White	**0.32** (0.07)
Hispanic	**−0.17** (0.04)
Female	**−0.33** (0.17)
Seattle	−0.01 (0.05)
Tacoma	0.06 (0.05)
Age	**0.02** (0.01)
Age squared	−0.00 (0.00)
Education level	0.00 (0.03)
Survey date	0.00 (0.00)
Intercepts:	
1|2	**−0.64** (0.00)
2|3	**0.09** (0.08)
3|4	**1.60** (0.09)
N =	892
AIC	1828

Note: Higher values on the response represent *less* support for NAFTA. Coefficients with p-values ≤ 0.05 are indicated in bold. Reference category for geographic area is Los Angeles/Long Beach. Reference category for race includes Asian Americans, African Americans, Pacific Islanders, and those that self-identified as "other."

ILWU members with the greatest union "exposure" are significantly more likely to report strong opinions about abstract trade policy issues than otherwise similar non-members. Second, ILWU members appear somewhat more skeptical of trade liberalization compared to matched individuals drawn from nearby communities. Third, ILWU members are significantly more skeptical of NAFTA than either the broader American population or matched non-members who live in nearby communities. This discrepancy between the ILWU members' responses to the generic trade restriction question and the NAFTA question closely parallels the ILWU's stated goals and objectives: ILWU leaders have consistently opposed specific free trade treaties while maintaining rhetorical commitment to "fair trade" and expanded work opportunities for the membership. Union members are correspondingly more likely to oppose the only specific treaty we asked about, NAFTA, while having less crystallized opinions about "new limits on foreign imports."

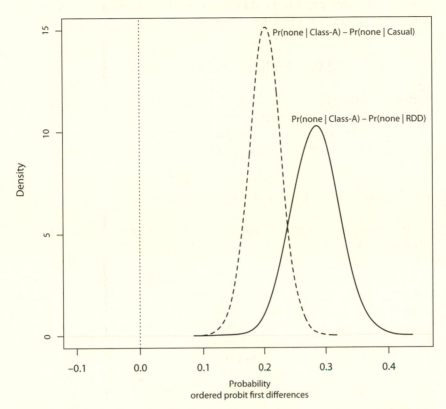

Effect of ILWU exposure on NAFTA confidence

Figure 7.7: Difference in the predicted probability of having no confidence in NAFTA, comparing Class-A/RDD and Class-A/Casual, holding other covariates at central tendencies

Also consistent with our argument about the impact of organizational participation over time, Class-A members are more likely to support increased restrictions on foreign imports—a belief that, if put in practice, would directly detract from their primary source of income. In addition, confidence in NAFTA significantly decreases among high-ranking members in the union compared to incoming casuals. Indeed, in two of the three surveyed locals, no Class-A men reported "a great deal of confidence" in the treaty. Our results indicate that increased tenure in the union is associated with member beliefs more in line with the union's overarching stance on international trade policy. Since it is hard to imagine why union leadership would be more salient for one group of members than another (especially comparing A and B members), it is not obvious why this pattern would emerge if union members were simply parroting the union leadership's line.

ILWU Affiliates' Political Behavior

Is there a discernable ILWU "effect" in affiliates' self-reported political behavior? We asked survey respondents about three major ways in which citizens in democratic societies can participate in politics: participation in a protest or march, contributing to political campaigns, and voting.

POLITICAL PROTEST

The first question in this category reads:

> "In the past twelve months, have you taken part in a protest, march, or demonstration on some national or local issue?"

Respondents could choose "Yes," "No," or "Don't know." Less than 1 percent of respondents indicated that they did not know if they had engaged in one of these actions, prompting us to drop observations in this category. Figure 7.8 shows the distribution of responses to this question. The left-hand panel shows the distribution of ILWU and RDD respondents. The right-hand panel shows the distribution among ILWU respondents by the affiliates' rank. Consistent with our findings in the models of trade policy opinions we see that ILWU respondents in our sample are more likely to have participated in a protest than matched observations of the RDD sample. The right panel, however, demonstrates that there remains a substantial difference between the Class-A, Class-B, and Identified Casual affiliates.

Table 7.3 displays parameter estimates from a logit model describing the probability that the respondent reported participating in a political demonstration in the last year. Reflecting the finding in the simple frequency distributions, we see from the table that Class-A and Class-B members are significantly more likely to have participated in a protest than *either* Identified Casuals or matched RDD respondents. Age, education, and gender do not appear correlated with protest behavior.

To interpret the magnitude of this relationship we construct two scenarios with covariates held at their appropriate central tendencies. The scenarios describe the difference between an ILWU (Class-A) and an RDD respondent who are both forty-six-year-old white males from Tacoma who have completed some college and taking the survey by

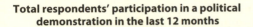

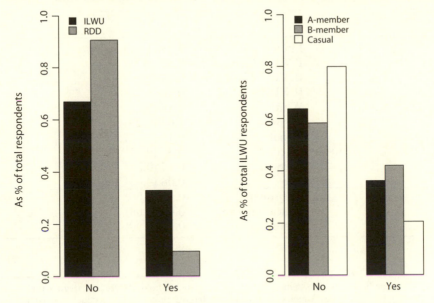

Figure 7.8: Distribution of self-reported protest behavior in the last 12 months

phone on August 7, 2009. As an odds-ratio, the ILWU affiliate is close to three times more likely to report having engaged in a political protest in the past twelve months as compared to the RDD respondent. We also compare an ILWU casual to a Class-A respondent with the same demographic characteristics described above; the Class-A member is 1.8 times more likely than the Casual to have reported participating in a political demonstration.

POLITICAL CONTRIBUTIONS

Findings for the protest variable may seem unsurprising since the ILWU itself asks members to protest, as we have repeatedly documented. But there are other types of political participation that we document. A second question asks: "In the past twelve months, have you contributed money to a candidate or political organization?" Again, respondents could answer "Yes," "No," or "Don't know," but less than 0.01 percent indicated that they did not know. Figure 7.9 shows the distribution of responses to this question. The left-hand panel shows the distribution of ILWU and RDD respondents. The right-hand panel shows the distribution among ILWU respondents by the affiliates' rank.

TABLE 7.3: Logistic regression on self-reported participation
in political demonstrations, imputed and matched data

	$\hat{\beta}$ (SE)
Intercept	**−3.41** (1.21)
ILWU affiliate	0.51 (0.27)
ILWU * Class A	**0.81** (0.24)
ILWU * Class B	**0.96** (0.26)
White	0.13 (0.22)
Hispanic	**1.01** (0.29)
Female	0.15 (0.25)
Seattle	0.37 (0.27)
Tacoma	−0.15 (0.28)
Age	0.06 (0.05)
Age squared	−0.00 (0.00)
Education level	0.09 (0.06)
Survey date	0.00 (0.00)
N =	892
AIC	977

Note: Coefficients with p-values ≤ 0.05 are indicated in bold. Reference category for geographic area is Los Angeles/Long Beach. Reference category for race includes Asian Americans, African Americans, Pacific Islanders, and those that self-identified as "other."

Table 7.4 displays parameter estimates from logistic regression describing the probability that the respondent reports contributing to a political candidate or organization in the past twelve months. In addition to the specifications included in the above models, we also include three dummy variables indicating whether the "past twelve months" at the time the survey was taken included the 2006 midterm elections, the 2008 presidential elections, or the 2010 midterm elections.

ILWU membership as either Class-A or B is positively and significantly associated with the increased likelihood that the respondent contributed to a political candidate or organization. Older, more educated, and Latino respondents were also more likely to report contributing. Those in Southern California were less likely to do so. To describe the magnitude of the "ILWU effect," we construct the same scenarios described in our discussion of political protest activities. The Class-A ILWU respondent is over three times as to report contributing to a political candidate or organization as compared to the RDD respondent. The same Class-A respondent is just under three times as likely as a Casual to report contributing.

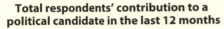

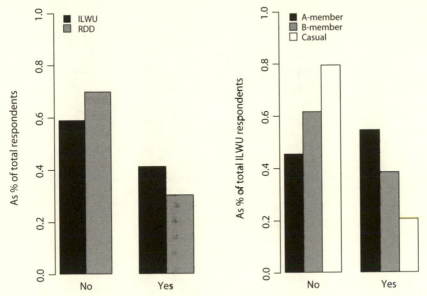

Figure 7.9: Distribution of self-reported political contributions

VOTING

As a final behavioral indicator, we look at self-reported voting. Specifically, the question reads:

> "In talking to people about elections, we often find that a lot of people were not able to vote because of many different reasons. How about you? Did you vote in this past November's election?"

Respondents could answer "Yes," "No," or "Don't know," but less than 2 percent of respondents did not know if they had voted in the previous election. Figure 7.10 shows the distribution of responses to this question. The left-hand panel shows the distribution of ILWU and RDD respondents. The right-hand panel shows the distribution among ILWU respondents by the affiliates' rank. Our matched sample reports very high voting rates, with 82 percent of ILWU affiliates and 77 percent of RDD respondents reporting having voted.

Table 7.5 displays parameter estimates from logistic regression describing the probability that the respondent reports voting in "past November's election." As in table 7.4, we control for the specific elections. Class-A

TABLE 7.4: Logistic regression on self-reported political
contributions, imputed and matched data

	$\hat{\beta}$ (SE)
Intercept	**−5.70** (1.19)
ILWU affiliate	0.04 (0.25)
ILWU * Class A	**1.62** (0.25)
ILWU * Class B	**0.67** (0.28)
White	0.22 (0.21)
Hispanic	**0.82** (0.30)
Female	−0.27 (0.26)
Seattle	**1.10** (0.27)
Tacoma	**0.92** (0.26)
Age	0.08 (0.05)
Age squared	−0.00 (0.00)
Education level	**0.22** (0.06)
Survey date	**0.00** (0.00)
Midterm 2006	0.47 (0.34)
Presidential 2008	0.19 (0.55)
Midterm 2010	**−0.98** (0.27)
N =	892
AIC	1025

Note: Coefficients with *p*-values ≤ 0.05 are indicated in bold. Reference category for geographic area is Los Angeles/Long Beach. Reference category for race includes Asian Americans, African Americans, Pacific Islanders, and those that self-identified as "other."

affiliation is positively and significantly associated with the likelihood that the respondent voted in the past election; a Class-A respondent is about 10 percent more likely than an RDD respondent to report having voted.

It appears that ILWU members are more politically active in terms of protest, political contributions, and voting when compared to otherwise similar RDD respondents to our survey.

Robustness Considerations

There are two important remaining questions that we can partially address with our data. First, are there unobserved confounders that might be generating our results? Second, have we identified an "ILWU effect" or simply a "union effect"? Both are interesting questions in their own right; the answer to the latter would not necessarily undermine the argument

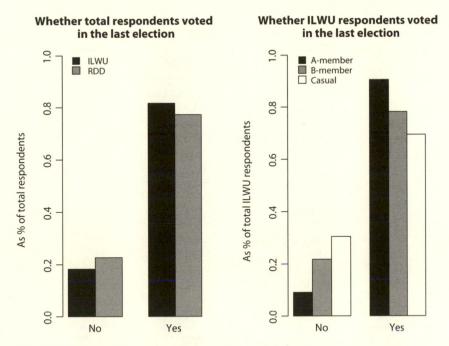

Figure 7.10: Distribution of self-reported voting behavior

we are making about the ILWU in particular. We fit additional models to gain some insight here.

To address the first issue, we use the following question from our survey: "Thinking about your family (mom, dad, uncles, aunts, and grandparents), have any members of your family been a member of a labor union?" Out of 557 RDD respondents who answered this question, 58 percent of respondents report having a family member in a union. This question partially addresses the possibility that people who come from union families may be both more likely to become ILWU members and to have systematically different political opinions and behaviors. The question has an obvious drawback that prevented us from including it in the initial analysis: we have no way of knowing whether the respondent's family member(s) joined unions before or after the respondent herself joined the ILWU. That is, we do not know if this is a "pre-treatment" covariate. We also do not know if the respondent was raised in a union family (parents or grandparents in a union) as opposed to having children or nieces/nephews in a union (or both). Nevertheless, we repeated the analysis but included this variable in both the matching pre-processing model and the analysis of the matched data.

TABLE 7.5: Logistic regression on self-reported
voter turnout, imputed and matched data

	$\hat{\beta}$ (SE)
Intercept	**-3.95** (1.16)
ILWU affiliate	-0.33 (0.26)
ILWU * Class A	**0.99** (0.30)
ILWU * Class B	0.34 (0.30)
White	**0.49** (0.24)
Hispanic	0.01 (0.36)
Female	**-0.64** (0.28)
Seattle	-0.56 (0.34)
Tacoma	-0.18 (0.34)
Age	**0.13** (0.05)
Age squared	-0.00 (0.00)
Education level	**0.44** (0.09)
Survey date	0.00 (0.00)
Midterm 2006	0.41 (0.45)
Presidential 2008	-0.59 (0.63)
Midterm 2010	-0.23 (0.36)
N =	892
AIC	747

Note: Coefficients with *p*-values ≤ 0.05 are indicated in bold. Reference category for geographic area is Los Angeles/Long Beach. Reference category for race includes Asian Americans, African Americans, Pacific Islanders, and those that self-identified as "other."

Results for the trade and NAFTA questions as well as all other robustness results described here are available from the online resources associated with this book.[20] Results for the imports restriction question are nearly identical to those reported in table 7.2. Importantly, the "union family member" variable is not a significant predictor of attitudes to import restrictions in the new model. Turning to the NAFTA question, the patterns of sign and significance described in table 7.3 remain after matching and conditioning on the "union family member" variable. In this instance those coming from a union family are significantly less likely to express confidence in NAFTA.

To address the "union effect" issue we take advantage of the following question from our survey: "Have you ever been a member of a labor

[20] Available at http://depts.washington.edu/ilwu/.

union?" Out of 600 RDD respondents who answered this question, 46 percent report having ever been a member of a union. We cannot match on this variable since all ILWU members will obviously answer "yes." We therefore match only using the subset of RDD respondents that report belonging to a union and then redo the parametric analysis. Detailed results are available online, but under this specification, "ILWU effect" remains for both the "import restrictions" and NAFTA questions. We find this striking, in part because non-ILWU union members are likely to find increased trade more threatening to their jobs security than the ILWU.

We omit results tables for the behavior variables analyzed earlier, but, again, results are quite similar. For both the political protest variable and the political contribution variable, our conclusions are unchanged regardless of whether we include "union family member" in the models, match only on union members, or both. The union family member is also significant in both of these models, suggesting that being in a union family further encourages these political activities. Not surprisingly, in the voting models, where we initially found no effective difference between ILWU and RDD respondents, we again find no difference between the two in the re-analysis, though Class-A affiliates are more likely to vote.

Conclusion

Do unions affect the political opinions of their members? Our study presents compelling evidence that they can. We examined the puzzling case of the ILWU, a union that has taken strong and consistent stances against a variety of trade-expanding policies and international agreements even though the union's membership appears likely to benefit from these agreements, at least in the short term. We linked the union's stance on these agreements to their long-standing and deeply ingrained organizational principle that "an injury to one is an injury to all." For decades the union leadership has consistently reinforced how the members have a community of fate with working people the world over, how their interests are bound together. The ILWU's trade position is a costly demonstration of its organizational commitments.

We then turned to an examination of the opinion of the rank and file in three of the ILWU's main locals. Using recently developed matching techniques, we compared ILWU members of varying levels of seniority to otherwise similar non-members. We found consistent evidence that ILWU members were more likely to have crystallized opinions about trade policy and they were more likely to favor trade restrictions and oppose trade agreements like NAFTA. Those having the longest and most intense exposure to the union differed the most from their non-ILWU matches. Further investigation showed that this difference is not due to an age cohort effect but seems to be directly related to exposure to the union. These findings are not an artifact of coming from union families; it also appears that the ILWU effect, at least on trade preferences, is *not* simply a special case of a broader "union effect." We then looked at three other forms of political behavior and found that more senior ILWU members are more likely to have reported engaging in protest activity, giving to political campaigns, and voting.

A key limitation of this analysis is our inability to measure the persistence of the ILWU effect, especially among individuals who might leave the union for non-political reasons. Nonetheless, our findings provide evidence of the consistency and breadth of preference provocation in the ILWU while members are active in the union. And it appears the union influence spills over to other political behaviors.

Appendices

A7.1: MATCHING DIAGNOSTICS

The plot in figure 7.11 shows the standardized bias for each included covariate before matching and after matching. Standardized effect sizes are defined as the difference between the treatment and comparison group means, divided by the treatment group standard deviation. The standardized biases for all covariates and the distance measure between groups (as defined through the genetic matching algorithm) are all under 0.1 in the matched data.

In addition, the histogram in figure 7.12 shows the distribution of propensity scores—defined as the probability of receiving the treatment given the covariates—in both the matched and unmatched datasets for ILWU (treated) and RDD (control) respondents.

Finally, the jitter plot in figure 7.13 displays each observation in the matched and unmatched treatment and control groups. The size of each point is proportional to the weight given to that observation. We discard observations in both groups for which there was not a successful match.

A7.2: SURVEY APPENDIX

This appendix reports in detail the initial research methodology proposed and the ultimate procedures followed in administering our survey to members of the International Longshore and Warehouse Union (ILWU) and the RDD sample.

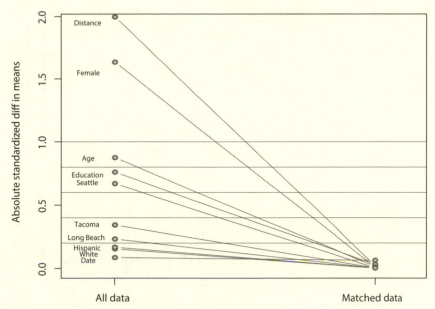

Figure 7.11: Standardized bias, pre- and post-matching

BACKGROUND

Longshore workers are grouped into four categories, based on seniority: casuals, "identified casuals," B, and A. The union and employer only track ID casuals, B, and A workers. The process of moving from ID casual to B includes 200 hours of longshore work and various trainings; some of this is waived for gender representation reasons.

The size of the labor force is decided by the Joint Port Labor Relations Committee, which includes both ILWU and PMA representatives. The JPLRC meets quarterly to review the size of the registration list in light of expected workload. The stated objective is to add small numbers of workers regularly rather than large additions infrequently. All ID casuals must pass the strength and agility test, physical, and drug test.

Following the rapid increase in shipping volumes through the West Coast ports in the late 1990s and early 2000s, the ILWU and PMA agreed to dramatically increase the size of the port labor force. For example, on July 29, 2004, the JCLRC agreed that LA/LB (Local 13 and 63) would add 3,000 identified casuals immediately. This number was later raised to 5,000. Similar though smaller expansions of the workforce were conducted in Seattle and Tacoma in 2006 and 2007, respectively.

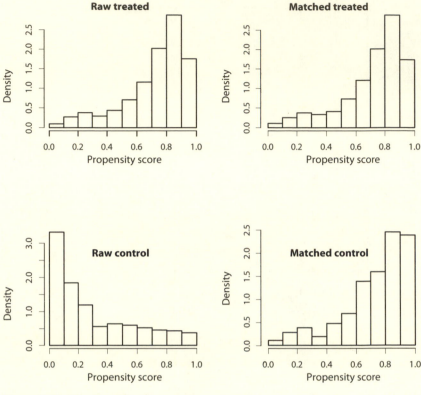

Figure 7.12: Distribution of propensity scores

To prevent possible lawsuits, primarily around gender imbalance issues, the ports decided to randomize the process by which they registered new identified casuals. For example, the Southern California selection procedure occurred as follows:

1. "Industry interest cards" were distributed, one to each A, B, and ID casual with at least 70 percent of the average working hours over the last six months. 500 interest cards were distributed to the PMA member companies.
2. Public notice was placed in *Los Angeles Times* on August 9, 2004 asking all those interested in working on the docks to submit postcards with name, address, and phone number to a P.O. box.
3. All interest cards and postcards postmarked by 8 August 11, 2004 were considered. Union officials estimate they received 375,000–500,000 cards. The accounting firm hired to manage the cards stopped counting at 150,000.

Distribution of propensity scores

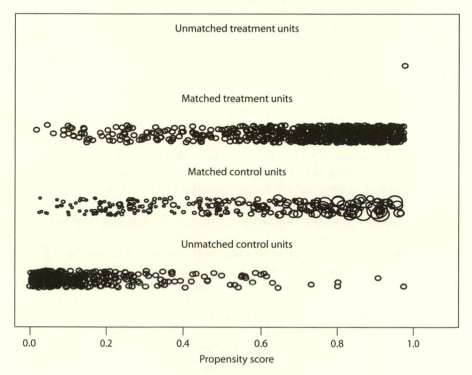

Figure 7.13: Visualizing matched and unmatched units by propensity score

4. Individuals submitting duplicates are disqualified (if known).
5. The area labor arbitrator conducted two drawings, with numerous observers from various community groups present. Other area labor arbitrators were also called down as additional observers.
   a. A number of the postcards were randomly selected from the postcard pool equal to the number of industry interest cards received.
   b. These two pools are then combined. The cards are drawn randomly and sequenced.
6. Individuals were then awarded ID casual status as their sequence number dictates.
7. Those selected in the second drawing but not eligible for immediate registration due to their sequence number are held back as a waiting list.

Those cards not selected are in sealed boxes and stored by the accounting firm. These cards are to be held for five years but are only to be opened by mutual consent of the ILWU and PMA.

Our initial research design focused on constructing a longitudinal survey consisting of a set of (1) existing ILWU Class-A members; (2) newly randomly selected Casuals; (3) those who put their names into the lottery for Casual status but were not selected; and (4) a non-longitudinal RDD sample from the same phone area codes in which the union members lived. In 2006, we secured permission from the ILWU leadership to conduct the survey. They required that we also secure the permission of the local union leaders in Seattle, Tacoma, and Los Angeles/Long Beach.

We began constructing our sampling design and contacting the locals with the longitudinal survey in mind. Because our research design was based on leveraging the randomized nature of union contact, we were less interested in securing a properly random sample of union members than in ensuring we had sufficient numbers of respondents at the different levels of seniority. Our union sample is ultimately a convenience sample.

We were ultimately unable to execute this design because the ILWU and PMA refused us access to the list of those not chosen under the lottery. Attempts to execute a longitudinal survey of ILWU members also failed. In order to protect the anonymity of the respondents, we relied on the ILWU to maintain the contact lists for the multiple intended waves of the longitudinal survey. This proved an overly burdensome task for ILWU support staff, making a longitudinal design infeasible. Furthermore, Los Angeles/Long Beach has annual leadership elections and regular turnover at the local leadership level. On two separate occasions a new leadership cadre was installed by the time we had secured permission to run our survey from their predecessors, implying substantial delay in the Southern California survey and undermining any possibility of coherent longitudinal "waves" across locals. Finally, the collapse in shipping volumes through the West Coast ports in 2008–2010 led many identified casuals to take work elsewhere, dropping off union rolls.

We therefore formally abandoned any attempt at a longitudinal design in 2010 and concentrated on generating as many survey respondents as possible, with the hope of using the RDD samples we had been gather periodically as the relevant comparison group.

RDD PHONE SURVEYS

We contracted with ISACorp (http://www.isacorp.com) to administer the telephone survey, both to the union and to generate an RDD sample. For the RDD sample they generated random phone numbers from area codes 206, 425, and 253 (Seattle and Tacoma). They also generated random phone numbers from telephone exchanges falling in San Pedro, California. Once they had numbers they made repeated attempts, often more than six, to contact someone.

There were two RDD calling waves in the Seattle-Tacoma region. The first ran between May 12, 2008 and June 6, 2008. They resolved 1,291 good phone numbers from which we received 274 completed surveys. The second wave ran from October 14, 2010 to November 1, 2010. In wave 2 they resolved 344 good phone numbers from which we received 151 completed surveys.

The single RDD calling wave in San Pedro was conducted between October 14, 2010 and November 1, 2010. They resolved 350 good phone numbers from which we received 150 completed surveys

UNION ROUND I PHONE SURVEY

Initial Sample Design and Target Ns in Seattle and Tacoma.

We first gained approval to run our surveys in Local 19 (Seattle) and Local 23 (Tacoma).

We aimed to sample a total of 200 dockworkers in each of the Seattle and Tacoma ILWU locals, for a grand total of 400 dockworkers.

Seattle has a total of 975 workers prior to the 2005 lottery, and added another 300–400 dockworkers in 2010–11. The 2008 breakdown is approximately 48%, 28%, 24% (A, B, ID).

Tacoma has a total of 1,269 workers after the 2005 lottery, with a breakdown of 42%, 30%, 38% (A, B, ID). Important to note: Tacoma has all the lottery winners as ID Casuals, with prior casuals moved up to B status after the lottery.

Accordingly, we sampled as follows from each local (available N in each pool in parentheses):

Seattle A: 40 (of 445); B: 40 (of 282); ID: 20 (of 248); Lottery: 100 (of ~350)

Tacoma A: 40 (of 533); B: 40 (of 382); ID (lottery): 120 (of 354)

The total target sample would contain 55% lottery winners, 20% each of As and Bs, and 5% ID casuals (non-lottery winners). In all, the target sample will represent 400 of the approximately 2,594 available dock workers (assuming 350 new recruits in Seattle after the lottery). This is an overall sampling rate of 15.4%.

Sampling Procedure

Upon granting approval, both local union presidents drafted letters describing their approval and the perceived benefit of our research to the union to be included in an opt-out packet distributed to each potential participant. As such, participation involved several levels of selection, detailed below:

1. Each union local generated a list of ID numbers for their members, separate from any identifying information and phone numbers.

2. A random drawing of the union generated IDs.
3. Each selected participant was contacted via letter by the local, allowing him or her to opt out of the study if they contacted the president's assistant within two weeks. The packet contained an IRB-approved study information sheet along with a letter from the president of each union local detailing his approval of the study and how it will be beneficial to the union and its membership.
4. Based on the letter, one of two actions occurred per each selected participant:
    a. *Opted In*: potential participants not contacting the union within two weeks were then part of the survey research firm's available phone pool. The local then provided phone numbers along with the IDs to us via email or fax. We then forwarded this information to the survey firm to begin calling.
    b. *Opted Out*: participants choosing not to participate were proportionately replaced via another random drawing from the list. Each local provided the IDs of the individuals, which were returned with replacements. Each of these newly selected individuals received an information packet and was granted a two-week window in which to opt out of the study.

Sampling

Within each of the list of opt-in members, the desired sample sizes were drawn from each pool of possible respondents without replacement. This was done separately for A's, B's, and ID Casuals.

Resampling

Each time new respondents need to be drawn from the pool, commonly due to opting out of the study or due to nonworking phone numbers, the IDs of these "dead" cases are added to the running list of already sampled cases to be removed from the available respondent pool. Once the non-active cases have been removed from the available respondent pool—allowing sampling without replacement—the original sampling procedures described above are employed with modifications for desired resample size for each group of A's, B's, or ID Casuals.

Based on the replacement sampling procedure used, we had a total resampling of 25 A's, 20 B's and 35 ID Casuals through July 2007. A total of 80 respondents out of a possible 629 sampled through July 2007, or 12.7%, have opted out of the study on the union side by notifying the local president's assistant (table 7.6).

The initial surveys, both RDD and to the union group, were conducted by phone by ISACorp.

TABLE 7.6: Resampling ILWU respondents by local and rank

Local	A's	B's	ID Casuals
23 (Tacoma)	17	13	35
19 (Seattle)	8	7	—

Round 1 Paper Survey

Additional phone survey administration to ILWU members was halted in early 2008 at the request of the ILWU leadership. 2008 was a contract negotiation year and the union was receiving membership complaints about the survey largely due to the fact that the survey firm's name was quite similar to that of a major shipping company (ISA and SSA).

To address the union's concerns about the telephone survey, we shifted to pencil-and-paper survey instruments when we resumed surveys in Locals 19 and 23 in late 2008. These surveys were administered in person by several members of the local's education committee at the morning shift pick-up in the union hiring hall.

We completed surveys of Local 23 in March 2008.

From November 2008 through February 2009, we received 27 paper surveys from casuals and B-status longshore workers in Local 19. Members of the research team administered these surveys during union educational events and shop steward meetings.

Round 2 Survey

In an attempt to conduct the second wave of the longitudinal survey, we re-opened survey administration in Local 23 (Tacoma) in July 2010 and Local 19 (Seattle) in November 2010. The delay was due to revived concerns among the local leadership about union confidentiality and the lack of Los Angeles/Long Beach participation. It became clear that the union staff would not be able to re-contact the previously surveyed individuals in a timely fashion, so we attempted to garner as many respondents as possible. All A's, B's, and casuals were, in principle, eligible to participate.

Local 23: In July 2010, members of the research team made a presentation at a union education event attended by nearly fifty members. They introduced the survey project. The Local 23 president encouraged membership to participate. Subsequent to that event the union education committee handed out surveys at several education events, before daily work registration, and at membership meetings through November 2010. All surveys were pencil-and-paper. Completed surveys were handed back to union administrative staff. Respondents were selected based on availability at meetings and union events. Only individuals wanting to participate did so. Participation was encouraged by raffling several pairs of college football tickets. We received a total of 100 responses during this effort.

Local 19: In October 2010, members of the research team approached the Local 19's (Seattle) Executive Board to renew survey administration (again, attempting to maintain the longitudinal design). We met resistance from some of the Local 19's Executive Board on the survey administration. This, combined with our inability to survey in LA/LB and the extended time period of the initial "wave," lead us to abandon the longitudinal design. We proposed administering the survey at stop work meetings at which our project was openly criticized. The Executive Board and the Local 19 membership ultimately voted that the survey could be administered, but we conjecture that that the controversy around the survey led to reduced participation.

In November 2010, members of the research team went to two union stop work meetings to solicit pencil-and-paper surveys from the A and B members in attendance. Surveys were distributed to the attendees and we left copies in the office for members and casuals to pick up. The surveys were handed out at the Local 19 union hall, but members were allowed to fill them out at home and return them to the hall.

Members of the research team went to the casual hall on several occasions during the morning dispatch in November 2010 to ask casuals to fill out surveys while they were waiting to be dispatched for work. Finally, the union put out a message reminding members to fill out the survey with the possibility of winning one of the football tickets we were raffling off.

There were approximately 100 people at both stop work meetings attended by the research team. In addition, we solicited another approximately 150 over the course of several weeks. We received a total of 59 responses during this effort. Approximately 30 of these responses came from those personally solicited by Amanda Clayton and Byron Haworth.

Local 13: We finally received permission to survey members in Los Angeles/Long Beach on August 26, 2010. All A's, B's, and casuals were eligible to participate.

There were two waves of attempts to solicit respondents at Local 13 (LA/LB). During the first wave (September 1–October 14), 5,000 fliers advertising the survey were distributed widely at the union business offices, dispatch hall, stop work meetings, and casual hall. Members were asked to come to the Memorial Hall for an event in which they would be served lunch and asked to complete the survey. The second attempt to solicit respondents involved mailing out fliers requesting members fill out the survey online. Fliers went out on June 15, 2011. The Local 13 administration sent a total of 6,500 fliers to the home addresses of all A's and B's. An additional 1,500 fliers were distributed at the casual dispatch hall. College football tickets were offered as raffle prizes for both of these attempts.

The first survey event took place on October 14, 2010 at the ILWU Local 13 Memorial Hall in San Pedro, California. A paper-and-pencil survey was administered. The second attempt to solicit responses was through an online survey (administered through the company, Survey Monkey). The online survey was available for members to fill out at their convenience during June–August 2011.

We received 93 paper-and-pencil surveys and 146 online responses.

CHAPTER 8

Signaling Solidarity?

Members of the ILWU observed May Day 2008 by refusing to appear for work, effectively closing down the ports from Bellingham, Washington to San Diego, California. The official union newspaper, the *Dispatcher*, claimed that this action was to protest what they considered to be an illegal, unjust, and costly war in Iraq. More than 10,000 longshore workers stayed away from work (Serjeant and Woodall 2008). The work stoppage was illegal under the union's contract, so workers lost a full shift's pay and the union was exposed to possible legal repercussions. In addition to closing the ports, many ILWU locals, including those in Seattle and Oakland, mounted major protest events that drew several thousand people up and down the West Coast.[1]

The *Los Angeles Times* editorial page expressed a cynical evaluation of the protests:

> More likely, it was a demonstration of union power directed at the Pacific Maritime Ass[ociatio]n. [PMA], the organization of cargo carriers, terminal operators and stevedore companies that oversees union contracts. The two sides later got past their biggest stumbling block, reaching agreement on the details of a healthcare plan. Still under discussion are such items as wages, pensions and safety procedures. The longshoremen would be wise not to try to push shippers too hard on these issues, given the stresses the industry faces in the current economy. ("Dockworkers Need a Deal" 2008)

The Pacific Maritime Association thought that "[The May Day strike] raised the question of whether this was an attempt to leverage contract negotiations" (Serjeant and Woodall 2008). For its part, the *Dispatcher* reported that "The May Day action had one important goal: to protest the war in Iraq. But it also produced some unexpected benefits, including a powerful display of membership solidarity, extraordinary public

---

[1] The ILWU locals in Los Angeles/Long Beach also shut down the ports on May Day but did not march; they had just participated in the LA County Labor Federation's Hollywood to the Docks march two weeks prior. This march was meant to unify all the LA-area unions facing contract expirations in 2008.

support, and extensive positive media coverage" (Merriless et al. 2008). Ultimately, the union and PMA successfully negotiated a new contract—the first under the leadership of ILWU president Robert McEllrath—in which the union achieved many of its objectives while avoiding the industrial conflict that plagued the 2002 negotiations.

In 1949, the WWF called a union-wide stop work meeting to protest the Australian government's imprisonment of Communist activists on sedition charges and the imprisonment of one activist for criticizing the Australian Stevedoring Industry Commission (ASIC) on the floor of the arbitration court. The ASIC was the arbitration authority charged with issuing industrial relations awards for the WWF; the judge ordering the activist's imprisonment, Kirby, was also the head of the ASIC. In the press, Kirby appealed directly to the Sydney WWF rank and file to defy Healy's call for a work stoppage. In the event, the stop work meetings were held. In Sydney, all but ninety-seven workers stayed away from work (as discussed in chapter 6).

Defending his call to use the WWF's industrial power to make a political point, Healy argued before the WWF's Federal Council that political and industrial action are linked: "[W]hen the Federation calls for a stoppage of a particular kind . . . somebody squeals about the cost, not realizing that *the solidarity shown while the stoppage is on is of the utmost value when dealing with other matters*" (Noel Butlin Archives 1949, 20, emphasis added). Dutchy Young, another Federal Councilor, went on to say, ". . . there is no line between the industrial and politics" (Young 1986).

The *Los Angeles Times* conjectures that the ILWU's political demonstration produces some sort of advantage in subsequent contract negotiations; the WWF example and statements by the leadership seem consistent with this idea. If the *"LA Times* conjecture" is correct, then political mobilization could be self-reinforcing in the sense that it helps leaders continue to deliver good economic outcomes for the members. The hypothesis that unions mobilize politically because they benefit economically, while not in direct conflict with our core argument, differs in spirit and has the virtue of relative parsimony. In this chapter we take that hypothesis seriously.

Examining an instrumental account for behavior that, on its face, appears ideologically motivated is not meant to imply that leaders or union members do not have strong political and moral commitments. Quite the opposite in fact, since the signaling argument begs a number of additional questions: (1) why use political protest to signal? Why not preemptively raise strike funds, engage in solidarity strikes, or simply burn money? (2) even if there is signaling value to political mobilization, why would a union stop work over the Iraq War as opposed to any number of other issues? (3) if using political strikes is so valuable as a signaling device, why are they so rare? We contend that the factors we have already discussed—political commitments of union leaders and the organizational governance that supports political rents—matter for all three. In chapter 2 we argued that political mobilization around issues far from the members' immediate interests or reasons for joining the union begins as a way of compensating successful leaders who have broader political commitments. A key implication of the theory is that the union's expansion into political activities is only sustainable so long as the organization continues to deliver good economic outcomes for the members. In chapters 6 and 7 we showed how being asked to contribute to the union's political activities in the context of an industrially strong organization can in fact provoke some members into revising their beliefs about their political efficacy and possibly their political preferences more broadly. The combination of preference provocation, contingent consent among the members, and the governance rules and leadership rents that attract politically motivated leaders reproduce the organization's behavior through time.

To consider the alternative "*LA Times* conjecture," we propose what we believe to be the most plausible way in which political activism might be instrumentally useful to the union: political mobilization is a cost-effective way to signal *the employer* (or its agent) about some relevant union attribute so as to derive benefit at the bargaining table. We develop testable hypotheses using insights from previously developed models of repeated bargaining and adverse selection and then examine the extent to which this approach helps us understand political strikes beyond the May Day example above.

We look at data from both the ILWU and WWF. For the ILWU we deploy a new, original dataset on ILWU work stoppages over the post-War period. In the ILWU case we find some evidence that the timing of large-scale political actions is consistent with a signaling logic, but there are two important caveats. First, this relationship is only observable in the data after the union suffers its first major industrial setback, a shock to its reputation of internal solidarity. Prior to that point, the union's use of industrial power for political ends shows no consistent relationship with the bargaining calendar. Second, given our data limitations, we are unable to demonstrate whether the ILWU's political mobilizations were, in fact, economically beneficial in terms of shorter bargaining rounds or "better" contracts, though we are able to make some simple comparisons between the economic outcomes for the ILWU and ILA.

We then compare our ILWU findings to an analysis of Australian government records of WWF strikes. This comparison is particularly important since the theoretical models in chapters 2 and 6 underplay the broader political-economic environment. Looking at union behavior when it comes to wage bargaining brings these contextual differences to the fore. The WWF inhabits a very different institutional environment and, as it turns out, uses its industrial power in the political arena in ways difficult to reconcile with the signaling model proposed. This mixed evidence and the cross-country differences lead us to conclude that it is possible for political mobilization to have some instrumental value, but that this is insufficient to explain the scope, timing, and volume of political mobilization in the activist unions we study. That said, the ability of the ILWU to continue to deploy its political capacity strategically may have helped it maintain its activist posture longer than the WWF.

Bargaining, Strikes, and Politics

Strikes have been extensively studied across the social sciences. Early work by economists focused on identifying important empirical relationships, including that between strike frequency and the business cycle. Advances in non-cooperative bargaining theory led to resurgence in the theoretical modeling of strikes, a literature we build on below. Political scientists and sociologists have looked at different aspects of strikes, such as the number of strikers mobilized, person-hours lost, and duration (Franzosi 1995) as well the extent to which strike powers are centralized in peak associations (Ahlquist 2010). Taken together, these features— frequency, duration, and mobilization—describe the "shape" of strike behavior, which is affected government partisanship, wage bargaining institutions, and other features of the political economy (Franzosi 1995). For example, strikes directed at government are typically infrequent and short in duration but involve large numbers of strikers compared to strikes against employers in a bargaining situation.

The notion of political strikes is an old, if ill-defined, one. An activist tradition dating back to Karl Marx and continuing with Rosa Luxemburg reflects on the role of strikes in revolutionary politics. Recently, scholarly interest in the political nature of strike activity is largely at the national level, either as "waves" of worker unrest that are presumably driven by some common underlying grievances or as mobilizations organized by union peak associations to protest and (hopefully) change government policies relevant to workers. In contrast, we focus on work stoppages at the level of the bargaining unit, typically the union, as opposed to national peak associations (see also Robertson 2004, 2007).

The relationship between unions' achievements in wage bargaining and their political commitments has received even less attention. A major exception is the work of Stepan-Norris and Zeitlin (1995, 2002). They find evidence that Communist-led and more internally democratic unions won better contracts than more conventional American unions during the CIO period. This important finding notwithstanding, we are left to speculate as to the mechanisms generating it.

But, as we showed in earlier chapters, not all unions or union leaders can effectively call political strikes. Union leaders with pre-existing reputations for radical political commitments are better able to elicit rank-and-file cooperation with their exhortations to join a protest, particularly when they are embedded in a union with appropriate governance institutions. Unions that have long avoided or been actively antagonistic to any actions not of immediate service to the material interest of members are less able to mobilize members for a political strike.

INFORMATION AND BARGAINING

It has long been recognized that if unions and employers are fully informed about each other's objectives and capabilities, and some profitable exchange exists, then there is no reason to resort to costly strikes. The union and employer have every incentive to come to terms without disrupting production. Under these assumptions, strikes must therefore be the result of irrational or mistaken actors (Hicks 1932). Current thinking about strikes—and the process of bargaining more generally—takes a different approach, one fundamentally related to the notion of incomplete information. If either or both of the two parties are uncertain about the relevant parameters, the bargaining process now becomes a means of communication; conflict, including strikes, can emerge in equilibrium both as a result of this asymmetric information and as a means for credibly transmitting information to the other party.

Economists commonly modeled strike duration using a structure in which the union makes repeated offers to the employer but is uncertain of the value the employer attaches to the workers' labor. The employer can accept or reject a settlement at each point in time, and delay is costly. In such a model, a strike, i.e., continued delay, is a way for the union to "price discriminate" between types of employers. Firms highly valuing the workers' skills will settle quickly, whereas those with a lower valuation will hold out longer. Empirical evidence for this model has been mixed, to put it kindly (Tracy 1986; Card 1990).

This standard modeling approach for strikes and bargaining is dissatisfying for several reasons. First, other forms of uncertainty beyond the employer's willingness to pay are plausible. As Kennan and Wilson (1993, 61–62) recognize, the ability for a union to sustain a strike requires an ability to maintain solidarity and morale. And, although strikes clearly occur over wage-and-benefits issues, they are often bound up in power struggles between the employer and the union over control of the shop floor or hiring. Many of the bitterest strikes have been over simple recognition of the union as a bargaining agent, not over wage increases. Uncertainty can just as easily be on the side of the employer: how "resolved" is the union to fight for what it values? How long will the rank and file maintain a united front with the leaders' policies and bargaining stance?

Second, most bargaining happens in the shadow of a possible strike and lockout, not in the midst of one. Powell (1996) investigates bargaining under incomplete information when the parties have the ability to exercise an outside option in addition to accepting the offer on the table or continuing to negotiate. Even in an infinite-horizon, alternating-offers bargaining structure Powell ends up with bargaining "shutdown" in which the dissatisfied party either accepts an offer or goes on strike at her first available opportunity. While information asymmetry can generate strikes in equilibrium, "its limited ability to explain delay, which is the simplest kind of inefficiency, should serve as a note of caution" (Powell 2002).[2] Any attempt to motivate signaling as a way to economize on costly bargaining delay in a one-shot bargaining situation relies on arbitrary assumptions about the extensive form, in particular who gets to make the first offer, and, therefore, who has some bargaining power.

POLITICAL STRIKES AS SIGNALS

We take a different approach, building on the fact that most wage bargaining relationships are repeated interactions. Specifically we build on insights in Calabuig and Olcina (2000), informally considering the possible implications of pre-bargaining signaling.[3] In their model, unions are assumed to vary in the extent to which they are internally solidaristic and resolved; the employer is uncertain about the union's strength.[4] Calabuig and Olcina (2000) are interested in characterizing the ability of weaker unions to mimic the wage demands of stronger unions and the corresponding extent to which the employer will take strikes over time in an effort to screen out the weaker types. They show that there is a (finite) upper bound on the number of strikes an employer is willing to take before conceding the union a reputation of strength. Strong unions must endure these strikes until the employer gives up—a cost of establishing its reputation for resoluteness. This result provides a formal motivation for the *LA Times* conjecture: given that the strong union will have to endure strikes while the employer attempts to determine the union's resoluteness, might it not try to send a credible but less costly signal?

---

[2] Leventoglu and Tarar (2008) alter the extensive form of the Powell (1996) model and are able to generate bargaining delay under some conditions

[3] The working paper versions of this chapter, available from the authors, presented a more formalized treatment.

[4] Calabuig and Olcina (2000) rely on "behavioural types." See Fudenberg and Levine (1989) and Schmidt (1993) results for "perturbed games."

Our contribution is to imagine that the combination of union governance institutions, leadership ability, and structural conditions that enable a union to mobilize the membership around political issues also reflect union resoluteness in wage bargaining. For example, politically radical union leaders like the ILWU's Harry Bridges repeatedly justify the union's involvement in politics by linking political causes with the union's industrial power. We are not assuming that all strong unions can signal; rather, we are saying that unions who can effectively mount political strikes are by definition strong. Unionists that have already built a solidaristic organization and expanded the organizational scope to include politics may be able to use this ability to time their political actions so as to signal their strength to employers without enduring as many industrial strikes. Political actions may be used as costly demonstrations of the union's solidarity that employers ignore to their own detriment. To the extent that political action improves average negotiated outcomes, political mobilization may become self-reinforcing.

The existence of any signaling relies on several important substantive assumptions: first, the union type (internal solidarity, resoluteness) is not directly observable. Second, resoluteness or solidarity correlates with the ability of the union to mount a symbolic political action. Third, there is always something worth protesting; the union can always send a signal if it so desires. Fourth, agreements (contracts) are enforceable ex post.

The theory of games under incomplete information also provides general logical constraints on when signaling would be profitable. First, we should have some reason to believe the employer is uncertain about the union's level of resolve. It must also be the case that the signaling benefit of political action outweighs the costs. On the other hand, for political action to be informative, the costs to mounting a political strike must be sufficiently steep that a weaker "type" would not want to mimic.

Political strikes are, of course, only one way in which unions might try to signal resolve or internal solidarity to employers. Unions might preemptively take up a collection for a strike fund. Union negotiators might attempt to win strike authorization from the membership before or during the bargaining process, or try to win promises of solidaristic action from other unions. The IBT, ILWU, and WWF do all these things. For example, immediately prior to the expiration of their contract in 2002, the ILWU conducted two "solidarity barbeques" with the IBT and ILA, two organizations with which the ILWU has had historically tense relations. Nevertheless, political strikes have additional features. Since these actions are not directly and obviously related to the immediate self-interest of the members, the union may be sending the message, "See what we can turn out for political causes. Just imagine what we'll do if our livelihoods are actually on the line."

IMPLICATIONS

The incorporation of signaling into the repeated bargaining model yields two immediate observable implications. First, bargaining pairs in which the union has successfully signaled its type using political mobilization should end up in fewer large industrial disputes. Second, large industrial disputes should not occur in bargaining rounds following political strikes.

The Calabuig and Olcina (2000) model assumes that the union strength and resoluteness are fixed through time; once a reputation for resoluteness has been established, there will be no need to signal (or strike) at all. It is more realistic to imagine that a union's resoluteness can fluctuate through time. When large shocks to the union occur—such as the election of a new leader, the introduction of a major new technology, the retirement or influx of a large cohort of members, or a change in the political-economic environment—the union's reputation may not be enough to maintain its bargaining power.

When events increase the uncertainty about the union's solidarity, the need to transmit information can induce more frequent signaling. This leads to two additional implications. First, events likely to cast doubt on the union's solidarity and resoluteness should increase the risk of both political strikes and industrial strikes. Second, because of the risk of a shock across periods, we should expect to see a higher likelihood of political work stoppages close to the onset of wage bargaining, especially when there has been a recent shock to the union.

Table 8.1 summarizes the empirical implications. We focus our empirical investigation on H8.2 and H8.4, though we have some evidence pertaining to H8.1 and H8.3.

TABLE 8.1: Hypotheses

H8.1	Bargaining pairs in which the union engages in political strikes will have fewer bargaining failures
H8.2	Probability of a bargaining failure is lower after observing a recent political strike
H8.3	External shocks will increase the risk of political strikes
H8.4	Political strikes are more likely near the onset of bargaining, especially after "reputation shocks"

The ILWU

Examining the relationship between bargaining and political strikes requires a level of detail not found in the standard work stoppages data from the U.S. Bureau of Labor Statistics and similar sources. Specifically, we need to know the timing of contract expiration at the level of the bargaining unit, the timing of work stoppages, and the purported cause or grievance for the work stoppage. We therefore focus on one particular bargaining pair: the ILWU and PMA. Since 1938 the ILWU has succeeded in putting all West Coast ports (and longshore locals) under a single contract, alleviating issues of contract timing across different union locals. Moreover, the ILWU and PMA keep detailed historical records and have generally shown a willingness to work with us in piecing together a dataset. Most important, the ILWU offers an example of a union that regularly produces large-scale actions on issues that appear to transcend narrow material interest, in line with the union's stated principle that "an injury to one is an injury to all." This activism has spanned eight decades, six different international presidents, and numerous political causes.

ILWU and ILA Compared

To assess H8.1 from the signaling model requires a comparison of the ILWU with a less resolute union or one unable to signal; the ILA offers a nice contrast. As described in chapter 3, the ILA has a long history of corruption and repeated industrial disputes. Nevertheless, we were unable to uncover any evidence of ILA involvement in a significant political protest or mobilization at any time since the 1940s, although the ILA website emphasizes that it boycotted Soviet shipping following the 1979 invasion of Afghanistan.

While an ILA-ILWU comparison is far from conclusive, the differences between them are suggestive. Consistent with H8.1 from the signaling model, the incidence of large-scale industrial conflict differs between them. Since 1948 there have been only two major bargaining failures on the West Coast—the 1971 strike and the 2002 lockout. In contrast, there were at least eight major ILA contractual strikes between 1959 and 1977, three of which were initiated by the rank and file and several of which centered on containerization (Jensen 1974; Monaco and Olsson 2004). In 2010, there were significant industrial disputes in the ports of Philadelphia and New York (Leach 2010). The bargaining situation can be quite tense; for example, in 2012 the ILA president issued a thinly veiled strike threat (Szakonyi and Bonney 2012). Beyond that, the ILA rank and file engaged in numerous wildcat strikes against the union leadership.

We can also say something about the industrial performance of the two unions. Table 8.2, reproduced from Waters (1993), compares the two

TABLE 8.2: ILA and ILWU compared

| | Avg. annual % change (1959–89) | |
	ILA	ILWU
Registered workers	–5.5	–2.0
Hours worked	–5.5	–1.8
Basic wage rate	6.3	6.5
Tons handled	1.5	6.7

Source: Waters 1993.

unions' relative performance on wages, hours, and membership during a period of significant technological upheaval. The ILWU was better at retaining membership and work opportunities while growing wages at roughly the same rate (from a higher base). By 1989, "the average actual wage income of ILWU members was greater at $30.84 per hour than for ILA members at $21.78" (Waters 1993, 269). West Coast employers also seem to have done better: labor productivity in West Coast ports is higher. The last row of table 8.2 indicates that shipping volumes grew slightly faster than wages for the ILWU-PMA but more slowly in the East. Waters (1993) estimates that by 1989, hourly labor costs to the PMA were $43.85, against $48.22 for the ILA's employers. This differential performance is difficult to explain away with simple references to shipping patterns. As figure 7.1 made clear, the major growth in Asia-West Coast shipping did not kick off until the 1990s, after Waters' estimates.

WORK STOPPAGES

The key variables for our study are indicators of significant work stoppages in the U.S. West Coast ports. Unfortunately there is no centralized, publicly available "official" record of port labor disputes for any significant length of time. In order to have a single consistent report of work stoppages, especially political, solidaristic, and other symbolic events, we collected the entire historical record of the ILWU newspaper, the *Dispatcher*. By relying on the union paper as our record of work stoppages, we recognize that we are likely not picking up all work stoppages. Localized events lasting a short time are less likely to be documented. Some work stoppages are illegal under the union contract and American labor law, exposing the union and its officers to legal sanction and fines. For example, in 1997 the ILWU members refused to work the cargo ship *Neptune Jade* that was loaded by non-union labor. The PMA sued individual members of the ILWU, including members of the leadership for

ILWU Local 10 (Oakland, California) for damages incurred during the picket, going so far as to subpoena union leaders and documents from the *Dispatcher* in order to identify the picketers by name (Stallone 1998; Price 1997).[5] The *Dispatcher* faces a clear incentive to ignore or downplay work stoppages that could cause legal problems for the ILWU. There is also the possibility that the union leadership, which exercises ultimate editorial control over the paper, reports only successful and authorized work stoppages.

Given these incentives, reports of stoppages appearing in the union paper are exactly those events that the union leadership wants to highlight. We have the added benefit of having the official union statement of the stoppage's purpose. The very fact that there are repeated mentions of these stoppages in the union paper, notwithstanding the risk of punitive action, implies that the union is trying to send some sort of message. The stoppages that are most likely to be consistent with the signaling model are exactly those loudly reported in the *Dispatcher*. We believe that the *Dispatcher* is a reasonably reliable source for data on the existence of symbolic work stoppages, though less so for purely industrial disputes, something we discuss further below.

We concentrate on the post-1948 period and consider only the longshore division of the ILWU. Many of the important covariates described below are only available after World War II. Also, prior to 1948, the ILWU and the Waterfront Employers' Association (WEA) were engaged in what can only be termed industrial warfare, with the ILWU attempting to expand and consolidate its control of work on the docks and the WEA repeatedly attempting to break the union. Prior to World War II, federally imposed arbitration awards, not contracts in the conventional sense, delimited working conditions. During World War II, the ILWU-WEA conflict was dormant due to the needs of the war effort, but it resurfaced in 1946 and then, crucially, in 1948. The 1948 strike was a disaster for the employers; as the strike dragged on, the WEA tempered its militant anti-union stance, named a more conciliatory negotiating team, and ultimately signed its first contract with the ILWU, ending the strike. This contract introduced the "instant arbitration" system that survives to the present and enables direct job action. There was not another coast-wide longshore industrial strike until 1971.

We aggregate the data to the quarterly level. In each quarter, we code a "1" if there is evidence of a work stoppage in that quarter and a "0" otherwise. The *Dispatcher* also reports the ports and union locals involved so we have a rough idea about the size and geographic scope of

---

[5] The attempted subpoena of *Dispatcher* records was denied and the PMA eventually dropped the suit.

the stoppage, though we have no consistent data on the number of participants or duration. We code any stoppage that involves two or more of the large West Coast ports[6] as "major," otherwise a stoppage is coded as "localized." Work stoppages are coded as "industrial" or "symbolic." Our default coding is "industrial"; in the absence of any declared political or solidaristic motivation for a work stoppage, we assume the work stoppage is an industrial grievance or dispute.

Symbolic strikes are further categorized as "political," "solidaristic," or "other." When there is evidence of a work stoppage in which (1) workers' representatives make no demand on employers; (2) there is no mention of an industrial grievance; and (3) there is some justification given in terms of political issues or objectives, broadly construed, we conclude that the union engaged in a political work stoppage in that quarter. Solidaristic work stoppages are ones in which the union stops work in order to respect the picket line of another union or in support of another striking union (e.g., the *Neptune Jade* dispute mentioned earlier). We consider these types of strikes to be analytically distinct from purely political work stoppages, as there is clearly an expectation of reciprocity when supporting another union currently on strike. That said, solidaristic striking may also serve to signal employers. It is worth noting the unions, such as the Teamsters, who resolutely avoid politics, also generally refuse to engage in sympathy actions. Finally, there are a handful of events that are clearly not industrial, overtly political, or solidaristic. For example, the union shut down the ports in 2001 to commemorate Harry Bridges' 100th birthday. Events of this sort we code as simply symbolic. Since 1948, we observe sixteen quarters in which there is some political work stoppage and thirty quarters where there is a symbolic event of some kind. We record forty quarters in which there are industrial work stoppages, mostly of a small scale as best we can tell. Only two of these (1971 and 2002) are full-fledged, coast-wide closings of all ports in the course of a strike (1971) or employer lockout (2002). In the analysis we focus on political strikes and make note of how findings differ if we expand the types of events to include these other symbolic acts.

COVARIATES

For H8.4 the key covariate of theoretical interest concerns the bargaining calendar. Ever since 1948, the ILWU has negotiated coastwise contracts approximately every three years, with contracts generally expiring in July. Based on reports in the Bureau of Labor Statistics *Current Wage Developments, Compensation and Working Conditions*, and from the contract documents themselves, we code the quarters in which contracts

---

[6] Los Angeles/Long Beach, Portland, San Francisco/Oakland, Tacoma, Seattle.

expired. From this we then calculate the number of quarters until the contract expires as our measure of the bargaining cycle. If the signaling logic outlined above holds, the coefficient on this variable should be negative in models predicting political strikes. We also construct an indicator variable that takes on 1 if the contract expires within the next 12 months and 0 otherwise; this coefficient should be positive if the union is using its political activities to improve its bargaining position.

Looking at potential shocks to the union's reputation (H8.3), there are several potentially relevant union-specific issues. First, union leaders might vary in their objectives, political and moral commitments, beliefs about the best union strategy, and ability to attract rank-and-file support. The election of a new president may increase the employer's uncertainty about the union's intentions and internal level of resolve. A new president may not initially be as credible when invoking the union's reputation for strength and political radicalism. Thus, the new president has a greater incentive to signal resolve to the employer, implying a greater probability of political strikes after the election of a new president, all else equal. We therefore construct a variable called "first contract." This variable takes on a "1" for all quarters after the election of a new president up to the first contract expiration on his watch. Every two or three years the ILWU holds its all-union convention, where policy is set and political resolutions passed. Union elections for International officers also occur in convention years (although not at the convention). The variable "convention year" is coded as "1" for the year leading up to a convention and "0" otherwise. While we have no a priori expectation about the directionality of this variable on the propensity for political strikes, coming up for election may impact leaders' strategic calculus when calling strikes.

After 1948, the union's position was secure, and there was little in the way of major industrial conflict for some time. The introduction of container shipping in the 1960s began to put pressure on the industry. The ILWU and PMA negotiated the landmark Mechanization and Modernization Agreement in 1960, but many within the union considered this agreement a bad deal. By 1971, the membership effectively demanded a strike over Bridges' expressed advocacy to the contrary. The 1971 strike was the union's only major industrial defeat and foreshadowed Bridges' retirement in 1977. To the extent there are reputational issues driving the need to signal, 1971 is a pivotal period. We will therefore explore whether the relationship between political mobilization and contract negotiations varied between the pre- and post-1971 periods.

The costs and benefits of calling political strikes may vary with the external political climate. A left-wing union like the ILWU may be more prone to strike when Republican policies are being implemented; they may be correspondingly less willing to embarrass a Democratic administration by shutting down the ports for political reasons.[7] We include indicator variables taking on "1" if the U.S. president is a Republican and "0" otherwise. We include a similar variable, GOP governors, that sum the number of Republican governors among California, Hawai'i, Oregon, and Washington State. Wars may also provide a reason to protest. We therefore code quarters in which the United States is at war (Korea, Vietnam, and the Gulf/Iraq wars). It may be the case that the union is trying to send political messages during major political campaigns or after a new president takes office, so we include an indicator for presidential election years.

There is substantial evidence that strike activity follows the business cycle. When times are good and labor markets tight, workers have greater bargaining leverage and are more prone to strikes (Ashenfelter and Johnson 1969; Farber 1978). We account for this in two ways. First, we track the business cycle in the shipping industry. Unfortunately, shipping volume data are not readily available for the major West Coast ports prior to 1974. So we use the annual percent change in industry value added for the transportation and warehousing industry, as reported by the U.S. Bureau of Economic Analysis. These data are only available at an annual level, so we apply the total yearly change to each quarter.[8] To account for the overall state of the job market we include the national unemployment rate.[9]

POLITICAL STRIKES AND THE BARGAINING CALENDAR

We turn first to the probability of a political strike, examining H8.4. We fit logistic regression models to a response variable coded as "1" if there was a political strike in a particular quarter and "0" otherwise. The models include quarterly fixed effects[10] and, since there may be temporal dependence, all models were fit with cubic orthogonal polynomials in

---

[7] However, it is unclear the extent to which the ILWU has any particular affinity for Democratic administrations. The ILWU refused to load ships taking scrap iron to Japan under FDR, supported Henry Wallace in the 1948 presidential election, and marched against the WTO ministerial in Seattle under Clinton.

[8] While this obviously overstates the quarterly changes, we are merely interested in characterizing whether times in the industry are good or bad, which this strategy accomplishes. Linear interpolation would be problematic due to the highly seasonal nature of the shipping industry. This seasonality has itself changed over time as trade with Asia has become increasingly important.

[9] State-level unemployment data are not available until 1976.

[10] It is well known that logit models are inconsistent when including fixed effects in short panels. In this case we have sufficient panel length (61 observations per quarter) to obviate this problem. In any event, key results are substantively unchanged when omitting the quarterly effects, though model performance degrades.

TABLE 8.3: Logit models of political strikes

	Model 1	Model 2	Model 3	Model 4	Model 5	Model 6
Post-'71 strike		**5.93**	**9.32**	**7.21**		
		(2.50)	(3.86)	(2.66)		
Contract year	0.84	1.41	2.15			
	(0.59)	(1.35)	(1.87)			
Time to new contract				**−0.26**	0.00	**−0.26**
				(0.10)	(0.07)	(0.11)
Post-'71 strike × contract year		**3.37**	**4.58**			
		(1.60)	(2.28)			
Convention year	0.70	0.90	1.24	**1.50**	0.25	**1.60**
	(0.58)	(0.66)	(0.72)	(0.71)	(0.85)	(0.78)
Unemployment	−0.23	**−0.68**	**−1.54**	**−0.67**	−0.34	−0.55
	(0.26)	(0.30)	(0.57)	(0.30)	(0.40)	(0.33)
First contract			0.16			
			(1.23)			
Density			0.30			
			(0.32)			
Δ Industry VA			0.19			
			(0.13)			
Growth			-0.31			
			(0.19)			
GOP governors			0.45			
			(0.62)			
GOP president			0.01			
			(0.86)			
Presidential election year			−0.02			
			(0.74)			
War			**−3.10**			
			(1.47)			
N	244	244	244	244	109	159
AIC	132.84	121.24	127.25	116.79	54.09	81.76
Time period	1948–2008	1948–2008	1948–2008	1948–2008	1948–1971	1972–2008

Standard errors in parentheses. Bolded estimate implies $p < 0.05$. Intercept, quarterly effects, quadratic year, and cubic event time polynomials estimated but not reported.

event time (Carter and Signorino 2010) as well as a quadratic polynomial in the calendar year. Deviance residuals exhibited no serial correlation.

Table 8.3 reports results. Models 1–4 are fit to the entire time period, 1948–2008. Models 1, 2, and 4 use only the covariates that consistently demonstrated predictive power across a variety of specifications. Model 3 adds a slate of additional covariates to demonstrate that our conclusions are not sensitive to their inclusion.

In model 1 we make no attempt to address the "reputation shocks" of the early 1970s. This model performs poorly and we see little evidence consistent with the signaling logic over the entire time frame. Results are dramatically different, however, when we compare union behavior before and after the 1971 strike. Model 2 displays the basic pattern reinforced across the other specifications. In this model we introduce a dummy variable indicating periods after the settlement of the 1971 strike and interact it with the contract-timing variable.[11] We find evidence that political strikes are more likely closer to contract expiration, but only after the union's stalemate in the 1971 strike. Among the other covariates, the only consistent predictor of political strikes is the unemployment rate, which suppresses work stoppages, as expected. Not surprisingly, model 2 is preferable to model 1, as the AIC indicates.

Models 3 and 4 represent alternate specifications. Model 3 includes all the covariates described in the previous subsection. Interestingly, none appear to have any systematic relationship with the ILWU's likelihood of mounting a political work stoppage; the negative coefficient on the war variable is driven by the long spell in which there is lack of reported political strikes in our dataset. This is largely, we believe, due to the negotiation and implementation of the M&M agreement, which happened to coincide almost exactly with the Vietnam War. The ILWU took a vigorous and public stance against the conflict in Vietnam, but did not report politically motivated work stoppages during this period. The first contract negotiated by a new ILWU president is signed in the expected direction but is insignificant. Model 4 replaces the contract year indicator with the continuous time-until-expiration variable. Using the more granular measure of contract timing obviated the need for the time period interaction.[12] Again, however, we see a strong relationship between the bargaining calendar and the union's self-reporting of political mobilization while the overall risk of political stoppages is elevated after the 1971 strike.

The implied size of these differences on the relative risk of a political stoppage is large. Using estimates from model 4 and holding all other covariate samples at mean values we see that the risk of a political strike in the quarter prior to contract expiration is about six times greater than one in which contract negotiations are two years in the future. Nevertheless, this risk increases dramatically after the 1971 strike. The risk of a

---

[11] No other variables showed evidence of a conditional relationship with political strike occurrence.

[12] Likelihood ratio tests provided no evidence that an interactive version of model 4 is preferred to the one presented here.

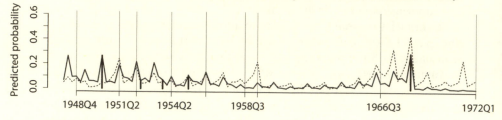

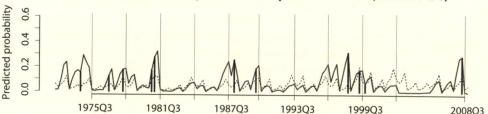

Figure 8.1: The negotiating calendar has little bearing on political strikes prior to the 1971–72 strike, but in later years the two are closely related

political strike in the quarter before contract expiration is more than 200 times greater after the 1971 strike than before.[13]

To better see the distinction between the pre- and post-1971 periods, models 5 and 6 are fit to the two periods separately.[14] The contract calendar, convention/election, and unemployment variables show strong predictive ability, but only in the post-1971 period. To visualize the substantive implications of these relationships, the panels of figure 8.1 display the political strike behavior of the ILWU during the pre-1971 (top) and post-1971 (bottom) periods. Light vertical lines represent contract expirations. Dark vertical segments depict political work stoppages with height proportional to the predicted probability of a political strike in that quarter as taken from model 5 (top) and model 6 (bottom). The solid curve in the background plots the predicted probabilities for each quarter, while the broken line plots predicted probabilities from model 1 as a point of reference. The plot illustrates how the bargaining calendar

---

[13] All these risk ratios are distinguishable from the null of no relationship at the 95% level or better.

[14] Due to perfect separation issues, models 5 and 6 were fit as Bayesian models with diffuse normal priors over the regression parameters.

became much more regularized after the 1971 strike. Politically motivated work stoppages reported in the *Dispatcher* clearly cluster nearer the end of contract periods in the later window but show little relationship in the earlier period, a fact picked up in Model 6 and clearly absent from model 1.

We might wonder whether 1971 appropriately identifies the shock to the union's reputation. Two other specific possibilities seem plausible: the retirement of Harry Bridges in 1977 and Ronald Reagan's firing of striking air traffic controllers in August 1981. We evaluate these possibilities using simple Chow tests for "structural breaks" in the series at 1972Q2, 1977Q3, and 1981Q3 on linear probability models corresponding to models 2, 3, and 4. We are able to reject the null of no structural break at 1972Q2 at $p < 0.02$ regardless of which measure of negotiation timing we use and whether we include the slate of covariates. We find no evidence against the null at either 1977Q3 or 1981Q3, increasing our confidence that the 1971 strike represented a significant shift in the union's perceived strength. No similar evidence points to Bridges' retirement or the PATCO strike as important in this regard.

More systematically, let θ designate the quarter such that the dummy variable $I(\theta) = 0$ in each period prior to θ and 1 thereafter. We fit models with the same covariates as in model 4, but replaced the post-1971 strike dummy with $I(\theta)$, interacted $I(\theta)$ with all non-time trend regressors and then let θ vary from 1950Q1 to 2006Q4. Figure 8.2 plots the model's log likelihood as a function of θ. It is clear that there is a significant change in the series in the quarters following the 1971 strike, as identified by the grey shaded region.[15] But more interestingly, the spike in value of θ that defines the change in "bargaining regime" occurs exactly between the end of the 1971 strike and the ILWU's political strike to protest the Pinochet coup in Chile. In substantive terms, the shift in bargaining regimes appears to coincide with the poor outcome of the 1971 strike, but the union's 1974 political mobilization effectively signals union strength. The difference between the post-1971, pre-Chilean strike period and other plausible shocks to the union's reputation described in the previous paragraph are clearly visible in the plot.

We also conducted all this analysis using solidaristic strikes, all symbolic strikes, major (multiple large port) symbolic and major political strikes as the response variables. We found similar but considerably weaker relationships between the bargaining calendar and solidaristic strikes, but no relationship for the convention year variable. Looking at symbolic work stoppages, findings were quite similar to those reported

---

[15] Substantive conclusions are unchanged from those based on results in table 8.3 if we alter the dummy in the reported models to any value in the 1972Q2:1974Q4 interval.

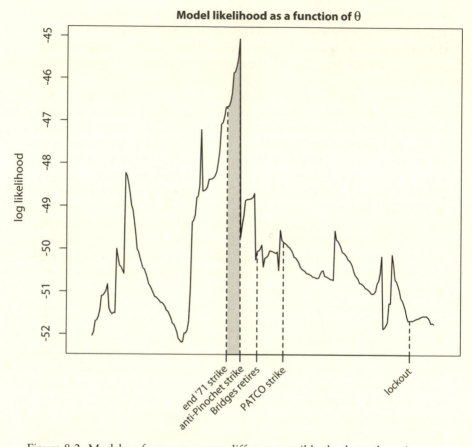

Figure 8.2: Model performance across different possible shocks to the union reputation. The immediate aftermath of the 1971 strike is clearly visible

above, although the magnitude of the contract variables was attenuated. But when we look at "major" symbolic and, especially political work stoppages, the relationship becomes much stronger for the contract calendar, convention year, and unemployment variables. We interpret these findings as reflecting the fact that the union has significantly less discretion in choosing when to act in solidarity with another union; the other union must be involved in a strike and choose to call on the ILWU. Political strikes and, to a lesser extent, other symbolic actions, however, are completely under the ILWU's control. Findings here demonstrate that there is a qualitative difference between political work stoppages and other types of "symbolic" action that could make politically motivated job actions particularly useful for signaling purposes.

The evidence thus far is consistent with H8.3 and partially so with H8.4, but features of the pre-1971 period deserve explanation. First, if political strikes are useful signals, why were there any political strikes prior to 1971? Between the 1948 and 1971 strikes, the union's internal solidarity was well known; there is little reason to believe that there was significant asymmetric information between the union and the PMA about the union's resoluteness. The political work stoppages in that period were therefore solely political statements. So were subsequent political stoppages, made possible by a long tradition of union commitment to social and political causes, a tradition maintained after Bridges left office. However, it seems that technological change, in part a cause of the 1971 strike, affected the PMA's perceptions of the ILWU's relative strength. Subsequent ILWU political mobilization, while consistent with the organization's stated principles, is also consistent with what we might expect if the union is sending a message to employers. We conjecture that the union's organizational mechanisms for involving itself in political affairs may be self-sustaining in part *because* it ends up having instrumental value for the members in terms of improved or more efficient bargaining outcomes.

Second, why do the data show a long gap in political strikes in the late 1950s and 1960s, a period of much wider upheaval?[16] This was exactly the period when higher barriers to political action were erected. The 1947 enactment of Taft-Hartley and consequent contract terms made it more difficult for the union to halt work except under highly specified industrial conditions. During the 1950s, the union was heavily engaged in combating federal government initiatives designed to screen workers off the dock for their Communist political affiliations. Through the 1960s, the union was involved in ongoing negotiation and implementation of an agreement on how to share the gains associated with the introduction of containerized shipping. In short, large-scale political stoppages took a back seat to protecting the union. Still, the union was hardly quiet. Members and locals engaged in demonstrations, passed resolutions at conventions, and refused to load individual ships for political causes that included the Korean War, apartheid in South Africa, the war in Vietnam, and the civil rights movement. Given the increased costs of political action, the union's existing reputation for strength, and the need to defend the union against political and technological incursions on its prerogatives, the ILWU membership expressed its political commitments in more localized ways during this period.

---

[16] The 1968 stoppage was called to protest the assassination of Martin Luther King, Jr.

POLITICAL AND INDUSTRIAL STRIKES

Is there any evidence for the key hypothesis that political strikes affect the likelihood of subsequent bargaining failures resulting in industrial disputes (H8.1 and H8.2)? The 1971 strike and 2002 lockout are the only instances in our dataset of bargaining breaking down into coast-wide industrial conflict. This small number is consistent with the notion that symbolic work stoppages prevent major industrial conflict from emerging. Also consistent with H8.2, there were no political or other symbolic strikes in our dataset in the three quarters leading up to either the 1971 or 2002 negotiating round; thus there is no evidence that bargaining broke down in the aftermath of a political work stoppage. We might also expect the union to be more willing to signal the employer in the contract rounds that immediately follow a major industrial dispute. It turns out that this did occur. In 1975, the bargaining round immediately following the 1971 strike, there was a major political stoppage, the anti-Pinochet action described above, four quarters prior to contract expiration. In the introduction to this chapter we discussed the May Day work stoppage in the run-up to the 2008 bargaining round.

We explored this further using the many smaller work stoppages reported in the *Dispatcher* that we have default-coded as "industrial." We again fit logistic regression models with these industrial work stoppages as the outcome. The key covariate from a theoretical perspective is our indicators of political work stoppages in the same quarter or the previous two; other covariates, including fixed effects and time polynomials, are as reported in model 4. We omit results tables, but, in general, the models were not good predictors of industrial stoppages.[17] We never found any evidence that lagged political strikes affect the likelihood of industrial work stoppages. Many of these smaller-scale stoppages appear to be over questions of safety; we conjecture that the union paper is reporting them to highlight safety risks for the members and to show evidence of the union actively intervening in questions of safety.

Consistent with a signaling explanation for the timing of political work stoppages, we observe that there were no major coast-wide bargaining failures in the quarters after political (or other symbolic) work stoppages. We do see political strikes preceding bargaining in the two negotiation rounds immediately following the major ILWU-PMA industrial disputes. Nevertheless, *Dispatcher* reporting on non-symbolic work stoppages provides no additional evidence that political strikes depress the likelihood of reported smaller-scale industrial disputes.

---

[17] Analysis of deviance (χ^2) tests were unable to reject the hypothesis that the null (intercept-only) model is preferred to any model including additional covariates.

The WWF

Examining the WWF provides a nice contrast with the ILWU while also letting us take advantage of more systematic Australian government data collection on work stoppages. However, the distinctive institutional environment of the unions complicates the comparison. Australian wage bargaining institutions differ significantly from those in the United States, the Australian government is more explicitly involved in industrial relations on the waterfront, and the relationships between labor unions and political parties are substantially more formal and explicit than in the United States. Any attempt to use the union's political actions as a signal in a bargaining situation with employers is therefore substantially more complex given that third parties can intervene. We have little reason to expect that our findings in the ILWU, with its direct and repeated bargaining relationship with the PMA, will hold for the WWF.

On the Australian waterfront, special industrial relations tribunals, supplementary negotiation, and bargaining outside the arbitration system interact to set wages and working conditions. The Australian Industrial Relations Commission, in place since 1904 (albeit with reforms and name changes over times), is specifically tasked with forestalling and mitigating industrial conflict (Hamilton 1991). Arbitration requires employers and unions to keep detailed information to present to the court to make or defend their cases for changes in wages or working conditions. A tribunal then hands down a formal finding in the form of an "award." As noted in chapter 4, the process is often costly and time-consuming and gives unions recourse only via protest or illegal work stoppages. There is no membership vote on the award, although there is often considerable membership input into the log of claims that forms the basis of the union's wage case.

The Australian federal and state governments play a bigger role in wage bargaining than in the United States (Deery and Plowman 1991) while the Australian labor movement plays a substantially more formal and explicit role in partisan politics that in the United States (Ahlquist 2011). In addition to its appointment of the members of the arbitration court, the government has seen fit to intervene quite directly in wage bargaining and industrial relations on the waterfront on several occasions. Indeed, by far the biggest work stoppage by the WWF was not against employers but against the Menzies government's 1954 attempt to introduce non-union labor onto the waterfront via legislation. Another notable period of government-union involvement came in the 1980s when the Australian Labor Party (ALP) and the Australian Council of Trade Unions (ACTU) signed a formal Accord in which the ACTU (and member unions, including the WWF) agreed to more centralized bargaining and union wage restraint in exchange for a "social wage"—union-preferred social policies and an expansion of health and pension benefits (Singleton 1990; Ahlquist 2011). In the early 1990s the ALP government and the ACTU began to unwind the Accord in an attempt to decentralize wage bargaining.

From the beginning of our data, in 1951, until 1990, the WWF negotiated one nationwide award with Association of Employers of Waterside Labour (AEWL), which applied to all the branches. The new awards and contracts began on May 5 every even-numbered year. As part of the nationwide trend to decentralization of bargaining and the rise of so-called enterprise contracts, the government instituted the Waterfront Industry Reform Authority (WIRA) in 1990. WIRA moved bargaining from the industry to the enterprise level and shifted WWF members from a collective contract to individual contracts with each stevedoring company, resulting in more than sixty different agreements negotiated and administered separately. In the early 1990s, the WWF merged with the Seaman's union to form the MUA, and the AEWL dissolved, further solidifying the shift to individual contracts and altering the role and leverage of the union substantially. Therefore, we only analyze the pre-WIRA period when examining any possible relationship between contract timing and political work stoppages in the case of the WWF.

Because of the more bureaucratized nature of wage bargaining in Australia, we have the benefit of government arbitration records of work stoppages. Specifically we rely on the *Monthly Reports* and *Quarterly Reports* of the Australian Stevedoring Industry Association (1949–77) and the *Stevedoring Industry Disputes and Nature of Issues* reports from the Australian Department of Transport (1978–89). These sources report estimates of worker-hours lost to work stoppages on the waterfront by port. They also allocate work-hours lost to "political reasons" and "sympathy."[18] These sources provided no explicit coding rules and we have no reason to believe that they coincide with the rules we used in coding the *Dispatcher*. For example, Australian sources code the 1954 strike as "political"; this strike directly targeted government over an industrial issue before it. The WWF had every intention and desire to alter the Australian government's policy. The 1954 strike seems more closely related to a large strike by public sector workers than the ILWU's (and

---

[18] In some instances, particularly in the 1950s, sources did not report the rationale for port-level stoppages but did report total work-hours lost to stoppages by port and then reported national level work-hours lost to all stoppages and national level work-hours lost to political or solidaristic stoppages. In these cases we calculated the national-level percent of lost work-hours due to political stoppages and then used that proportion to estimate the port-by-port man-hours lost to political stoppages. Our conclusions are unchanged if we simply leave these observations out of the dataset.

WWF's) symbolic industrial actions for political ends. Unfortunately, we lack the ability to distinguish work-hours lost to symbolic political action from those lost to strikes against the Industrial Relations Commission, government policy, or legislation directly pertaining to the union's industrial position. Nevertheless, these data provide an opportunity to compare how unions deploy industrial power for political ends in different institutional environments.

As before, anything not coded as political or sympathy we treat as an industrial issue. Data are aggregated at the quarterly level. In figure 8.3 we display the distribution of work-hours lost to political strikes (on the log scale, with 1 added) for five important Australian ports over the 1950–90 period: Sydney, Melbourne, Brisbane, Newcastle, and Port Kembla. The distribution is clearly bimodal with a large spike at 0.

We capture this process using a hurdle negative binomial model. Our specification uses a logit model to describe the probability that we observe

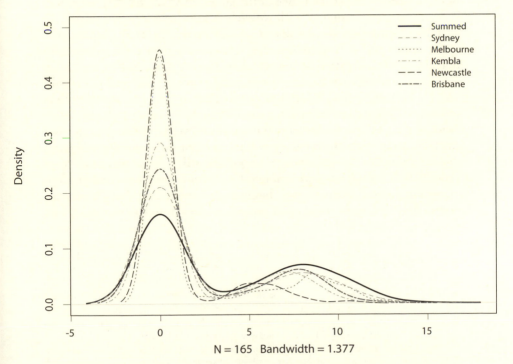

Figure 8.3: The distribution of man-hours lost to political strikes on the Australian docks, on the log scale (with a small constant added)

any political stoppage and then a truncated negative binomial model for the count of hours lost, conditional on observing a work stoppage. We use ψ to denote the vector of regression parameters for the hurdle process, while β is the vector of parameter estimates for the count process and ν is the shape parameter of the negative binomial distribution.

We begin by modeling the relationship between political strikes and the contract cycle.[19] To measure the contract cycle we include dummies for whether the contract expires in the current or subsequent quarter, respectively. We also include real GDP per capita growth from the Penn World Tables (Heston, Summers, and Aten 2006) as our business cycle indicator,[20] and indicators for the Accord period, ALP government, Australian federal elections, and the first contract under a new WWF general secretary. We interact the ALP government and election indicators to see if the WWF behaves differently during elections with an ALP incumbent compared to those with Coalition incumbents. In the count model we include a linear calendar time trend.[21] In the hurdle logit model we include cubic polynomials in event and calendar time. As noted, our data sources coded the 1954Q4 strike against the government's proposed Stevedoring Industry Act as a political work stoppage. This strike is one of the largest in WWF history. We report in footnotes when results differ if we exclude this quarter from analysis.

Table 8.4 reports the results of this analysis. The lower half of the table reports the ψ from the hurdle process, describing the probability that there was a political stoppage in any of the five ports in a quarter. The upper half reports the β from the negative binomial portion, describing the number of man-hours lost conditional on there being a political stoppage. Unlike our findings for the ILWU, we see that WWF political work stoppages are closely related to political events. While the electoral calendar on its own shows no systematic relationship with the probability of a political strike, we find that political strikes are bigger in election years *with a Labor Party incumbent*. Consistent with others (Beggs and Chapman 1987; Morris 1996; Chapman 1998), we find that the Accord period saw a lower probability of political strikes (lower half of the table)

---

[19] Interpretation of findings is unchanged if we include the (log) WWF membership as a covariate in the model or if we fit OLS models to work-hours lost (in the 5 ports discussed) per WWF member. We prefer the specification presented in table 8.3 because (1) WWF membership data include all ports, not just the five ports for which we have data; (2) including the membership data induces a loss of 17 observations; (3) work-hours lost per WWF member shows a pronounced bimodality. The OLS specification fails to capture this and, as a result, the business cycle and first contract effects we see in table 8.4.

[20] Australian unemployment data do not become available until 1960; we use real GDPpc growth to maximize the number of observations in the analysis.

[21] Based on the BIC, models with the linear trend were strongly preferred over models with quadratic and cubic polynomials in time.

TABLE 8.4: Hurdle negative binomial model for
work-hours lost to political strikes

Negative binomial model of work hours lost

	$\hat{\beta}$	$\hat{\sigma}_{\hat{\beta}}$
Contract expire$_t$	−0.09	0.68
Contract expire$_{t+1}$	−2.46	0.69
Growth	*0.10*	0.06
Accord	*−1.18*	0.70
ALP government	−0.77	0.53
Election	−0.98	0.85
ALP × Election	**3.04**	1.35
First contract	**1.85**	0.84
log ν	**−0.66**	0.16

Logit hurdle model of political strikes

	$\hat{\psi}$	$\hat{\sigma}_{\hat{\psi}}$
Contract expire $_t$	**−2.02**	0.76
Contract expire $_{t+1}$	*−1.20*	0.72
Growth	0.01	0.06
Accord	**−4.92**	1.75
ALP government	1.00	1.08
Election	−1.24	0.97
ALP × Election	−0.06	1.62
First contract	0.64	1.17
N =	160	
AIC	1651	

Bolded entries achieve $p < 0.05$; italics achieve $p < 0.1$.

Intercepts, linear calendar time trend (negative binomial), and cubic event time polynomials (logit) estimated but omitted.

with fewer work-hours lost (upper half). The size of political stoppages is pro-cyclical, but the probability of a political stoppage shows no relationship with macroeconomic growth performance.

WWF findings contrast starkly with those for the ILWU vis-à-vis signaling behavior: WWF political strikes were *less* likely and smaller in the quarters during and preceding the expiration of the WWF award, significantly so in the quarters preceding award expiration. While the existence of political stoppages is unrelated to the tenure of the WWF general secretary, we do find that political strikes are bigger under new leaders. We believe that the contrast between the ILWU and WWF is related to the stark institutional differences already discussed. WWF political strikes, as recorded in these data, are undertaken largely for political ends, often directly policy related, whereas in the ILWU large-scale political work stoppages have become more closely tied to the bargaining calendar.

We also examine the relationship between work-hours lost in political stoppages with those in industrial disputes. We again model this process using a hurdle negative binomial. We include the log of the work-hours lost in political stoppages in the previous quarter (+1). We experimented with several time polynomials as well as with the interaction term between the ALP government and elections. The time polynomial structure in table 8.5 reflects the specification most preferred on a BIC basis. The ALP-election interaction term never approached significance in any specification, so it is omitted.

We find that prior political strikes show no discernable relationship with either the likelihood of industrial stoppages or the size of the industrial dispute. That the "effect" of WWF political stoppages fails to conform to the *LA Times* conjecture is unsurprising, given our findings in table 8.4; nevertheless, the increased likelihood of subsequent industrial disputes remains a puzzle.

Industrial strikes do correlate with political events, though not in exactly the same ways as in table 8.4. Industrial stoppages are both less common and smaller in election years, but the partisanship of the incumbent shows no relation to industrial stoppages, either on its own or conditional on the electoral calendar. Industrial disputes also respond to the Accord process as expected: dispute size is significantly smaller under the Accord.

Although we know that the political activist commitments of the WWF are similar to those of the ILWU, we see evidence of the two unions using distinct logics in the use of political action. Using government-coded data describing WWF work stoppages, we see that the union's use of its industrial power, especially to make political statements, is strongly influenced by political opportunities, including election timing and the partisanship of the government. We see some indicators of a political logic to its activism but no evidence that WWF political stoppages follow the signaling logic we developed to describe the bargaining environment faced by the ILWU. The variation in institutional contexts appears to have real consequences for the strategic use of political action.

Conclusion

This chapter systematically explored an important alternative argument for explaining unions' expansion of their activities into politics. We explored the "*LA Times* conjecture" in which unions that have developed

TABLE 8.5: Hurdle negative binomial model for
work-hours lost to industrial strikes

Negative binomial model of work-hours lost

	$\hat{\beta}$	$\hat{\sigma}_{\hat{\beta}}$
Contract expire$_t$	**0.91**	0.28
Contract expire$_{t-1}$	0.43	0.26
log(Political Strike hours lost)$_{t-1}$	0.02	0.02
Growth	0.03	0.02
Accord	**−1.26**	0.61
ALP government	0.03	0.31
Election	**−1.06**	0.30
log ν	0.02	0.10

Logit hurdle model of industrial strikes

	$\hat{\psi}$	$\hat{\sigma}_{\hat{\psi}}$
Contract expire$_t$	−0.24	2.23
Contract expire$_{t-1}$	−1.10	1.50
log(Political Strike hours lost)$_{t-1}$	0.48	0.34
Growth	0.25	0.29
Accord	0.00	1.30
ALP government	−0.95	2.51
Election	**−3.41**	1.62
$N =$	160	
AIC	3311	

Bolded entries achieve $p < 0.05$.

Intercepts, linear calendar time trend (negative binomial), and cubic event time polynomials (logit) estimated but omitted.

the power to mount large-scale political protests can use this ability to improve their outcomes in bargaining with employers. We clarified the empirical expectations needed to test the argument. Examining the empirical evidence for both the ILWU and WWF, we found ambiguous results for the signaling logic. We presented empirical evidence using data from the ILWU-PMA bargaining pair from 1948–2008. We found that in the early post-War period, when the union had a militant leader and arguably had a reputation for strength emerging out of the 1948 strike, political strikes were unrelated to the bargaining calendar which was itself less regularized. But after the union's (and Bridges') first major industrial setback in 1971, the union's highly visible political actions became more tightly related to contract negotiations. When we tried to discern whether observed political strikes had any relationship with subsequent industrial work stoppages we found some evidence for a relationship. Neither of the major industrial disputes on the West Coast since 1948 occurred in the aftermath of a symbolic job action.

We then used a different data source to examine the WWF's strike behavior in a contrasting institutional environment, one in which the government inserts itself directly into industrial relations via legislation, the Australian Industrial Relations Commission, and direct bargaining with the union federation in the form of the Accord. Unsurprisingly we find that the WWF's reported use of political work stoppages in the five major ports for which we have data looks quite different from the ILWU. The WWF's actions seem to respond more readily to political events, including elections timing. The WWF's political work stoppages, as coded by others, appear to be serving a different purpose than in the ILWU.

The balance of evidence, then, points to the conclusion that the possible instrumental benefits of political action are insufficient to explain the existence of union mobilization around causes far from the immediate interests of the members. Rather, we interpret our findings as reinforcing our larger argument: to the extent there are possible strategic benefits for mounting political strikes during wage bargaining, these benefits can only accrue to organizations that have *already* built the governance institutions and selected leaders that can credibly mount such symbolic actions. The ILA is in a similar structural position as the ILWU and WWF yet it does neither. This suggests that the structural position of an organization is insufficient to account for an expansion of organizational scope to include politics. Organizational governance and the preferences and objectives of leaders interact with structural opportunities and constraints to enable or retard political mobilization.

Leaders with strong ideological commitments embedded in organizations with governance institutions that allow the rank and file to coordinate are necessary for effectively calling political strikes. But the model presented in earlier chapters predicts that this limits both the frequency and causes around which the union can mobilize. The organization's governance institutions delineate the issues around which the leader can call on the members while providing the members with the ability to evaluate the leader's demands. Leaders, however ideologically committed, must pick their battles carefully; their ability to extract political rents depends on their continued delivery of good economic outcomes.[22] Members will only tolerate mobilization up to a point. It may be that impending

---

[22] In conversations with the authors, one former ILWU leader referred to shutting down the docks as the "nuclear option."

contract negotiations provide a golden opportunity for unionists to serve both God and Mammon: unions with ideological commitments can use the signaling value of political strikes to make their political statements while also effectively serving the membership and perhaps attracting the participation of members who may not otherwise share the union's political stance.

The contrast between the ILWU and WWF shows that the political institutions in which the unions live have important effects on how unions choose to deploy the industrial strength to make political points. In the United States, striking and industrial action are heavily regulated; striking outside of specific negotiation periods is generally legally costly and secondary boycotts and sympathy strikes are generally prohibited under the Taft-Hartley Act. The ILWU has succeeded in negotiating (and defending) contract provisions—including monthly "stop work" union meetings and the right to respect the picket lines of others—that allow them some flexibility to use their industrial position to make political statements. Such contract provisions appear to be rare among American unions. The fact that the ILWU has fought to retain these contract provisions is an indication that the union values the ability to take political and solidaristic stands. Being able to consistently call upon the rank and file to contribute resources to symbolic political actions requires appropriate leadership embedded in a governance structure that allows members to develop common knowledge and the ability to coordinate. But this is not enough. Thus, while there appear to be some cases in which unions can leverage reputation for political militancy to affect negotiations with employers, this does not appear to be a general or sufficient rationale for understanding all union political mobilization.

Appendix

ALP government: =1 if Australian prime minister is a member of the Australian Labor Party

Industrial work stoppage: =1 if there was historical evidence (as discussed in the text) of any work stoppages not classified as "political," "solidaristic," or "symbolic"

Political work stoppage: =1 if there was historical evidence of a political work stoppage (as discussed in the text)

Contract expiration: =1 if the ILWU coast-wide longshore contract expires in that quarter and 0 otherwise (United States Bureau of Labor Statistics, N.d.a,N)

Time to contract expiration: Number of quarters until a coast-wide labor agreement between the ILWU and PMA expires

Contract year: =1 in the three quarters prior to the expiration of an ILWU-PMA coast-wide labor contract

Convention: =1 in years of an ILWU International Convention and election, taken from library microfilm records of convention proceedings and the *Dispatcher*

First contract: =1 in every quarter until the first contract expiration after a new ILWU president or WWF general secretary is installed

President: =1 if the U.S. president is a Republican and 0 otherwise

Real GDP per capita growth: annual real GDPpc growth rate, applied at the quarterly level, taken from the Penn World Tables

GOP governor: Sum of the number of Republican governors in office in each quarter among California, Hawai'i, Oregon, and Washington

Election year: =1 in quarters of calendar years in which U.S. presidential election/Australian Federal elections are held

% Δ Industry VA: Annual % change in industry value added in current dollars (United States Bureau of Economic Analysis, 2009)

Unemployment: U.S. national unemployment rate (Bureau of Labor Statistics 2009)

War: =1 if the United States was involved in each of the major foreign wars, respectively. Vietnam is dated from the coup against Diem.

CHAPTER 9

Conclusions and Implications

We have demonstrated how union membership can influence the kind and quality of political behavior. We have shown how some unions can repeatedly induce their members to act (or refrain from acting) on behalf of those outside the group. But our interest is not limited to unions. One reason for studying unions is that they face, in miniature, many of the same challenges and possibilities confronted by other stakeholder organizations, ranging from religious and nationalist groups to political parties to states and firms. Our investigation has implications for unions but also for the relationship among leadership, governance institutions, and behavior in those membership organizations where the costs of exit are high.

Although the transport sector unions we studied varied in their political commitments, they shared features that made it possible to test (and develop) our theory: a common position in the economy; heterogeneity in members' political beliefs; an organization whose principal goal is distinct from the political commitments some of them evoke; and, over time, increasing costs of exit from the unions. The last three in this list are also the scope conditions for extensions of our findings to other unions and other membership organizations. In addition, these conditions clarify what we do not attempt to explain: instances in which individuals self-select into an organization devoted to costly political ends, e.g., the Communist Party or a terrorist organization. Such individuals reveal strong political commitments and willingness to act on them by joining groups that share their commitments. Preference provocation is moot. The question of why they make additional sacrifices they did not initially expect to be asked to make is more relevant, and our model does perhaps offer insights on this issue.

Given these scope conditions, our next task is to assess the transportability of these concepts and claims. The most abstract formulation of the model emphasizes, first, the establishment of governance institutions, organizational principles, and leadership rents that made it possible to demand more of members and, second, reproduction of organizational scope and behavior over time by evoking contingent consent and provoking preferences. For the ILWU and the WWF/MUA, the specifications of these features include a cohort of ideological leaders at a pivotal moment in the union's history, leaders willing to sacrifice salary and governance autonomy in order to signal credibility and accountability; a highly participatory democracy enabling challenges to leadership, contingent consent, and political learning; and, finally, work and neighborhood institutions that create ties, networks, and interdependencies among members and with leaders that ensure reproduction of the organizational scope, in these cases an expansive community of fate. Other organizations may have functional alternatives for achieving credibility and accountability, for producing contingent consent and political learning, and for creating social ties and interdependencies.

Our theory and our data also reveal two preconditions for political activism. Leadership cohorts, at the least those that create the organizational governance institutions, begin with strong ideological priors. They must constantly demonstrate their ability to help members achieve material gains, which is, after all, the raison d'être of the union. Organizations that evoke political commitments have founding leaderships who solved crucial strategic problems for the organization while also possessing strong ideological principles. Further, organizations tend to select successive leaders who will act consistently with its governance institutions while also satisfying the group's objectives, be they votes, policy shifts, or pastoral care.

Although we cannot explore all possible kinds of organizations our theory might help illuminate, we will consider a few, before turning to some additional challenges to and implications of our claims.

Union Behavior

One immediate extension of the model is to unions outside the transport sector. Unions are important organizations in their own right, living at the nexus of politics and the market for human effort. At the macro-level, where union membership is widespread: proportional electoral institutions are more common (Cusack 1997; Boix 1999), Left and Social Democratic parties govern more frequently (Western 1997), social spending is greater, and economic redistribution is more profound (Bradley et al. 2003; Lee and Roemer 2005), particularly towards minority citizens (see, e.g., Card, Lemieux, and Riddell 2007; Agnone 2010). At the micro-level unions affect pay, working conditions, and opportunities for employment (see, e.g., Freeman and Medoff 1984; Rosenfeld 2006; Beramendi 2007; Freeman 2007). Where they are embedded in a broader set of institutions, unions play an important role in generating a highly skilled workforce (Hall and Soskice 2001; Iversen 2005; Mares 2006).

Unions also affect the quality of the polity. They influence political participation directly (Verba, Schlozman, and Brady 1995; Nagler and Leighley 2007; Rosenfeld 2010) and can affect civic engagement more indirectly by creating both the political knowledge and norms that encourage involvement (Abrams, Iverson, and Soskice 2010). Robert Putnam (2000) classified unions as secondary mass-based organizations that did not sufficiently engage membership to count as important sources of social capital. However, at least some unions—the ILWU and WWF/MUA among them—generate exactly the kinds of social networks and citizen obligations Putnam is so eager to encourage, and so do many unions in other parts of the world (e.g., Ross 1981; Seidman 1994; Korpi, O'Connor, and Olsen 1998; Murillo 2001; Levitsky 2003; Iversen 2005). While the ILWU and WWF may represent one tail of a continuum, especially within the U.S. context, unions can represent an enormous reservoir of economic and political resources enabling workers to simultaneously improve their economic situation and engage in collective action on behalf of a larger community of fate.

A concerted attack on unions' ability to attract and retain members is taking place among those advanced industrial polities where market competition is uncoordinated, that is, relatively unconstrained (Hall and Soskice 2001), unions are fragmented, and laissez-faire ideologies are most prevalent. Both Australia and the United States fit this description. In Australia, labor market reforms in the early 1990s instituted enterprise bargaining after nearly a decade of centralized wage setting and altered the union landscape profoundly. The Howard government went even further, passing legislation aimed at undermining union strength for the purported purpose of reducing so-called labor market rigidities. In the United States, there has been little change in federal law since the late 1950s. Nevertheless there have been effective and successful campaigns against unions throughout the country. The National Labor Relations Board (NLRB) has become hopelessly politicized (Moe 1985), to the point where, at the time of this writing, Congress and the president cannot even agree to staff it sufficiently to let it perform its tasks. In the absence of functioning labor market regulatory institutions, the number of union representation elections has plummeted (Farber and Western 2002). Employers routinely and increasingly rely on explicit and nominally illegal attacks on union workers and organizers (Levi 2003; Bronfenbrenner 2009). In January 2012, Indiana became the twenty-third "right to work" state by passing legislation removing a worker's obligation to contribute to the union that represents him in collective bargaining.

To counteract these attacks and arrest the decline of organized labor, there have been numerous calls for fundamental transformation in American and Australian unions toward a broader social justice/social movement orientation (Fletcher and Gapasin 2008; Tattersall 2010). But these calls ring hollow in the absence of an understanding of how this might occur and the organizational and structural constraints social movement unions face.

By holding leaders accountable and requiring the union to improve the well-being of its members, labor organizations generate a capacity to demand contributions and solidarity around issues that extend well beyond what serves the narrow interests of those immediately being served. Appropriate governance institutions can expand the community of fate. But this recipe does not apply to all unions: the unions that are both willing and able act on their political commitments can do so in no small part because of their pivotal position in the economy and international supply chains. The fact that dependence on transport sector workers remains high and that their actions can actually interrupt the flow of goods gives their unions an advantage, should they choose to use it, in reducing the cost and raising the symbolic value of political action. It is substantially harder to build a base of support among members when the very fight for survival has not yet been won.

Yet, the transport sector is not unique in its importance to the economy or in the survival of its unions. Extractive industries, the energy sector, parts of the public service, and, in this "just-in-time" economy, workers on the assembly lines of high-demand goods are in similarly strategic positions in the global economy. They may have to make concessions during economic downturns, but they can still be successful in protecting, even improving, the lot of their members. They can certainly build and sustain a community of fate, but how broad it will be depends on what leadership demands, how it governs, and whether members consent. The development of the union may be a consequence of structural and political factors; the community of fate is contingent on a combination of serendipity—the principles of the leaders who solve the strategic problems at a pivotal moment—and governance institutions that evoke or sometimes transform goals and preferences. A case in point is the transformation of the Service Employees International Union (SEIU) in the late 1990s. In at least some locals, leadership has been recruited (as opposed to emerging from within the membership) to energize the base and to win material successes members need and demand. They have destroyed the rigidities and displacement of goals that had made the unions fit the Michelian model (Voss and Sherman 2000) but not, as it turns out, the reliance on oligarchic leadership. While it is true that many of the members became involved in activities supporting immigrant rights, this is similar to the Teamsters fighting for certain forms of social insurance. These goals are in the interests of the unions—albeit a broadened interest beyond merely wages, hours, and benefits. The unions are fighting for collective goods from which their members will directly benefit or they are proving their value to those they hope to organize, or both.

Ultimately both their size and competition with other labor organizations limited the actual changes the ILWU and the WWF could effect in the world. Where unions have been able to affect policy more broadly, they tend to be embedded in bigger organizational structures that are themselves more closely tied to political actors. Coalitions of unions, generally in the form of labor confederations, may ensure the combination of greater material success and the introduction of an expanded community of fate, but the difficulties of achieving, let alone sustaining, such coalitions, are difficult and often insuperable (Ahlquist 2010, 2012). It is harder yet when there are larger social goals at issue, alliances with community groups become both necessary and possible (Levi 2001; Tattersall 2010). The existence of a strong social democratic party is one important source of coalitional action, and this was traditionally the way some European unions were able to move beyond a narrow and personal job focus to a broader view of interest that encompassed national and even global concerns. A variety of mechanisms made this possible, including permissive electoral institutions (Kitschelt 1994), national movements and platforms around particular causes, public intellectuals who articulate wider goals and engage with union leadership (Fishman 2004), and interdependence of workers within the country and across national borders as a consequence of shared regulatory regimes. Critically, formal linkages between labor movements and political parties provide career paths (and policy rents) for some politically ambitious union leaders, generating an incentive to take a broader view of the consequences of union actions. For example, there is evidence that the personal and career linkages between the Australian Council of Trade Unions and the Australian Labor Party (ALP) enabled the ALP to win union support for and maintain compliance with its wage and price Accord (Ahlquist 2011).

Other Membership Organizations

The extension of the argument to membership organizations other than unions appears easy enough in situations where there are gains to members from joining, the costs of exit are high, and the governance institutions offer the possibility of participation and challenge to decisions. Issues arise, however, as soon as we suggest the obvious examples, e.g., religious groups or political parties that ask members to invest in actions that are beyond the mission that justified their joining. In religious organizations, benefits can take decidedly non-material form, and leadership can be very top down. In political parties, participatory democracy is seldom the rule; indeed it is the transformation of social movements into elite dominated political parties that inspired Michels' "iron law of oligarchy" (Michels 1962 [1919]). For both, dependence on the organization can restrict rather than expand the community of fate.

The commitments, networks, and opportunities available through inclusion in an organization can create intense loyalty or, at least, a reluctance to leave. Exit becomes even less likely when seniority and community confer positive advantages to staying or when serious threats to livelihood, limb, or life create high and negative costs of withdrawal. The link between exit and loyalty (Hirschman 1970) is well-established, as is the extent to which solidarity increases with dependence on the organization (Hechter 1987). But loyalty and solidarity are not unalloyed virtues. Leaders may be able to take advantage of the members' dependency and steep exit costs to extract maximal rents while retaining an insular and closed community. Members may be willing to tolerate more oligarchic governance when not being asked to take action on behalf of non-members.

What happens when high costs of exit co-exist with institutions that promote leadership accountability and processes of political learning? If leaders possess the "right" motivations and are embedded in governance institutions to solve the informational and incomplete contracting problems that plague any organization, then in-group solidarity and dependence can enhance a leader's ability to induce members to look beyond their immediate interests.

Taking religious organizations as an example, the cases that seem to best fit our model are those in which membership confers, in addition to spiritual returns, a community and various forms of social insurance and pastoral care; the religious leader is contracted by or otherwise beholden to the congregation;[1] and the leader attempts to persuade the congregants to engage in political actions that are not the reason they belong to that denomination and congregation. Among the many possible examples are Baptist ministers and Jewish rabbis urging participation in the civil rights movement in the segregated U.S. South, Catholic priests promoting liberation theology in Latin America, and local Imams promoting resistance to the Shah in pre-revolutionary Iran. Augmenting religious activities with other social services can even increase a group's ability to act militarily (Berman and Laitin 2008). Although they all used their bully pulpits, religious leaders still had to persuade their members to go along with them. As we know from the U.S. civil rights movement and many other actions (Granovetter 1983; Chong 1991), as well as from the

---

[1] We follow Putnam and Campbell (2010) here in using this term inclusively for organizations of all religious groups.

research on unions reported here, leaders and their cohort are often the first movers in political actions, paying extremely high costs and often acting out of ideological or principled motivations that exceed those of their membership. Yet, to convince members to go along, leaders must supply, first, information about the world and, second, a model explaining how members' actions could result in some reasonable probability of making a difference. Often this requires convincing members of the existence of a political opportunity, an opening for effective action (see, e.g., McAdam 1982; McAdam, Tarrow, and Tilly 2001).

One important distinction between religious organizations and unions is that sorting and self-selection may be relatively easy for those seeking congregations, at least in the absence of theocracies. Iannaccone (Iannaccone 1992, 1994; Iannaccone, Olson, and Stark 1995), in particular, emphasizes the value of screening and selection in church congregations for generating internally valued religious goods, something that may reduce or inhibit expanding the scope of action beyond worship. In examining how American congregations influence the political persuasions of their congregants in terms of both parties and issues, Putnam and Campbell discover considerable self-selection, movement and sorting (2010, 35). They conclude that it is not the congregations or their pulpits per se that influence political behavior so much as the social networks in which congregants are embedded:

> Religious social networks matter as much as they do, we posit, because they serve as echo chambers. Social interaction among like-minded co-religionists reinforces and even hardens one's beliefs, even if the process is subtle. Many of those beliefs will have no political relevance . . . When they do, being embedded within a social network where common opinions are shared on such issues will only heighten their salience. (Putnam and Campbell 2010, 437)

Whether the Putnam and Campbell findings are true beyond the United States is for others to determine. As for our findings on unions, while social networks are key, self-selection for political beliefs is not. More important, it remains an empirical question whether it is possible to explain the provocation of collective political activism, in contradistinction to political attitudes, without the kinds of processes and mechanisms we identify.

Self-selection is also a key attribute of political parties (at least in democracies), but the literature examining the emergence of "programmatic" and "clientelistic" parties (Kitschelt et al. 1999; Kitschelt and Wilkinson 2007; Kitschelt et al. 2010; Stokes et al. 2013; Diaz-Cayeros, Estevez, and Magaloni forthcoming) resonates with our distinction between "business" and "social movement" unions. It does appear that the development of unions with more encompassing communities of fate were important for the development of programmatic parties, especially of the European Social Democratic variety (Pontusson 1991; Kitschelt 1994; Boix 2012). What is less clear is the extent to which our argument has much to contribute to understanding this distinction among actual party organizations. We hope scholars of political parties will clarify the extent to which our model helps or is irrelevant to an explanation.

Firms

Our argument builds on economic models of the firm, although we explicitly modified some assumptions to apply to more general forms of collective action. Has our extension brought us any additional insights that we can apply to firms, especially since we rarely, if ever, see firms calling on employees to mobilize around non-economic activities? In membership organizations, which firms are not, leaders' major responsibility is to promote members' interests, not profits. In unions, for example, industrial success means improving worker welfare; in firms, industrial success implies greater return to stockholders.

Still, there are many instances in which we see managers attempting to engender a "community of fate" within the firm, typically trying to convince workers that the interests of the firm and the interests of the workers are aligned (Cole 1979; Videla 2006). Some firms do seem able to develop reputations for treating employees well and generating loyalty, but we would expect this to be an unstable equilibrium, perturbed easily by profit demands and by changes in management. Indeed Miller (1992; also Videla 2006) shows that such relationships are exceedingly fragile and workers often bear all the risk when deciding whether an employer's promises and claims are true. Greenberg (2010) reveals how even a long-lasting and apparently mutually beneficial community of fate between employers and employees at Boeing is transformed by a merger with the very different corporate culture of McDonnell Douglas Corporation.

In some, still relatively rare cases, firms are willing to define themselves as part of a more expansive community of fate. Cases exist in which CEOs choose to sacrifice some profit, sometimes even long-term profit, in order to keep workers employed or to meet higher standards than is normal in the industry. Robert Owen did this and went broke. Lincoln Electric, a famous contemporary example, has a no layoff policy and is surviving. Joe Bozich of Knights Apparel built the Alta Gracia factory in the Dominican Republic; the workers receive a living wage, and so far the firm is doing well.

The State

The arguments we have put forward may have applications for state-building and for government processes within established states. States are also, in a sense, membership organizations that demand payments in the form of taxes and conscription in return for government provision of protection and other goods and services. Unions, sometimes, and governments, nearly always, resort to coercion to inhibit free riders and produce public goods. Unions use the dues check-off and, when they can, require dues (or payment in lieu of dues) for all those covered by the collective bargaining agreement. Governments legally require tax payment and punish evaders. In both unions and states, exit is costly, and the political beliefs of the citizens/subjects are often extremely heterogeneous.

States often ask more of their citizens than compliance with laws and taxes. Government leaders may demand great sacrifices at times of war or economic depression. Even in peacetime, some make calls for extraordinary public service, such as serving in the Peace Corps or VISTA in the United States, engaging in voluntary work brigades as in Cuba, or undertaking energy conservation and recycling in countries throughout the world. Some ask for citizen compliance with highly invasive programs such as vaccinations or the Indian government's attempt to build a national identity database. Clearly some governments are better able than others to win low-cost compliance with these requests.

The founding leadership coalitions of emerging states have several commonalities with the pivotal leaders of the unions described here. Leaders of both formative states and unions build coalitions that allow them to fight successfully to win the battles essential to gain control over the governing apparatus. They then use those coalitions or build others in order to actually govern. What coalitions they form and with whom has consequences for the kind of governance institutions that emerge.[2] Not unusually, the path is that of the ILA; a few benefit from the dues and efforts of the many. The Teamster way is more conducive to growth of the whole corpus, albeit accompanied by unequal division among the leaders and the led. Very occasionally a government is grounded in a more fully inclusive process, enfranchising much of the population and making it easier for them to influence policy.

Poor strategic decisions about incorporation in the governing coalition can be disastrous, as Julius Caesar learned when Brutus delivered his deathblow. Good decisions can create initial stability in the most unlikely of situations, as when Nelson Mandela absorbed some of his former

---

[2] Recent work of importance in the huge literature on state-building includes North, Wallis, and Weingast (2009), Fukuyama (2011), and Acemoglu and Robinson (2012).

enemies into his government. Both Caesar and Mandela were smart and able, and both, it can be argued, were seriously attempting to build an enduring and welfare-enhancing government. Yet, mistakes can be made.

Leaders of states clearly enjoy rents, and citizens tolerate them to varying degrees. More often, the choice of coalition reflects a thoughtful decision about how to extract resources to the benefit of the leadership cohort. As one of us argued several decades ago (Levi 1988), rulers (or, more generally, formal leaders) maximize revenue, but how they spend the returns varies widely and depends on a combination of personal goals, incentives, and political constraints. In other words, the nature of the rents, particularly personal rents, can vary considerably. In some cases, they spend returns on themselves or a small set of cronies, but in others the wealth produced is shared more generally among the population. Numerous authors have attempted to assess the conditions under which governments predate or are developmental (see, e.g., Evans 1989; Campos and Root 1996; Moore 1998; Kang 2002; Moore 2004; Acemoglu and Robinson 2012), but the question remains an open one.

As with unions, the reasons for this variation rest largely with the personal motivations of and the institutional constraints on formal leaders. Rulers' actions are generally delimited by institutional constraints and the bargaining power of other powerful actors (Levi 1988; Bueno de Mesquita et al. 2003). However, some leaders may also possess ideologies and principles they then attempt to embody in the rules and norms of the state (Levi and Epperly 2009). In contemporary state-building efforts, Gandhi and Mandela come to mind, but so does Mobutu, who started with such principles but whose love of power trumped his earlier and more ethical motivations. Too many union leaders fit the Mobutu model—and far too many heroes of the revolution who become the heads of state.

What we have seen with unions is as true with states. The pivotal moments in their histories can have institutional persistence through time. The principles leaders incorporate into the governance institutions sometimes provide mechanisms for trying to ensure that the institutions survive and that leadership remains accountable, particularly if the rents are structured and constituents empowered in ways that ensure that successors uphold similar organizational principles.

In all governments, leaders who fail to deliver to key constituents—be they warlords or voters—are likely to find themselves out of power. Only those who succeed in satisfying the material or policy demands of those they are supposed to be serving have a chance of being able to induce willing compliance with governmental extractions and policies. In the best functioning polities, a virtuous circle exists in which governments provide promised goods and services, citizens then comply quasi-voluntarily with tax and other extractions, which enables governments to provide more in goods and services, inducing more citizens to quasi-voluntarily comply (Levi and Sacks 2009). Crucial to this story is the delivery of positive returns. For taxpayers this generally means provision of basic security and the political underpinnings for prosperity: infrastructure, a stable system of justice, education and health services, and the like. But, as we discussed in the case of the ILA, leaders can win their rents from others than those they govern. Rulers relying on military and economic support from abroad have less incentive to care about the population and greater ability to employ repression (see, e.g., Bates 2001, 2008). They can actually or effectively own salt mines, petroleum fields, or other major sources of revenues, thus enhancing their autonomy from constituents.[3] The ILA leadership's historical connections to high-profit criminal activity on the docks yield concentrated economic rents in ways that resonate with the "resource curse" literature.

A quid pro quo from government, while necessary, is not a sufficient condition for contingent consent. Quasi-voluntary compliance and contingent consent are more widespread when citizens deem fair the process for determining who gets what and when (Levi 1997; Levi and Sacks 2009). Both members and external observers of the ILWU and WWF/MUA viewed the union's governance procedures and equitable distribution of work as fair. Not even those actively opposing the leadership attacked the unions' governance institutions as tilted. In governments, fairness is embodied in the extent to which due process exists, bureaucracies are neutral in their distribution of goods and services, and there is a process (usually representative) by which citizens can influence given policies and not just vote on leaders. What constitutes fairness varies across societies and time. Nonetheless, any government that does not meet widely held expectations on these matters is likely to suffer resistance and dissent, passive and active.[4]

Of equal import for determining who is willing to quasi-voluntarily comply may be the extent to which government is able to influence the size and concerns of communities of fate. Evan S. Lieberman's (2003, 2009) research reveals how differences in the social construction of political communities affected government policies and citizen responses in South Africa and Brazil. What is particularly interesting is the variation

---

[3] Whether the discussion is about premodern states or the contemporary "resource curse," a large and growing literature details the manipulation of available resources by the formal leaders of government. For the first, see, e.g., North (1981), Levi (1988), Kiser (1994). For the second, see, e.g., Ross (2006), Goldberg, Wibbels, and Mvukiyehe (2008), Luong and Weinthal (2010), Haber and Menaldo (2011), Ross (2012).

[4] This argument also draws on Rothstein (1998), Cook, Hardin, and Levi (2005), chapters 8 and 9, Rothstein (2011), and Tyler (1990).

in these communities of fate around different issues: Brazil has more difficulty eliciting compliance with tax than AIDS policy, and South Africa is the other way around. For Lieberman, the answer lies in the boundaries of the groups who believe they share risk and the obligations associated with risks. In our terminology, the key is how interdependencies are perceived.

With the provision of valued collective goods, the establishment of fairness, according to prevailing norms, and the construction of appropriate communities of fate, governmental leaders then have an opportunity to achieve compliance with laws, regulations, and taxes. Not only is the state more likely to prosper, but so is the leader, whose rents—be they in votes, budgets, personal income, or successful demands for action—are likely to improve. They are also more likely to succeed at importuning extraordinary political action, such as engagement in wars or other forms of self-sacrifice, particularly if they resort to the evocation of threats, quandaries, and the politics of fear (Weingast 1997, 2005; Schofield 2006). However, reliance on fear and resentment tends to require a narrowing of the community of fate to those who share ethnic, religious, racial, and national attributes (Bates, de Figueiredo, and Weingast 1998; Petersen 2002). In situations where citizens feel relatively secure, ceteris paribus, and where government is believed to be relatively trustworthy, individuals are likely to respond to a call such as John F. Kennedy's, "Ask not what your country can do for you—ask what you can do for your country." They are more likely to expand their communities of fate.

All of this needs additional study, but theorists of state-building and good government can learn from the experiences of these unions. They could learn more if our model was able to illuminate the leader's use of extra-legal violence against members and potential members, a feature we neither theorized adequately nor investigated systematically in the union case. Extra-legal violence was notably absent in the WWF and ILWU but most definitely present in the IBT and ILA. However, at least in the IBT, the members seemed to tolerate intimidation and even explicitly illegal coercion against others. This provides an avenue for future research: under what conditions can a leader win the consent of the members to use or threaten extra-legal violence in the service of larger organizational goals?

Other Implications

Our investigations have revealed some additional features of activist unions that are worth further discussion. How these organizations use their history as a political resource, effect political learning, and structure their democracies all have implications for the range of behaviors available to organizations, be they voluntary or governmental.

HISTORY AS POLITICS

It has long been recognized that organizations and governments of all types employ a whole suite of symbolic images, logos, flags, and historical narratives (Edelman 1964; Bennett 1979; Ross 2007). Union expenditure of resources on preserving and teaching their histories is purposeful and by no means universal. In both the ILWU and the WWF/MUA, references to the past abound as a reminder of the need for constant vigilance and struggle. In comparison, the IBT and ILA devote negligible resources to historical preservation and education.

We can conceive of this construction and repetition of a specific historiography as organizational attempts to expand the community of fate through time, lengthening time horizons. These stories not only emphasize how current union members benefit from the actions and sacrifices of early generations. They also reinforce how the actions of members today will affect the lives and opportunities of their children, something of high salience when fathers, sons, daughters, nieces, and nephews are working together on the docks. It is also a means for framing the conflict with employers and for producing solidarity, pride, and dignity among those who share or at least look to a common past.

As with communities of fate, appeals to history may be for good or ill. The ILWU and WWF/MUA appear to use history effectively as a means of creating a common identity and as a model of laudatory behavior. But history can also be used to justify racial purity or the dominance of one country over others. Nationalist pride may be a source of significant mobilization, but the question is always for what end.

Sometimes, of course, historical appeals are simply empty rhetoric, as when dictators refer to their key role in the victory over colonial oppressors and their current task of protecting against external enemies; there are far too many Mobutu's, Gadaffi's, and their like throughout history who justify contemporary oppression with glorification of an historical role. There are far too many union or religious or community leaders who use past successes to justify present corruption or repression. The political uses of history have received inadequate analytic attention as an important resource in conflict, state-building, and other political processes.[5] Our cases show that further work should be done, not just at the level of the nation-state. Much of the interesting variation is visible at the level of membership organizations.

---

[5] Rothstein (2000) is a partial exception, and so is Levi (2010).

Mechanisms of Accountability and Participation

Important in sustaining the organizational governance institutions of the ILWU and WWF/MUA are accountability and participation, and in the unions they take the specific forms of local autonomy, rank-and-file democracy, and limits on officer compensation. These unions exemplify the features of a virtuous circle of government: the combination of economic provision, leadership accountability, and a strong participatory democracy giving members effective decision-making power and encouraging their cooperation.[6] The positive consequences we observe of the accountability and participatory mechanisms complement extant research on their salutary effect on the quality of citizenship (Bachrach 1967; Pateman 1970; Mansbridge 1980; Cohen and Rogers 1983; Fung 2006).

Unions generally vary in their processes for accountability and participation in similar ways to governments. Social scientists have a lot to say about how differences in rules of enfranchisement and active participation affect who gets influence in the polity and who gets what services and protections. The union cases reinforce our priors that the more an organization delivers, is accountable, acts according to prevailing norms of fairness, and involves its members in important policy and strategy, the greater the willingness of citizens to comply on a variety of dimensions, ceteris paribus. Our research also lends support to Knight and Johnson (2011), who argue that democratic practice can improve policy-making and institutional choice.

Political Learning and Mobilization

A major aim of our book is to illuminate by what mechanisms organizational membership and, by extension, government citizenship affect the targets and intensity of political mobilization. Such mechanisms include, among others, the invitation to participate, information provision, and the activation of norms, all of which contribute to political learning and, consequently, political mobilization.

The echo chamber, noted by Putnam and Campbell (2010), is undoubtedly part of the explanation of how beliefs and preferences are reinforced, but it is not always the case that individuals are simply receiving positive feedback of their pre-existing opinions. We found evidence of evocation of beliefs and preferences members either did not realize they had or came to hold as a consequence of membership. The important

---

[6]   Grossman (2012) and Grossman and Baldassarri (2012) are engaged in a series of interesting field experiments that reveal a strong positive effect of inclusive and participatory rules for selecting leaders on the responsiveness of leaders and on citizen cooperation with the provision of collective goods.

mechanism is being asked to participate in a *specific* and *bounded* activity in the context of an organizational structure that lends credibility to the requestor and to the information she provides to justify the requested member actions. Often this process includes, as it did with the ILWU and WWF, an invitation for members to consider new and previously unimagined behavior (also see Perrin 2006).

Information provision is obviously important because individuals learn of events of which they were previously unaware but about which they may come to care. In some cases, the mere knowledge activates existing norms. In others it provides the basis for more discussion of how one should react. However, the likelihood of group action is largely dependent, as we have argued throughout, on the belief that there is something one can do collectively to express the relevant community's view of the situation. How individuals in an organization acquire information, learn new perspectives, and come to believe that they can act depends on openness to messages of the leader. A leader who has established her trustworthiness in delivering the goods, limiting her monetary rents, and being responsive and answerable to members can earn the right to push her constituents to think about and even act in ways they might not have considered otherwise.

There are other processes that affect openness to leadership demands and messages. A number of cognitive biases might influence the decisions of members, as Herbert Simon (1947) noted years ago and as students of behavioral economics increasingly document (e.g., Ostrom 1998; Thaler and Sunstein 2008; Kahneman 2011). We earlier cited the "halo effect," which enables well-respected leaders to expand their influence and acceptance beyond the domains in which they have already proved successful. Equally important may be individual emotional responses. The desire to avoid the perceived shame from not contributing is one possible and powerful motivator to action; this explains why at least some young people sign up for war or jihadist actions. The pride of membership that Wood (2001) discovers among insurgents and that we have documented among unionists can be equally compelling. The feeling of efficacy around important normative and moral issues appears to enhance and be a major source of this sense of pride.

Other psychological mechanisms that can affect political learning have to do with the interaction between internal and external motivation. The conventional wisdom holds that when external incentives, usually economic, are strong enough, they may "crowd out" the intrinsic normative incentives that might otherwise facilitate learning and action. This is a variant of the famous Titmuss claim that payment for blood donations depletes voluntary donations (Titmuss 1971). Others have explored this issue in a variety of contexts in which payment for a service reduces voluntary contributions (see, e.g., Frey 1994; Barzel 2001) or monetary incentives can degrade and corrupt civic virtue (Sandel 2012).

The recent experimental literature, however, finds the relationship between monetary and other incentives to be quite complex; implicit and emotional incentives and various social factors can lead to complementarities rather than substitution of intrinsic and extrinsic motivations (Fehr and Falk 2002; Bowles and Polanía-Reyes 2011; Fehr and Hoff 2011). Our cases reveal some circumstances in which leaders succeed in stimulating members to believe that improving their own economic condition is compatible with improving that of others, and advances in psychology should help us to better explain why. Moreover, we illuminate instances where the emphasis on moral motivations may even crowd out monetary incentives; economism appears to be trumped by norms of fairness or the pride inherent in selfless acts on behalf of others.

Communities of Fate

We began with a puzzle about why some organizations are able to expand the community of fate to encompass non-members, mobilizing around issues that are not the reason members joined. We end with some findings and answers that reaffirm how important governance institutions are but also reveal the respective roles of leadership and followership in reinforcing and maintaining those governance institutions. Social networks and emotional attachments play important roles; equally important are organizational commitments to the provision of education and information. Perhaps one of the most important findings is that, where self-selection is not the basis of membership or citizenship, even trusted and principled leaders must first provide for the material well-being of their constituents before they can effectively expand the scope of actions around which they can readily expect member compliance.

The union examples allow us to begin to disentangle which institutional features and mechanisms matter for what outcomes. Institutions are key to the nature of organizational governance that promotes political action, in particular how the organization manages (or even attempts to manage) leader accountability and trustworthiness, credible information provision, reinforcement of community and social networks, and opportunities for voice, interrogation, and collective decision-making. When combined with a perceived efficacy of action, followers become effective citizens, sometimes even embedded in a larger community of fate.

The major takeaways from this project are that:

It is possible to build organizational governance institutions that improve the material well-being of constituents while also evoking from them commitments to a larger public good.

Although members come to the organization with goals and beliefs, organizational membership can induce a revision and restructuring of member's beliefs in important ways.

Leadership plays a pivotal role in this process, but only if leaders are constrained, both internally and structurally. The key features we identify in two successful cases may not constitute an easy or easily replicable project, but it is a feasible and achievable one. We can learn from how these unions expand the community of fate to promote political and social commitments that narrow self-interest cannot explain. We can then import some of those observations into the investigation of other unions, an array of membership organizations, and even into state-building projects.

Throughout this book, we have focused on how to expand the community of fate of the union membership, how to evoke from citizens beliefs and preferences that make them feel obligated to a wider polity that includes those outside their friends, family, and similar others. We have learned that there are even conditions under which their prior preferences and beliefs are transformed and broadened. We are well aware that a community of fate can be used for good or ill. It is a basis for mobilizing people to act, and sometimes their actions do more harm than good.

As with social capital (Putnam 1995)[7] and ethnicity-based mobilization, the effects of creating a community of fate are not always positive. The ILWU, WWF, and IBT all make exit from the union costly and the advantages of membership a net gain. While not everyone may agree with their goals, methods, or politics, all three unions are (or have become over the years) fully consistent with the norms, laws, and practices of the democracies in which they are located. This is not true for all membership organizations that cultivate high membership dependence. The Nazis, the Taliban, or Basque terrorist groups (Sanchez-Cuenca 2001) are among the many examples of the dark side of organizations that cultivate a commitment to a larger public good that is, in fact, a public bad. The capacity to promote solidarity, coordinate, and solve collective action problems may expand a group's community of fate but with harmful consequences for those considered outside of or inimical to the community (Hardin 1995). It defines the community of fate as exclusive rather than a broad church that encompasses those in the larger polity in need of assistance.

Inevitably, the process of constructing communities of fate involves drawing boundaries between groups: who is "like us" and who is not?

---

[7] For critiques, see Levi (1996) and Tarrow (1996).

The ILWU and WWF/MUA succeeded in building a very expansive community of fate, one that was able to transcend salient racial and geographic boundaries relatively successfully. But there is nothing inherent in the strategic and organizational logic that we develop that implies that this must be the case. To the extent a community of fate is defined as those sharing ethnic or religious ties, an extra-organizational community of fate may only serve to broaden conflict.

Our cases of an expanded community of fate stand in contradistinction to communities that narrow the scope of their members, but they also make clear how difficult it can be to build and sustain widely inclusive communities. By understanding the complex of factors that enable organizations to expand membership's interests to encompass those of unknown others while engendering a sense of efficacy and pride in group actions that go beyond the reasons members joined, we can begin to define the conditions under which it might be possible for other organizations and even governments to generate polities in which more of their constituents will act in the interests of others.

Bibliography

A.P. 1988. "Teamsters Are Said to Scrap A Rule on Two-Thirds Vote." *New York Times*, October 21, p. 2.

Abadie, Alberto, and Guido W. Imbens. 2011. "Bias-Corrected Matching Estimators for Average Treatment Effects." *Journal of Business and Econometric Statistics* 29 (1):1–11.

Abrams, Samuel, Torben Iverson, and David Soskice. 2010. "Informal Social Networks and Rational Voting." *British Journal of Political Science* 41(2):229–25.

Acemoglu, Daron, Simon Johnson, James A. Robinson, and Pierre Yared. 2008. "Income and Democracy." *American Economic Review* 98 (3):808–42.

Acemoglu, Daron, and James A. Robinson. 2012. *Why Nations Fail: The Origins of Power, Prosperity and Poverty*. New York: Crown Publishers.

Agnone, Jon-Jason. 2010. Racial Inequality in Wealth: Do Unions Matter? PhD diss., Sociology, University of Washington, Seattle.

Ahlquist, John S. 2010. "Building Strategic Capacity: The Political Underpinnings of Coordinated Wage Bargaining." *American Political Science Review* 104 (1):171–88.

———. 2011. "Navigating Institutional Change: The Accord, Rogernomics, and the Politics of Adjustment in Australia and New Zealand." *Comparative Political Studies* 44 (2): 127–55.

———. 2012. "Who Sits at the Table in the House of Labor? Rank-and-File Citizenship and the Unraveling of Confederal Organizations." *Journal of Law, Economics, and Organization* 28 (3):588–616.

Ahlquist, John S., Amanda B. Clayton, and Margaret Levi. Forthcoming. "Provoking Preferences: Unionization, Trade Policy, and the ILWU puzzle." *International Organization*. Winter.

Ahlquist, John S., and Margaret Levi. 2011. "Leadership: What It Means, What It Does, and What We Want to Know About It." *Annual Review of Political Science* 14 (1):1–24.

Alt, James E., Jeffry A. Frieden, Michael Gilligan, Dani Rodrik, and Ronald Rogowski. 1996. "The Political Economy of International Trade: Enduring Puzzles and an Agenda for Inquiry." *Comparative Political Studies* 29 (6):689–717.

Alt, James E., and Michael Gilligan. 1994. "The Political Economy of Trading States: Factor Specificity, Collective Action Problems and Domestic Political Institutions." *Journal of Political Philosophy* 2 (2):165–92.

American Association of Port Authorities. 2011. "North American Container Port Traffic 1990–2010." Available from http://www.aapaports.org/Industry/content.cfm?ItemNumber=900#Statistics.

———. 2011. *American Association of Port Authorities Free Trade Agreements*. Available from http://www.aapa-ports.org/Issues/USGovRelDetail.cfm?itemnumber=16975.

Anonymous. 1941a. "8,000 Hot Dogs Free for U.S. Service Men." *Washington Teamster*, September 26.

———. 1941b. "Takes $5,100." *Washington Teamster*, September 12.

Arian, David. 1992. "Speech to the U.S. House of Representatives Committee on Interior and Insular Affairs." Available at California State Northridge special collections.

Arrow, Kenneth J. 1974. *The Limits of Organization*. New York: Norton.

Ashenfelter, Orley, and George E. Johnson. 1969. "Bargaining Theory, Trade Unions, and Industrial Strike Activity." *American Economic Review* 59 (40):35–49.

Ashworth, Scott. 2005. "Reputational Dynamics and Political Careers." *Journal of Law, Economics, & Organization* 21 (2):441–66.

Ashworth, Scott, and Ethan Bueno de Mesquita. 2008. "Electoral Selection, Strategic Challenger Entry, and the Incumbency Advantage." *Journal of Politics* 70 (4):1006–25.

Australia Commission on the Stevedoring Industry. 1946. Stevedoring Industry Inquiry: Report of Commission on the Stevedoring Industry. Chaired by Judge Alfred W. Foster. Melbourne: Stevedoring Industry Commission.

Australia Committee of Inquiry into the Stevedoring Industry. 1957. Report of Committee of Inquiry, 7th March 1957. Chaired by J. B. Tait. Canberra: Government Printing Office.

Australia Commonwealth Court of Conciliation and Arbitration. 1908–1956. "Bound Transcripts of Proceedings and Rules in Cases: Annual Single Number Series." Melbourne: Australian Industrial Registry.

Australian Stevedoring Industry Board. 1950. "First Report." Sydney: Commonwealth of Australia.

Bachrach, Peter. 1967. *The Theory of Democratic Elitism; A Critique*. Boston: Little, Brown.

Baehr, Peter. 2008. *Caesarism, Charisma and Fate*. New Brunswick, NJ: Transaction Publishers.

Baker, George, Robert Gibbons, and Kevin J. Murphy. 2002. "Relational Contracts and the Theory of the Firm." *Quarterly Journal of Economics* 117:39–83.

Bamberger, Nowell D. 2005. "Waterfront Unionism in Seattle and Tacoma, 1887–1958: A Comparative Study in Radicalism." Seattle: University of Washington.

Barro, Robert. 1973. "The Control of Politicians " *Public Choice* 14:19–42.

Barzel, Yoram. 2001. *A Theory of the State*. New York: Cambridge University Press.

Bates, Robert H. 2001. *Prosperity and Violence*. New York: Norton.

———. 2008. *When Things Fall Apart*. New York: Cambridge University Press.

Bates, Robert H., Jr. de Figueiredo, Rui J. P., and Barry R. Weingast. 1998. "The Politics of Interpretation: Rationality, Culture and Tradition." *Politics & Society* 26 (4):603–42.

Bates, Robert H., Avner Greif, Margaret Levi, Jean-Laurent Rosenthal, and Barry R. Weingast. 1998. *Analytic Narratives*. Princeton, NJ: Princeton University Press.

"Battling Corruption in the ILA: A Partial Chronology." 2008. In *Union Democracy Review*. Brooklyn: Association for Union Democracy.

Bawn, Kathleen. 1999. "Constructing 'Us': Ideology, Coalition Politics and False Consciousness." *American Journal of Political Science* 43 (2):303–34.

Beasley, Margo. 1996. *Wharfies: A History of the Waterside Workers' Federation of Australia*. Rushcutters Bay, NSW: Halstead Press.

Beck, David. 1946. "Forward with America: The Program and Policies of the Western Conference of Teamsters as Our Country Prepares for a Great Era of Peacetime Production." Opening of the 10th Western Conference of Teamsters, Seattle.

———. 1947. "What Labor Wants." *American Legion Magazine*, May 7.

———. 1949. "To Keep Our Freedom Safe." Minneapolis: IBT.

———. 1957. "Report of General President Dave Beck at the 17th Convention of the IBT."

———.1988. Dave Beck interviewed on tape by Ronald Magden in Seattle, Washington. Tapes now contributed to the Labor Archives of Washington State, University of Washington, Seattle.

Beggs, John J., and Bruce Chapman. 1987. "An Empirical Analysis of Australian Strike Activity: Estimating the Industrial Relations Effects of the First Three Years of the Prices and Incomes Accord." *Economic Record* 63 (180):46–60.

Bennett, W. Lance. 1979. "When Politics Becomes Play." *Political Behavior* 1 (4):331–59.

Beramendi, Pablo. 2007. "Inequality and the Territorial Fragmentation of Solidarity." *International Organization* 61:783–820.

Berman, Eli, and David Laitin. 2008. "Religion, Terrorism, and Public Goods: Testing the Club Model." *Journal of Public Economics* 92:1942–97.

Besley, Timothy. 2006. *Principled Agents? The Political Economy of Good Government*. New York: Oxford University Press.

Bicchieri, Cristina. 2006. *The Grammar of Society*. New York: Cambridge University Press.

Blair, Douglas H., and David L. Crawford. 1984. "Labor Union Objective and Collective Bargaining." *Quarterly Journal of Economics* 99(3):547–66.

Boix, Carles. 1999. "Setting the Rules of the Game: The Choice of Electoral Systems in Advanced Democracies." *American Political Science Review* 93:609–24.

———. 2012. "El Auge de la Socialdemocracia." In *Democracia y Socialdemocracia*, ed. Adam Przeworski and Ignacio Sanchez-Cuenca. Madrid: Centro de Estudios Politicos y Constitucionales.

Bonacich, Edna, and Jake B. Wilson. 2008. *Getting the Goods—Ports, Labor, and the Logistics Revolution*. Ithaca, NY: Cornell University Press.

Bonney, Joseph. 2003. "Cease-fire!: A Month-Long ILA Strike Ends, But Not Before Taking a Heavy Toll on Evergreen and Its Customers." *Journal of Commerce*, June 16–22. Available from archives of *http://www.joc.com/maritime-news*.

———. 2004. "Close Call for ILA Contract: Master Contract is Approved, but Dissidents Are Pleased with their Strong 'No' Vote." *Journal of Commerce* June 13, 2004. Available from archives of *http://www.joc.com/maritime-news*.

Booth, Alison L. 1995. *The Economics of the Trade Union*. Cambridge, UK: Cambridge University Press.

Bowles, Samuel. 1998. "Endogenous Preferences: The Cultural Consequences of Markets and Other Economic Institutions." *Journal of Economic Literature* 36 (1):75–111.

Bowles, Samuel, and Herbert Gintis. 2002. "Social Capital and Community Governance." *Economic Journal* 112:419–36.

Bowles, Samuel, and Sandra Polanía-Reyes. 2012. "Economic Incentives and Social Preferences: Substitutes or Complements?" *Journal of Economic Literature* 50 (2):368–425.

Bracken, Kevin. 2006. Conversation with Kevin Bracken, Melbourne Branch Secretary, MUA. Melbourne, 24 March 2006.

Bradley, David, Evelyne Huber, Stephanie Moller, Francois Nielsen, and John D. Stephens. 2003. "Distribution and Redistribution in Postindustrial Democracies." *World Politics* 55:193–228.

Brady, David W., John Ferejohn, and Jeremy C. Pope. 2005. "Congress and Civil Rights Policy: An Examination of Endogenous Preferences." In *Preferences and Situations*, ed. Ira Katznelson and Barry Weingast. New York: Russell Sage Foundation.

Brenner, Mark. 2010. "Unions' Top-Heavy Salaries a Drag on Organizing." In *Labor Notes*. Detroit: Labor Education and Research Project.

Bridges, Harry. 1955. "On the Beam." *Dispatcher* 13, no. 19 (September 16, 1955), 2.

Brigden, Cathy 2005. "The Melbourne Trades Hall and the Split." In *The Great Labor Schism: A Retrospective*, ed. Brian Costar, Peter Love, and Paul Strangio. Melbourne: Scribe.

Bronfenbrenner, Kate. 2009. "No Holds Barred: The Intensification of Employer Opposition to Organizing. " In *EPI Briefing Paper*. Washington, DC: Economic Policy Institute.

Bueno de Mesquita, Bruce, Alastair Smith, Randolph M. Siverson, and James D. Morrow. 2003. *The Logic of Political Survival*. Cambridge, MA: MIT Press.

Bueno de Mesquita, Ethan. 2010. "Regime Change and Revolutionary Entrepreneurs." *American Political Science Review* 104 (03):446–66.

Bureau of Economic Analysis. 2009. "Gross Domestic Product by Industry." Washington, DC: U.S. Department of Commerce. Available from http://www.bea.gov/industry/gdpbyind_data.htm (cited February 15, 2013).

Bureau of Labor Statistics. 2009. *Current Wage Developments, Compensation and Wage Developments*. Washington, DC: U.S. Department of Labor. Available from http://www.bls.gov/opub/cwc/ (cited February 13, 2013).

———. 2009. "Labor Force Statistics from the *Current Population Survey*." Washington, DC: U.S. Department of Labor. Available from http://data.bls.gov/cgi-bin/surveymost?lf (cited February 13, 2013).

———. Periodic reports. *Compensation and Working Conditions*. Washington, DC: U.S. Department of Labor.

Burgmann, Verity. 1995. *Revolutionary Industrial Unionism: The Industrial Workers of the World in Australia*. Cambridge; New York: Cambridge University Press.

———. 2005. "From Syndicalism to Seattle: Class and the Politics of Identity." *International Labor and Working-Class History* 67 (1):1–21.

Noel Butlin Archives Centre, Australian National University: Waterside Workers' Federation of Australia, T62/4. 1937. "Minutes of the Federal Conference of the Waterside Workers' Federation of Australia." Sydney: Waterside Workers Federation of Australia.

———. 1954. "Fifth Biennial National Conference. Held at the Waterside Workers' Building." Sydney: WWF.

———. 1949a. "Melbourne Branch Rules." Melbourne: Waterside Workers Federation of Australia.

———. 1949b. "Minutes of the Meetings of the Federal Council of the Waterside Workers' Federation of Australia." Sydney: Waterside Workers Federation of Australia.

———. 1950. "Third Biennial National Conference." Sydney: Waterside Workers Federation of Australia.

———. 1954. "Fifth Biennial National Conference. Sydney: Waterside Workers Federation of Australia.

———. 1958. "Sixth Biennial National Conference." Sydney: Waterside Workers Federation of Australia.

———. 1964. "Minutes of the Meeting of the Federal Council of the Waterside Workers' Federation." Sydney: Waterside Workers Federation of Australia.

Byrne, Phil. 2011. "National Returing Officer's Report 2011." *Maritime Workers' Journal*, 13–15.

Calabuig, Vicente, and Gonzalo Olcina. 2000. "Commitment and Strikes in Wage Bargaining." *Labour Economics* 7:349–72.

Campbell, Ian. 1962. "ALP Industrial Groups—A Reassessment." *Australian Journal of Politics and History* 8 (2):182–99.

Campos, Jose-E., and Hilton Root. 1996. *The Key to the Asian Miracle: Making Shared Growth Credible*. Washington, DC: Brookings Foundation.

Card, David. 1990. "Strikes and Wages: A Test of an Asymmetric Information Model." *Quarterly Journal of Economics* 105 (3):625–59.

Card, David, Thomas Lemieux, and W. Craig Riddell. 2007. "Unions and Wage Inequality." In *What Do Unions Do? A Twenty Year Perspective*, ed. J. T. Bennett and B. E. Kaufman. Rutgers: Transaction Publishers.

Carter, David B., and Curtis S. Signorino. 2010. "Back to the Future: Modeling Time Dependence in Binary Data." *Political Analysis* 18 (3):271–92.

Chandra, Kanchan. 2004. *Why Ethnic Parties Succeed: A Comparative Study*. New York: Cambridge University Press.

Chang, Han-pi. 1997. *Taiwan: Community of Fate and Cultural Globalization*. Munster: Lit Verlag.

Chapman, Bruce. 1998. "The Accord: Background Changes and Aggregate Outcomes." *Journal of Industrial Relations* 40 (4):624–42.

Cherney, Robet. 1994. "Harry Bridges, Labor Radicalism, and the State." In *Occasional Paper Series*. Seattle: Harry Bridges Center for Labor Studies, University of Washington.

Cho, Wendy K. Tam, James G. Gimpel, and Joshua J. Dyck. 2006. "Residential Concentration, Political Socialization, and Voter Turnout." *Journal of Politics* 68 (1):156–67.

Chong, Dennis. 1991. *Collective Action and the Civil Rights Movement*. Chicago: University of Chicago Press.

Chong, Dennis, and James N. Druckman. 2007. "Framing Theory." *Annual Review of Political Science* 10:103–26.

Chwe, Michael. 2001. *Rational Ritual*. Princeton, NJ: Princeton University Press.

Cialdini, Robert B., and Noah J. Goldstein. 2004. "Social Influence: Compliance and Conformity." *Annual Review of Psychology* 55 (1):591–621.

Clayton, Amanda B. 2011. "'A World Apart': Union Member Residence Patterns and Political Preferences." Paper presented to American Political Science Association, Seattle.

Cohen, Joshua, and Joel Rogers. 1983. *On Democracy*. New York: Penguin Books.

Cole, Robert E. 1979. *Work, Mobility, And Participation: A Comparative Study of American and Japanese industry*. Berkeley: University of California Press.

Cook, Karen S., Russell Hardin, and Margaret Levi. 2005. *Cooperation Without Trust?* New York: Russell Sage Foundation.

Cooper, Carl L. 1944. "Council Group to Probe Taxicab Strike Charges." *Seattle Post-Intelligencer*, November 25, 3.

Costar, Brian, Peter Love, and Paul Strangio, eds. 2005. *The Great Labor Schism: A Retrospective*. Melbourne: Scribe.

Croke, Brian. 2001. "Prelates and Politics: the Carroll Style." *Journal of the Australian Catholic Historical Society* 21:31–46.

Croke, Chris. 2011. "Waterside Workers Federation." Sydney: United States Studies Centre at the University of Sydney. Student memo; available from http://depts.washington.edu/ilwu/.

Crumlin, Paddy. 2011. "Logging On." *Maritime Workers' Journal*, 5.

Cusack, Thomas R. 1997. "Partisan Politics and Public Finance: Changes in Public Spending in the Industrialized Democracies, 1955–1989." *Public Choice* 91 (3–4):375–95.

de Figueiredo, Jr., Rui J. P., and Barry R. Weingast. 1999. "The Rationality of Fear: Political Opportunism and Ethnic Conflict." In *Civil Wars, Insecurity and Intervention*, ed. Barbara Walter and Jack Snyder. New York: Columbia University Press.

Deery, Stephen J. , and David H. Plowman. 1991. *Australian Industrial Relations*. New York: McGraw Hill.

Dembo, Jonathan. 1986. "The West Coast Teamsters' and Longshoremens' Unions in the Twentieth Century." In *Labor in the West*, ed. Hugh T. Lovin. Manhattan, KS: Sunflower University Press.

Denzau, Arthur T., and Douglass C. North. 1994. "Shared Mental Models: Ideologies and Institutions." *Kyklos* 47 (1):3–31.

Dewan, T., and D. P. Myatt. 2008. "The Qualities of Leadership: Direction, Communication, and Obfuscation." *American Political Science Review* 102 (3):351–68.

Diamond, Alexis, and Jasjeet S. Sekhon. Forthcoming. "Genetic Matching for Estimating Casual Effects." *Review of Economics and Statistics*. Posted online October 10, 2012.

Diaz-Cayeros, Alberto, Federico Estevez, and Beatriz Magaloni. Forthcoming. *Strategies of Vote Buying: Democracy, Clientelism and Poverty Relief in Mexico*. New York: Cambridge University Press.

Dickson, Eric. 2006. "Rational Choice Epistemology and Belief Formation in Mass Politics." *Journal of Theoretical Politics* 18 (4):455–98.

Dixon, Chicka. 1995. *Chicka Dixon interviewed by Gary Foley*. Canberra: National Library of Australia History Collection (transcript of sound recording). ORAL TRC 3282.

Dobbs, Farrell. 1972. *Teamster Rebellion*. New York: Monad Press.

———. 1973. *Teamster Power*. New York: Pathfinder.

———. 1977. *Teamster Bureaucracy*. New York: Pathfinder.

"Dockworkers Need a Deal." 2008. *Los Angeles Times*, June 28.

Druckman, James N., and Arthur Lupia. 2000. "Preference Formation." *Annual Review of Political Science* 3 (1):1–24.

Dunlop, John T. 1944. *Wage Determination Under Trade Unionism*. New York: A.M. Kelley.

Ebbinghaus, Bernhard, and Jelle Visser. 2000. *Trade Unions in Western Europe since 1945*, ed. Peter Flora, Franz Kraus, and Franz Rothenbacher. New York: Grove's Dictionararies.

Edelman, Murray J. 1964. *The Symbolic Uses of Politics*. Urbana: University of Illinois Press.

Editorial. 1937. "An Open Letter to Harry Bridge." *Voice of the Federation*, 23 September.

Ehrlich, Sean. 2010. "The Fair Trade Challenge to Embedded Liberalism." *International Studies Quarterly* 54 (4):1013–33.

Ehrlich, Sean, and Cherie Maestas. 2010. "Risk, Risk Orientation, and Policy Opinions: The Case of Free Trade." *Political Psychology* 31 (October): 657–84.

Eidlin, Barry. 2009. "'Upon This (Foundering) Rock': Minneapolis Teamsters and the Transformation of US Business Unionism, 1934–1941." *Labor History* 50 (3):249–67.

Ensminger, Jean, and Jack Knight. 1997. "Changing Social Norms: Common Property, Bridewealth, and Clan Exogamy." *Current Anthropology* 38:1–24.

Evans, Peter B. 1989. "Predatory, Developmental, and Other Apparatuses—A Comparative Political-Economy Perspective on the Third-World State." *Sociological Forum* 4 (4):561–87.

Farber, H. S., and Bruce Western. 2002. "Ronald Reagan and the Politics of Declining Union Organization." *British Journal of Industrial Relations* 40 (3):385–401.

Farber, Henry S. 1978. "Bargaining Theory, Wage Outcomes, and the Occurrence of Strikes." *American Economic Review* 68:262–71.

"Federal Rules, Questions to be Submitted." 1938. *Maritime Worker*, 1.

"Feds File Racketeering Lawsuit Against Longshore Union." 2005. In *Labor Notes*. Detroit: Labor Education and Research Project.

Fehr, Ernst, and Armin Falk. 2002. "Psychological Foundations of Incentives." *European Economic Review* 46 (4/5):687–724.

Fehr, Ernst, and Karla Hoff. 2011. "Introduction: Tastes, Castes and Culture: The Influence of Society on Preferences." *Economic Journal* 121:F396–F412.

Ferejohn, John. 1986. "Incumbent Performance and Electoral Control." *Public Choice* 50 (1–3):5–25.

———. 1991. "Rationality and Interpretation: Parliamentary Elections in Early Stuart England." In *The Economic Approach to Politics*, ed. Kristen Renwick Monroe. New York: Harper Collins.

———. 1999. "Accountability and Authority: Toward a Theory of Political Accountability." In *Democracy, Accountability and Representation*, ed. Adam Przeworski, Susan C. Stokes, and Bernard Manin. New York: Cambridge University Press.

Finlay, William. 1988. *Work on the Waterfront: Worker Power and Technological Change in a West Coast Port*. Philadelphia: Temple University Press.

Fiorina, Morris P., and Kenneth A. Shepsle. 1989. "Formal Theories of Leadership: Agents, Agenda Setters, and Entrepreneurs." In *Leadership and Politics*, ed. Bryan D. Jones. Lawrennce: University Press of Kansas.

Fishman, Robert M. 2004. *Democracy's Voices: Social Ties and the Quality of Public Life in Spain*. Ithaca, NY: Cornell University Press.

Fisman, Raymond F., Shachar Kariv, and Daniel Markovits. 2005. "Distinguishing Social Preferences from Preferences for Altruism." Working paper, Yale School of Management's Legal Scholarship Network.

Fitzgibbon, Charlie. 1986. *Charlie Fitzgibbon interviewed by Richard Raxworthy in the Labor Council of New South Wales oral history project. Canberra: National Library of Australia Oral History Collection* [transcript of sound recording].

Fletcher, Bill Jr., and Fernando Gapasin. 2008. *Solidarity Divided*. Berkeley: University of California Press.

Foisie, Frank P. 1934. *Decasualizing longshore labor and the Seattle experience*. Seattle: Waterfront Employers of Seattle.

Franzosi, Roberto. 1995. *The Puzzle of Strikes*. New York: Cambridge University Press.

Freeman, Richard. 2007. *America Works: The Exceptional Labor Market*. New York: Russell Sage Foundation Press.

Freeman, Richard B., and James L. Medoff. 1984. *What Do Unions Do?* New York: Basic Books.

Frey, Bruno S. 1994. "How Intrinsic Motivation Is Crowded Out and In." *Rationality and Society* 6 (3):334–52.

Frohlich, Norman, Joe A. Oppenheimer, and Oran Young. 1971. *Political Leadership and Collective Goods*. Princeton, NJ: Princeton University Press.

Fudenberg, Drew, and David K. Levine. 1989. "Reputation and Equilibrium Selection in Games with a Patient Player." *Econometrica* 57:759–78.

Fukuyama, Francis. 2011. *The Origins of Political Order: From Prehuman Times to the French Revolution*. New York: Farrar, Straus, and Giroux.

Fung, Archon. 2006. *Empowered Participation: Reinventing Urban Democracy*. Princeton, NJ: Princeton University Press.

Gallup. 2012. *Most Important Problem* 2012. Available from http://www.gallup.com/poll/1675/most-important-problem.aspx (cited October 22, 2012).

Gallup, George. 1957. "Poll Shows Hoffa Has Lost Ground: Gallup Survey Among Teamster Groups Discloses Many Want No Part of Him Gallup Survey." *Los Angeles Times*, September 24, p. 2.

Galston, William A. 2001. "Political Knowledge, Political Engagement, and Civic Education." *Annual Review of Political Science* 4 (1):217–34.

Ganz, Marshall. 2009. *Why David Sometimes Wins: Leadership, Organization, and Strategy in the California Farm Worker Movement*. New York: Oxford University Press.

Garnel, Donald. 1972. *The Rise of Teamster Power in the West*. Berkeley: University of California Press.

Gentile, Antonina. 2010. "Historical Varieties of Labor Contention and Hegemony in Transnational Docker Campaigns." PhD diss., Department of Political Science, Johns Hopkins University, Baltimore.

Gibbons, Robert. 1998. "Incentives in Organizations." *Journal of Economic Perspectives* 12:115–32.

———. 2005. "Four Formal(izable) Theories of the Firm?" *Journal of Economic Behavior & Organization* 58 (2):200–45.

Gillingham, J. B. 1956. *The Teamsters Union on the West Coast*. Berkeley: Institute of Industrial Relations, University of California.

Gillingham, Paul. 1970. "The Early History and Development of Industrial Relations in the West Coast Longshore Industry, 1919–1934." Master's thesis, History, University of Washington, Seattle.

Gintis, Herbert. 2003. "Solving the Puzzle of Prosociality." *Rationality and Society* 15 (2):155–87.

Glaberson, William. 1990. "US Racketeering Suit to Focus on Dock Union." *New York Times*, February 2.

Goldberg, Ellis, Erik Wibbels, and Eric Mvukiyehe. 2008. "Lessons from Strange Cases." *Comparative Political Studies* 41 (4–5):4–5.

Golden, Miriam. 1997. *Heroic Defeats: The Politics of Job Loss*. New York: Cambridge University Press.

Goldthorpe, John H., David Lockwood, Frank Bechhofer, and Jennifer Platt. 1968. *The Affluent Worker: Political Attitudes and Behaviour*. London: Cambridge University Press.

———. 1969. *The Affluent Worker in the Class Structure*. London: Cambridge University Press.

Gould, Roger V. 1993. "Collective Action and Network Structure." *American Sociological Review* 58 (2):182–96.

Gramsci, Antonio, and Joseph A. Buttigieg. 1992. *Prison Notebooks*. New York: Columbia University Press.

Granovetter, Mark. 1978. "Threshold Models of Collective Behavior." *American Journal of Sociology* 83 (6):1420–43.

Granovetter, Mark S. 1983. "The Strength of Weak Ties: A Network Theory Revisited." *Sociological Theory* 1:201–33.

Greenberg, Edward S. 2010. *Turbulence: Boeing and the State of American Workers and Managers*. New Haven, CT: Yale University Press.

Greif, Avner. 2006. *Institutions and the Path to the Modern Economy: Lessons from Medieval Trade*. New York: Cambridge University Press.

———. 2012. "A Theory of Moral Authority: Moral Choices under Moral Networks Externality." Working paper, Stanford, CA: Stanford University.

Griffith, Gary. 1997. "Obituary: Ted Roach (1909–1997)." *Illawarra Unity— Journal of the Illawarra Branch of the Australian Society for the Study of Labour History* 1 (2):30–4.

Grossman, Guy. 2012. "Causal Effects of Leader Selection Rules on Leader Responsiveness and Cooperation: Evidence from Ugandan Community Organizations." Working paper, Department of Political Science, University of Pennsylvania.

Grossman, Guy, and Delia Baldassarri. 2012. "The Impact of Elections on Cooperation: Evidence from a Lab-in-the-Field Experiment in Uganda." *American Journal of Political Science* 56 (4):964–85.

Haber, Stephen, and Victor Menaldo. 2011. "Do Natural Resources Fuel Authoritarianism? A Reappraisal of the Resource Curse." *American Political Science Review* 105 (1):1–26.

Hagan, John. 1991. "Destiny and Drift: Subcultural Preferences, Status Attainments, and the Risks and Rewards of Youth." *American Sociological Review* 56 (5):567–82.

Hainmueller, Jens, and Michael J. Hiscox. 2006. "Learning to Love Globalization: Education and Individual Attitudes Toward International Trade." *International Organization* 60 (2):469–98.

Hall, Peter A. 1986. *Governing the Economy: The Politics of State Intervention in Britain and France*. Oxford: Oxford University Press.

Hall, Peter A., and David Soskice, eds. 2001. *Varieties of Capitalism*. New York: Oxford University Press.

Hamilton, Reg. 1991. "Strikes and the Australian Industrial Relations Commission." *Journal of Industrial Relations* 33 (3):34–68.

Hardin, Russell. 1995. *One for All*. Princeton, NJ: Princeton University Press.

Harry Bridges Center for Labor Studies, Waterfront Workers History Project. 2009–2010a. *1950 Newsreel of Harry Bridges*. Available from http://depts.washington.edu/dock/interviews_harry_bridges.shtml (cited August 16, 2011).

———. *The Waterfront Worker—Complete Collection 1932–1936*. 2009–2010b. Available from http://depts.washington.edu/labpics2/repository/v/waterfront _workers/wworker/ (cited August 16, 2011).

Hass, Eric. 1955. *Dave Beck: Labor Merchant*. New York: Socialist Labor Party.

Hechter, Michael. 1987. *Principles of Group Solidarity*. Berkeley: University of California Press.

Heckathorn, Douglas D. 1990. "Collective Sanctions and Compliance Norms— A Formal Theory of Group-Mediated Social-Control." *American Sociological Review* 55:366–85.

———. 1993. "Collective Action and Group Heterogeneity—Voluntary Provision Versus Selective Incentives." *American Sociological Review* 58:329–50.

Heidtman, Ina. 2006. Personal Interview. Sydney, 27 September.

Henrich, Joseph, Robert Boyd, Samuel Bowles, Colin Camerer, Ernst Fehr, and Herbert Gintis, eds. 2004. *Foundations of Human Sociality—Economic Experiments and Ethnographic Evidence from Fifteen Small-Scale Societies*. New York: Oxford University Press.

The Herdsman. November 29 1948. Available from http://www.time.com/time/ printout/0,8816,804876,00.html (cited October 5. 2012).

Hermalin, Benjamin E. 1998. "Toward an Economic Theory of Leadership." *American Economic Review* 88 (5):1188–1206.

———. 2001. "Economics and Corporate Culture." In *International Handbook of Organizational Culture and Climate*, ed. S. Cartwright, C. L. Cooper, and P. C. Earley. Chichester: John Wiley & Sons.

———. 2007. "Leadership for the Long Term." *Journal of Economic Behavior & Organization* 62 (1):1–19.

Heston, Alan, Robert Summers, and Bettina Aten. 2006. "Penn World Tables Version 6.2."

Hicks, John Richard. 1932. *The Theory of Wages*. New York: St. Martin's Press.

Hirschman, Albert. 1970. *Exit, Voice, and Loyalty: Responses to Decline in Firms, Organizations, and States*. Cambridge, MA: Harvard University Press.

Hiscox, Michael J. 2006. "Through a Glass and Darkly: Attitudes Toward International Trade and the Curious Effects of Issue Framing." *International Organization* 60 (3):755–80.

Ho, Daniel, Kosuke Imai, Gary King, and Elizabeth Stuart. 2007. "Matching as Nonparametric Preprocessing for Reducing Model Dependence in Parametric Causal Inference." *Political Analysis* 15 (3):199–236.

Holmstrom, Bengt. 1982. "Moral Hazard in Teams." *Bell Journal of Economics* 13 (2):324–40.

Huckfeldt, Robert, and John Sprague. 1987. "Networks in Context: The Social Flow of Political Information." *American Political Science Review* 81 (4):1197–1216.

———. 1988. "Choice, Social Structure, and Political Information: The Information Coercion of Minorities." *American Journal of Political Science* 32 (2):467–82.

Iannaccone, Laurence R. 1992. "Sacrifice and Stigma: Reducing Free-riding in Cults, Communes, and Other Collectives." *Journal of Political Economy* 100:271–91.

———. 1994. "Why Strict Churches are Strong." *American Journal of Sociology* 99 (5):1180–1211.

Iannaccone, Laurence R., Daniel V. A. Olson, and Rodney Stark. 1995. "Religious Resources and Church Growth." *Social Forces* 74, no. 2 (December):705–31.

IBT (International Brotherhood of Teamsters). *Teamsters*. 2010. Available from http://www.teamster.org/ (cited February 15, 2013).

ILA Rank and File Committee. 1945. "Vote No on Phony Contract!" New York.

ILWU. 1938. *Constitution and By-Laws of the International Longshoremen's and Warehousemen's Union District 1 Affiliated with the C.I.O.* San Franciso: ILWU (amended periodically at the Conventions of the ILWU).

———. n.d. *The ILWU Story and International Solidarity*. Available from http://www.ilwu19.com/history/the_ilwu_story/international_solidarity.htm.

ILWU Pensioners, Seattle. 2007a. Interviews with Pensioners of ILWU in Seattle, March 2, 2007.

———. 2007b. Interviews with Pensioners of ILWU in Seattle, February 7, 2007.

International Brotherhood of Teamsters, Chauffeurs, Warehousemen, and Helpers of America. 1957. "Proceedings of the 17th Convention," 724.

———. 1961. Proceedings of the 18th Convention.

International Labour Reports. 1984. Manchester: Mayday Publications.

International Longshore & Warehouse Union. 2006. "How the Union Works: The Structure of the International Longshore & Warehouse Union." San Francisco: ILWU. Communications Department and the Department of Research and Education. http://www.ilwu.org/wp-content/uploads/2010/12/how-the-union-works.pdf (cited February 15, 2013).

Iversen, Torben. 1999. *Contested Economic Institutions: The Politics of Macroeconomics and Wage Bargaining in Advanced Democracies*. New York: Cambridge University Press.

———. 2005. *Capitalism, Democracy and Welfare*. New York: Cambridge University Press.

James, Ralph C., and Estelle Dinerstein James. 1965. *Hoffa and the Teamsters: A Study of Union Power*. New York: D. Van Nostrand Company.

Jensen, Vernon H. 1974. *Strife on the Waterfront: The Port of New York since 1945*. Ithaca, NY: Cornell University Press.

Johnson, Ted. 1993. "Port and Labor Split on NAFTA: Trade: Harbor officials envision significant growth in import export volume, with a positive effect on employment. Union officials fear that lucrative jobs will be among the exports to Mexico." *Los Angeles Times*, September 17.

Johnson, Victoria. 2000. "The Cultural Foundation of Resources, the Resource Foundation of Political Cultures: An Explanation for the Outcomes of Two General Strikes." *Politics & Society* 28 (3):331–65.

———. 2008. *How Many Machine Guns Does It Take to Cook One Meal? The Seattle and San Francisco General Strikes*. Seattle: University of Washington Press.

Jones, Bryan D. 2001. *Politics and the Architecture of Choice*. Chicago: University of Chicago Press.

Jones, George Michael. 1957. "Longshore Unionism and Puget Sound: A Seattle-Tacoma Comparison." Master's thesis, History, University of Washington, Seattle.

Jugum, Martin. 1994. *Presentation to "The Legacy of Harry Bridges and the Tradition of Dissent."* Seattle: Harry Bridges Center.

Jung, Moon-Kie. 2006. *Reworking Race: The Making of Hawaii's Interracial Labor Movement*. New York: Columbia University Press.

Kagan, Robert A. 1990. "How Much Does Law Matter: Labor Law, Competition and Waterfront Labor Relations in Rotterdam and US Ports." *Law and Society Review* 24 (1):35–70.

Kagel, Sam. 1999. "'The 1934 Strike' As Told by Sam Kagel, A Member of the 1934 Joint Marine Strike Committee." In *Working Paper No. 12*. Seattle: Harry Bridges Center for Labor Studies.

Kahneman, Daniel. 2003. "Maps of Bounded Rationality: A Perspective on Intuitive Judgment and Choice." In *The Nobel Prizes 2002*, ed. Tore Frängsmyr. Stockholm: Nobel Foundation.

———. 2011. *Thinking, Fast and Slow*. New York: Farrar, Straus, and Giroux.

Kang, David C. 2002. *Crony Capitalism, Corruption, and Development in South Korea and the Philippines*. Cambridge, MA: Cambridge University Press.

Katznelson, Ira. 2006. "'To Give Counsel and to Consent': Why the King (Edward I) Expelled His Jews (in 1290)." In *Preferences and Situations*, ed. Ira Katznelson and Barry Weingast. New York: Russell Sage Foundation.

Kelly, Devin. 2009. Wharf Rats and Lords of the Dock: How Dock Regime and Union Institutions Effect Dockworker Response to New Technology. Master's thesis, Department of Sociology, University of Washington, Seattle.

Kennan, John, and Robert Wilson. 1993. "Bargaining with Private Information." *Journal of Economic Literature* 31 (1):45–104.

Kerrissey, Jasmine, and Evan Schofer. 2010. "Union Membership and Political Participation in the United States." In *Annual Meeting of the American Sociological Association*. Atlanta, GA.

Kim, Hyojoung, and Peter S. Bearman. 1997. "The Structure and Dynamics of Movement Participation." *American Sociological Review* 62:70–93.

Kimeldorf, Howard. 1988. *Reds or Rackets? The Making of Radical and Conservative Unions on the Waterfront*. Berkeley: University of California Press.

———. 1992. "World War II and the Deradicalization of American Labor: The ILWU as a Deviant Case." *Labor History* 33 (2):248–78.

King, Gary, James Honaker, Anne Joseph, and Kenneth Scheve. 2001. "Analyzing Incomplete Political Science Data: An Alternative Algorithm for Multiple Imputation." *American Political Science Review* 95 (1):49–69.

Kiser, Edgar. 1994. "Markets and Hierarchies in Early Modern Tax Systems: A Principal-Agent Analysis." *Politics & Society* 22 (3):284–315.

Kitschelt, Herbert. 1994. *The Transformation of European Social Democracy*. New York: Cambridge University Press.

Kitschelt, Herbert, Kirk Hawkins, Juan Pablo Luna, Guillermo Rosas, and Elizabeth Zechmeister. 2010. *Latin American Party Systems*. Cambridge; New York: Cambridge University Press.

Kitschelt, Herbert, Zdenka Mansfeldova, Radoslaw Markowski, and Gabor Toka. 1999. *Post-Communist Party Systems: Competition, Representation, and Inter-Party Cooperation*. New York: Cambridge University Press.

Kitschelt, Herbert, and Steven Wilkinson. 2007. *Patrons, Clients, and Policies: Patterns of Democratic Accountability and Political Competition*. Cambridge; New York: Cambridge University Press.

Knight, Jack, and James Johnson. 2011. *The Priority of Democracy: A Pragmatist Argument*. Princeton, NJ: Princeton University Press & Russell Sage Foundation Press.

Korpi, Walter, Julia Sila O'Connor, and Gregg Matthew Olsen. 1998. *Power Resources Theory and the Welfare State: A Critical Approach: Essays Collected in Honour of Walter Korpi*. Toronto: University of Toronto Press.

Kremer, Michael, and Benjamin A. Olken. 2009. "A Biological Model of Unions." *American Economic Journal: Applied Economics* 1 (2):150–75.

Kreps, David M. 1990. "Corporate Culture and Economic Theory." *Perspectives in Positive Political Economy*, eds. James E. Alt and Kenneth Shepsle. New York: Cambridge University Press.

Kuran, Timur. 1995. *Private Truths, Public Lies*. Cambridge, MA: Harvard University Press.

Kurzban, Robert. 2003. "Biological Foundations of Reciprocity." In *Trust and Reciprocity: Interdisciplinary Lessons from Experimental Research*, ed. Elinor Ostrom and James Walker. New York: Russell Sage Foundation.

Lannon, Jr., Albert. 1968. Statement of the Washington Representative, International Longshoremen's and Warehousemen's Union, Before the Committee on Ways and Means, U.S. House of Representatives, June 11, 1968. 90th Congress. Second Session. pp. 864–68.

———. 1970. Statement of ILWU Washington Representative, Trade Hearings, Committee on Ways and Means, U.S. House of Representatives, May 19, 1970. 91st Congress. Second Session. pp. 1185–88.

Larrowe, Charles P. 1955. *Shape-up and Hiring Hall; A Comparison of Hiring Methods and Labor Relations on the New York And Seattle Water Fronts.* Berkeley: University of California Press.

Lawler, Edward J., Shane R. Thye, and Jeongkoo Yoon. 2009. *Social Commitments in a Depersonalized World.* New York: Russell Sage Foundation.

Lawson, J. N. 1939. "Report into Conditions of the Waterfront at the Principal Ports of the Commonwealth." ed. Department of Trade and Custom: Commonwealth of Australia.

Leach, Peter T. 2010. "NY–NJ Terminals Shut for Second Day by ILA Strike." In *Journal of Commerce*, September 29, 2010. Available from http://www.joc .com/maritime-news/ny-nj-terminals-shut-second-day-ila-strike_20100929 .html (cited February 14, 2013).

Lee, Woojin, and John E. Roemer. 2005. "The Rise and Fall of Unionised Labour Markets: A Political Economy Approach." *Economic Journal* 115:28–67.

Leiter, Robert D. 1957. *The Teamsters Union: A Study of Its Economic Impact.* New York: Bookman Associates.

Lenin, V. I. 1963 [1902]. *What Is to Be Done?* Translated by S.V. Utechin and Patricia Utechin. Oxford: Clarendon Press.

Leventoglu, Bahar, and Ahmer Tarar. 2008. "Does Private Information Lead to Delay or War in Crisis Bargaining?" *International Studies Quarterly* 52:533–53.

Levi, Margaret. 1988. *Of Rule and Revenue.* Berkeley: University of California Press.

———. 1996. "Social and Unsocial Capital: A Review Essay of Robert Putnam's Making Democracy Work" *Politics & Society* 24 (1):45–55.

———. 1997. *Consent, Dissent and Patriotism.* New York: Cambridge University Press.

———. 2001. "Capitalizing on Labor's Capital." In *Social Capital and Poor Communities*, ed. Mark E. Warren, Susan Saegert, and Phil Thompson. New York: Russell Sage Foundation.

———. 2003. "Organizing Power: Prospects for the American Labor Movement." *Perspectives on Politics* I (1):45–68.

———. 2005. "Inducing Preferences within Organizations." In *Preferences and Situations: Points of Intersection Between Historical and Rational Choice Institutionalism*, ed. Ira Katznelson and Barry R. Weingast. New York: Russell Sage Foundation.

———. 2010. "The Past as a Source of Political Power in the Present." In *History and Memory*, ed. Sashi Joshi. Indian Institute for Advance Studies, Shimla.

Levi, Margaret, and Brad Epperly. 2009. "Principled Principals in the Founding Moments of the Rule of Law." In *Global Perspectives on the Rule of Law*, ed. James Heckman, Robert Nelson, and Lee Cabatingan. London: Routledge.

Levi, Margaret, and David Olson. 2000. "The Battles in Seattle." *Politics & Society* 28 (3):217–37.

Levi, Margaret, David Olson, Jon Agnone, and Devin Kelly. 2009. "Union Democracy Reexamined." *Politics & Society* 37 (2):203–28.

Levi, Margaret, and Audrey Sacks. 2009. "Legitimating Beliefs: Concepts and Measures." *Regulation & Governance* 3 (December):311–33.

Levinson, Mark. 2006. *The Box: How the Shipping Container Made the World Smaller and the World Economy Bigger.* Princeton, NJ: Princeton University Press.

Levitsky, Steven. 2003. *Transforming Labor-Based Parties in Latin America: Argentine Peronism in Comparative Perspective.* New York: Cambridge University Press.

Lewis, Mike. 1987. "Workers' Rights and Trade Adjustment Assistance Programs Hearing before the Committee on Finance." Washington, DC: U.S. Government Printing Office.

Lichbach, Mark. 1995. *The Rebel's Dilemma.* Ann Arbor: University of Michigan Press.

———. 1997. *The Cooperator's Dilemma.* Ann Arbor: University of Michigan Press.

Lieberman, Evan S. 2003. *Race and Regionalism in the Politics of Taxation in Brazil and South Africa.* New York: Cambridge University Press.

———. 2009. *Boundaries of Contagion: How Ethnic Politics Have Shaped Government Responses to AIDS.* Princeton, NJ: Princeton University Press.

Lipset, Seymour Martin. 1994. "The Social Requisites of Democracy Revisited." *American Sociological Review* 59:1–22.

Lipset, Seymour Martin, Martin Trow, and James Coleman. 1956. *Union Democracy.* Garden City, NJ: Anchor Books, Doubleday & Company.

Lipsky, Michael. 1968. "Protest as a Political Resource." *American Political Science Review* 62 (2):1144–58.

Little, R.J.A., and Donald Rubin. 2002. *Statistical Analysis with Missing Data.* 2nd ed. Hoboken, NJ: Wiley Interscience.

Lockwood, Rupert. 1975. *Black Armada.* Sydney: Australasian Book Society.

———. 1990. *Ship to Shore: A History of Melbourne's Waterfront and Its Union Struggles.* Sydney: Hale & Iremonger Pty Limited.

Lowenstein, Wendy, and Tom Hills. 1982. *Under the Hook: Melbourne Waterside Workers Remember Working Lives and Class War 1900–1980.* Prahan, Victoria: Melbourne Bookworkers.

Luong, Pauline Jones, and Erika Weinthal. 2010. *Oil Is Not a Curse: Ownership Structure and Institutions in Soviet Successor States.* New York: Cambridge University Press.

Luxemburg, Rosa. 1971 [1916]. *The Mass Strike: The Political Party and the Trade Unions, and the Junius Pamphlet.* New York: Harper & Row.

Macintyre, Stuart. 1998. *The Reds: The Communist Party of Australia from Origins to Illegality.* Sydney: Allen & Unwin.

———. 2004. "Arbitration in Action." In *The New Province of Law and Order: 100 Years of Australian Industrial Conciliation and Arbitration,* ed. Joseph Isaac and Stuart Macintyre. New York: Cambridge University Press.

Magden, Ronald. 1991a. *A History of Seattle Waterfront Workers, 1884–1934.* Seattle: International Longshoremen's and Warehousemen's Union 19 of Seattle, the Washington Commission for the Humanities.

———. 1991b. *The Working Longshoreman.* Tacoma, WA: International Longshoremen's and Warehousemen's Union, Local 23 of Tacoma.

Magden, Ronald, and A. D. Martinson. 1982. *The Working Waterfront: The Story of Tacoma's Ships and Men*. Tacoma, WA: International Longshoremen's and Warehousemen's Union, Local 23 of Tacoma.

Mallory, Greg. 1997. "Ted Roach, 1909–1997." In *Green Left Weekly*. Australia.

———. 2005. *Uncharted Waters: Social Responsibility in Australian Trade Unions*. Brisbane: Boolarong Press.

Mansbridge, Jane J. 1980. *Beyond Adversary Democracy*. New York: Basic Books.

Mansfield, Edward, and Diana Mutz. 2009. "Support for Free Trade: Self-Interest, Sociotropic Politics, and Out-Group Anxiety." *International Organization* 63 (2):425–57.

Mares, Isabela. 2003. *The Politics of Social Risk*. New York: Cambridge University Press.

———. 2006. *Taxation, Wage Bargaining, and Unemployment*. New York: Cambridge University Press.

Maritime Union of Australia. 2011a. "MUA members participate in Occupy Sydney and Occupy Melbourne." http://mua.kindee.mooball.net/news/mua-members-participate-in-occupy-sydney-and-occup/ (accessed February 18, 2012).

Maritime Union of Australia. 2011b. "*Patrick Workers Vote Down Patrick Offer.*" http://www.mua.org.au/ (accessed February 18, 2012).

Maritime Union of Australia. 2006. National Veterans' Organization Group interviews. Sydney, 28 March.

Markey, Ray, and Stuart Svensen. 1996. "Healy, James." In *Australian Dictionary of Biography*, ed. John Ritchie. Melbourne: Melbourne University Press.

Markholt, Ottilie. 1998. *Maritime Solidarity: Pacific Coast Unionism, 1929–1938*. Tacoma: Pacific Coast Maritime History Association.

Martin, Donald L. 1980. *An Ownership Theory of the Trade Union*. Berkeley: University of California Press.

Martin, John Bartlow. 1959. "The Making of a Labor Boss." *Saturday Evening Post*, July 4, p. 27.

Marwell, Gerald, and Pamela E. Oliver. 1993. *The Critical Mass in Collection*. Cambridge: Cambridge University Press.

Mason, Scott. 2011. Interview with Current President of Local 23 (Tacoma), June 16, 2011.

Masters, Marik F., and John Thomas Delaney. 1987. "Union Political Activities: A Review of the Empirical Literature." *Industrial and Labor Relations Review* 40 (3):335–53.

Mayda, Anna Maria, and Dani Rodrick. 2005. "Why Are Some People (And Countries) More Protectionist Than Others?" *European Economic Review* 49 (6):1393–1430.

Mayhew, David. 1974. "Congressional Elections: The Case of the Vanishing Marginal." *Polity* 6:295–317.

McAdam, Doug. 1982. *Political Process and the Development of Black Insurgency, 1930–1970*. Chicago: University of Chicago Press.

McAdam, Doug, Sidney Tarrow, and Charles Tilly. 2001. *Dynamics of Contention*. New York: Cambridge University Press.

McCallum, John D. 1978. *Dave Beck*. Mercer Island, WA: The Writing Works.

McDaniel, Eric L. 2008. *Politics in the Pews: The Political Mobilization of Black Churches*. Ann Arbor: University of Michigan Press.

McEllrath, Robert. 2012. *ILWU Opposes Korea-United States Free Trade Agreement* 2011. Available from http://www.ilwu.org/?p=1626.

McGinn, Kathleen. 2006. "History, Structure, and Practices: San Pedro Longshoremen in the Face of Change." In *Exploring Positive Relationships at Work: Building a Theoretical and Research Foundation*, ed. J. Dutton and B. Ragins. Mahwah, NJ: Lawrence Erlbaum Associates.

McWilliams, Brian. 1999. *Speech at the WTO Labor Rally* Available from http://www.ilwu19.com/history/wto/speech.htm (cited October 21, 2012).

Merriless, Craig, Russ Miyashiro, Tom Price, and Jennifer Sargent. 2008. "We Stood Up for America, the Troops, and Against the War." *Dispatcher* 66(6), 1, 4-6.

Merton, Robert K. 1968 [1957]. *Social Theory and Social Structure*. 3rd ed. Glencoe, IL: Free Press.

Michels, Robert. 1962 [1919]. *Political Parties: A Sociological Study of the Oligarchical Tendencies of Modern Democracy*. New York: Free Press.

Miller, Gary. 1992. *Managerial Dilemmas*. New York: Cambridge University Press.

Miller, Raymond Charles. 1969. "The Dockworker Subculture and Some Problems in Cross-Cultural and Cross-Time Generalizations." *Comparative Studies in Society and History* 11 (3):302–14.

Mills, C. Wright. 1948. *The New Men of Power*. Chicago: University of Illinois Press.

Minolt, Berry. 1992. *Harry Bridges—A Man and His Union*: CreatSpace. film, DVD.

Moe, Terry M. 1985. "Control and Feedback in Economic Regulation: The Case of the NLRB." *American Political Science Review* 79 (4):1094–1116.

Moldea, Dan E. 1978. *The Hoffa Wars: Teamsters, Rebels, Politicians, and the Mob*. New York: Paddington Press.

Monaco, Kristen, and Lindy Olsson. 2004. "Labor at the Ports: A Comparison of the ILA and ILWU." Springfield, VA: METRANS Transportation Center. Available through the National Technical Information Service.

Moore, Mick. 1998. "Death without Taxes: Democracy, State Capacity, and Aid Dependence in the Fourth World." In *The Democratic Developmental State: Politics and Institutional Design*, ed. Mark Robinson and Gordon White. New York: Oxford University Press.

———. 2004. "Revenues, State Formation, and the Quality of Governance in Developing Countries." *International Political Science Review* 25 (3):297–319.

Morgan, Murray. 1982. *Skid Road: An Informal Portrait of Seattle*. Seattle: University of Washington Press.

Mori, Pier A., and Piero Tedeschi. 1992. "Economic Models of Trade Unions: An Introduction." In *Economic Models of Trade Unions*, ed. P. Garonna, Pier A. Mori, and Piero Tedeschi. London.

Morris, Alan. 1996. An Economic Analysis of Industrial Disputation in Australia, Thesis, Applied Economics, Victoria University of Technology, Melbourne.

Mullenholz, William, and William Fitzgerald. 1958. *Attempt by Dave Beck While General President of the International Brotherhood of Teamsters, to Give Seattle Every Possible Benefit that Would Accrue from a Well Administered Investment Program*. Seattle: International Brotherhood of Teamsters.

Murillo, Maria Victoria. 2001. *Partisan Coalitions and Labor Competition in Latin America: Trade Unions and Market Reforms*. New York: Cambridge University Press.

Murray, Robert. 1970. *The Split: Australian Labor in the Fifties*. Melbourne: Cheshire Publishing.

Muste, A. J. 1928. "Factional Fights in Trade Unions: A View of Human Relations in the Labor Movement." In *American Labor Dynamics in the Light of Post-War Developments*, ed. J.B.S. Hardman. New York: Harcourt, Brace.

Myrdal, Morgan. 2007. "Updated Dave Beck Memo." Department of Political Science, University of Washington, Student memo; available from *http://depts .washington.edu/ilwu/*.

Nagler, Jonathan, and Jan E. Leighley. 2007. "Unions and Class Bias in the U.S. Electorate, 1964–2004." *Journal of Politics* 69:430–41.

Nelson, Bruce. 1988. *Workers on the Waterfront: Seamen, Longshoremen, and Unionism in the 1930s*. Urbana: University of Illinois Press.

———. 1998. "The 'Lords of the Docks' Reconsidered: Race Relations among West Coast Lonshoremen, 1933–61." In *Waterfront Workers: New Perspectives on Race and Class*, ed. Calvin Winslow. Urbana: University of Illinois Press.

Nelson, Tom. 1957. "The Hungry Mile." Sydney: Sydney Branch, WWF.

Neuberger, Richard L. 1938. "Labor's Overlords." *American Magazine*, March 16–17, 166–70.

"New Officers Elected at ILA International Convention." 2007. *ILA News Report*, 15.

New York Waterfront Commission of New York Harbor. 1954. *Annual report— The Waterfront Commission of New York Harbor*.

Norris, Pippa. 2000. *A Virtuous Circle: Political Communications in Postindustrial Societies*. Cambridge; New York: Cambridge University Press.

North, Douglass C. 1981. *Structure and Change in Economic History*. New York: Norton.

———. 1990. *Institutions, Institutional Change, and Economic Performance*. New York: Cambridge University Press.

———. 2005. *Understanding the Process of Economic Change*. Princeton, NJ: Princeton University Press.

North, Douglass C., John Wallis, and Barry Weingast. 2009. *Violence and Social Orders: A Conceptual Framework for Interpreting Recorded Human History*. New York: Cambridge University Press.

North, Douglass C., and Barry R. Weingast. 1989. "Constitutions and Commitment: The Evolution of Institutions Governing Public Choice in Seventeenth Century England." *Journal of Economic History* 49 (4):803–32.

Oliver, Pamela E., and Daniel J. Myers. 2002. "Formal Models in the Study of Social Movements." *Methods of Research in Social Movements*, ed. Burt Klandermans and Susan Staggenborg. Minneapolis: University of Minnesota Press.

Olson, Mancur. 1965. *The Logic of Collective Action*. Cambridge, MA: Harvard University Press.

Olvera, Bobby, Jr. 2011. Interview. Local 13 Business Office, San Pedro, CA, 15 January 2011.

Ostrom, Elinor. 1990. *Governing the Commons: The Evolution of Institutions for Collective Action*. New York: Cambridge University Press.
———. 1998. "A Behavioral Approach to the Rational Choice Theory of Collective Action." *American Political Science Review* 92 (1):1–22.
Oswald, Andrew J. 1982. "The Microeconomic Theory of the Trade Union." *Economic Journal* 92 (367):576–95.
Page, Scott E. 2006. "Path Dependence." *Quarterly Journal of Political Science* 1 (2):87–115.
Pateman, Carole. 1970. *Participation and Democratic Theory*. Cambridge: Cambridge University Press.
Perlman, Selig. 1928. *A Theory of the Labor Movement*. New York: Augustus M. Kelley.
Perrin, Andrew J. 2006. *Citizen Speak: The Democratic Imagination in American Life*. Chicago: University of Chicago Press.
Petersen, Roger. 2002. *Understanding Ethic Violence: Fear, Hatred, and Resentment in Twentieth Century East Europe*. New York: Cambridge University Press.
Pierson, Paul. 2000. "Increasing Returns, Path Dependency and the Study of Politics." *American Political Science Review* 94 (2):251–67.
PMA. 2011. "PMA 2010 Annual Report." San Francisco: Pacific Maritime Association.
Pontusson, Jonas. 1991. *The Limits of Social Democracy: Investment Politics in Sweden*. Ithaca, NY: Cornell University Press.
Poteete, Amy R., Marco A. Janssen, and Elinor Ostrom. 2010. *Working Together: Collective Action, the Commons, and Multiple Methods in Practice*. Princeton, NJ: Princeton University Press.
Powell, Robert. 1996. "Bargaining in the Shadow of Power." *Games & Economic Behavior* 15:255–89.
———. 2002. "Bargaining Theory and International Conflict." *Annual Review of Political Science* 5:1–30.
Price, Tom. 1997. "The Saga of the Neptune Jade: Scab Cargo Shunned 'round the world'." *Dispatcher* 55(9), 11.
Project, Harry Bridges. 2009. *To Make a Long Story Short: The Life and Times of Sam Kagel*. Los Angeles: Harry Bridges Project.
Przeworski, Adam. 1985. *Capitalism and Social Democracy*. New York: Cambridge University Press.
———. 1991. *Democracy and the Market*. New York: Cambridge University Press.
Przeworski, Adam, and John Sprague. 1986. *Paper Stones: A History of Electoral Socialism*. New York: Cambridge University Press.
Putnam, Robert D. 1995. "Bowling Alone: America's Declining Social Capital." *Journal of Democracy* 6 (1):65–78.
———. 2000. *Bowling Alone*. New York: Simon & Schuster.
Putnam, Robert D., and David E. Campbell. 2010. *American Grace: How Religion Divides and Unites Us*. New York: Simon & Schuster.
Radcliff, B., and P. Davis. 2000. "Labor Organization and Electoral Participation in Industrial Democracies." *American Journal of Political Science* 44 (1):132–41.

Radcliff, Benjamin. 2001. "Organized Labor and Electoral Participation in American National Elections." *Journal of Labor Research* 22 (2):405–14.

Raskin, A. H. 1971a. "Collecting Evidence." *New York Times*, June 13.

———. 1971b. "What the 'Little Fellow' Says to the Teamsters Is What Counts." *New York Times*, May 30.

Resnik, Susan. 1999. *Blood Saga: Hemophilia, AIDS, and the Survival of a Community*. Berkeley: University of California Press.

Rilling, James K., and Alan G. Sanfey. 2011. "The Neuroscience of Social Decision-Making." *Annual Review of Psychology* 62 (1):23–48.

Robertson, George. 2007. ""This Rrankest Kind of UnAmericanism:" International Longshoremen's and Warehousemen's Union and the Fight Against Waterfront Screening, 1949–1957. Seattle: University of Washington. Student memo; available from http://depts.washington.edu/ilwu/.

Robertson, Graeme. 2004. "Leading Labor: Unions, Politics and Protest in New Democracies." *Comparative Politics* 36 (3):253–72.

———. 2007. "Strikes and Labor Organization in Hybrid Regimes." *American Political Science Review* 101 (4):781–98.

Rodden, Jonathan. 2010. "The Geographic Distribution of Political Preferences." *Annual Review of Political Science* 13 (1):321–40.

Romer, Sam. 1962. *The International Brotherhood of Teamsters: Its Government and Structure*. New York: Wiley.

Rosenfeld, Jake. 2006. "Widening the Gap: The Effect of Declining Unionization on Managerial and Worker Pay, 1983–2000." *Research in Social Stratification and Mobility* 24:223–38.

———. 2010. "Economic Determinants of Voting in an Era of Union Decline." *Social Science Quarterly* (Blackwell Publishing Limited) 91 (2).

Rosenstone, Stephen J., and John Mark Hansen. 1993. *Mobilization, Participation and Democracy in America*. New York: Macmillan.

Ross, George. 1981. "What Is Progressive about Unions? Reflections on Trade Unions and Economic Crisis." *Theory and Society* 10 (5):609–43.

Ross, Marc Howard. 2007. *Cultural Contestation in Ethnic Conflict*. Cambridge; New York: Cambridge University Press.

Ross, Michael. 2006. "A Closer Look at Oil, Diamonds, and Civil War." *Annual Review of Political Science* 9 (1):265–300.

Ross, Michael Lewin. 2012. *The Oil Curse: How Petroleum Wealth Shapes the Development of Nations*. Princeton, NJ: Princeton University Press. Available from http://public.eblib.com/EBLPublic/PublicView.do?ptiID=827801.

Rothstein, Bo. 1998. *Just Institutions Matter*. London: Cambridge University Press.

———. 2000. "Trust, Ssocial Dilemmas and Collective Memories." *Journal of Theoretical Politics* 12 (4):477–501.

———. 2011. *The Quality of Government: Corruption, Social Trust, and Inequality in International Perspective*. Chicago; London: University of Chicago Press.

Russell, Thadeus. 2001. *Out of the Jungle: Jimmy Hoffa and the Remaking of the American Working Class*. New York: Alfred A. Knopf.

Sachse, Cary B. 2007. "Social Justice Issues Examined Memo." Seattle: University of Washington. Student memo; available from http://depts.washington.edu/ilwu/.

Saiegh, Sebastian. 2009. "Political Prowess or 'Lady Luck'? Evaluating Chief Executives' Legislative Success Rates." *Journal of Politics* 71 (4):1342–56.

Sanchez-Cuenca, Ignacio. 2001. *ETA contra el Estado*. Barcelona, Spain: Tusquet Editores.

Sandel, Michael J. 2012. *What Money Can't Buy: The Moral Limits of Markets*. New York: Farrar, Straus and Giroux.

Schelling, Thomas C. 1978. *Micromotives and Macrobehavior*. New York: Norton.

Scheve, K. F., and M. J. Slaughter. 2001. "What Dtermines Individual Trade-Policy Preferences?" *Journal of International Economics* 54 (2):267–92.

Schmidt, Klaus M. 1993. "Reputation and Equilibrium Characterization in Repeated Games with Conflicting Interests." *Econometrica* 61 (2):325–51.

Schofield, Norman. 2006. *Architects of Political Change: Constitutional Quandaries and Social Choice Theory*. New York: Cambridge University Press.

Schwartz, Harvey. 1978. *The March Inland*. Berkeley: Inks Press.

———. 1980. "A Union Combats Racism: The ILWU's Japanese-American 'Stockton Incident' of 1945." *Southern California Quarterly* 62:161–6.

———. 2009. *Solidarity Stories*. Seattle: University of Washington Press.

Seidman, Gay. 1994. *Manufacturing Militance: Workers' Movements in Brazil and South Africa, 1970–1985*. Berkeley: University of California Press.

Serjeant, Jill, and Bernard R. Woodall. 2008. "U.S. West Coast Ports Working after Day-time Strike." Reuters, available from http://www.reuters.com/article/2008/05/02/idUSN01451100 (cited February 14, 2013).

Shapiro, Ian, and Sonu Bedi, eds. 2007. *Political Contingency: Studying the Unexpected, the Accidental, and the Unforeseen*. New York: New York University Press.

Sheridan, Tom. 1994. "Australian Wharfies 1943–1967: Casual Attitudes, Militant Leadership and Workplace Change." *Journal of Industrial Relations* 36 (2):258–84.

———. 1997. Groupers and Wharfies 1945–1968. Paper read at Frontiers of Labour, at Perth.

———. 2006. *Australia's Own Cold War: The Waterfront Under Menzies*. Melbourne: Melbourne University Press.

Silver, Beverly J. 2003. *Forces of Labor: Workers' Movements and Globalization since 1870*. New York: Cambridge University Press.

Simon, Herbert A. 1947. *Administrative Behavior*. New York: MacMillan.

Singleton, Gwynneth. 1990. "The Accord and the Australian Labour Movement." Melbourne.

Sloane, Arthur A. 1991. *Hoffa*. Cambridge: The MIT Press.

Smith, Warren, and Zoe Reynolds. 2009. Conversation with MUA federal officers: Warren Smith, Assistant National Secretary, and Zoe Reynolds, Media and Projects Coordinator. Sydney, September 22.

Stallone, Steve. 1998. "PMA finally Drops Neptune Jade Lawsuit." *Dispatcher* 56(10), 3.

Stepan-Norris, Judith, and Maurice Zeitlin. 1995. "Union Democracy, Radical Leadership, and the Hegemony of Capital." *American Sociological Review* 60 (6):829–50.

———. 2002. *Left Out: Reds and America's Industrial Unions*. New York: Cambridge University Press.

Stier, Anderson, and Malone, L.L.C. 2002. *The Teamsters: Perception and Reality. An Investigative Study of Organized Crime Influence in the Union*. Washington, DC.: Prepared for the International Brotherhood of Teamsters.

Stokes, Susan C., Thad Dunning, Marcelo Nazareno, and Valeria Brusco. 2013. *Brokers, Voters, and Clientalism*. New York: Cambridge University Press.

Stovel, Katherine. 2001. "Local Sequential Patterns: The Structure of Lynching in the Deep South, 1882–1930." *Social Forces* 79 (3):843–80.

Streeck, Wolfgang. 2002. "Labor Unions." In *International Encyclopedia of the Social and Behavioral Sciences*, ed. Neil J. Smelser and Paul B. Baltes. Oxford: Elsevier Science.

Stutzer, Alois, Lorenz Goette, and Michael Zehnder. 2011. "Active Decisions and Prosocial Behaviour: A Field Experiment on Blood Donation." *Economic Journal* 121 (556):F476–F93.

Swenson, Peter. 1989. *Fair Shares: Unions, Pay, and Politics in Sweden and Germany*. Ithaca, NY: Cornell University Press.

Szakonyi, Mark, and Joseph Bonney. 2012. "Strike Is Possible, ILA's Daggett Warns." In *Journal of Commerce*, March 6, 2012. Available from http://www.joc.com/container-shipping/strike-possible-ilas-daggett-warns (cited February 14, 2013).

Tarrow, Sidney. 1994. *Power in Movement*. New York: Cambridge University Press.

———. 1996. "Making Social Science Work Across Space and Time: A Critical Reflection on Robert Putnam's Making Democracy Work." *American Political Science Review* 90 (2):389–97.

Tattersall, Amanda. 2010. *Power in Coalition: Strategies for Strong Unions and Social Change*. Ithaca, NY: Cornell University Press.

Thaler, Richard H., and Cass R. Sunstein. 2008. *Nudge: Improving Decisions About Health, Wealth, And Happiness*. New Haven, CT: Yale University Press.

Thelen, Kathleen. 1999. "Historical Institutionalism in Comparative Politics." *Annual Review of Political Science* 2:369–404.

Tilly, Charles. 1978. *From Mobilization to Revolution*. Menlo Park, CA: Addison-Wesley.

Titmuss, Richard M. 1971. *The Gift Relationship*. New York: Pantheon Books.

Toman, Rene de la Pedraja. 1994. *A Historical Dictionary of the US Merchant Marine and Shipping Industry*. Westport, CT: Greenwood Publishing.

Tracy, Joseph S. 1986. "An Investigation into the Determinants of U.S. Strike Activity." *American Economic Review* 76 (3):423–36.

Turnbull, Peter. 2000. "Contesting Globalization on the Waterfront." *Politics & Society* 28 (3):367–91.

Tyler, Tom R. 1990. *Why People Obey The Law*. New Haven: Yale University Press.

Ugles, Herald. 2012. Personal Interview. Seattle, January 9.

Union Facts. 2011. Available from http://www.unionfacts.com/union/Longshoremens_Association (cited February 21, 2012).]

U.S. Bureau of Economic Analysis. 2011. "U.S. International Transactions Accounts."

U.S. Korea FTA Business Coalition. 2008. *Letter to the U.S. Congress from the US–Korea FTA Coalition.* Available from http://www.uschamber.com/sites/default/files/hill-letters/080910_uskorea_fta.pdf.

Verba, Sidney, Kay Schlozman, and Henry E. Brady. 1995. *Voice and Equality: Civic Voluntarism in American Politics.* Cambridge, MA: Harvard University Press.

Videla, Nancy Plankey. 2006. "It Cuts Both Ways: Workers, Management and the Construction of a 'Community of Fate' on the Shop Floor in a Mexican Garment Factory." *Social Forces* 84 (4):2099–2120.

Vosko, Leah F., and David Scott Witwer. 2001. "'Not a Man's Union': Women Teamsters in the United States during the 1940s and 1950s." *Journal of Women's History* 13 (3):169–92.

Voss, Kim, and Rachel Sherman. 2000. "Breaking the Iron Law of Oligarchy: Union Revitalization in the American Labor Movement." *American Journal of Sociology* 106 (2):303–49.

Vrana, Gene. 2011. Personal Interview. Seattle. March 1, 2010.

Walker, Robin. 2011. "UW Labor Archives Preserves Workers' History." ILWU website. http://www.ilwu.org/?p=3276 (cited February 19, 2013).

Wallerstein, Michael, and Bruce Western. 2000. "Unions in Decline? What Has Changed and Why." *Annual Review of Political Science* 3 (1):355–77.

Walter, Stefanie. 2010. "Globalization and the Demand-Side of Politics: How Globalization Shapes Individual Perceptions of Labor Market Risk and Policy Preferences." In *IPES Annual Meetings.* Harvard University.

Ward, Estolv Ethan. 1978, 1979. "Louis Goldblatt: Working Class Leader in the ILWU, 1935–1977, v. 2." Berkeley: Regional Oral History Office, The Bancroft Library, Univerity of California.

Ward, Michael D., Katherine Stovel, and Audrey Sacks. 2011. "Network Analysis and Political Science." *Annual Review of Political Science* 14 (1):245–64.

Waters, Robert C. 1993. "Leadership and Its Consequences: Technical Change in the Longshore Industry." *Industrial Relations* 32 (2):262–71.

Waterside Workers of Australia. 2006a. Veterans, Melbourne Branch, Group interviews. Melbourne, 24 March.

Waterside Workers of Australia. 2006b. Veterans, Sydney Branch, Group interviews. Sydney, 29 March.

Waterside Workers of Australia 2006c. Veterans, Sydney Branch, Group interviews. Sydney, 29 March.

———. 2005. "Persuasion, Preference Change, and Critical Junctures: The Microfoundations of a Macroscopic Concept." In *Preferences and Situations,* ed. Ira Katznelson and Barry Weingast. New York: Russell Sage Foundation.

Weingast, Barry R. 1997. "The Political Foundations of Democracy and the Rule of Law." *American Political Science Review* 91 (2):245–63.

Weir, Margaret. 1994. "Urban Poverty and Defensive Localism." *Dissent* (Summer):337–42.

Wellman, David. 1995. *The Union Makes Us Strong: Radical Unionism on the San Francisco Waterfront.* New York: Cambridge University Press.

Wenzl, Joe. 2011. Personal Interview. Seattle. August 25, 2011.

Western, Bruce. 1997. *Between Class and Market.* Princeton, NJ: Princeton University Press.

Westine, Carl Gustaf. 1937. The Seattle Teamsters. Master's thesis, History, University of Washington, Seattle.

Wildavsky, Aaron. 1987. "Choosing Preferences by Constructing Institutions." *American Political Science Review* 81:3–21.

Williams, Annie. 2007. "Eye of the Storm: Our Fight for Justice and a Better Contract." United States: International Longshore and Warehouse Union.

Williams, Victor. 1975. *The Years of Big Jim*. Victoria Park, WA: Lone Hand Press.

Williamson, Oliver E. 1993. "The New Institutional Economics: Taking Stock, Looking Ahead." *Journal of Economic Perspectives* 38:595–613.

———. 1996. *The Mechanisms of Governance*. New York: Oxford University Press.

Wilson, James Q. 1973. *Political Organizations*. New York: Basic Books.

Wilson, Rick K., and Carl M. Rhodes. 1997. "Leadership and Credibility in N-Person Coordination Games." *Journal of Conflict Resolution* 41 (6):767–91.

Witwer, David. 2000. "The Different Meanings of Corruption in the Context of the Teamsters Union." *Journal of Labor Research* 21 (2):287–303.

———. 2002. "Race Relations in the Early Teamsters Union." *Labor History* 43 (4):505–32.

———. 2003. *Corruption and Reform in the Teamsters Union*. Urbana: University of Illinois Press.

Wood, Elisabeth Jean. 2001. "The Emotional Benefits of Insurgency in El Salvador." In *Passionate Politics: Emotions and Social Movements*, ed. Jeff Goodwin, James M. Jasper, and Francesca Polletta. Chicago: University of Chicago Press.

———. 2003. *Insurgent Collective Action and Civil War in El Salvador*. New York: Cambridge University Press.

———. 2007. "Modeling Contingency." In *Political Contingency: Studying the Unexpected, the Accidental, and the Unforeseen*, ed. Ian Shapiro and Sonu Bedi. New York: New York University Press.

Union Facts.Com. http://www.unionfacts.com (cited October 20, 2011).

Young, Dutchy. 1986. *Dutchy Young interviewed by Richard Raxworthy in the Labor Council of New South Wales oral history project* [transcription of sound recording].

Zald, Mayer N., and John D. McCarthy. 1979. *The Dynamics of Social Movements: Resource Mobilization, Social Control, and Tactics*. Cambridge, MA: Winthrop Publishers.

Zaller, John. 1992. *The Nature and Origins of Mass Opinion*. New York: Cambridge University Press.

Ziblatt, Daniel. Forthcoming. *Conservative Political Parties and the Birth of Modern Democracy in Europe*. New York: Cambridge University Press.

Index

Accord, the, 251–52, 254
accountability of union leaders, 6, 40;
    activist unions and, 46; compliance and,
    274; credibility and, 32, 262; direct
    elections and, 36–37, 59, 88–90, 92–93;
    governance institutions and, 36–37, 56,
    97–101, 135, 264 (*see also specific*);
    ILWU governance institutions and,
    88–91; local autonomy and, 95–97;
    mechanisms of, 270, 274; member
    compliance and, 6, 274; and mobiliza-
    tion, 78; political activism and, 46, 78,
    80; political ideology of leadership and,
    118; rents and, 36–37; signals of leader-
    ship, 264; tolerance of dissent or op-
    position and, 93–95; unions as legally
    accountable for strike actions, 105
active decision hypothesis, 161–62
Adcock, Tony, 179
AFL-CIO: Gompers and philosophy of
    AFL, 57; and international trade policy,
    193–95, 198
agency, pleasure of, 163, 164, 169
Alford, Gus, 109, 132
Anastasia, Anthony, 74, 76
arbitration: Australian government and
    regulation of, 104–5, 110, 133, 182,
    231, 251–52; and direct action, 98–101;
    ILA and, 85; ILWU and, 85, 98–101,
    240; National Longshoreman's Board
    and arbitration of 1934 strike, 99;
    WWF and, 104–7, 110–12, 133, 182,
    251–52
Arian, David, 100, 115, 195
Arrow, Kenneth J., 32
Association of Employers of Waterside
    Labour (AEWL), 252
asymmetry, relational and informational,
    26–29
Australia: Aboriginal rights and, 113;
    Australian government and regulation
    of arbitration in, 104–5, 110, 133, 182,
    231, 251–52; pig iron dispute, 107,
    113; unions and criminal element in,

81. *See also* Waterside Workers Federa-
    tion (WWF)
Australian Council of Trade Unions
    (ACTU), 112, 251–52
Australian Industrial Relations Commis-
    sion, 251, 253, 258
Australian Labor Party (ALP), 14, 17,
    104–6, 110, 131–32, 135, 185n2,
    251–59, 265. *See also* Groupers (ALP's
    Industrial Group)
Australian Stevedoring Industry Associa-
    tion (ASIA), 252
Australian Stevedoring Industry Board
    (ASIB), 103, 111
Australian Stevedoring Industry Commis-
    sion (ASIC), 110, 111, 231
autonomy of locals, 57, 61; and activism,
    96–97, 135; and elections, 95–96; and
    expanded community of fate, 96–97;
    IBT and, 57, 61, 124; ILWU, 89–91,
    95–97, 115, 118–19, 274; as organi-
    zational governance institution, 89; as
    rank-and-file democracy, 118–19; and
    tolerance of dissent/opposition, 95–97;
    WWF/MUA and, 116, 118–19, 274

bargaining, 5; contract expiration and
    bargaining calendar, 58, 241–42,
    246–47; models of, 234–35; non-
    cooperative bargaining theory, 233;
    and potential for strike as context, 235;
    recognition of union as goal, 234–35;
    in state-building and governing, 270;
    transparency of process, 58, 89; as
    union function, 53
bargaining power: political actions as
    signal of, 20, 230–33, 243–45, 256;
    pre-bargaining signals of, 235–36;
    reputation and, 237; shocks and shifts
    in perceived, 83, 237; in state-building
    and governing, 270
Beck, Dave (Daniel David), 46, 55–56,
    60–69, 77–78; approval of rank-and-file

example," as signaling tactic, 31–32; call to action and, 24; Communism as ideological influence on, 17, 38, 43, 104, 122–23; competition for leadership position, 35–37, 47–52; credibility of, 32–33, 262; direct elections and competition for, 59; election of new leader as shock to union reputation, 242; elections and, 11; equilibrium and activist demands, 24; and expanded community of fate, 22–24, 38, 44, 46, 79–80, 84–87, 156, 262–63, 277; generalized salience and, 26; governance institutions as selected by, 41–42, 74–75; governance institutions as shaped by, 42–43; "halo effect," 27n5, 181, 275; ideology and political activism, 262; as influence on organizational action, 29–31; informational theories of, 27–28, 35–36, 43; institutionalization of leaders' beliefs, 11; as instrumental, 27; leaders as influence on political opinion, 161–62; mobilization and, 10, 24, 38, 44, 46, 78–80, 84–87, 156, 262–63, 277; monetary rents for, 43; motivation and, 23–26; oligarchic, 54, 62, 93, 264, 266; organizational function of, 23; as relational, 26; rents (*see* rents); reputation and, 32–33; role in organization building, 6–7; and sacrifice as signaling tactic, 31; salaries paid union leaders, 37, 72–73, 75–76, 107, 115, 168, 175, 261–62; salience of, 31–32; signaling and, 28; structural theories of (spatial voting model), 27–28; succession, factors influencing, 60–71, 74–76; and trust of rank-and-file membership, 23–24

Lelli, Phil, 128n8, 129
Lenin, 3–4, 38, 43
Lewis, John L., 127
Lieberman, Evan S., 271–72
lobbying, political by unions, 5–6
locals, IBT: Local 544 (Minneapolis), 122–24; Local 574 (Minneapolis), 122
locals, ILA, 84; Local 38-12 (Seattle), 125–26, 128; Local 38-97 (Tacoma), 125–27, 128
locals, ILWU: Local 6 (Oakland Warehouse), 102, 179; Local 8 (Portland), 102; Local 10 (San Francisco/Oakland),

13, 94, 95–96, 100, 101, 170, 175, 239–40; Local 13 (Los Angeles/Long Beach, San Pedro), 96, 102, 142, 147, 170, 177, 221, 228–29; Local 19 (Seattle), 95, 126, 129–30, 172, 180, 225, 227–28; Local 23 (Tacoma), 115, 130, 145–46, 225, 227; Local 26 (Los Angeles Warehouse), 179–80; Local 63 (Los Angeles/Long Beach clerks), 115; Local 142 (Hawaii), 85
locals, WWF Branches: Brisbane Branch, 173, 253; Hobart Branch, 181–83; Melbourne Branch, 81, 83, 104, 109, 112, 116–17, 130–35, 142, 168–69, 173, 176, 181–83, 253; Newcastle Branch, 107, 253; Port Kembla Branch, 107, 113, 117, 179, 253; Sydney Branch, 79, 103–4, 106, 113, 116–18, 130–34, 142, 152, 168–69, 171, 173–76, 182, 231, 253
Lockwood, Rupert, 138, 173
logistics revolution, economic impacts of, 185
Los Angeles Times (newspaper), 222, 231–32, 235, 256–57
Lowenstein, Wendy, 132, 171, 176
lying, 32–33, 45–49, 162–63

Magden, Ron, 125n5, 130
Maritime Union of Australia (MUA): amalgamated with WWF, 79n1, 117, 252; autonomy of locals, 116, 118–19, 274; as case, 10–11; community of fate and, 119, 261–63, 278; mandatory participation in elections, 117; member education, 138–39, 176–77; organizational structure of, 117; political mobilization of, 20, 116, 118; recruitment by, 139n11; residential patterns, 140, 142, 152; signaling and political actions by, 20
Maritime Worker (newspaper), 82, 106, 109, 138, 168
Mason, Scott, 197
McClellan Committee, 66, 70–71
McDaniel, Eric L., 10
McEllrath, Robert, 72n10, 196, 230–31
McWilliams, Brian, 12–13, 115, 196
Mechanization and Modernization (M&M), 95, 99, 242. *See also* containerization

on members, 261; larceny by leaders, 60; as leadership incentives, 39–40, 43; and material interests of rank-and-file members, 55–56; mobilization and, 40; monetary, 40, 41, 43, 77, 275 (*see also* salaries *under this heading*); and organizational governance institutions, 38–42; political activism as, 135, 163, 258; provision of good economic outcomes as prerequisite for, 258; salaries paid union leaders, 37, 72–73, 75–76, 107, 168, 175, 261–62; state governments and demands for, 269–70

reputation: and bargaining power, 237; costs paid for, 48n31; and demands for political activism, 97–98, 234; development as rational choice, 50–51; "halo effect" and, 27n5, 181, 275; honesty/lying and, 32–33, 45–49, 162; incentives for development of, 163; information and, 42–43, 162; leaders and (*see* reputation, leadership and); organizational governance and, 42–43; and political activism, 259; and reduced signaling, 32n14; rents and, 33, 36; repeated game and incentive for development of, 50–51; and "shocks" to union, 242, 245; and signaling, 242, 245, 247–48; and strikes, 257; and strikes as signals, 235–37; of union for resoluteness, 237

reputation, leadership and, 14, 18–19, 32–33, 275; consistency with organizational rules and principles, 24; rents and, 18–19, 32; repeated game and valuation of future, 32

residence patterns: and union membership, 140–54

"resource curse," 271

revolutionary model, 3–4

Ricardo-Viner model, 190, 198

Ricks, Marvin, 171

"right to work" legislation, 263–64

Roach, Ted, 82, 104–13, 130–31, 138, 175

Ryan, Joseph, 42, 73–77, 84

sacrifice: as signal tactic, 31

safety issues, 55, 72, 97, 103, 106–7; as negotiation issue, 100; work stoppages and safety issues, 99, 112, 126, 250

scrap iron dispute, protest of Japan's invasion of Manchuria, 1, 12, 79, 86, 107, 113, 243n7

screening: and church congregations, 11–12, 267; for Communists during Red Scare, 86, 171–73, 249; union membership screening process, 11–12, 19; and union strength, 235

Seaman's Union of Australia, 252

Seattle General Strike, 62, 128–29

self-interest, 12; and trade stance of ILWU, 20

self-sacrifice, 1, 10, 31, 272

self-selection, 261; membership, 1–2, 15–16; and partisan politics, 267–68; religious organizations and, 267; screening processes and, 267

seniority ranks (A-list, B-list, Casual) in ILWU: as affecting political views, 187, 203–4, 206–9, 212–13; description and distinctions, 89, 139–40, 177, 187–88; and voting rights, 115–16

Service Employees International Union (SEIU), 264

shape-ups, 72, 74, 76

Shea, Cornelius P., 56

Sherman, Lou, 179–80

signaling: accountability of union leaders and, 264; collection for strike funds as, 236; ILA-ILWU comparison and evidence of, 238; as leadership, 28, 31–32; political actions as, 20, 230–33, 235–37, 243–45, 256; pre-authorization of strike as, 236; pre-bargaining signals, 235–36; repetition and, 32n14; reputation and, 32n14, 235–37, 242, 245, 247–48; sacrifice as signal, 31; solidaristic action as, 236

Simon, Herbert, 275

Skoglund, Carl, 122

slowdowns, 12, 112, 114

Smith Act, 124

social pressure, as motivation for membership, 16

social relational or network approach: compliance and, 16

solidaristic action: state regulation and prohibition of, 259

South African apartheid, 13, 79, 96–97, 173, 174, 249

Spell, Conrad, 115